BUSINESS LAW:
A HANDS-ON APPROACH

NEAL R. BEVANS

WEST LEGAL STUDIES

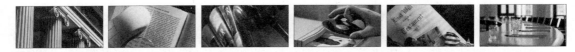

Options.
Over 300 products in every area of the law: textbooks, CD-ROMs, reference books, test banks, on-line companions, and more – helping you succeed in the classroom and on the job.

Support.
We offer unparalleled, practical support: robust instructor and student supplements to ensure the best learning experience, custom publishing to meet your unique needs, and other benefits such as West's Student Achievement Award. And our sales representatives are always ready to provide you with dependable service.

Feedback.
As always, we want to hear from you! Your feedback is our best resource for improving the quality of our products. Contact your sales representative or write us at the address below if you have any comments about our materials or if you have a product proposal.

Accounting and Financials for the Law Office • Administrative Law • Alternative Dispute Resolution • Bankruptcy • Business Organizations/Corporations • Careers and Employment Civil Litigation and Procedure • CLA Exam Preparation • Computer Applications in the Law Office • Contract Law • Court Reporting • Criminal Law and Procedure • Document Preparation • Elder Law • Employment Law • Environmental Law • Ethics • Evidence Law • Family Law • Intellectual Property • Interviewing and Investigation • Introduction to Law Introduction to Paralegalism • Law Office Management Law Office Procedures Legal Nurse Consulting • Legal Research, Writing, and Analysis • Legal Terminology • Paralegal Internship • Product Liability • Real Estate Law • Reference Materials • Social Security Sports Law • Torts and Personal Injury Law • Wills, Trusts, and Estate Administration

---

West Legal Studies
5 Maxwell Drive
Clifton Park, New York 12065-2919

For additional information, find us online at:
www.westlegalstudies.com

THOMSON
DELMAR LEARNING

BUSINESS LAW:
A HANDS-ON APPROACH

NEAL R. BEVANS

THOMSON

DELMAR LEARNING™

Australia Canada Mexico Singapore Spain United Kingdom United States

THOMSON
DELMAR LEARNING

WEST LEGAL STUDIES

Business Law: A Hands-On Approach
by Neal R. Bevans

Vice President, Career Education Strategic Business Unit:
Dawn Gerrain

Director of Editorial:
Sherry Gomoll

Editor:
Shelley Esposito

Senior Developmental Editor:
Melissa Riveglia

Editorial Assistant:
Brian E. Banks

Director of Production:
Wendy A. Troeger

Production Editor:
Matthew J. Williams

Director of Marketing:
Wendy E. Mapstone

Marketing Specialist:
Gerard McAvey

Marketing Coordinator:
Erica Conley

Cover Design:
Joe Villanova

For permission to use material from this text or product, contact us by
Tel   (800) 730-2214
Fax   (800) 730-2215
www.thomsonrights.com

Library of Congress Cataloging-in-Publication Data

Bevans, Neal R., 1961-
  Business law : a hands-on approach / by Neal R. Bevans.– 1st ed.
     p. cm. – (The West Legal Studies series)
  Includes bibliographical references and index.
  ISBN 1-4018-3353-5 (pbk.)
1. Commercial law–United States. 2. Contracts–United States. 3. Business law–United States. I. Title. II. Series.
  KF889.B48 2006
  346.7307–dc22

                                                    2005011613

NOTICE TO THE READER

TABLE OF CONTENTS

CHAPTER **3**   **The Legal Concept of Acceptance   47**

CHAPTER 10   Discharge, Performance, and Cancellation of a Contract   231

CHAPTER 11   Remedies in Contract Law   257

CHAPTER 12: Drafting Contracts   284

PREFACE

This text is designed to act as an introductory text to business law, providing a practical, hands-on guide that gives the student a firm foundation in commercial practices, with an eye toward the kind of law that a legal professional (not a business major) should know.

Features of the Text

The text has numerous features that take advantage of the varying learning styles that students apply to learning. Based on the recognition that students who apply their newly acquired knowledge often retain it much better than those who do not, this text takes a strong "hands-on" approach to business law by emphasizing practical applications of important concepts. The theoretical bases of the material are provided and then the student is asked to apply this material in the following ways:

- Each chapter analyzes the elements of business law and business structures from basic contracts to UCC transactions
- Significant cases are excerpted and explored in great detail
- Web sites for further research or discussion are provided
- Step-by-step analysis of the creation of contracts is presented, as well as the common clauses contained in them
- Chapter discussions are based on actual business problems
- Numerous hypotheticals and practical examples are offered to bring home the issues discussed in each chapter.
- Practical assignments are given, based on real-world problems faced by business people and attorneys on a daily basis.
- Numerous sidebars are presented in each chapter addressing a wide variety of issues
- The end of chapter exercises, hands-on assignments, and practical applications emphasize the theoretical concepts presented in the text.
- A "Business Case File" appears in each chapter that profiles various businesses and how they carry out their daily activities and how legal concerns often feature in their business decisions.
- The material is also topical, including discussions about ethical concerns and emerging technology, e-mail. and an entire chapter devoted to e-commerce

Key Features of Each Chapter:

Each chapter has numerous features that are designed to assist the student in acquiring a solid footing in business and contract law. These chapter-specific features include

- **Learning objectives stated at the beginning of each chapter**

  The learning objectives for the chapter are stated clearly and succinctly at the beginning of each chapter. These learning objectives help the student and the instructor focus on the critical issues for each chapter and provide the student with a method for evaluating the studentís mastery of the material.

- **Terms and legal vocabulary are defined immediately for the student**

  The first time a key word or legal term is mentioned in the text, a definition of it appears in the margin. This helps students grasp the meaning without breaking into the flow of the reading by having to turn to the glossary.

- **Figures and tables are offered to illustrate crucial points and are designed to capitalize on different student learning styles**

  The author provides numerous figures and tables to develop certain points from the material. This feature takes advantage of the different learning styles among students, allowing those geared to a more visual learning style the opportunity to absorb the material appropriately.

- **Hypothetical questions to help students develop their understanding of the material**

  The author uses hypothetical questions and other scenarios to illustrate the points under discussion in each chapter. These scenarios also provide excellent in-class discussion questions.

- **A complete case that explores a topic raised in the chapter**

  Each chapter contains a complete appellate case taken from state and federal jurisdictions nationwide that show how the topics discussed in the chapter are applied in the legal arena.

- **Numerous sidebars**

  Each chapter also contains numerous sidebars. These explore aspects of the text in greater detail, explaining how homicide detectives review a crime scene for instance, or detailing significant crime statistics.

- **End of chapter questions, activities, and assignments to increase student comprehension and retention of the concepts presented in the chapter**

  End of chapter exercises include review questions, practical applications of theoretical concepts, and additional material to assist the student in continuing to apply the concepts presented in the chapter.

■ **Ethics File**

Ethics is crucial for any legal professional. Each chapter explores an important ethical question and explains the relevance of ethical systems for the day-to-day practice of law.

■ **"Paralegal Checklists" based on actual activities carried out by attorneys and paralegals in creating various business structures**

Checklists provided throughout the book act as a guideline for the student. The checklists are based on material raised in the chapter and help focus the student on critical aspects of each chapter.

■ **"Business Case File," that profiles a real business and the legal problems and concerns the owners encountered, and continue to encounter, in running it.**

Each chapter also profiles a different business, from a bed and breakfast to an economic development corporation. These business profiles help the student understand the real people behind the legal issues and how the various aspects of business law have practical applications.

■ **"Help this Business," presenting a wide variety of typical business problems and the legal methods to address these problems.**

Working from the Business Case File in each chapter, this feature requires the student to do additional work on a typical legal problem using information learned in that chapter. This feature helps the students make an additional connection with the material presented.

■ **Web sites for further research or discussion**

At the end of each chapter is an extensive list of Web resources focusing on the issues raised in that chapter. Students are provided with links to various governmental and other Web sites that help them expand on the discussion in the text and also allow them to get as in-depth on any particular issue that suits them.

■ **Appendix containing a wide variety of business forms, letters, contracts, and so on**

The appendix contains numerous forms of business documents to allow the student the opportunity to see how the theory of contract law is applied on a practical basis.

■ **Glossary containing definitions of all terms used in the text**

All of the terms and phrases defined throughout the text are also provided in a handy glossary.

Pedagogy

The text is written in clearly presented language that engages the student, keeps the reader's interest, and presents information in a variety of styles to take advantage of different learning styles. Each new concept is presented in a multilayer fashion, first with the basic concepts and then adding greater complexity once the intellectual foundation is laid. Charts and diagrams are provided to illustrate concepts as they are discussed and to provide the instructor with additional material for class discussion. Sidebars, tables, and interviews are also presented to supplement the chapter information in a different format for students who may not fully grasp the concepts on initial presentation. Finally, practical, hands-on assignments and discussion questions are presented to reiterate and emphasize the concepts. This allows for greater comprehension and retention by the student. The author fills the text with a balance of theoretical discussions and practical examples, all presented in a well-written, enjoyable style.

Non-gender-specific language

In recognition of the impact of gender specific language, the author has adopted the following convention in the text: each even-numbered chapter uses "he" in general discussions and examples, whereas the odd-number chapters use "she" for the same purposes.

Instructor's Manual

The author has developed an impressive instructor's manual to accompany the text available both in print and online at www.westlegalstudies.com. Recognizing the needs of instructors for multiple resources, the author has provided the following features:

- Suggested syllabi and lesson plans
- Annotated outlines for each chapter
- Answers to all end-of-chapter questions
- Test bank

  The test bank includes a variety of test questions, including:
  - Essay questions (five per chapter)
  - Short answer (10 per chapter)
  - Multiple choice (25 per chapter)
  - True-False (10 per chapter)

Online Companion

Available to students at www.westlegalstudies.com are supplemental resources including the following:

- Study Tips
- Chapter Outline
- Web sites
- Powerpoint slides

About the Author

Neal Bevans is a former private attorney and Assistant District Attorney in Atlanta, Georgia. A veteran of over 150 trials, Mr. Bevans has tried every major felony from rape, murder, and narcotics to armed robbery. One of his cases was televised nationally on Court TV (Georgia v. Mobley). He has been a college instructor for over eight years. A writer of fiction and nonfiction material, his textbook Criminal Law and Procedure for Paralegals was published in 2002. He also has published numerous magazine articles about many aspects of the legal field. He is a contributing columnist to Legal Assistant Today magazine.

CHAPTER 1

INTRODUCTION TO CONTRACTS

Focus of this chapter: This chapter introduces the basic concepts of business and contract law. The basic details of contractual law are developed and a foundation is laid for discussion in future chapters.

Chapter Objectives:
At the completion of this chapter, you should be able to:

- List and explain the basic elements of all contracts
- Describe the differences between unilateral and bilateral contracts
- Explain the application of the "Mailbox Rule"
- Describe the methods by which contracts are created
- Explain the Statute of Frauds
- Provide a basic definition of "contract"
- Describe the difference between an offer and an acceptance
- Define void versus voidable contracts
- Explain the difference between an executory and an executed contract
- Explain the function of ethical rules

Introduction to Contracts

Business is the lifeblood of a capitalist society. We have all entered into a contract at some point in our lives. We have all been employed, or bought a car, financed a boat, put in an offer on a house, or been married. Each one of these situations involves some aspect of contract law. This book is designed to demystify the subject of contract and commercial law and to provide practical information for paralegal students. Before we can begin to outline the essential elements of a contract and define the various methods used to create one, we must first answer a more basic question:

What Is a Contract?

The legal definition of a **contract** is a promise (or set of promises) that, when breached by one party, gives the other party a legal remedy. This definition is rather vague. Many jurisdictions have opted for a definition that takes the relationship of the parties into account. For instance, the Uniform Commercial Code, which we will discuss in greater depth in later chapters, defines a contract as the total legal obligation that results from an agreement.

In this chapter, the focus is on basic contracts. However, there are some contracts that fall into special categories and will be discussed in later chapters. These contracts have formal requirements and are often governed by specific statutes. Examples of these technical contracts are:

- Negotiable instruments
- Letters of Credit
- Contracts under "seal"

The Basic Elements of All Contracts

All contracts consist of some basic elements. These include:

- Mutual assent (a valid offer and acceptance)
- Consideration
- Legality of subject
- Capacity

In this chapter, we will introduce the basic components of these elements. In later chapters, each of these elements will be developed in much greater depth.

Mutual Assent

mutual assent: A party's willingness to enter into a contractual obligation and an agreement as to the general terms in the contract.

Mutual assent is the final product of a valid offer and acceptance. The concept of mutual assent takes into account the agreement of the parties to enter into a contract. It also refers to the right of a party to decide whether or not to contract with someone else. A person cannot be forced to enter into a contract. Such force overcomes the consent of the party and makes the contract void.

Mutual assent or mutual agreement consists of a valid, legal offer and a valid, legal acceptance. We will begin our discussion with offers.

Sidebar:
Mutual assent is also often referred to as "meeting of the minds"

Offer

offer: Make a proposal; present for acceptance or rejection.

What constitutes an offer? Under the law, an **offer** is an expression by a party (usually called the *offeror*) that he or she is willing to enter into a bargain. It contemplates that if the offer is accepted, the party will carry through on the details in the offer.

In order to be a valid offer, it must be specific as to terms and performance. The terms must be spelled out in sufficient detail so that the person receiving the offer understands what is being offered. The offer also must be specific in terms of performance. Who will actually perform? What will each party to the contract actually do?

HYPOTHETICAL 1-1   The non-offer offer

I will give you something nice if you are good.

Is this a valid offer?

Answer: No. The offer is not specific as to terms or performance. It fails to define exactly what is being offered or how the offeror could satisfy the conditions and receive a benefit (or even what the benefit is).

This is not to say that an offer must be overly technical and precise to be considered a valid offer. Consider the scenario in Hypothetical 1-2.

HYPOTHETICAL 1-2   Paying half

Miguel approaches his neighbor, Ed, and tells him, "If you'll pay for half of the expenses, I'll build a chain link fence along our shared property line." Is this a valid offer?

Answer: Yes. Miguel's offer is specific as to terms: paying half of the expenses in exchange for a specific performance, that is, Miguel's action in constructing the fence.

A valid offer does not have to take into account every possible permutation of human nature or unforeseen consequences. For instance, Miguel is not required to include stipulations in his offer such as, "assuming that both of us stay alive for the next month," or "a fence of 110 feet, made of 2 inch mesh chain link, with a minimum of 8 supporting posts." The language in an offer will be construed by its normal meaning. Later, as we explore offers in greater depth, we also will see that the courts have a stated preference for construing language so that a contract exists. Given this preference, there is a great deal of latitude in how an offer is phrased.

> **Sidebar:**
> In order to form a contract, there must be an offer and acceptance.

The Power of Acceptance

An offer must be specific and definite. When it is, it creates a legal right in the person receiving the offer. This right is called the **power of acceptance**. Simply put, the power of acceptance refers to the right of the person receiving the offer to accept it and create a binding contract. An offer that does not create the power of acceptance in another is not a valid offer. Examples of statements that often are confused with offers are the preliminary discussions or negotiations about buying or selling a business. These discussions are not offers and do not become offers until someone puts forward specific terms and then places him- or herself in the position of entering a binding agreement.

power of acceptance: the right conferred on a person who has received a valid offer.

Offers Can Be Made by Words, by Actions, or Any Combination of Both

An offer can be made without any words at all. Example: Rick is at a noisy club and motions to the bartender for service. The bartender points at a beer and holds up three fingers. Rick interprets this to mean that the beer costs $3. He hands over the $3 and the bartender hands Rick the beer. Although they probably do not realize it, both men have just negotiated and completed a contract. When the bartender handed over the beer, would he have the legal right to the $3? Absolutely. The fact that neither man actually said anything to one another is irrelevant. Similarly, if Rick paid his $3 and was then handed a glass of water, instead of a beer, would he be legally entitled to a beer? Again, the answer must be yes. In fact, Rick could argue successfully that he is entitled to the beer that the bartender pointed to when Rick got his attention.

How Long Is an Offer Valid?

Generally, an offer expires by its own terms, or after a reasonable period of time. A "reasonable period of time" depends on all of the surrounding circumstances in a particular case. An offer also can cease to exist when the person making it withdraws the offer.

ACCEPTANCE

acceptance: Agreeing to an offer and thus forming a contract.

A valid offer creates the power of acceptance in another. When this **acceptance** is properly communicated to the offeror, a contract is formed. However, there are many circumstances in which an acceptance is not legally valid.

An acceptance is not valid when:

- It is made by unauthorized means (telephone call when writing is required, for example)
- It alters the material terms of the offer
- It includes a condition or a qualification
- It has been previously rejected
- It is a counteroffer

In situations in which there is no specific mode of acceptance required, the acceptance is normally made in the same medium as the offer. A verbal offer can be accepted verbally; a written offer can be accepted in writing. In unspecified situations, a verbal acceptance also may be sufficient when the offer is in writing.

However, an offer can place strict limitations on the method of communicating an acceptance. The offer can state, for instance, that acceptance must be made in writing. In such a case, a telephone call would not be legally sufficient.

When the offeror negotiates a point in the offer by changing one of the material terms, the offeror is essentially rejecting the offer.

HYPOTHETICAL 1-3   Rick's Offer

Rick goes to a used car lot and sees a car that he likes. When the salesman approaches, Rick asks "How much?" The used car salesman says, "Ten thousand." Another potential buyer is standing nearby and hears this exchange. Rick tells the used car salesman, "I'll go eight thousand, but that's it." While the used car salesman is thinking this over, the other person chimes in. "I'll pay $10,500 for that car." Rick, now believing that he may lose the car, says, "Okay, I'll take it for ten thousand."

Is this a valid offer and acceptance?

Answer: No.

When Rick changed a material term (i.e., the offering price), he rejected the offer. (Actually, Rick made a counteroffer, which then placed the used car salesman in the position of accepting Rick's counteroffer).

A material term refers to an essential element of the transaction. Normally, a material term refers to price, subject, or time of performance. It is not a material change in terms in the example above, for instance, for Rick to pay with cash instead of a check. When the change is not on a material term, courts generally are flexible in interpreting the offer and acceptance. However, there is one point on which there is no flexibility: the acceptance must be communicated.

Communicating an Acceptance

The person accepting the offer (the offeree) must communicate this acceptance to the offeror. Courts will not consider the intent of the parties, or what they hoped to do, or wanted to do; the fact of acceptance must be established. To communicate an acceptance, an offeror must unequivocally signal his acceptance of the offer to the person who actually made the offer. Sometimes, such as when the offer contains specific limitations on the mode of communication, an offer can be communicated only by the manner prescribed.

HYPOTHETICAL 1-4   The Newspaper Offer

Miguel places an ad in the local newspaper. It reads, "I will sell my 1999 Ford Explorer to the first person to appear at my house with $4,000 in cash."

Arnold reads the ad in the paper and immediately places a telephone call to Miguel. "I'll buy it!" he yells. Arnold adds that he will be at Miguel's house in less than ten minutes. As soon as Miguel hangs up the telephone, Burt knocks on Miguel's front door and when Miguel answers it, he presents Miguel with $4,000 in cash and asks for the keys to the car. When Arnold shows up later, he finds that Miguel has already sold the car. Arnold wants to sue Miguel for failure to abide by the contract. Will Arnold win the suit?

Answer: No.

Miguel's offer was specific as to the manner of acceptance. Miguel specifically stated that acceptance must come in the form of physically appearing at his home, with the required amount of money. Miguel also stated that he would sell his car to the first person to arrive who met those conditions. Arnold did not validly accept Miguel's offer because he telephoned, instead of appearing, and he was not the first person to arrive at Miguel's home with the $4,000.

The Mailbox Rule

Mailbox Rule: A rule that holds that an acceptance is legally valid at the time that it is posted; this rule is subject to several exceptions

The so-called **Mailbox Rule** is a rule that modified the general law of communicating an acceptance. This rule states that an acceptance is legally effective when it is deposited in the U.S. postal system. Consider this scenario:

HYPOTHETICAL 1-5   The Computer Contract

John offers to sell Mary a shipment of the latest model laptops for a stated price. Mary likes the offer and writes out her acceptance. She mails the acceptance on Tuesday morning, 9 A.M. At 3 P.M. on Tuesday, John decides that he can get a better price from a large computer retail store and faxes Mary a revocation of his offer. Mary's acceptance has already been mailed. Under the Mailbox Rule, Mary's acceptance was legally effective at the time that she mailed it (because it was out of her hands and she was unable to retrieve it). John's revocation was not legally effective, because an offeror cannot revoke an offer that has already been accepted.

The Mailbox Rule was created because, without it, any offer accepted by mail would not be effective until received. A mailed acceptance could take one to three days to reach the person addressed. In those three days, many things could happen, all of which could cause confusion without some rule dictating when the acceptance becomes effective. The Mailbox Rule works the other way, as well. Mary cannot rescind her acceptance after she mails it to John. As far as the law is concerned, she has accepted the offer when she put it in the mail and a contract was then created.

Can a Person Accept by Silence?

Generally, courts have held that mere silence is not sufficient to constitute a valid acceptance. A person must take some action that indicated his or her willingness to enter into a contract. Failure to do anything is usually interpreted as unwillingness to contract. Under this application, the following offer would not result in a valid contract.

HYPOTHETICAL 1-6   Miguel's Neighbor's Silent Acceptance

Miguel knows that his neighbor likes Miguel's house. Miguel writes up a letter with specific details about price and financing for the neighbor to purchase Miguel's home. He includes a sentence in the offer that states, "If you would like to purchase my home, do nothing. I will assume your lack of response to indicate that you wish to purchase under the terms stated."

When the neighbor claims that he did not accept Miguel's terms, Miguel sues for lack of performance under a contract. The court rules that no contract was ever created, so Miguel cannot enforce it.

Some offers contain specific provisions detailing how acceptance must be communicated. In such situations, an acceptance communicated in another way will often be legally insufficient. An offer may contain language stating that acceptance can only be made in writing. A verbal acceptance under that situation would be inadequate and would not result in a binding contract.

Terminating the Power of Acceptance

A person's power of acceptance can be terminated by:

- A revocation of the offer by the offeror
- A rejection of the offer by the offeree
- Lapse of time
- Death or subsequent incapacity of either party
- The failure of a required condition

When a person makes an offer, he or she almost always has the right to revoke it. A revocation of the offer can be made in the same breath as the offer. A revocation can come at any time prior to acceptance.

When the offeror rejects the offer, there is no longer any power of acceptance.

> **Sidebar:**
> Every contract involves some kind of promise. However, not every promise creates a contract.

HYPOTHETICAL 1-7   The Plate Collection

Miguel approaches Mary and makes the following offer: "I'll sell you my Limited Edition Collector Plates for $50." Mary declines. Later, Mary sees an article in a magazine about the tremendous increase in value for all collector plates, especially the limited edition kind. She calls Miguel and says, "I've changed my mind. I want those plates." But Miguel has read the same article and refuses to sell. Mary brings a suit to force Miguel to sell her the plates for $50. Will she win the suit?

Answer: No.

When Mary declined Miguel's offer, the offer was dead. Mary could not legally attempt to accept it after having rejected it.

COUNTEROFFERS

When a person makes a counteroffer, the original offer is rejected. Counteroffers are new offers, not an acceptance of the original offer. When a person makes a counteroffer, the power of acceptance shifts to the other party. Usually, the courts consider continued negotiations to be counteroffers. Miguel offers his car for sale for $4,000. Barry likes the car but not the price. Barry says that he will pay $3,000. Miguel counters with $3,500. What has occurred here?

Miguel's first offer was for $4,000. When Barry countered with $3,000, he rejected Miguel's offer and made his own offer for that amount. A counteroffer creates a new potential contract by shifting the power of acceptance from Barry to Miguel. The situation changes again when Miguel counters with $3,500. At this point, he has rejected Barry's counteroffer and created a new offer, shifting the power of acceptance back to Barry. This offer/counteroffer shift can occur many times during the negotiation of a contract (see Exhibit 1-1).

✗   I promise to study Business Law every day. *(Not an offer)*

✓   If you make an A in your Business Law course, I will pay you $50. *(Offer)*

EXHIBIT 1-1: Examples of valid and invalid offers.

LANGUAGE REQUIRED TO CREATE A CONTRACT

There is no magic formula of words that must be used in order to create a contract. Courts have been very liberal in their interpretation of agreements between parties. For instance, the term "contract" is not required to create a contract. The terms used are not important. What is important is that the basic elements are present, including offer and acceptance, consideration and capacity of the parties. Contracts can be created orally, in writing, or any combination of the two. Words such as "consideration" and "mutual assent" are not required. In addition, there are no special forms or other formal requirements to create most contracts.

CONSIDERATION

consideration: The basic reason for a contract; a person gives up something of value in exchange for receiving something of value through the contract.

Contracts must contain **consideration**. What is consideration? Simply put, consideration is the core of the bargain expressed in the contract. B does something he is not obligated to do in exchange for A doing something that she is not legally obligated to do. Notice that we have used the phrase "not legally obligated to do." When a person is legally obligated to carry out some action, it cannot be the basis of consideration.

HYPOTHETICAL 1-8   Miguel's Stolen Car

Example: Miguel's car is stolen and he puts an ad in the paper, "$100 for any information leading to the arrest and conviction of the person who stole my car last week." A police officer answers the ad and tells Miguel that he is the lead investigator in the case and states that he has just arrested the person who stole Miguel's car. He demands the $100. Is there legal consideration?

Answer: No.

The officer was legally obligated to investigate the case and to make an arrest when he had sufficient probable cause. Because he was legally obligated to carry out the action, there is no consideration for the contract. This is why police officers are generally barred from collecting on rewards posted in criminal cases.

Would the same result occur in Hypothetical 1-8 if the person who answered Miguel's ad were a private citizen? In that case, the answer would be no. A private citizen has no legal obligation to investigate crimes. In this case, if Miguel failed to pay the $100, the private citizen could bring a suit to force Miguel to pay and would most likely win.

Why is there a requirement of consideration? In any contract, both parties must incur some legal obligation, often termed **detriment**. A person who incurs no detriment in a contract has no legal obligation. Without legal obligation, the contract cannot be enforced. Consideration, therefore, is the glue that binds the contract together (see Exhibits 1-2 and 1-3).

> **Sidebar:**
> When someone is legally obligated to take an action, it cannot be the basis of consideration.

> **detriment:** the bargained for exchange in a contract, where the parties take on some responsibility that they are not legally obligated to undertake.

> **Sidebar:**
> Consideration is often described as "bargained for exchange."

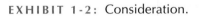

Right, interest, or benefit

    Forbearance, loss, or responsibility

EXHIBIT 1-2: Consideration.

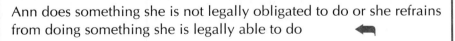

Ann does something she is not legally obligated to do or she refrains from doing something she is legally able to do

    Bob does something he is not legally obligated to do or refrains from doing something he is legally able to do

EXHIBIT 1-3: Analyzing consideration.

However, in most cases, the law does not set a minimum or maximum amount of consideration, only that the consideration be "something of value." This tends to downplay the importance of consideration in evaluating a contract. Courts generally do not inquire about the sufficiency of the consideration, that is, whether the consideration was commensurate with the responsibilities assumed under the contract. In most jurisdictions, any consideration, no matter how slight is enough.

CAPACITY

When a person has legal **capacity**, it simply means that he or she has the legal authority to enter into binding, legal agreements. This means that a person must know what he or she is doing. A person cannot agree to a contract "by mistake," or be tricked into consenting to a contract. If a person is unconscious or unable to understand the proceedings, for instance, when a person is acting under the influence of alcohol or some other drug, the agreement will usually be invalidated.

Individuals are legally incapable of entering into a contract when they:

- Suffer from mental illness or mental defect
- Have had a legal guardian appointed to handle their transactions
- Are under the age of 18 (the age of majority in most jurisdictions)
- Are intoxicated by alcohol or other drugs

SUBJECT OF CONTRACT MUST BE LEGAL

The subject of the contract must be legal. A contract that involves illegal activity will not be enforced through the court system, for obvious reasons.

HYPOTHETICAL 1-9   The Cocaine Contract

Example: Ron is planning to sell a kilo of cocaine to Stan. Stan has agreed to pay $20,000 for the cocaine. Ron produces the cocaine, which Stan takes, and then fails to pay the money. Ron cannot use the court system to enforce his contract.

Contracts for the sale of cocaine are rare. It is far more common for the illegal subject to involve unfair consumer practices, such as illegally high interest rates charged on financed purchases, or forced waivers of all rights by a consumer who purchases an item.

Types of Contracts

There are many different types of contracts. In this section, we examine contracts in terms of performance.

CLASSIFYING A CONTRACT BY PERFORMANCE

A contract usually envisions some type of performance, either the delivery or the exchange of goods or other actions. However, in this section, we examine contracts that require actions in order to be created.

Unilateral Contracts

Contracts can be categorized by the type of actions anticipated by both parties to the transaction. A **unilateral contract** is one such contract. In a unilateral contract, the offeror makes a promise in anticipation of some action by the other party.

unilateral contract: A contract in which one party makes a promise in exchange for an action by the other party.

HYPOTHETICAL 1-10 The Missing Cat Reward

Example: Miguel posts a reward for his missing cat, Missy. The reward poster reads: "Will pay $100 for the safe return of this cat." He puts a photo of Missy on the poster. This is an offer for a unilateral contract. What Miguel is promising is the payment of $100 in exchange for someone's action. Miguel is not interested in another promise. He does not want someone to promise to return his cat; he wants his cat. The action of producing the cat is how someone accepts Miguel's offer. At the moment that some other person takes action, a contract is created. The person producing the cat would have a legal right to the $100, since he has accepted the offer.

Although most contracts are bilateral, there are at least two common transactions that are categorized as unilateral contracts. Rewards, shown earlier, are unilateral contracts. So are promissory notes. Promissory notes are given when someone borrows money from another and agrees to repay the amount, usually plus interest, by a specific date.

Sidebar:
A unilateral contract is a promise in exchange for an action. A bilateral contract is a promise in exchange for a promise.

Bilateral Contracts

In contrast to a unilateral contract, a **bilateral contract** involves a promise in exchange for another promise. Most contracts are bilateral contracts. One person offers a promise in exchange for another promise. The Restatement of Contracts downplays the differences between unilateral and bilateral contracts by refusing to use these terms.

bilateral contract: A contract that offers a promise in exchange for another promise.

Executory and Executed Contracts

An executory contract is one that has not yet been completely performed. An executed contract is one in which all required actions have been completed. The reason for the distinction is that different remedies are triggered for executory contracts than for executed contracts. A party to a contract that has not yet been performed might request that the court order the other party to abide by the original agreement (referred to as "specific performance"). A party to an executed contract may only be able to sue for damages resulting from substandard goods or some other violation of the contract provisions.

Void and Voidable Contracts

A **void** contract is a contract that is invalid. A void contract cannot be enforced. Parties to void contracts cannot sue for damages or equitable remedies. An example of a void contract is our previous example of a contract

void: Without legal effect.

for the sale of illegal narcotics. Such a contract is void as soon as it is made, because it involves an illegal substance. By contrast, **voidable** contracts are enforceable, at least to an extent. A voidable contract is a contract that could be invalidated, but has not yet been ruled void. A voidable contract is valid until challenged. An example of a voidable contract is set out in hypothetical 1-11.

HYPOTHETICAL 1-11   The Child Star's Statue

Jim is a sculptor. One day, Haley, a famous actor, comes to Jim's studio and asks Jim to do a statue of him that he can display at his home. Jim creates the sculpture and then requests payment. Only then does he learn that Haley, who looks older, is actually only 16 years old. Because Haley is below the age of majority in his state, their contract is voidable. Haley can still pay for the sculpture and Jim can still deliver it. On the other hand, Haley could decide to void the contract on the grounds of his age.

Sidebar:
The Statute of Frauds should actually be called the "Statute to Prevent Frauds," because that was the purpose of the original legislation, which became law in England in 1677 (see Exhibit 1-4).

Statute of Frauds: Any of various states' law, modeled after an old English law, that require many types of contracts to be signed and in writing to be enforceable in court.

Putting it in Writing: The Statute of Frauds

Generally, there is no requirement that a contract be reduced to writing. An oral contract can cover a wide range of arrangements, sometimes involving million's of dollars. However, there are some statutes that require specific types of contracts to be put into writing. Each jurisdiction has its own version of the **Statute of Frauds**. The Statute of Frauds is a statute that requires certain types of contracts to be reduced to writing before they are considered legally enforceable.

Sidebar:
Entertainer Dean Martin had an oral agreement with his agent that lasted for four decades. It was never in writing and was never contested by either man. Because it was not a type of contract that was required to be in writing under the Statute of Frauds, their arrangement was perfectly legal, if a little unconventional.

- Prenuptial agreements
- Promise to the pay the debt of another
- Contracts that, by their terms, cannot be performed in less than a year
- Contracts involving the sale or transfer of real estate

EXHIBIT 1-4: Types of contracts that must be in writing under the Statute of Frauds.

The Case of Charity

Carlson v. Krantz[1]

STONE, J.

Action on contract wherein, after verdict for plaintiff, defendant appeals from an order denying his motion for judgment notwithstanding or a new trial. Defendant is a minister of the gospel and in 1911, in which year the alleged contract was made, was the pastor of a church at Duluth. Plaintiff is single and until 1911 had been very much of a wayfaring man, much of his life having been spent before the mast. Being a slave to the liquor habit, but having the desire to reform, he sought the aid of defendant, who had long been his dependable friend and spiritual adviser. The effort was not in vain, and no question is made of the initial disinterestedness of the efforts of defendant on behalf of plaintiff, which had characterized the acquaintance between the two for some time prior to the making of the alleged contract.

Defendant owns a fractional quarter section of wilderness land on the shores of Grand Lake, in St. Louis County. Its potentialities as a summer residence or agricultural property are suggested but not clear. Defendant acquired it before 1911 and has owned it ever since. Except as hereinafter stated, it has never been improved and neither he nor his family has made personal use of it. If it was acquired as a long time investment, the purpose has been achieved so far as duration is concerned.

Plaintiff's story is that in 1911, at his own solicitation, defendant took him out to this land, which we shall designate as the farm, and first installed him in the home of a neighbor, where defendant paid his board. At plaintiff's solicitation, defendant soon built a substantial log cabin on the farm, admittedly for the use of plaintiff and to afford him a habitation where he could keep aloof from the temptations of the old life from which he was attempting escape. That purpose is not only clear but also conceded to have been the dominating purpose of the transaction, whether it was contract or mere charity. After

the house, a substantial barn and root cellar were added, a well sunk and some fencing done. The cost of all the improvements was borne by defendant except that some of the common labor was done by plaintiff. Plaintiff continued his residence on the land, with unimportant interruptions, until 1924. Then, if there was a contract, it was breached by defendant, who required plaintiff to vacate or at least refused longer to maintain him on the farm. During all this period defendant had no income from the place. Neither did he make any use of it save that on a few occasions he and one or two of the younger members of his family were there for short periods. Defendant bought and paid for a horse which plaintiff used on the premises. Likewise, he bought a cow for plaintiff's use. Defendant furnished food supplies, clothing, and other necessities required by plaintiff, including money for incidental expenses.

On his part, plaintiff remained on the place and did some work there, but in extent and value it lacks much of being commensurate either with the duration of his stay or the amount defendant has expended on him. He has done not to exceed 15 acres of clearing, and not to exceed 10 acres have ever been cropped. The rest plaintiff claims to have "parked." Some fruit trees have been planted. Further detail is unnecessary, but it is safe to generalize to the effect that, considering that plaintiff was on the place for 13 years, the physical improvement resulting from his efforts has been relatively insignificant, a situation explained probably by physical disability and advancing years.

The contract claimed for plaintiff is that, in consideration of his agreement to go onto the place and live there as a sort of caretaker, there being very little attempt in the record to state what real obligation he assumed, the defendant promised to maintain him on the farm, furnishing sufficient money for food, clothing, and incidental expenses as long as he should live. In other words, if the contract was made as claimed by plaintiff, he thereby became a life tenant on the farm without obligation to pay rent, even to the extent of keeping up taxes, and without any obligation to do a single thing beneficial for his lessor, defendant, except that it is vaguely suggested that he assumed the duties of a caretaker and guard against the hazards of trespass and fire.

Defendant, on his part, denies the contract, but admits his interest in plaintiff, his efforts to reform him, and his installation of the man on the farm in the hope that he would thereby have an opportunity for an outdoor life aloof from former associations and temptations, and the opportunity for reform which plaintiff solicited him to furnish.

Due to circumstances which are unfortunate rather than discrediting, plaintiff's testimony is very unsatisfactory, so much so that the learned trial court doubted its sufficiency to "warrant a finding of a contract expressed in words." It was thought, however, that the evidence was sufficient to take the case to the jury "on the question of contract implied from the offer of defendant to furnish Carlson with support for life and its acceptance by his going on the land and working as he did."

It is one thing to say that defendant offered to support his repentant and needy parishioner for life and that plaintiff accepted the offer, but it is entirely another thing to say that either of them intended to bind himself contractually. To us, it seems preposterous that defendant contracted with plaintiff to make the latter a life tenant on a farm which plainly he might want to sell at any time. In other words, it is easy to understand the relationship between plaintiff and defendant as one of accommodation and charity, but it passes understanding when it is considered as one of contractual obligation of the kind here sought to be imposed. That consideration has become so strong with us that we feel that the interests of justice require a new trial.

The case was submitted to the jury upon the theory of a contract expressed by both words and conduct. The jury was permitted to consider it a case of services rendered at the request of defendant without an agreement as to their value, but with the mutual understanding that they were to be paid for. Upon that issue,

it should be observed that the fact that services are rendered, even on request, does not create liability where the circumstances repel the inference that compensation was intended. So when services are performed or acts done, even on request, merely from kind or charitable motives, the law will not imply a promise to pay for them. It follows that when the use of property is accorded one on a promise of maintenance made solely through charitable or kind motives, no contract results. Even though in such a case the words used have a contractual sound, yet if clearly the parties do not intend to assume contractual obligation, no contract results. Again, in such a case, it is easy for an interested party, in retrospect, to give to a mere expression of intention a promissory and contractual effect. That may well have taken place here. If in this case defendant, out of anxiety to save plaintiff from his old habits, had expressed the intention of caring for him for life, it would have been easy for a man of much better education than that of plaintiff, out of self-interest, to convert that expression into a promise. Such an issue is ordinarily one for the trier of fact, but if this case is resubmitted to a jury, it might be well to explain not only that agreements entered into solely for kindly and charitable as distinguished from contractual purposes cannot result in legal obligation, but also that care should be taken not to attach promissory and contractual effect to what was at the time merely an expression of intention concerning future action.

Order reversed.

Case Questions:

1. In this case, the court commented that the plaintiff's physical improvement of the land was not significant. Was this an important part of the court's decision in this case? Why or why not?

2. Why justification did the court give in deciding that no contract existed?

3. Is it true that the relationship gave no benefit to the defendant?

4. Is this really a case of charity and not a contractual relationship? Why or why not?

5. What situation or agreement would have justified a different decision in this case?

The Case of the Angry Attorney

J. ROBERT LYNCH, Justice[2]

The plaintiff, an attorney, has brought this action to recover the value of legal services alleged to have been performed for the defendant. The complaint seeks $5,214.87 with interest from June 1, 1962, the date of an alleged demand for payment and the date upon which the plaintiff contends that his cause of action accrued. The defendant contests the merits of the complaint. It also asserts a defense of the six-year statute of limitations. The plaintiff was first employed to act as its attorney by the defendant in 1952 or 1953, as the plaintiff has testified not on any retainer basis, but by being called upon to handle individual matters as they arose. About June 1958, the defendant, through its officers, asked the plaintiff to do something about its real property tax assessments which it felt were excessive. The plaintiff told the defendant that his fee for handling its assessment problems would be one-half of any first year tax saving he effected at the grievance board level; that, if a tax certiorari had to be prosecuted in the courts, his fee would be at the election of the defendant, either the entire amount of the first year's tax saving that he accomplished or one-half of the first two years' tax savings.

The plaintiff prosecuted a protest of the 1959 assessment by a tax certiorari proceeding to the point where he obtained a reduction of the assessment in a memorandum opinion from Hon. George T. Vandermeulen, Official Referee, dated March 1st, 1960. No order was ever entered upon this opinion to effectuate a tax saving. Instead, the plaintiff used the opinion as a lever against the grievance board to attempt to force a reduction in at least a similar amount, and hopefully a greater amount, with respect to the subsequent years' assessments. He states that this strategy was approved by the defendant which hoped to obtain a greater reduction than that allowed by the official referee.

The plaintiff's letter to the defendant was actually dated July 31st. It summarized his accomplishments:

"We have received notification from Mr. Richard Fitchette, Chairman of the Town of Alexandria Board of Assessors that your tax assessments have been reduced for 1962. . . . . Since this case commenced, we have obtained a total assessment reduction on Holland Street of $22,600.00 and on the Boat Works of $16,900.00, or a total reduction in assessments of $39,500.00. This represents a tax saving each year of approximately $1,975.00."

The letter went on to suggest that any further legal proceedings were at least temporarily halted. "I did, however, advise the board that if they granted the above reduction this year, we would not bring a tax certiorari proceeding this year. As I told you, they have discharged their former attorney, and I am sure that they are as anxious as you folks to avoid any future litigation."

Having been given a summary of the plaintiff's accomplishments with the implication that there was to be no "future litigation" and having been told that the plaintiff had effectuated a first year tax savings of "approximately" $1,975, the defendant tried to get a bill from him for his services. By letter of October 20, 1961, it asked for a statement of services up to September 1, 1961. This letter also disputed the plaintiff's assertion that he had saved the defendant $1,975 in taxes.

The plaintiff gave the defendant no written bill. He testified that he gave an oral statement to the defendant reciting the same amount for his services that he later asked in Schedule A annexed to the complaint. At least he says that he thinks he did, because he contends that this was not really a bill in the sense of being a demand for payment but was merely a statement to show what the defendant owed him so that the latter could include it as an expense in that year's income tax return which was on an accrual basis, and because he usually gave orally such a figure to the defendant annually. We cannot credit this testimony, nor accept this explanation, because the letters from the defendant to the plaintiff make it obvious that it wanted a bill, and, if it wanted it for its tax return, it also wanted it so it could pay it.

When it had not received such a statement as a result of its October 20th letter, the defendant wrote the plaintiff another letter on November 3, 1961. It stated that the defendant was "very anxious to get the 1961 business straightened out. If I do not hear from you promptly, I will take it for granted that your bill is as outlined in the (defendant's letter of October 20th)," i.e., based on a claimed tax savings of approximately $1,975.

This letter elicited no response from the plaintiff and on January 26, 1962, the defendant sent the plaintiff a check for $987.50 (one-half of $1,975). The plaintiff has never cashed the check nor has he returned it.

The plaintiff testified that the defendant told him it wanted no further assessment proceedings and asked him to submit a bill. He states that he made up a bill claiming $2,136.95 plus disbursements of $454.87. It recited that its basis was "tax savings for 1961–62: $39,500.00 = 54.10/m $2,136.95." The bill was dated June 1, 1962, and contained an itemization of the services rendered and the date each was rendered.

The testimony proves a contract between the parties, "an obligation attached by the mere force of law to certain acts of the parties, usually words, which ordinarily accompany and represent a known intent" (*Hotchkiss v. National City Bank of New York*,

D.C.N.Y., 200 F. 287, aff'd, 231 U.S. 50, 34 S.Ct. 20, 58 L.Ed. 115, as restated in *Matter of Ahern v. South Buffalo Ry. Co.*, 303 N.Y. 545, 561, 104 N.E.2d 898, 908). We add the proviso that the full intent of the parties must be capable of reasonably certain ascertainment, else the contract alleged would be too uncertain to be meaningful or binding. (9 N.Y.Jur., Contracts, s 46, pp. 575–76.) Here, resort to the circumstances of the meeting between the plaintiff and the defendant, and the statements engendered there, leads inescapably to the conclusion that a binding contract was created. The subsequent interaction of the plaintiff and defendant in processing a review of the tax assessment was an overt manifestation of their mutual assent to the terms of the employment of the plaintiff that they had discussed.

Case Questions:

1. Does the court determine that a contract exists in this case? If so, why?

2. Explain the basic dispute between the plaintiff and defendant in this case.

3. What does this court say about how a contract should manifest the intention of the parties?

4. Is the problem with this case that there were no specifics about when a contractual relationship developed?

5. What facts does the court rely on in finding that a contract existed?

ETHICS FILE: Introduction to Ethics

Paralegals must be as concerned about ethics as the attorneys with whom they work. As a paralegal, you often will be given broad responsibilities, but your training in the complicated ethical requirements of the legal system may not have been all you would have hoped. One way of addressing ethical requirements is to be aware of the ethical codes established by the national paralegal associations. There are two major national paralegal associations, the National Federation of Paralegal Associations (NFPA) and the National Association of Legal Assistants. Practicing paralegals and paralegal students are eligible to join either or both of these organizations. Benefits of membership include newsletters, annual conventions and a ready-made network of friendly professionals who can often assist a paralegal with difficult or unusual legal matters. Both organizations have created model rules of ethical behavior for paralegals. The Web sites for both are provided.

Business Case File

Corner Oak Manor Bed and Breakfast

Karen and Andy Spradley

Karen and Andy Spradley took a vacation 15 years ago and stayed at a bed and breakfast in California. When they were there, the idea suddenly dawned on them they could open their own bed and breakfast.

"We didn't know anything about running a business," said Karen. "We had to do a lot of research, especially about laws. There were dozens of things we had to consider. For one thing, we bought a one hundred year old house and decided that we'd put our bed and breakfast in it. The first thing we had to consider was the zoning regulations. In any business, there are all kinds of laws and rules and regulations that you have to learn about. We got it all together and have been running our B&B for fourteen years now. I'm glad we did it, but it wasn't easy."

—*Karen Spradley, Corner Oak Manor, Bed and Breakfast, Asheville, North Carolina*

Chapter Summary:

Contracts involve basic elements that must exist in every contract in order for it to be legally valid. These elements include mutual assent, which is composed of a valid offer and a valid agreement. The contract must be supported by consideration, which is the exchange of something of value between the parties. Parties to a contract must have the legal capacity to enter into a contract. A contract also must have a legal object in mind; contracts for illegal activities will not be enforced. Contracts are often categorized by the method of creation, such as unilateral contracts that involve a promise from one party in exchange for an action by the other. By contrast, bilateral contracts involve the promise from one party in exchange for the promise of the other party. In many situations, there is no requirement that a contract be put in writing to be enforceable, unless the subject of the contract falls into one of the categories under the Statute of Frauds. In that situation, a contract will only be legally viable when the parties reduce it to writing (see Exhibit 1-5).

✔ **PARALEGAL CHECKLIST**

- ☐ Names of the parties
- ☐ Addresses of the parties
- ☐ Language expressing intent to enter into an agreement
- ☐ Language expressing that there is some form of consideration
- ☐ A detailed description of the terms, prices, and duties imposed on the parties
- ☐ Language expressing the length or term of the contract
- ☐ The date the contract become effective

EXHIBIT 1-5: Features that a contract should contain.

WEB SITES

National Association of Legal Assistants
http://www.nala.org/
Provides extensive information about paralegal careers, specializations and other helpful information.

American Association for Paralegal Education
http://www.aafpe.org/
Serves paralegal educators and institutions. Offers useful links and information about paralegal education.

UCC Online
http://www.law.cornell.edu/ucc
Legal Information Institute's home page on the Uniform Commercial Code.

Westlaw
www.westlaw.com
Provides extensive and comprehensive references for legal research. A pay site.

Legal Information Institute—Overview of Contract Law
http://www.law.cornell.edu/topics
Provides excellent overviews on a wide variety of legal topics, including contract law.

REVIEW QUESTIONS

1. What are the basic elements of a contract?
2. Explain the "Mailbox Rule."
3. List three situations in which a person is not legally competent to enter into a contract.
4. What is the Statute of Frauds? Provide four examples.
5. Explain consideration.
6. What is the difference between a "void" and a "voidable contract?"
7. What are some contracts required to be put into writing before they are legally enforceable?
8. Why is it necessary to have a rule that protects children from entering into contracts?
9. How does a counteroffer affect the original offer?
10. When an offer specifies that acceptance must come in the form of a letter and a person accepts by telephone, there is no contract. Why? What would justify such a rule?
11. What is meant by the "power of acceptance?"
12. Can a person accept an offer without actually communicating the acceptance?
13. What is the difference between a bilateral contract and a unilateral contract?
14. What are examples of actions that would terminate an offer?
15. How is consideration different from capacity?
16. Why must the subject of a contract be legal?
17. Is an executed contract a void contract?
18. What are some of the national paralegal associations and what role do they play in providing ethical models for paralegals?
19. Explain the result in the "Case of the Charity." Why did the court rule that no contract existed?
20. If only specific types of contracts are required to be in writing, why do so many people write out contracts anyway?

HANDS-ON ASSIGNMENT

Spend some time going through your local telephone book or online. How many attorneys are listed under "Corporation and Business Law"? How does the number of firms compare with those who are listed under "Personal Injury"? What conclusions can you draw from this comparison?

PRACTICAL APPLICATION

In a typical automobile purchase, how are the various elements of a contract satisfied?

HELP THIS BUSINESS

A guest staying at Corner Oak Manor disputes his bill. He tells the Spradleys that since there was no written contract between himself and the Innkeepers that there is no binding contract. Based on what you have learned in this chapter, how can you help the Spradleys?

KEY TERMS

contract	detriment
mutual assent	capacity
offer	unilateral contract
power of acceptance	bilateral contract
acceptance	void
Mailbox Rule	voidable
consideration	Statute of Frauds

ENDNOTES

[1] 214 N.W. 928 (Minn. 1927)

[2] *Shaad v. Hutchinson's Boat Works, Inc.*, 84 Misc.2d 631,376 N.Y.S.2d 861 (N.Y.Sup. 1975)

 For additional resources, visit our Web site at www.westlegalstudies.com

CHAPTER 2

OFFERS

Focus of this chapter: This chapter focuses on the law as it applies to making an offer, including how an offer is defined, whether advertisements are considered offers, termination and revocation of offers, and the effect of counteroffers.

Chapter Objectives:
At the completion of this chapter, you should be able to:

- Define what an offer is
- Explain how an offer is made
- Describe the importance of the offeror's intention when making the offer
- Explain the difference between offers and invitations to make an offer
- List and explain the various ways that an offer can be terminated
- Explain revocation of offers
- Describe the effect of a counteroffer on the original offer
- Describe the type of language needed to make an offer
- Explain how an advertisement may become an offer
- Describe the various ways that a party would prove revocation/rejection of an offer

Introduction to Offers

Is this section, we examine the various legal aspects of offers. How definite must an offer be? What does the law require for a valid offer? These questions and many others will be answered in the next few sections.

Defining an Offer

An offer is an expression by one person of his willingness to enter into a bargain with another person. A valid offer communicates the idea that the other person, by accepting the offer, will enter into a valid contract.[1] However, when a person realizes that an offer is made in jest, or by someone with no intention of actually entering into a contract, there is no offer, because the requisite intent is missing.

When the courts consider the validity of an offer, the objective facts are always examined. The question asked by the court is, "would a reasonable person, under these facts, consider the statement to be an offer?" If the answer to that question is no, then there is no offer and thus no binding contract.[2] Courts will not consider the **offeror's** subjective reasons in making his offer. Even if the offeror later claims that he was just "fooling around," a statement that appears to be a valid offer will be considered one, despite the offeror's claim to the contrary.

offeror: The person making the offer

Preliminary business discussions or communications about entering into a contract are not offers. To be legally effective, an offer must be definite about terms and conditions. A valid offer is specific and can be enforced by law.[3] This is not to say that offers cannot have a degree of creativity and flexibility.

HYPOTHETICAL 2-1   Rainy Day Offer

Rene approaches Rick and says, "If it rains today, I'll clean out your gutters for $5. If it doesn't rain, I'll clean your gutters for $10."

Is this a valid offer?

Answer: Yes. Even though the offer is made in the alternative, giving different conditions and different results, it is still definite enough to be enforceable.[4]

Proving an Offer

When presenting proof at trial that an offer was made, it is not fatal to the plaintiff's case that he cannot remember the defendant's exact wording when he made the offer. After all, the court will examine both the words and the actions of both parties. Generally, if both parties behave as though they had entered into a contract, this behavior will be strong evidence that both sides, at least at one point in time, believed that a legally binding contract existed.[5] The actual determination about whether specific words created a contract is left to the jury.

When do preliminary discussions cross the line into a valid offer and acceptance? For instance, in the give and take of a business conference, when does the law consider that the parties have entered into a contract? Courts have not come up with any standard to be applied to all contractual negotiations that settles this question. Instead, each case must be considered on its own merits. Testimony about what was said and what was subsequently done form the crucial points in making this determination, but there is no hard-and-fast rule that will work in all situations.[6]

HYPOTHETICAL 2-2   For Sale by Owner

Miguel decides to sell his home. Rather than deal with a broker, he simply puts a "For Sale" sign in his front yard. Stan sees the sign and decides that Miguel's house is worth about $90,000. He knocks on Miguel's door and tries to hand Miguel a check for that amount. Miguel refuses to accept the check and Stan sues for breach of contract. Did a contract exist?

Answer: No. The question here is the significance of Miguel's sign. When a homeowner puts a "For Sale" sign in his yard, is he making an offer, or inviting offers? Courts consider such signs to be invitations to make an offer and therefore they are not legally enforceable offers.

GENERAL OFFERS VERSUS GENERAL INVITATIONS TO MAKE AN OFFER

When examining this area of law, it is important to make a distinction between general offers and general invitations to make an offer. A general offer is made to a nonspecific person. For instance, Miguel puts a sign in his front yard that states, "Will sell to the first person to appear with $100,000 in cash." Unlike the previous scenario, in which Miguel's "For Sale" sign was simply an invitation to make an offer, Miguel's sign is actually an offer. Why? For one thing, it is specific and definite. Although it is not made to a specific person, it is legally valid. Miguel would be obligated to sell his home (which seems to be the clear intent of his sign) to the first person to show up with the correct amount of money. Simply because an offer is not made to a specific person does not affect its legality.

HYPOTHETICAL 2-3   The Newspaper Ad

The following advertisement appeared in the local newspaper: "Bolstridge Corporation is accepting bids on the refurbishment of its main factory complex located at 100 Macon Way. All bids must be in writing."

Is this an offer or an invitation to make an offer?

Answer: It is an invitation to make an offer. How can we be sure? For one thing, advertisements are almost always construed to be invitations to make an offer. Despite that, we can examine the details and come to the same conclusion. Does the statement show a clear and definite intent to enter into a contract? Could someone 'accept' this advertisement without any further information? If not, then it is not a valid offer.[7]

However, the situation in Hypothetical 2-3 changes dramatically when the Bolstridge Corporation reviews the bids and accepts one. At that point, the bid is an offer that has been accepted by the corporation.

THE INTENT TO CONTRACT

At its simplest, a statement becomes an offer when it shows the speaker's intent to enter into a contract. The offeror's intent is absolutely essential to the transaction, but the court is in no better position to read the offeror's mind than anyone else. The only way to determine the offeror's intent is to examine his or her actions. How does the offeror's intent manifest itself? In this case, actions really do speak louder than words. If the offeror behaves in a manner consistent with making an offer, that behavior will have a telling effect with the court.

An offeror is free to make an offer to the public at large. There is no requirement that a valid offer must be addressed to a particular person. Even though advertisements and notices in newspapers are usually not offers, they can be drafted in such a way as to be considered a valid offer and would therefore give anyone the right to accept.[8] General offers or offers made to the public at large are usually unilateral contracts, that is, a promise in exchange for an action. Consider Hypothetical 2-4.

Sidebar:

When a general offer is made, how do the courts determine who the parties to the contract are? The test normally applied in this situation is: who has consideration? Put another way, who did something that he was not obligated to do, or refrained from doing something he could legally do, in response to the offer?[9] Consideration is discussed in depth in Chapter 4.

HYPOTHETICAL 2-4   The Lost Puppy

Marcia has lost her puppy. She posts signs throughout her neighborhood that states: "Lost Golden Retriever puppy. Will pay $10 to whoever brings him to 21 Robin Lane." Is this a valid offer?

Answer: Yes. Marcia has made a general offer to the public that can be accepted by anyone who produces her puppy.

Language Used to Make an Offer

There must be some specific statement or act that will qualify as an offer. Of course, it is helpful if the offeror actually uses the statement, "I offer you," or, "I hereby, without condition, extend the following offer to you ... " However, this language is not required for a valid offer to exist. In situations in which the offeror's acts or statements are ambiguous, it is up to the court (and often a jury) to interpret the facts of the case.[10]

Interpreting the words and actions of the parties can sometimes involve sifting through a great deal of testimony and other proof. Suppose, for example, that Miguel, the offeror, has a unique way of expressing himself. When he says, "I can get you that car for $1,000," he means that he is offering the car for sale for that amount of money. People who are familiar with

Sidebar:

There are no specific words that are required for a valid offer; however, there are words that will definitely not make a statement a valid offer. For instance, use of the words "invitation to bid," or "advertisement," often will be construed by the courts as expressly removing the statement from consideration as a valid offer.[11]

Miguel's unusual way of expressing himself could testify at trial as to what that statement means.

Mutual Assent

In considering whether a contract exists between two parties, courts will often consider the issue of mutual assent. The courts will ask, "Was there a valid offer and, if so, was there a valid acceptance?" If the answer to both of these questions is yes, the court is a long way toward determining mutual assent. But mutual assent involves more than a mere legally valid offer and acceptance. We will explore the issue of mutual assent in a later chapter. However, when the ambiguities in a contract rise to the level of showing that the parties did not have a proper meeting of the minds about what the contract was about, this can invalidate the contract.[12] When we speak of **meeting of the minds**, we look at the offer and acceptance as though they exist independently of the people making and accepting the offer. Consider Hypothetical 2-5.

meeting of the minds: The general agreement between parties to a contract as to material terms.

HYPOTHETICAL 2-5   Car Sale

Miguel wants to sell his car and knows that John is interested in acquiring it. He offers to sell John his car for $2,000, and John immediately accepts. A few moments after making the offer, however, Miguel begins to have second thoughts. He is no longer sure that he wants to sell the car. When John appears with the $2,000, Miguel claims that there is no longer a "meeting of the minds," because he has second thoughts about the entire proposition. Is there a contract?

Answer: Yes. When speaking of a meeting of the minds, we refer to the precise instant of the offer and the acceptance, not to any subsequent developments, second thoughts, regrets, or any other manifestations. What is important is that at the moment of the offer and acceptance, both parties were agreeing to the same proposition. In this way, we look at the offer and acceptance divorced from almost all other considerations.

Miguel's second thoughts about selling his car do not affect the legality of his offer and John's subsequent acceptance. As far as the law is concerned, there is a binding contract and Miguel's failure to perform (i.e., by selling his car) is actionable. John may sue for breach of contract, and, as we will see in a later chapter, may be entitled to specific performance (a court order forcing Miguel to sell his car).

The fact that some of the terms in the contract are vague, or that the parties later contested the validity of certain aspects of the contract in court, does not mean that there was no meeting of the minds at the time of the offer and acceptance.

Advertisements

In most situations, advertisements are not offers. They are usually interpreted by the courts as invitations to make an offer. The important question in determining whether an advertisement is an offer is whether a person could simply accept the ad without any further discussion and create a binding contract. In most situations, advertisements do not fall into this category. In reviewing the facts of a particular case, the courts will often look to the advertiser's intent. Was the ad placed as a way of encouraging people to come to the store and buy merchandise, or was it the manifestation of intent to contract? In most situations, an advertisement is simply a ploy to attract buyers.

Among the tests that have developed over the years is an examination of the precision or definiteness used in the advertising. Consider these two ads:

"Fine Corinthian China, set of 6, a low, low $39.95, normally $69.95!"

"Set of fine Corinthian China, set of 6, first three people through the door on Tuesday morning will be able to purchase at a low, low $39.95, normally $69.95!"

The first ad is not an offer. How can we be sure? For one thing, there is very little in the way of definiteness. The ad looks, and was designed to be, an invitation for buyers to come to the store and peruse the merchandise and perhaps even to buy a set of china.

But our analysis changes sharply with the second example. Although the same china is advertised, there is additional detail provided that changes it from an invitation to make an offer to a legally binding offer. How do we know? Look at the detail provided. How would someone accept this offer? The **offeree** would have to be one of the first three people through the doors of the business on Tuesday morning, with $39.95. The advertisement provides a level of definiteness that is normally absent from circulars and newspaper ads. Actually, the second advertisement is an offer for a unilateral contract. There is a promise (the sale of a set of six pieces of Corinthian china for $39.95 in exchange for an action: being one of the first three people through the door with the correct amount of money).

Because advertisements are generally not considered to be valid, legal offers, when an advertisement makes a mistake, such as advertising an expensive item at a ridiculously low price, the customer cannot insist on purchasing at that price, because there is no contract to be enforced.

offeree: The person to whom the offer is made

HYPOTHETICAL 2-6   The Really Cheap Tires

Example: "Chris Tire Sales announces the sale of a complete set of Saturn, high grade steel-belted radial tires, installed, balanced, with free lifetime rotation for $5.00!"

Miguel sees this advertisement and cannot believe his good fortune. He badly needs a new set of tires on his car and had been saving the several hundred dollars it would take to get them. He immediately drives down to Chris Tire Sales and sees a long line of customers stretched down the street. He quickly joins the line. A few minutes later, a representative of the tire store comes out and announces that the ad was a misprint. The ad, he explains, should have said three hundred and five dollars, not five dollars. There is a collective groan from the crowd and as the others disperse, Miguel moves forward and demands that he receive a set of tires for the stated price of $5.00, telling the man that the tire store made a valid, legal offer and Miguel has accepted it. The man refuses. Miguel files suit, seeking enforcement of the advertisement and asking that the tire store comply by placing a new set of tires on his car for $5. What does the judge rule?

Answer: Miguel loses. The judge rules that the advertisement was not an offer. Therefore, the misprint had no relevance to Miguel's purported acceptance.

STATING A PRICE IN AN ADVERTISEMENT

Suppose that an ad actually gives a stated price? For instance, after Miguel tried to sell his own house and met with no success, he contacted a local real estate broker and listed his home with her. She suggested that Miguel list his home in the Multiple Listing Service, which shows all of the homes for sale in the area and is seen by all local real estate agents. As part of the listing, she lists the following information: "3 bedroom, 2 bath, 2,400 square feet, $105,000."

Maria sees this listing and decides to view Miguel's home. When she does, she likes what she sees. At the end of the tour, she turns to Miguel's realtor and says, "I accept. I can have the $105,000 in about a week." Is Miguel obligated to sell his home to Maria? No. Advertisements, even those that contain price quotations are still considered to be invitations to make an offer, not actual offers in themselves.[14]

What about price quotations given in other contexts? Suppose that you pick up a catalog that shows office furniture for sale. You see a desk that you particularly like and you submit a purchase order for the desk, listing the correct model and product number. Do you have a contract with the furniture company? Again, the answer is probably no. The reason is that price quotations are almost always considered to be invitations to make an offer and most courts would construe the purchase order as an offer made by you that could be accepted (or rejected) by the office furniture store.[15]

Does the wrong price in an advertisement amount to an offer?

The Case of the Cheap China[16]

FRANCIS G. CALDEIRA, J.

On February 11, 1981 the defendant advertised for sale, in *Newsday*, "Sango" china dishes. The advertisement listed the sale price of service for 12 at $39.95 with the regular price listed as $280. The plaintiff attempted to purchase the dishes from the defendant for $39.95; the defendant would not sell at that price. Thereafter, the plaintiff commenced this small claims action seeking to recover $280. The plaintiff has failed to prove any actual damages. No proof was submitted that she purchased the dishes elsewhere. She has not sought to recover the difference in the purchase price and the price advertised; rather, she has simply sought to recover $280. Further, the plaintiff may not recover on a breach of contract theory because the advertisement "is nothing but an invitation to enter into negotiations, and is not an offer which may be turned into a contract by a person who signifies his intention to purchase some of the articles mentioned in the advertisement." But these conclusions do not end consideration of the matter. Article 22-A of the General Business Law must be considered. Sections 350-a and 350 of the General Business Law, contained in that article, define and prohibit false advertising. Effective June 19, 1980, subdivision 3 of section 350-d was added to the General Business Law. This section provides, in part: "Any person who has been injured by reason of any violation of section three hundred fifty or three hundred fifty-a of this article may bring an action in his own name to enjoin such unlawful act or practice and to recover his actual damages or fifty dollars, which ever is greater. The court may, in its discretion, increase the award of damages to an amount not to exceed three times the actual damages up to one thousand dollars, if the court finds the defendant willfully or knowingly violated this section." This provision raises several issues not fully explored or argued by the parties in this small claims case but which determine whether the plaintiff is entitled to recover. The first question is whether the defendant engaged in the practice of falsely advertising. A second question is whether the plaintiff has been injured. More specifically, this question is whether the plaintiff has been "injured" though she has not proven breach of contract damages. Clearly she was unable to purchase the china dishes for the price advertised. Section 350-a of the General Business Law provides: "The term 'false advertising' means advertising, including labeling, which is misleading in a material respect; and in determining whether any advertising is misleading, there shall be taken into account (among other things) not only representations made by statement, word, design, device, sound or any combination thereof, but also the extent to which the advertisement fails to reveal facts material in the light of such representations with respect to the commodity to which the advertising relates under the conditions prescribed in said advertisement, or under such conditions as are customary or usual." In deciding whether the defendant has violated sections 350 and 350-a the key question is whether the advertisement was "misleading in a material respect." It seems clear that the plaintiff need not prove intent to deceive to establish false advertising. First, section 350-a does not define "false advertising" in terms of intent. Second, subdivision 3 of section 350-d permits the court to increase damages otherwise recoverable if it finds that the defendant willfully or knowingly falsely advertises. The advertisement in question was a full page appearing in *Newsday*. In bold print to the right side of the page the advertisement reads, "40% to 50% off regular prices Mikasa Sango and Yamaka." Listed below are four specific sets of china with regular and sale prices shown. The first is a 20-piece set regularly $100 on sale for $59.95. The second is a 40-piece set regularly $140 on sale for $59.95. The third is a set of service for 8 regularly $120 on sale for $69.95. The fourth is the item in controversy. It shows a set of service for 12 regularly $280 on sale for $39.95. In *People v. Volkswagen of Amer.* (47 AD2d 868) the Appellate Division discussed the meaning of misleading advertising in the context of this article of the General Business Law. In so doing, the court cited several cases including *People v. Glubo* (5 NY2d 461). In that case, the Court of Appeals construed section 421 of the former Penal Law, which provided, in relevant part (pp. 469–470): "Any person . . . who, with intent to sell . . . merchandise . . . or anything offered by such person . . . directly or indirectly, to the public for sale or distribution, or with intent to increase the consumption thereof makes, publishes, disseminates, circulates, or places before the public, or causes, directly or indirectly, to be made, published disseminated, circulated, or placed before the public, in this state . . . over any radio station or in any other way, an advertisement, announcement or statement of any sort regarding merchandise . . . or anything so offered . . . which advertisement contains any assertion, representation or statement of fact which is untrue, deceptive or misleading, shall be guilty of a misdemeanor." Then, quoting *People v. Richter's Jewelers* (291 NY 161) interpreting the same provision the court stated (p. 472), "[i]n any event, though innocent error might render the offense venial, a statement of fact which is untrue, deceptive, or misleading, placed upon a tag 'with intent to sell or in any wise dispose of merchandise' constitutes a violation of section 421 of the Penal Law even when the statement is made without 'actual evil design or contrivance to perpetuate fraud or injury upon others.' The statutory offense is committed by 'material misrepresentations intended to influence the bargain' though at times such misrepresentations may be due to lack of care rather than dishonesty."

Thus, even in construing a Penal Law provision, the court found that intent to deceive was not an element in a case of false advertising. Accordingly, this court finds that judicial interpretation of article 22-A and the clear language of the statute dictate the conclusion that the plaintiff need not establish an intent to deceive.

Therefore, to establish a right to recover damages in this action the plaintiff need only establish that the advertisement was misleading in a material respect and that she was "injured." No dispute exists that the defendant would not sell the dishes for the price advertised. Perhaps it could be argued that the price in question was so low that it could not be taken for anything but an obvious mistake and thus, could not be misleading. But, this argument must be rejected. Sections 349 and 350 of the General

Business Law were enacted to safeguard the 'vast multitude which includes the ignorant, the unthinking and the credulous'. . . The test is not whether the average man would be deceived. Further, the $39.95 price is not so clearly an error as may first appear. As noted, the bold print on the right side of the advertisement indicates "40% to 50% off regular prices." Below, four specific items are shown. Two of the four advertise more than 50% off the regular price. The second item is advertised regularly for $140 on sale for $59.95. Certainly, this price is apparently reasonable enough to lead even "an average man" to believe the $140 dishes could be purchased for $59.95. If the 40% to 50% limitation does not apply here, it is difficult to pick the point at which the advertised sale price would be obviously too low to be that which was intended. Indeed, it is as likely that the error is in the listing of the percentages as it is in the prices. Thus, even on the limited proof submitted, the plaintiff has established that the defendant's advertisement was misleading in a material way within the meaning of article 22-A of the General Business Law.

The next question is whether the plaintiff has been injured within the meaning of subdivision 3 of section 350-d of the General Business Law. As noted above, the plaintiff did not prove actual damages. But it appears that a plaintiff need not prove actual damages to prove he is a "person who has been injured." As this section is written, it seems that a person who is mislead or deceived by an advertisement which is misleading in a material way is an injured person. The statute entitles the plaintiff to recover "his actual damages or fifty dollars, whichever is greater." The statute could have been written to limit the right to recover damages to any person who has suffered actual damages. But the statute speaks of a person who is injured and it explicitly grants a right to recover $50 without requiring the plaintiff to establish actual damages of that amount. Further, the Governor's memorandum in support of the bill indicates that by providing for a minimum damage recovery section 350-d (as well as newly added subdivision [h] of section 349 relating to deceptive acts or practices) is intended to encourage private suits. Thus, it seems that the Legislature intended $50 to be easily recoverable. The plaintiff is, therefore, entitled to recover that amount. The implications of this construction of the statute are awesome. Even running corrective advertising will not provide a defense by the terms of the section, other than to the extent it establishes that a person was not deceived or mislead. Very little in the way of reliance on the misleading advertisement need be shown. Possible liability for a mistake in advertisements in *Newsday* or any other newspaper so widely disseminated could be virtually limitless. But it does seem that this is the mandated result. Section 350-d of the General Business Law may be in need of legislative review and revision. However, in the present case, the plaintiff is entitled to judgment in the amount of $50.

Case Questions:

1. Is this a case about false advertising?
2. Does the court require that the plaintiff prove intent in alleging her claim?
3. If the store's advertisement was an obvious mistake that anyone of average intelligence would assume was a simple typographical error, does that relieve the store of liability? Why or why not?
4. Why is the plaintiff entitled to recover $50?
5. Explain the court's rationale in this decision.

MISTAKES IN ADVERTISEMENTS DO NOT CREATE OFFERS

Because a mistake in an advertisement is not an offer, what should the business owner do? Although it is true that he or she can refuse to sell at the mistaken price, the owner may not want to sour his customers on his business. He can do any of the following:

- Sell the goods at the advertised, and mistaken, price
- Post a sign prominently in his window stating that the advertisement was an error and offer a discount on the item, if the advertised price is unreasonably low

Does the business owner have an action against the newspaper that published the mistaken material? His action against the newspaper cannot be based on a contractual theory, such as a claim that the business owner was compelled to enter into a contract with customers who wrongly assumed that the asking price was legitimate. The reason that the business owner cannot make this claim is because the law does not recognize that the advertisement was an offer in the first place.

WHEN DOES AN ADVERTISEMENT BECOME AN OFFER?

An advertisement may be considered an offer when the words used express some intent on the part of the merchant to assume legal liability. What kind of wording would this be?

Sidebar:
"Bait and switch" is a term used to refer to unscrupulous business owners who deliberately publish advertisements for items well below market value, just to encourage shoppers to come to the store. When they arrive, they are told that the item has "sold out" but a substantially similar model, which is only "slightly" more expensive than the advertised item is available.

HYPOTHETICAL 2-7   Offer for a New Car

Early Bird Motors published the following ad in the local paper:

"If you purchased a 2004 model from us during January of this year, you can trade up to a 2005 for no extra cost. You must present proof of purchase that shows you purchased your automobile between January 1 and January 3 of this year, including registration and receipt. Your car must be in running condition (determined by our mechanics). This offer is only good from October 1 through October 31."

Is this advertisement actually a valid, legal offer?

Answer: Yes. What makes this advertisement different from others that are not considered to be offers? For one thing, there are very specific details. Instead of simply advertising various items for sale, this advertisement presents enough detail, and to specific persons, so that it could be accepted. How would someone accept this offer? The person would first have had to purchase a 2004 model during January. Then, by presenting proof of purchase between the listed dates, the person would be entitled to receive a 2005 model at no extra charge. That detail certainly sounds as though Early Bird Motors is intending to enter into a contract. In fact, in the case on which this hypothetical is based, the court did rule that the car dealership presented a valid offer that could be accepted.

Rejecting an Offer

Once a person has rejected an offer, it cannot be accepted. As far as the law is concerned, a rejected offer is legally invalid and once gone, it cannot return unless a new offer is made.[17] Rejection can come in many forms. The offeree can simply state that he rejects the offer. The offeree also can reject by actions that would indicate to a reasonable person that he has rejected the offer, such as shaking his head, turning away, storming out of the room, and so on.[18] However, it is not a rejection for the offeree to ask for time to consider the offer. It is a rejection if the offeree does not accept within a stated time limit, or after the passage of a "reasonable" amount of time after the offer has been made (see exhibit 2-1).

✓ **PARALEGAL CHECKLIST**

Any or all of the following can prove rejection of an offer:

☐ Testimony from the offeror about the offeree's actions/words that indicated a refusal of the offer

☐ Testimony from third parties about the offeree's actions and how they were consistent with someone who had rejected the offer

☐ Cross-examination of the offeree about his actions, such as
   - communicating his "acceptance" in an unauthorized method
   - making material changes in the offer, thus converting it into a counteroffer
   - conditions or other limitations on his acceptance

EXHIBIT 2-1: Proving rejection.

Counteroffers

counteroffer: A rejection of an offer and a new offer made back.

When a person makes a **counteroffer**, he is rejecting the first offer and substituting it with one of his own (Exhibits 2-2 and 2-3).

- Offeree asks that one more of the terms be slightly altered[i]
- There is some vagueness about the terms of the offer, such as type of payment, and so on

---

EXHIBIT 2-2: Statements and other negotiations that do not constitute counteroffers.

---

[i] *Turner v. Mccormick*, 56 W. Va. 161, 49 SE 28 (1904).

- Offeree prepares a new contract with different terms than original offer[i]
- Offeree gives a conditional acceptance, such as "I will only accept if you also throw in your stamp collection"[ii]

EXHIBIT 2-3: Statements and other negotiations that do constitute counteroffers.

---

[i] *Thomas v. Life Ins. Co.*, 219 La 1099, 55 So 2d 705 (1951).
[ii] Restatement, Contracts 2d §39.

HYPOTHETICAL 2-8   The Coin Sale

Example: Maria wants to buy Leonard's coin collection. Maria offers Leonard $100 for the collection. Leonard states that the collection is worth more than $100. Leonard says, "I'd consider selling at three hundred." What is the current status of offer and acceptance between Maria and Leonard?

Maria made an offer of $100.

Leonard refused it and made a counteroffer of $300.

One way of approaching this question is to ask, "Who has the right to accept the offer?" In a typical negotiation, the right (referred to as the power of acceptance, covered in the next chapter) shifts from one person to another, until the offer is accepted.

Another way that we can be sure that Leonard has made a counteroffer is to examine the following scenario:

Maria says, in response to Leonard's counteroffer of $300, "that's ridiculous!" "Okay," Leonard says, "I'll sell for $100."

"No, I'm not going to buy from you, now. You're a jerk!"

Is there a binding contract between Maria and Leonard now?

Answer: No. When Leonard made his counteroffer of $300, the original offer was taken off the table. As far as the law is concerned, the offer of $100 is dead and therefore cannot be acted on. At the moment that Leonard made his counteroffer what he was really saying is: "I hereby reject your offer of $100 and substitute instead my offer of $300." Of course, people don't usually speak like that, so the wording must be inferred from the actions of Maria and Leonard.

THE VALIDITY OF A COUNTEROFFER

A counteroffer must meet the same requirements as an offer (i.e., specificity as to terms and expressing an intention to enter into a binding agreement with another). A counteroffer must also give the other person the right to accept. If any of these elements are absent, there is no counteroffer. When the counteroffer is rejected, all offers stand rejected. The first offer was rejected by the counteroffer and when the counteroffer was rejected, all offers were effectively canceled. At this point, the original offeror is free to make another offer, or even to make the original offer again. The parties return to the same footing that they were in prior to any offer having been made.

Knowledge of the Offer

Although it sounds like common sense, it is important to point out that the offeree can only accept an offer if he knows of its existence. Therefore, the offer must be communicated. The offeree cannot later claim that he accepted an offer that was never communicated either directly or indirectly to him. (For example, such as when the offeree hears that another person accepted an offer that was never communicated to him, but involves an offer he would have accepted).

Sidebar:
"Speech-Act-Theory" holds that an offer and an acceptance are not expressions so much as they are acts. The expression of an offer followed by actions in conformity with that action are what prove that mutual assent occurred between the parties. The parties' subjective intent will not affect this analysis, except to the extent that the offeror must have had the intent to contract at the time that he made his offer.

ETHICS FILE: **Business and Ethics**

Although it often appears that ethics and business are not compatible, most business people would disagree. Nonethical conduct might result in a short-term gain but a long-term loss. Business people, and those who represent them, must always keep honesty and integrity in the forefront of their practices. Ethical standards are essential to good business practices. Without trust and honesty, many businesses would fail in a short period of time. In future chapters, we will explore the ethical issues that confront both business people and legal professionals.

The Case of the Contentious Credit Card

MAURICE WAHL, Justice. *Texaco, Inc. v. Goldstein* 34 Misc.2d 751, *752–756,
229 N.Y.S.2d 51,**52–56 (N.Y.Mun.Ct.1962)

The plaintiff seeks to recover a judgment against the defendant predicated upon purchases made pursuant to the terms and conditions of a credit card issued by the plaintiff to the defendant on or about June 11, 1959.

The plaintiff is a major oil company engaged in the production and distribution of petroleum and related products throughout the United States. Dealers operating gas stations and engaged in private enterprise, retail the petroleum products of the plaintiff in the operation of their stations, and by means of dealer agreements with the plaintiff are authorized to vend products of the plaintiff.

Texaco, Inc., as a device to stimulate sales, issued a credit card enabling the holder to purchase its products at any authorized Texaco station. The practice is that the party to whom the card issues thereafter receives a monthly statement covering all purchases made in prior months.

On the reverse side of the card, the agreement between the customer and the company is contained and the relevant portion appears as follows: "This credit card confirms the authorization of credit during the period shown, to the person, corporation, or firm whose name is embossed on the reverse side thereof. Such person, corporation, or firm assumes full responsibility for all purchases made hereunder by any one through the use of this credit card prior to surrendering it to the company or to giving the company notice in writing that the card has been lost or stolen. Retention of this card or use thereof constitutes acceptance of all the terms and conditions thereof."

Upon the defendant's application, a card was issued to him by the plaintiff, bearing a certain number with an expiration date of the last day of May, 1961.

Thereafter, the defendant was deprived of the card by theft, but failed to report the loss to the plaintiff. A dealer marketing plaintiff's products picked up the card on or about December 23, 1960, at Chicago, Illinois, where it had been tendered by an illicit possessor, for the purpose of purchase of petroleum products. The dealer then notified the plaintiff that the card had been reclaimed, and plaintiff in turn notified the defendant that his card was being used by another in the Chicago area. The plaintiff then confirmed a telephone conversation with the defendant by a letter dated January 23, 1961.

From the date the card was missing to the date of the telephone notification by plaintiff to defendant of its recovery, some $569.98 in charges were made with the said credit card, which charges constitute the subject of this action.

The issues raised here are whether the defendant is liable pursuant to the terms and conditions as set forth on the reverse side of the credit card, for the unauthorized purchases made by another person, prior to notification to the plaintiff by the defendant of the loss of the credit card.

In the case of Eimco Corp., the Court there held that a party should not be bound by clauses printed on the reverse side of a document unless it be established that such matter was properly called to its attention and that it assented to the provisions there stated, but in the same case the Court recognized the fact that whether the intent of the parties was to have the matters on the face of the contract include the matters on the reverse side is a question to be decided on the trial.

Further, in the Eimco case the sale and purchase were not pursuant to any formal contracts jointly executed by the parties but were initiated by written orders on its printed form by Eimco and accepted by Derring on its printed form. The procedure followed is not the same or even similar to the procedure followed in the case at issue. In the case at bar, the defendant submitted an application to plaintiff requesting the issuance to him of a credit card.

The application contained none of the terms of the agreement between the parties but amounted to a mere invitation to do business. At this point, neither the plaintiff nor the defendant were bound by any contractual agreement. The contractual agreement followed later when the plaintiff issued its credit card to the defendant to be accepted by him in accordance with the terms and conditions therein set forth, or at his option to be rejected by him. Such rejection need take the form of returning the card, or simply its nonuse. The issuance of the card to the defendant amounted to a mere offer on plaintiff's part, and the contract became entire when defendant retained the card and thereafter made use of it. The card itself then constituted a formal and binding contract.

The agreement expressed in the provisions of the credit card in the case at bar, are not unreasonable. The plaintiff assumes the risk of all loss after it receives notice of the loss or theft of the credit card; the defendant assumes the risk of loss prior to such notice.

With the increasing use of the credit card and its growing importance to the economy, the imposition of a high duty of diligence upon the major oil companies in general, most of whom use the same or similar systems of credit card transactions, would result in an impairment of an important segment of our economic structure. We must take into consideration that for the most part, the dealers to whom the cards are presented are independent contractors engaged in private enterprise. The plaintiff undertakes to honor credit card purchases by persons presenting them to the individual dealers for credit. In each such transaction however, the plaintiff is in no way involved; it had previously agreed to purchase from the dealer, such charges at par and the plaintiff has no control of either the dealer or the purchaser using the card, until the credit charge invoice actually reaches the company for payment to the dealer on presentation by him. Accordingly, the negligence of the card holder becomes most important. The intent of the parties is that in the event of the issuee's or obligor's loss of his card, or it having been stolen, that he be required to treat his credit card with at least the same importance, or perhaps greater importance than he would with his currency. Assuming the defendant were to have lost some currency, he alone bears the risk of loss, and his loss is fixed by the amount of currency he lost. Should he, however, lose his credit card, the amount of loss would not be fixed, and the risk of loss is not only borne by him but also by the Company when he actually complies with the conditions of the issuance of the card to him. This is a risk the company is apparently willing to assume, and the only requirement by the company is that the card holder exercise a proper degree of care in the handling of his card. Unless actual notice of loss is given to the company, it can have no way of knowing of such loss, and to require some 30,000 dealers to suspect the loss of any particular credit card and use diligence against its abuse, is not within the requirements of plaintiff as the issuer of the credit card. Unlike credit cards used in the restaurant and hotel fields, where personal use to the issuee is usually restricted, any holder of the credit card can use the same.

It is the opinion of this Court that the application to the plaintiff, by the defendant, for the issuance to him of a credit card, and the acceptance by him and use thereafter of the card, constitutes the offer and acceptance resulting in an entire contract. The liability of the defendant to the plaintiff arises out of the contract contained on the credit card itself.

Judgment for the plaintiff in the sum of $569.98.

Case Questions:

1. The court compares a credit card to what other form of payment?

2. According to the court, why are credit cards important?

3. How is a contractual relationship created in a typical credit card arrangement?

4. When does a cardholder's obligation to the credit company end?

5. What action could the cardholder have taken in this case to avoid liability?

Terminating the Offer

terminate: to end an offer before any legal action has been taken on it.

An offer can **terminate** in any of a number of ways. Here the word "termination" carries a specific meaning. An offer that has been terminated has no legal effect. Termination is a general term that covers any type of ending, whether initiated by the parties or imposed by the courts. Later, we will see that revocation by the offeror is only one type of termination. The offer may contain language stating that it will expire within a given period, or by a specific date. When no date is provided, an offer terminates after a "reasonable period" (see Exhibit 2-4).

An offer is legally terminated when:

- the offeror withdraws the offer before it is accepted

- the offeror takes some action inconsistent with his previously stated desire to enter into a contract (i.e., withdraws from the negotiations, closes his business, ceases all communications, etc.), and this information is relayed to the offeree[i]

- an offer is terminated by the death of the party making it

- the offeree changes the terms of the proposed offer[ii]

EXHIBIT 2-4: Terminating an offer.

[i] Restatement, Contracts 2d §43.
[ii] *Keeler v. Murphy,* 117 Cal App 386. 3 P2d 950 (1931).

Sidebar:
It is not fatal to a contract that some of the details of the exchange were not worked out beforehand. The courts will allow a certain amount of vagueness in some of the contract details as long as the main points (offer and acceptance) can be proven.[19]

The offeror is usually permitted to withdraw (or revoke) his offer at any time prior to acceptance. He or she also may withdraw an offer by taking some action that demonstrates that he no longer intends to enter into a binding contract. Finally, because an offer is the offeror's manifestation of his intent to contract with another person, his death makes this intent impossible to perform.

However, the rule changes when the subject involves an irrevocable offer. In such a situation, the offer survives the death of the person making it. In option situations, for instance, the death of the party does not revoke the option.

Revoking an Offer

revoke: when the person making the offer terminates it before it has been accepted.

An offeror can **revoke** his offer any time before it is accepted. A revocation of an offer is a specific type of termination. A person who makes an offer has the right to revoke it. This broad statement is subject to certain limitations, however. As we will see in our discussions of the so-called Mail Box rule (discussed in Chapter 3) an acceptance that has been mailed to the offeror but not yet received may still be valid, even when the offeror has revoked the offer.

As far as the law is concerned, an offer that is validly withdrawn cannot create any power of acceptance in any other party. Therefore, it is legally impossible to accept a revoked offer.[20] However, this rule is also subject to certain exceptions. For example, if there is a statute that specifically mandates that a type of offer is irrevocable for a certain period of time, then it cannot be revoked until the time period has passed.

When the offeror decides to revoke the offer, he must communicate this intention to the offeree before the offeree accepts. If he fails to communicate his revocation and the offeree accepts, a contract is created. Where a revocation is sent by mail, fax, or e-mail, it is not effective until the offeree has received it.

A written revocation also can be effective when the offeree's authorized agent receives it. The jury is usually called on to decide when, how, and if the offeree received this revocation before he accepted the offer.

What information must a revocation contain? Under the law in most jurisdictions, a revocation must contain express language that indicates the offeror no longer wishes to enter into a contract. Some jurisdictions allow a revocation to be implied by the offeror's language in the revocation.

HYPOTHETICAL 2-9   The Fax Revocation

Example: Miguel faxes Maria an offer to sell his stamp collection to her for $400. Before Maria accepts Miguel's offer, Miguel faxes her again with the following message:

"I don't want to have anything more to do with you in any way.

"—Miguel"

This language, although it fails to make any assertions about revoking his previous offer to Maria certainly seems to indicate Miguel's desire to revoke his offer.

What if the situation changes?

Maria receives Miguel's offer and is considering it when she hears Miguel has declared bankruptcy. Miguel later calls Maria and in a despondent tone tells her, "It's all over. Everything I worked for is gone. I can't sell anything to anyone." Then Miguel hangs up the phone. Is Maria free to free to accept Miguel's previous offer?

Answer: In most jurisdictions, no. Although Miguel failed to mention anything about revoking his offer, a reasonable interpretation of his statements is that Miguel is unable to honor any of his contracts and is therefore unable to perform under the terms of his previous offer.

Revoking a Unilateral Contract Offer

Unilateral contracts involve a promise in exchange for an action. As such, an offer for a unilateral contract can be revoked at any time prior to someone taking action.

When an offer for a unilateral contract is made to the public at large, it must be revoked in the same manner as it was first made.

Example: Miguel posted a reward for his missing cat but, after five days, he began to realize that he rather liked his apartment cat-free. He drives around to the five places where he posted "reward-offered" signs and scrawls the word "revoked" across the face of each. Later that day, Tony appears with Miguel's missing cat. Tony asks for the reward money, but Miguel says that the offer was revoked. Can Tony legally demand the reward money? No. Because Miguel posted his revocation of his offer in the same manner that he originally advertised it, there is a legally valid revocation.

Sidebar:
Partial performance under a unilateral offer may, in some instances, support a contract.

Time Limits on Offers

When an offer has an express time limitation, such as "this offer will expire by 12 midnight on the 15th day of this month," the failure of a party to accept by that time will terminate the offer. When an offer does not state a specific time limit, courts follow the rule that the offer will expire after a "reasonable time." How the courts determine what a reasonable period of time is depends a great deal on the circumstances of each case. Some offers involve materials that have a built in shelf life. An offer for the purchase of fresh vegetables will have a different (and shorter) reasonable expiration date than an offer to purchase an automobile. There also may be customs that have developed over time in different industries that establish a de facto time limitation on an offer. For instance, it is common for offers involving used cars to expire within 24–48 hours, whereas an offer to buy stocks could expire within minutes of being made.

There are exceptions to the "reasonable time" expiration rule. For instance, the parties could specifically state that the offer has no expiration date. In such a situation, the offer would be deemed a "continuing" offer. In such a situation, the offer would remain pending until accepted, however long that may be.[22]

Revoking an Irrevocable Offer

An offer can be revoked even when the revocation apparently violates the terms of the offer. For instance, an offer can be withdrawn under any of the following circumstances:

- It contains language stating that the offer "cannot be withdrawn"
- It contains language giving the offeree a set amount of time to accept (and is revoked before that time period passes)
- It states that the offer will remain open for a stated period of time (and is revoked before that time)

However, if the offer is supported by consideration, a different rule applies. We will discuss consideration in greater detail in a later chapter, but a few words about the topic will be helpful. Consideration is the reason for the contract. When a party has consideration, it means that he or she has given up something in the expectation of getting something else. In cases in which the offer involves consideration, it cannot be revoked unless it abides by its own terms (see Exhibit 2-5).

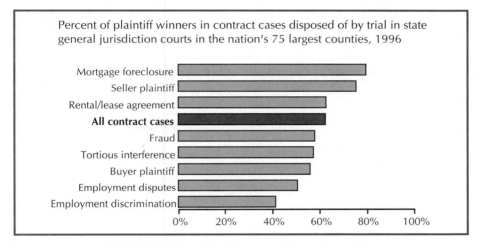

Percent of plaintiff winners in contract cases disposed of by trial in state general jurisdiction courts in the nation's 75 largest counties, 1996

EXHIBIT 2-5: Plaintiff winners in contract cases nationwide.

Source: Contract Trials and Verdicts in Large Counties, 1996. Civil Justice Survey of State Courts, 1996, U.S. Department of Justice.

Options

An **option** is a kind of mini-contract, in which one person gives another the right, for a stated period, to purchase an item for a specific amount. In order to be valid, an option must have consideration; something of value (usually money) must change hands to support the option. Essentially, an option is a contract for a later offer. The parties agree that for a stated period, one party will have the right to accept an offer for a stated amount. The person giving the option is giving up his right to sell to someone else in exchange for value. Once an option's period has expired, the person is free to sell to anyone, for any price. However, during the period of the option, which could last from as little as a few days to several years, the person who has received consideration is barred from offering the property to anyone else.

Options give the potential buyer the right to a certain amount of time to consider if he or she wishes to actually buy the item, while preventing others from buying it.

option: a contract in which one person pays money for the right to buy something from, or sell something to, another person at a certain price and within a certain time period.

In many situations, such as when an option involves real estate, the money paid to the property owner is applied to the purchase price of the item. If the buyer does not exercise his right to buy under the option, he forfeits the money paid as consideration for the option. Options are used in many different commercial areas.

Why would anyone wish to obtain an option? Here's an example:

John believes that the area in the northern part of the county is going to undergo a dramatic increase in value because of a new highway that will be built in the next two years. However, he does not know exactly where the highway will be placed. If he buys the right pieces of property, he can develop roadside and exit ramp convenience stores and gas stations and become rich. However, if he buys the wrong properties—ones that have no access to the highway—they will be useless to him. John knows that other land speculators will soon find out about the highway; he needs time to investigate without the chance of losing a particularly good piece of property. John approaches several of the landowners in what is currently rural countryside and offers each one $100 for a two-year option to buy their property at "fair market value." By doing so, he locks in those pieces of property for himself. The landowners, who may know nothing about the proposed highway, see the option money as a windfall. After all, none of them plan on selling within two years, so they are more than happy to give John an option to purchase. If, any time during the next two years, they do decide to sell, they must first deal with John.

When a person gives an option, he does not transfer any ownership rights. The option purchaser has no greater right to the property in question than any third party. The only right transferred by an option is the owner's right to sell the item to someone else for a stated period.

REVOKING AN OPTION

An option that has been accepted cannot be revoked before the time limit stated in the option agreement. What essentially happens in an option situation is that the person agrees that for a specified time he gives up his right to revoke the offer.[23]

When an offer has a set expiration date, it is classified as a continuing offer. When an offer has a set expiration date and is supported by consideration, it becomes an option. The reason it is so important to determine the exact status of a continuing offer is that a continuing offer can be revoked before the time period running, but an option cannot.

Options create an interesting legal question. What category of contract does an option fall into? The answer is that options are both offers and contracts: They are both continuing, irrevocable offers and unilateral contracts. After all, the purpose of the option is guarantee a future action, that is, selling the property to a specific person.[26]

Options can become very complicated. There are rolling options, no cash options, options in exchange for options and even a market in selling options to others.

Business Case File

Constance Boutique

Constance Boutique is a contemporary women's fashions store. It sells fashionable dresses and accessories. Owned by Constance Ensner, the store specializes in what Constance refers to as "feminine punctuation." She also prides herself on dealing directly with her customers.

"People like that one-on-one touch. It's also about style. I have employees, but customers will ask for me. They'll think that I'm the one who puts them together the best. I was such a force in this store for so long. They'd come in and I'd say, 'No, you don't want to do that; you should do this.' We're stylists. We help women figure out what to wear. With women, there are so many directions. There's a lot of hands on. That's why specialty stores are what they are. They're more expensive, usually, but it's better quality clothing and they offer more service. We're like fashion therapists. Someone might want a whole new image. They know that they want a new look, but they don't know how to do it. I'm approaching it more artistically. It's a cool business. We ask questions like, 'What's your lifestyle?' 'What do you need your clothes to do for you?' There's a lot of getting to know the customer and building a rapport over the years."

This personal touch has paid nice dividends for Constance, who is in her 19th year of running Constance Boutique. Interestingly enough, she had no business background before opening her store. When it came to contracts, she took a layperson's approach. When she received an offer for a service or a product, she made sure to pin down the details. "I had no business background, at all," she said.

"I studied pattern making and design all my life. I always loved clothes. I did sketches and imaginary wardrobes when I was ten. I made clothes for my dolls. I made my own clothes. I did custom sewing for people. The idea of opening up a clothing store just came as a natural progression.

Constance Ensner

"The hardest thing about opening a business for me was establishing and working within a budget. I'm very right brained. The creative stuff is what's exciting to me. Staying organized, staying on top of it, is one of the hardest things about being a sole proprietor. You wear so many hats. You're the janitor; you're the artistic director; you're the accountant."

Law firms that work with creative people, such as Constance, must remember that they often approach problems from a completely different perspective than a person trained to think like a legal professional.

"The business is like your child," Constance said. "You have very distinctive ways and systems that work for you. You can be kind of a control freak when you have your own business."

Business owners, especially sole proprietors, face unique issues that must be acknowledged by the legal team. You should remember that a business owner might have other people tied in very closely with the business. For example, Constance has an accountant. "You need to get a good accountant. I farmed a lot of the paperwork for my business out to my accountant." If you were working with a client such as Constance, it would be helpful to know that some of her records also would be found with her accountant and, in the case of a pending lawsuit, should be made part of the legal file.

(continued)

Constance also echoes a sentiment held by many business people. In addition to the demands on her time that the business brings, there is also a strong tendency to be tied to the store. "Sometimes the business turns into this roller coaster and you can't get off."

Chapter Summary:

Offers can come in many forms. An offer indicates the offeror's intent to enter into a binding contract. Once accepted, an offer transforms into a contract. It is important to note, however, that there are many situations in which a statement appears to be an offer, but is actually classified in other ways. A general invitation to make an offer solicits offers from others but is not an offer in itself. Advertisements are also not classified as offers. They are usually interpreted to be invitations to buyers to make offers. However, when an advertisement contains sufficient detail and reveals the merchant's intent to enter into a contract, it can constitute a legally valid offer. There is no required language that must be used to make a legally valid offer. Courts are generally very liberal in construing negotiations and statements as offers. However, no matter what language used, the offer must indicated a willingness to enter into a contract and when accepted must demonstrate a meeting of the minds between the parties. An offer can be revoked at any time prior to acceptance. It can also be terminated by its own terms, the passage of time or by several other reasons. A counteroffer revokes the original offer and substitutes a new offer. Finally, a specialized category of offers exists: options. An option is a type of mini-contract in which a person agrees to surrender his right to make an offer to anyone else for a stated time.

WEB SITES

Small Business Administration
http://www.sba.gov/
Provides extensive information about starting, financing, and managing a business.

U.S. Census Bureau—Business Statistics
http://www.census.gov/epcd/www/smallbus.html
Statistics about business from the U.S. Census Bureau. **Chicago-Kent School of Law**

Chicago-Kent School of Law
http://www.kentlaw.edu
Provides information on a wide variety of topics, including contract law
and mini lectures on offer and acceptance.

Hieros Gamos
http://www.hg.org
An overview of commercial law.

Findlaw.com
www.findlaw.com
Provides a broad overview of contract law.

REVIEW QUESTIONS

1. What is the legal definition of an offer?
2. What is the difference between an offer and an invitation to bid?
3. How detailed must an offer be?
4. Is a newspaper advertisement an offer?
5. Explain the term "power of acceptance."
6. Define the requirements of a valid offer.
7. When the plaintiff seeks to prove that an offer has been made, what evidence should he produce at trial?
8. What is a general offer? How is a general offer different from a general invitation to make an offer? How is an offer for a unilateral contract different from an offer for a bilateral contract?
9. Is the posting of a reward an offer?
10. Why isn't an advertisement generally considered to be an offer? Under what circumstances can an advertisement be considered an offer?
11. What are some of the methods that an offeror can use to revoke an offer?
12. How does a counteroffer affect the original offer?
13. How does the power of acceptance shift between offers and counter offers?
14. What are some of the methods used to terminate an offer?
15. When a valid option has been negotiated, what does this do to the power to revoke the offer?
16. What is the difference between a continuing offer and an option?
17. Explain the court's rationale in "The Case of the Cheap China."
18. How are business practices related to ethical practices?

19. Create a chart showing how the "power of acceptance" shifts in the course of negotiations where Party A makes an offer, Party B makes a counteroffer, Party A counters that offer with another, and Party B finally accepts.

20. When would a mistaken advertisement create a legally valid offer?

HANDS-ON ASSIGNMENT

Draft an offer that you could present to a local attorney, offering "freelance" paralegal services. What types of details should you make sure appear in your offer?

PRACTICAL APPLICATION

Wavy Waters, a local boat manufacturer and retailer, published the following advertisement: The winner of next week's Lake James sailboat regatta will be awarded a 20-foot, Wavy Waters 20-horsepower, three-person sleeper sailboat at no expense."

John participates in the sailboat race and wins. He calls up Wavy Waters and asks when he can expect delivery of his sailboat. The manager at Wavy Waters tells John that there has been a problem with their inventory and they will not be giving John a free boat after all. Does John have a valid contract with Wavy Waters? Why or why not?

Answer: Yes. There is a contract. The advertisement is an offer for a unilateral contract. John accepted the contract by fulfilling the proposed action: winning the race. Wavy Waters will have to give John the specified boat or it will be in violation of the contract.

HELP THIS BUSINESS

Miguel wants to form his own telecommunications business. He approaches a local telephone company and asks them how much it would cost to run one hundred telephone lines into his home. The telephone company states that it would cost $4,200 per month for such a service. Miguel says, "Okay. Let's do it." Once they set up an installation time, the customer service representative then faxes Miguel a contract form, listing all of the details that they have discussed. Miguel scratches through $4,200 per month and instead writes in $42 per month. Smiling to himself, he faxes the contract back to the telephone company. A few weeks later, when the company demands the first payment of $4,200, Miguel tells them that actually agreed to $42 per month. Is Miguel right? Why or why not?

KEY TERMS

offeror	terminating the offer
offeree	revoking an offer
meeting of the minds	option
counteroffer	

ENDNOTES

[1] Restatement, Contracts 2d §24.

[2] *Noland Co. v. Graver Tank & Mfg. Co.* (CA4 SC) 301 F2d 43 (C.A.S.C. 1962.).

[3] *Powell v. Beck,* 366 Mich 627, 115 NW2d 317 (1962)

[4] *H. S. Crocker Co. v. McFaddin,* 148 Cal App 2d 639, 307 P2d 429 (1957)

[5] *Rutledge v. Hoffman,* 81 Ohio App 85, 75 NE2d 608 (1947)

[6] *Newton v. Coe-Mortimer Co.,* 20 Ga App 736, 93 SE 235 (1917)

[7] *S.S.I. Investors, Ltd. v. Korea Tungsten Mining Co.,* 80 App Div 2d 155, 438 NYS2d 96, affd 55 NY2d 934, 449 NYS2d 173, 434 NE2d 242 (1981)

[8] *Las Vegas Hacienda, Inc. v. Gibson,* 77 Nev 25, 359 P2d 85 (1961)

[9] Restatement, Contracts 2d §29.

[10] Restatement, Contracts 2d §22

[11] *Retterer v. Bender,* 106 Ohio App 369, 154 NE2d 827 (1958)

[12] *Nelson v. Davis,* 102 Wash 313, 172 P 1178 (1918)

[13] *Retterer v. Bender,* 154 N.E.2d 827 (Ohio, 1958)

[14] *Brown Machine, Div. of John Brown, Inc. v. Hercules, Inc.* 770 SW2d 416 (1989)

[15] *Master Palletizer Systems, Inc. v. T.S. Ragsdale Co.,* 725 F Supp 1525 (DC Colo.1989)

[16] *Geismar v. Abraham & Strauss,* 109 Misc.2d 495 (1981)

[17] Restatement, Contracts 2d §38.

[18] 27 Am. Jur. Proof of Facts 2d 605.

[19] *Langer v. Lemke,* 78 ND 383, 49 NW2d 641 (1951)

[20] *Morgan v. Patillo,* 24 F2d 204 (1928)

[21] *Wagenvoord Broadcasting Co. v. Canal Automatic Transmission Service, Inc.,* 176 So 2d 188 (1965).

[22] Restatement, Contracts 2d §42

[23] *Warner Bros. Pictures, Inc. v. Brodel*, 31 Cal 2d 766, 192 P2d 949, 3 ALR2d 691, cert den 335 US 844, 93 L Ed 394, 69 S Ct 67, reh den 335 US 873, 93 L Ed 417, 69 S Ct 165 (1948).

[24] Restatement, Contracts 2d §25

[25] *Western Union Tel. Co. v. Brown*, 253 US 101, 64 L Ed 803, 40 S Ct 460 (1920)

[26] *Palo Alto Town & Country Village, Inc. v. BBTC Co.*, 11 Cal 3d 494, 113 Cal Rptr 705, 521 P2d 1097 (1974).

 For additional resources, visit our Web site at www.westlegalstudies.com

CHAPTER 3

THE LEGAL CONCEPT OF ACCEPTANCE

Focus of this chapter: This chapter focuses on the law of acceptance. Once an offer has been made, the analysis then shifts to the sufficiency of the acceptance. How, when, and under what circumstances can an acceptance can be made? This chapter also explores some of the important limitations on a person's power of acceptance and the stipulations that an offeror can insert into an offer to limit this power.

Chapter Objectives:
At the completion of this chapter, you should be able to:

- Explain what constitutes a valid acceptance
- Define the essential elements of a valid acceptance
- Describe who is empowered to accept
- Explain the limitations on a person's power of acceptance
- Define the Mailbox Rule
- Explain how the rules of ethics affect not only attorneys but also paralegals
- Describe the methods a paralegal would use to confirm that a valid acceptance has been made
- Define how and under what circumstances an offer can have alternative terms
- Explain the result when a purported acceptance contains an ambiguous term
- Describe how stipulations and conditions can affect acceptance

Introduction to Acceptance

As we have already seen, in order to have a valid contract there must be both an offer and an acceptance of the offer. It is the offer-plus-acceptance equation that results in mutual assent and thus a binding contract. The courts have termed this the "meeting of the minds." When a person accepts an offer, it shows that he intends to be governed by the terms of the contract. As we saw in the last chapter, an offer can be made in a wide variety of ways. In this chapter, we will explore the more limited ways in which an offer can be accepted.

When a person accepts an offer, he or she is agreeing to all of the terms expressed in that offer. If a person changes the terms of the offer, this results in a counter offer, not an acceptance. If a person does not like a particular term in the offer, he or she is free to reject the offer. A conditional acceptance, that is, one based on a proposed change in one of the terms of the offer, is normally interpreted to be a counteroffer. The original offeror must accept this counteroffer before a binding contract results.

Although it sounds like a very basic concept, when a contract is under dispute, the parties must prove that there was a valid acceptance before they can allege that a contract existed. If the plaintiff is the offeror, then the defendant in the lawsuit is the offeree. In such a case, the plaintiff would have to prove that the defendant made a valid acceptance of the offer. If he can prove that allegation, then the courts will be forced to the conclusion that a contract existed. Once that conclusion is made, the court will then move on to a consideration of whether the defendant breached the contract terms. If a breach can be proven, the court can assess damages against the defendant. We discuss breach and damages in a later chapter (see Exhibit 3-1).

- The person accepts the offer verbally

- The person has power and authority to accept the offer

- The person indicates by words or gestures that he accepts the offer

- There are no added conditions or modifications to the offer

- The person communicates the acceptance

- The person uses an accepted form of communication to accept the offer

---

EXHIBIT 3-1: Actions that indicate acceptance.

Sufficiency of Acceptance

Although a proper acceptance is a crucial element to the formation of a contract, the acceptance itself must satisfy certain basic requirements. Under the law, the acceptance must be legally sufficient. Legal sufficiency takes into account several factors. At its simplest, an acceptance must present some proof that the person accepting the offer has manifested agreement to the terms of the offer. Occasionally, such as when there is no clear evidence that a person gave a verbal acceptance, his acceptance can be inferred from his actions. When a person takes actions that are consistent with having accepted an offer and creating a contract, the courts will often interpret these actions to mean that the person intended to accept the offer.[1]

It is not enough that a person intends to accept an offer. The person must show some objective action that clearly signals this intent. The person's acceptance must be presented by words or actions that are consistent with this desire to accept the offer. In most situations, it is not necessary that the person actually use the words, "I accept," but it is essential that the person present some objective manifestation of the intent to be bound by the contract.

Communicating an Acceptance

For a person to accept an offer, he must do more than simply state that he wishes to enter into a contract. He must communicate that acceptance to the person who made the offer.[2]

HYPOTHETICAL 3-1   Miguel's New Car

John has made an offer to Miguel for the purchase of Miguel's car. Miguel has decided to accept John's offer. Miguel tells a close friend that he is going to accept. However, Miguel fails to communicate with John. Is this a valid acceptance?

Answer: In this situation, there is no binding contract, because Miguel failed to communicate his acceptance to the person who actually made the offer.

When an offer fails to state a particular mode or method of communicating the acceptance, any method will be sufficient. For instance, an oral offer can be accepted in writing and a written offer can be accepted orally. However, in some situations, an offer may stipulate the exact method of acceptance. In those situations, an acceptance must follow the prescribed mode or it will be legally insufficient.[3]

HYPOTHETICAL 3-2   John's Motorcycle

Mary faxes an offer to John to purchase John's motorcycle. Her offer clearly states that in order to accept this offer, John must submit a return fax to Mary with the words "I accept" written on the fax. After John receives the fax, he telephones Mary and leaves a message on her answering machine. In his message, John states that he accepts Mary's offer and will bring the motorcycle by her house later that evening. Is there a binding contract?

Answer: No. Skipping over the question of whether or not leaving a message on Mary's answering machine is communicating an acceptance, John has failed to abide by the express terms of Mary's offer. Mary included a specific stipulation that John could only accept by faxing his acceptance to her. In such a situation, John's telephone call is not legally sufficient.

WHAT WORDS ARE REQUIRED TO INDICATE ACCEPTANCE?

Although the law does not require that the person actually use the words "I accept," the person accepting the offer people must not only communicate but also communicate in such a way that the person who made the offer understands that it has been accepted. The person who made the offer is entitled to know that he now has a binding contract. Therefore, the acceptance must be unambiguous. As we have already seen, a counteroffer is a new offer that rejects the original offer.

There is an important point to raise here. If an offer definitively states that only one form of communication is acceptable, then that form of communication must be followed. However, if the offer merely suggests a method of communication, but does not require it, a person may accept in any manner.

Acceptance without Words

Can an offeree accept an offer without saying anything? The answer is clearly yes. If the offer specifically states that in order to accept this offer a person must take some action, then the person's words are irrelevant. In fact, when an offer requires performance of some action as the form of acceptance, use of the words "I accept" are actually not binding.[4]

HYPOTHETICAL 3-3   Acceptance by Action

Miguel sends a letter to Mary in which he offers to buy her broken computer for $100. He specifically states in the offer, "If you wish to accept my offer, you must paint your mailbox yellow. Once I see that your mailbox is painted yellow, I will come to your house and pay you the one hundred dollars in exchange for your computer." Is this a legally valid offer?

Although this offer is unusual, it is legally binding. If Mary telephones Miguel and says, "I accept" this would be insufficient to form a contract. Miguel's unusual condition must be met before a binding contract exists. The only way, under Miguel's offer, for Mary to accept is to paint for her mailbox yellow.

Stipulations requiring actions instead of words in offers are common in unilateral contracts. As we have already seen, rewards and other offers for unilateral contracts focus on actions, not words. However, when the offer calls for a bilateral contract, that is, a promise in exchange for a promise, silence is usually not a permissible method of acceptance.

HYPOTHETICAL 3-4   Acceptance by Silence

Tia sends John a letter that states, "I would like to enter into a contract with you to run a computer business. If you agree with the terms set out below, do nothing. I will assume from your silence that you agree to all terms." When John fails to respond to Tia's letter, has a binding contract been created between them?

Answer: In most situations, no. When a bilateral contract is contemplated, the offeree's acceptance must be manifested in some way. John's failure to respond in any way is more likely to be an indication of rejection under the law than an acceptance.

THE "POWER OF ACCEPTANCE"

When an offer has been created, it creates the **power of acceptance** in another person. The power of acceptance is a term used by the courts to describe the rights of a party to accept an offer and thereby create a binding contract. The power of acceptance can shift from one person to another during the course of negotiations.

power of acceptance: The right conferred on a person who has received a valid offer.

HYPOTHETICAL 3-5   The Computer Business

Miguel and John are discussing a possible business venture. John suggests that if Miguel can provide modified computers, John can sell these computers to businesses for a substantial profit. Miguel tells John that he can produce about 10 computers per week. John says that if Miguel can produce these 10 computers per week, he will buy them from Miguel at $400 per computer. Is there an offer pending? If so, who has the power of acceptance?

Answer: At this point, Miguel has the power of acceptance. John has put forward an offer to purchase computers from Miguel at $400 per unit. Miguel can either decide to accept that offer or reject it. If Miguel accepts this offer, his power of acceptance will create a binding contract.

Now, suppose the facts in Hypothetical 3-5 change slightly. Miguel begins to think that $400 per computer is too low a price. Instead, he counteroffers with $600 per unit. Who has the power of acceptance now?

Answer: John. Miguel has made a counteroffer that essentially rejects John's offer and replaces it with his own. At this point, John now has the power of acceptance, so if he accepts Miguel's counteroffer a binding contract will result.

As you can see in this example, the power of acceptance can shift between the parties during the course of the negotiations. The power of acceptance will ripen into a contract at the point where a valid offer has been made and it is accepted. As each counteroffer is rejected, the power of acceptance shifts between the parties (see Exhibit 3-2).

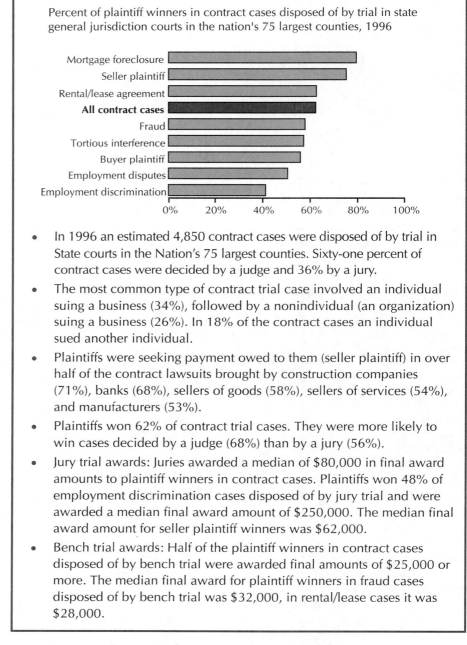

- In 1996 an estimated 4,850 contract cases were disposed of by trial in State courts in the Nation's 75 largest counties. Sixty-one percent of contract cases were decided by a judge and 36% by a jury.

- The most common type of contract trial case involved an individual suing a business (34%), followed by a nonindividual (an organization) suing a business (26%). In 18% of the contract cases an individual sued another individual.

- Plaintiffs were seeking payment owed to them (seller plaintiff) in over half of the contract lawsuits brought by construction companies (71%), banks (68%), sellers of goods (58%), sellers of services (54%), and manufacturers (53%).

- Plaintiffs won 62% of contract trial cases. They were more likely to win cases decided by a judge (68%) than by a jury (56%).

- Jury trial awards: Juries awarded a median of $80,000 in final award amounts to plaintiff winners in contract cases. Plaintiffs won 48% of employment discrimination cases disposed of by jury trial and were awarded a median final award amount of $250,000. The median final award amount for seller plaintiff winners was $62,000.

- Bench trial awards: Half of the plaintiff winners in contract cases disposed of by bench trial were awarded final amounts of $25,000 or more. The median final award for plaintiff winners in fraud cases disposed of by bench trial was $32,000, in rental/lease cases it was $28,000.

EXHIBIT 3-2: Summary of contract trails nationwide.

Source: Contract Trails and Verdicts in Large Counties, 1996. Civil Justice Survey of State Courts, 1996, U.S. Department of Justice.

The Case of the Confusing Counteroffer[5]

OPINION

BUSTAMANTE, Judge.

Defendant Allen (hereafter Seller) appeals from an order of summary judgment in favor of Plaintiff Long (hereafter Buyer) in an action for breach of a residential purchase agreement. Judgment was entered against Seller and his former wife, co-owners of the property at issue. Only Seller has appealed. We affirm.

DISCUSSION

Buyer made several offers to Seller and his former wife (collectively, Owners) to purchase their residence. Ultimately, Buyer made a written offer dated March 1, 1994, that was set to expire on March 3, 1994, at 6:00 P.M. unless the Owners delivered a written acceptance to Buyer before that time. The Owners signed the offer (the Agreement) on March 4, 1994, and returned it to Buyer on that date via her real estate agent. Both parties acknowledge that the Owners' execution of the Agreement on March 4 constituted a counteroffer. They dispute, however, whether uncontroverted facts establish that Buyer's performance constituted an "acceptance" that bound the Owners to the terms of the counteroffer.

The ultimate question of whether the Owners' counteroffer became a binding promise and resulted in a contract requires us to consider whether the evidentiary facts conclusively establish that Buyer accepted the counteroffer. See *Orcutt v. S & L Paint Contractors, Ltd.*, 109 N.M. 796, 798, 791 P.2d 71, 73 (Ct.App.1990) (offeree's acceptance must be clear, positive, and unambiguous). Acceptance of an offer is a manifestation of assent to the terms of the offer, made by the offeree, in a manner allowed, invited, or required by the offer. Id. (citing Restatement (Second) of Contracts § 50 (1981)).

Seller initially contends that the specific terms of the Owners' counteroffer required a written acceptance. Seller refers us to paragraph 4.11 of the Agreement which states that "[a]ll notices and communications required or permitted under this Agreement shall be in writing." Paragraph 4.11 is a general provision which describes the mechanics for giving notice "required or permitted under this Agreement," including addresses and facsimile telephone numbers. The paragraph also defines the effective time of notices depending on the method of delivery. The paragraph does not on its face address the manner of acceptance or time within which acceptance of the counteroffer is required. We believe that the act of acceptance of the counteroffer is not a communication under the document as provided in paragraph 4.11. Rather, acceptance is an act creating an agreement. The Agreement does not otherwise address in any way Buyer's mode of response and, in our view, simply does not specify that the counteroffer can only be accepted in writing. The counteroffer thus invited acceptance by any manner reasonable under the circumstances, such as by promise or performance. See Restatement, supra, § 30(2) (form of acceptance invited) and § 32 (in case of doubt, offeree may accept by promise or performance).

The fact that the transaction involved the sale of land and thus was within the statute of frauds does not persuade us by itself that a written acceptance was required. The Agreement, already signed by Buyer on March 1, identified each party and the subject land and also specified the pertinent terms and conditions of the transaction. See *Pitek v. McGuire*, 51 N.M. 364, 371, 184 P.2d 647, 651–52 (1947). Seller suggests that Buyer's actions were not the type of partial performance which would take the transaction out of the statute of frauds. We disagree. The Agreement satisfied the requirements set forth in *Pitek*, and Seller, the party to be charged in this case, signed the document. Nothing more is required to satisfy the statute of frauds. See id.; *Balboa Constr. Co. v. Golden*, 97 N.M. 299, 303, 639 P.2d 586, 590 (Ct.App.1981); Restatement, supra, § 131.

We turn next to the facts bearing on the issue of Buyer's acceptance of the counteroffer by her performance. To the extent the pertinent facts are not in dispute and all that remains is the legal effect of those facts, summary judgment is appropriate. See *Westgate Families v. County Clerk*, 100 N.M. 146, 148, 667 P.2d 453, 455 (1983). The following facts are undisputed. Paragraphs 1.4(A) and 1.9 of the Agreement required Buyer to deliver a $5,000 earnest-money deposit to a named title company as soon as practical. The check was received by the title company on March 8, 1994. Buyer arranged for professional inspections of the property as urged in paragraph 2.5 of the Agreement. Pursuant to paragraph 2.1 of the Agreement, Buyer sought and obtained a financing commitment for her purchase of the property. Paragraph 1.10 specified that the closing take place within ten business days of April 8, 1994, and that the parties arrange for delivery and execution of the necessary documents and funds. Buyer appeared at the title company office on April 14, 1994, and signed all the documents necessary to close the transaction. In our view, these facts establish conclusively that Buyer accepted the Owners' counteroffer by performance of what the counteroffer requested. See Restatement, supra, §62 (where offer invites offeree to choose between acceptance by promise and acceptance by performance, beginning of invited performance is an acceptance by performance).

We recognize that Seller's affidavit states he never received any communication from Buyer specifically claiming or purporting to accept the counteroffer. However, the fact that Buyer may not have communicated her verbal or written promissory acceptance explicitly is not fatal to Buyer's position. The Restatement makes it clear that notification to the offeror of acceptance is not necessary unless the offer requests notice or the offeree has reason to know the offeror has no adequate means of learning of the performance with reasonable promptness and certainty. Restatement, supra, § 54. We have already determined the offer did not require any particular form of acceptance. Further, Seller does not assert and has made no showing that he had no means of learning about Buyer's acceptance. Most tellingly, however, it cannot be disputed that Seller had actual notice of Buyer's acceptance. The following facts are undisputed. On March 9, 1994, at Seller's request, Buyer's real

estate agent faxed a copy of the Agreement to Seller's attorney. The cover sheet for the fax included the statement, "We are moving very fast to get everything done." Seller directed Buyer's agent to deliver Buyer's earnest-money-deposit check to the title company and Seller knew the check was delivered. Seller was kept informed regarding property inspections and Buyer's efforts to secure financing. Seller was aware that Buyer's real estate agent arranged for a survey of the property at the Owners' expense. Seller arranged for the April 14, 1994, closing appointment at the title company. Buyer was not aware of any obstacle to closing the purchase until she appeared at the title company to sign closing documents. These facts conclusively establish that Seller was aware in the normal course of business of Buyer's acceptance by performance.

Seller argues that the statement in Buyer's affidavit that she "entered into a valid contract with Defendants" on March 4 is a conclusion of law beyond Buyer's competence. We address this contention only to note that the trial court was not required to rely on Buyer's statement as proof of the existence of a binding contract.

CONCLUSION

We hold as a matter of law that Buyer accepted the counteroffer by performance, thus making the Owners' promises binding. Accordingly, we affirm the trial court's order of summary judgment for Buyer.

IT IS SO ORDERED.

Case Questions:

1. Did the buyer accept the counteroffer made in this case? Why or why not?

2. According to this court, what is the definition of acceptance of an offer?

3. The sellers contend that only a written acceptance was possible. How does the court address this issue?

4. According to the court, does the Statute of Frauds require that an acceptance must be made in writing?

5. What does the court mean when it refers to the buyer's acceptance "by performance?"

Conditions That Limit Acceptance

Offers can contain all manner of conditions regarding acceptance. For instance, an offer could contain a condition on the manner of acceptance. It could state that the offer could only be accepted in a particular way or at a particular place at a particular time. Under this situation, any acceptance that fails to live up to all the conditions is not legally valid and there is no contract. The offeror is always free to amend his offer or to waive a special condition.

Restrictions on the Method of Communicating the Acceptance

When an offer does not provide any limitations on the manner and mode of communicating the acceptance, it can be accepted in any manner. However, in some situations, an offer may stipulate the exact mode of acceptance. In those situations, the acceptance must follow the prescribed mode or it will be legally insufficient.

Time Limits on Acceptance

When an offer does not contain any language expressly limiting the time on which an offer can be accepted, the offer will remain open for a "reasonable period of time." This reasonable period of time is often interpreted by the courts on a case-by-case basis. As we have already seen, an offer can contain an express time limit. An offer can expire by its own terms or after a reasonable period of time has passed. In situations where an offer remains open, the person has the power to accept at any point in time.[6]

> **Sidebar:**
> Once a person has accepted an offer, he cannot revoke his acceptance.

Waving a Stipulation or Condition

The person making the offer is always free to amend his offer, or to waive a special condition. This right rests with the offeror, not the offeree. Therefore, the offeror can tell the offeree that he waives all conditions, prescribed methods of communicating the offer, and so on, in the original offer.

Acceptance Must Be Unambiguous

Although the law does not require that the person actually use the words, "I accept," the person accepting the offer must not only communicate with the offeror but also that he use language that is an unambiguous acceptance. The offeror is entitled to know that he has a binding contract with another person. If a person uses the words "maybe" and "perhaps," or his language is so ambiguous that it is impossible to discern his acceptance, the courts will usually interpret this as a rejection of the offer. As we have already seen, a counteroffer also is considered to be a rejection of the original offer.

Accepting Alternative Terms

An offer can include alternative terms. For instance, the person making the offer could state that "I will sell you my house on Maple Avenue for

$50,000 or I will sell you my home on Brown Street for $60,000. You can choose either or both houses." In such a situation, the offeree is authorized to make a valid acceptance of one or both of the houses. There is nothing precluding the person from accepting the offer on the Maple Street house while rejecting the offer on the Brown Street house. An offer also can contain an indefinite quantity. For example, an offer could be sent to a merchant with a blank line before the number of items to be ordered. By filling in the blank with a specific number, that person is accepting the offer for a specific quantity. The fact that the person making the offer did not specify an amount does not make the offer legally invalid.

In situations in which the quantity of items to be purchased is left blank, the law construes the situation to be that the offeror has already agreed, before sending out the offer, to any reasonable amount that the merchant decides to write in the blank. However, the situation can become murkier if the written quantity far exceeds what was expected. We will address that issue in the next chapter.

Accepting by Mail

When an offer has been extended that contains no limitations on the form of communication, the offeree is usually free to accept the offer by posting it in the U.S. mail. Unless an offer contains language specifically mandating a form of communication, acceptance by mail is considered to be legally valid. However, as we all know, it may take one to three days for a letter to reach its intended recipient. Suppose that the person making the offer changes his mind between the time that it is mailed to him and the time that he receives it? This common problem was the reason for the creation of the so-called Mailbox rule. The Mailbox Rule is a very simple rule that is used by the courts nationwide. Under the Mailbox Rule, the law creates a legal fiction: the fiction is that an acceptance is fully communicated at the time that it is posted, not at the time at which it is received. This means that when a person accepts by mail, this acceptance is legally valid the moment the letter leaves his hands and enters the U.S. postal system, even though it may not actually be received for several days. The Mailbox Rule was created to deal with the problem of how to determine who has validly accepted an offer when there are two people sending an acceptance and one of them sends the acceptance by mail and the other sends his acceptance by some other means.

HYPOTHETICAL 3-6   Theo's Paintings

Theo contacts Maria and John and offers to sell one of them his rare collection of folk art paintings. He tells them that he will sell for $1,000 to whomever accepts first. Both Maria and John think over the proposal. At 3 P.M. on the next day, Maria writes a letter to Theo in which she states that she accepts his terms and includes a check for $1,000. At 3:15 P.M. on the same day, John faxes a letter to Miguel in which he indicates that he will accept the offer and will send him a check for $1,000. Which person is entitled to the paintings?

Answer: Maria. In this situation, Theo has not imposed any limitations on the manner of communicating an acceptance. Maria is free to accept by mail or any other means. Because Maria posted her acceptance 15 minutes earlier than John's fax, Maria is entitled to the paintings, even though Theo does not actually receive her acceptance until the following day.

Sidebar:
In cases in which proof of the date and time of a mailing are crucial, the smartest move is to send the letter by certified or registered mail, after making sure that it has been stamped with both the date and time. This will help prove when the letter was actually mailed, if it comes down to a question of who has priority in the acceptance. (For an excellent overview of the types of proof required, see 7 Am. Jur. Proof of Facts 417.)

The justification for the Mailbox Rule is simple: unlike almost all other forms of communication, a letter, once mailed, is virtually impossible to retrieve. Once Mary has posted her letter, she is unable to retrieve it, or to make changes to it. With telephones, faxes, and e-mails, a change in the text of the message can be made almost immediately, or a follow-up communication can quickly clear up any discrepancies. This is not true with regular mail.

EXCEPTIONS TO THE MAILBOX RULE

One of the important exceptions to the Mailbox Rule is triggered when an acceptance contains language that is ambiguous. For instance, when a purported acceptance is mailed to the offeror and changes the terms of the offer, or places conditions on the acceptance, the Mailbox Rule is no longer applicable.

Sidebar:
The Mailbox Rule is also called the "Posted Acceptance Rule."

Rejecting an Offer

It should be obvious that an acceptance cannot be made when an offer has been revoked. When an offer has been revoked, there is no power to acceptance and therefore there is no way that a person can accept. In a similar way, once a person has accepted an offer, an acceptance cannot be revoked. A contract is created with a valid acceptance. Neither party is free to revoke because a contract has been created and there are new legal obligations on both parties. The offer and acceptance phase of contract formation is now over. As far as the law is concerned, there is neither a pending offer nor an issue regarding acceptance. Instead, there is now a contract that must either be honored or the parties may sue one another for failure to perform.

In some situations, an offeree may reject an offer through actions instead of words. For instance, suppose the offeree takes some action inconsistent with the formation of a contract. If the offeree demonstrates that he does not wish to be bound by a contract, his actions will often speak for him. His actions will be judged by the standard of what a reasonable, hypothetical person would have believed from observing his actions. Later, he cannot accept the offer when his actions have indicated his intention to reject it. Obviously, in any particular case, whether or not the offeree's actions amounted to a rejection of the offer would be a question for the jury.

HYPOTHETICAL 3-7   The Computer Business, Part Two

During their discussions about forming a computer business, Miguel becomes visibly upset and storms out of the room. At the point that he left, John had made a counteroffer to purchase Miguel's computers at $525 apiece. John interpreted Miguel's actions to be a rejection of this counteroffer. John then contacted a local computer manufacturer and began negotiations with the company. The company informs John that it can provide 200 computers per week at a cost of $450 per computer. John decides to go into business with the company. At this point, Miguel returns and says that he accepts John's counter offer of $525 per computer. Is there a binding contract between John and Miguel?

Answer: No. Although Miguel did not specifically say that he rejected John's offer, a reasonable interpretation of his actions would be that he did not wish to accept the offer and by storming out of the room, he indicated his rejection of that offer. Because he had rejected the offer, he no longer had the power of the acceptance. At this point, John was free to negotiate with anyone else.

What is true for acceptance is also true for the offer. Once an offer has been accepted, the offer cannot be revoked. When a valid offer has been accepted, it creates a new contract and the offer and acceptance phase is now over. If, at that point, the person making the offer attempts to revoke it, that revocation has no legal significance. At this point, a contract has been created and the offeror will now be subject to a lawsuit for failure to perform under that contract. The parties are free to modify their contract in any way that they see fit, but this does not mean that they can modify their original offer and acceptance. The parties are even free to rescind the contract; however, this does not take away the fact that a contract had been created (see Exhibit 3-3).

Modifying the Terms after Acceptance

Suppose that, after making a valid acceptance, the person who made the offer wishes to modify the contract in some way. Is the offeree obligated to accept these new modifications? The answer is no. Now that a contract has been formed, both parties must agree to any modifications of the contract. If one of the parties is not willing to modify the contract, then no modification can be had.

When an acceptance contains no language modifying or altering the terms of the original offer, the person who made the offer has the right to assume that the acceptance was an unequivocal acceptance of all of the terms presented in the offer. The person giving the acceptance cannot later claim that he only partially accepted. It is presumed under the law that an unconditional acceptance agrees to all of the terms of the offer.

When an acceptance does contain modifications or conditions, courts will usually interpret this as a counteroffer. If this counteroffer is accepted, the contract is formed containing these new conditions.

Table 2. Types of plaintiffs or defendants, by types of contract cases in state courts in the nation's 75 largest counties, 1996

| | Percent of each type of plaintiff | | | |
	Individual	Government	Business*	Hospital
All contract cases	100%	100%	100%	100%
Fraud	17.1	11.3	9.7	10.4
Seller plaintiff	19.8	14.7	51.3	53.7
Buyer plaintiff	22.8	—	10.3	16.9
Mortgage foreclosure	1.0	—	1.8	—
Employment discrimination	11.0	13.0	0.7	—
Other employment dispute	9.5	30.7	2.0	3.6
Rental/lease agreements	8.8	23.5	12.1	3.7
Tortious interference	3.9	3-4	6.2	1.9
Other contract	6.0	3.4	6.0	9.9
Number of cases with each type of plaintiff	2,661	37	2,091	54

| | Percent of each type of defendant | | | |
	Individual	Government	Business*	Hospital
All contract cases	100%	100%	100%	100%
Fraud	14.2	4.1	14.5	—
Seller plaintiff	45.9	8.4	29.4	20.7
Buyer plaintiff	8.6	5.5	22.5	3.9
Mortgage foreclosure	1.3	—	1.4	3.1
Employment discrimination	1.0	42.0	6.7	21.8
Other employment dispute	2.8	16.5	7.0	33.4
Rental/lease agreements	15.2	7.9	8.0	7.7
Tortious interference	3.8	1.1	5.7	1.6
Other contract	7.2	14.5	4.9	7.8
Number of cases with each type of defendant	1,543	184	3,051	64

Note: Plaintiff or defendant type is whichever type appears first in this list: (1) hospital/medical company, (2) business, (3) government agency, (4) individual. For example, any case involving a hospital defendant is categorized as a hospital even if there were also business, individual, or government defendants in the case.
Detail for litigant types was available for 99.8% of all contract trial cases. Detail may not sum to 100% because of rounding.
— No cases recorded.
* Includes insurance companies, banks and financial companies, construction and real estate development companies, service and goods sellers, manufacturing companies, and other businesses.

EXHIBIT 3-3: Types of plaintiffs or defendants in contract cases nationwide.

Source: Contract Trials and Verdicts in Large Counties, 1996, Civil Justice Survey of State Courts, 1996, U.S. Department of Justice.

The Case of the Overpriced Oil[7]

BANKS, Justice, for the Court:

In the fall of 1990, the plaintiffs, Jack and Dot Edwards (hereinafter, the Edwardses), had been engaged in the operation of a convenience store in Walnut Grove, Mississippi, for approximately two years. They had decided to find a supplier for petroleum products in order to sell gasoline at their store. During the latter part of November or early December 1990, Pat Thaggard, a friend of the Edwardses, introduced them to David Knapp, a representative of Wurster Oil Company, which was headquartered in Louisiana, but had been doing business in Mississippi. Knapp met with the Edwardses to survey their property and discuss the possibility of Wurster Oil supplying them with gasoline. A couple of days later, Knapp met with the Edwardses again, discussing the process of installing the equipment necessary to sell the gasoline. Jack and Dot Edwards, as well as their daughter and son-in-law, Sandra and Delbert Lathem, were present during the meeting. Knapp presented the Edwardses with a copy of the Gasoline Sales Lease and the Gasoline Sales Agreement, both of which contained several blank spaces. The Edwardses signed the documents, while David Knapp, Delbert Lathem, and Sandra Lathem witnessed them. However, the documents were not signed by any representative of Wurster Oil which would bind Wurster to the contract.

After the documents were signed by the Edwardses, they were delivered to Jim Thornton, secretary-treasurer and part owner of Wurster Oil Company. After receiving the documents, Thornton visited Walnut Grove to determine whether the Edwardses had an acceptable location which fit the company's criteria. Thornton discussed with the Edwardses and the Lathems the improvements necessary to be made to the land for the sale of gasoline. After meeting with the Edwardses, Thornton decided to approve the contract and notified Petron, Inc. of Alexandria, Louisiana, an oil services construction company, to make the improvements and install the equipment on the Edwardses' property. On January 15, 1991, Petron made an initial bid of $105,238.39.

The improvements were made and the Edwardses had begun selling Wurster Oil products by February 1991. Under the terms of the Gasoline Sales Agreement, the Edwardses were to be compensated on a split-the-profits basis and receive a commission equal to half of the profits for all gasoline and petroleum products sold by them for Wurster Oil. However, the agreement referenced an Exhibit "B", which states that the Edwardses were to be held responsible for half of the cost of the improvements through the withholding of half of their commission. Thus, they would effectively receive one-fourth of the profits from the sale of the gasoline.

The major dispute in this case arises from the portion of Exhibit "B" that was left blank when signed by the plaintiffs. The plaintiffs assert that the entire section of the agreement was blank, except for the signature lines. The defendants, however, assert that the entire section was filled in, except for the signatures of the parties and the amount of the cost of the improvements. The final cost of the improvements was $122,913.91 as submitted by Petron to Wurster Oil on April 25, 1991.

In March of 1991, after receiving two or three commission checks from Wurster Oil, Mrs. Edwards informed Jim Thornton of her dissatisfaction with the amount that they were receiving, after realizing that they were only receiving half of the commission they thought they were due. She also requested a copy of the contract they had signed, a copy of the cost of the installation of the equipment, and a calculation of the deductions that were made from their checks. All were received in the latter part of April, 1991, after Thornton had obtained the total cost from Petron. After Mrs. Edwards initially voiced her dissatisfaction with the deductions from their commission, Jim Thornton discussed the contract with her on several other occasions and offered to allow the Edwardses to pay for the installation of the equipment themselves, at a price of $122,913.91, or find another company which would do so.

On January 10, 1992, the Edwardses filed suit against Wurster Oil in chancery court, alleging that Exhibit "B" was "hopelessly contradictory" to the terms of the Gasoline Sales Lease and the Gasoline Sales Agreement, and therefore should be declared void. They further requested an accounting for the method used in calculating the per-gallon charge for the gasoline sold by the Edwardses on behalf of Wurster and a judgment against Wurster Oil for all commissions unlawfully withheld by Wurster Oil, as well as punitive damages, attorney's fees, and costs of court.

In the disposition of the lawsuit, the Chancellor held that the agreements completed by Wurster Oil "made material additions to the agreements as signed by the Edwardses and constituted a counteroffer. The Chancellor further noted that "[u]pon receiving the final agreements, the Edwardses had the right to reject them or accept them as they were."

The Chancellor then held: [b]y thereafter permitting the defendant to continue to deduct from their share one-half of the cost of the improvements [from May to the time of suit], the Edwardses accepted the counteroffer . . . [T]he actions of the Edwardses have been consistent with their having a subsisting contract with Wurster Oil Company . . . Pertinent in this regard is the fact that the plaintiffs waited until January 10, 1992 (over eight months), after receiving a copy of the contract before filing suit.

The Chancellor also held that the Edwardses were entitled to recover the amounts owed to them as a result of an audit that was to be conducted to determine whether the plaintiffs had been underpaid under the contract. The court denied the plaintiffs' request for attorney's fees and costs of court, and failed to make any finding regarding whether Exhibit "B" existed as the plaintiffs assert at the time they signed it or as the defendants assert.

The Edwardses appeal to this Court to consider whether the chancellor erred in ruling that they had accepted the counteroffer of Wurster Oil as evidenced by the Gasoline Sales Lease and the Gasoline Sales Agreement.

Whether the chancellor properly concluded that the Edwardses made an "offer" to which Wurster Oil replied with a "counteroffer" is of little consequence to the disposition of this case. The relevant issue to be decided by this Court on appeal is whether the chancellor's ultimate conclusion that the Edwardses' conduct after receiving the documents showing all of the terms from Wurster Oil constituted their acceptance of the contract is manifestly erroneous.

A contract is not formed until an offeree accepts. It is a well-settled principle of law that "acceptance of a contract as binding upon a party may be shown by his actions, and any definite and unequivocal course of conduct disclosing that the party has acceded or assented to it, is as binding on him as had he endorsed his assent in formal writing . . ." In *Crabb v. Wilkinson*, 202 Miss. 274, 32 So.2d 356 (1947), this Court confronted a similar circumstance where the appellees executed to the appellants two written instruments, one granting an oil and gas lease on all the lands involved within the lease, and one granting a mineral deed which conveyed to the appellants "an undivided one half interest in and to all the oil, gas, and other minerals in and under" the lands involved in the lease. The appellees filed suit, alleging that the latter document had been executed on the false "pretense that it was merely a copy of the oil and gas lease, and that the copy was desired for appellants' files." After the appellees inquired as to the reason for their receiving only one-half of the rental due on their property, they were shown copies of the agreements which explained that under the mineral deed they were entitled to one-half the annual rent and the appellants were entitled to the other one-half of the annual rent.

The appellees were then given the choice of refusing the rent, denying the validity of the mineral deed, or accepting the rent, which would have the effect of recognizing the right of the appellants to receive one-half of the rent by virtue of the mineral deed. The appellees chose to accept one-half the rent for the two years that the tender was made; nevertheless, this Court stated that "their action in accepting the $16 on the first rental renewal was all that was necessary to be shown for the reason that an election to affirm once made is thereafter irrevocable." The Court repeated the rule announced in *Koenig*, and noted that "at the time of their conduct in affirmance, they [the appellees] had before them in written form all facts material to that affirmance."

In a more recent case, *Turner v. Wakefield*, 481 So.2d 846 (Miss.1985), this Court again confronted the issue of ratification of contracts which are allegedly based on fraud. The appellee alleged that it had been fraudulently induced into the execution of a promissory note to the appellant. The appellee, however, continued to make payments on the note for eleven months after being advised of its potential invalidity. This Court stated that "a contract obligation obtained by fraudulent representation is not void, but voidable." *Id.* at 848–849. The Court held that "upon discovery thereof [of fraud], the one defrauded *must act promptly and finally* to repudiate the agreement; however, a continuance to ratify the contract terms constitutes a waiver." *Id.* at 849 (emphasis added). Thus, this Court's holding was in accord with its previous holdings in *Koenig and Crabb* that acts recognizing a contract as subsisting constitute acceptance of the terms of that contract. It is noteworthy that in *Turner,* the appellee pleaded financial hardship and ignorance of the law as reasons for his failure to terminate his payment under the note.

As was alleged in the previous cases, the Edwardses assert that Wurster Oil's actions constituted fraud. The Chancellor, however, had substantial credible evidence to form the conclusion that the plaintiffs demonstrated a "definite and unequivocal course of conduct" which would disclose that they had acceded to the contract with Wurster Oil. The record reveals that upon realization that the Edwardses were being required to pay fifty percent of the installation cost through the deduction of fifty percent of their commission, Mrs. Edwards immediately informed Jim Thornton of her disapproval of the arrangement in March of 1991. Furthermore, she requested a copy of the contract they had signed, a copy of the cost of the installation of the equipment, and a calculation of the deductions that were made from their checks, which were all received in the latter part of April of 1991.

After Mrs. Edwards voiced her dissatisfaction with the deductions from their commission, Jim Thornton offered to allow the Edwardses to pay for the installation of the equipment themselves at a price of $122,913.91, or they could find a company which would do so. The Edwardses assert that they were not financially able to do this. As in *Turner,* however, financial hardship may not be relied upon to explain the failure to cease compliance with a disputed contract. Thus, the Edwardses had to resort to other methods of obtaining relief.

Although a section of the Gasoline Sales Agreement provides that "[a]ll gasoline and all sums collected by Dealer [Jack Edwards and Dot Edwards] for gasoline sold hereunder shall be, become and remain the sole and exclusive property of the Owner," the plaintiffs could reasonably have retained a portion of the gasoline receipts that they believed they deserved and awaited suit by Wurster Oil. In the alternative, the plaintiffs could also have immediately sought legal representation and asserted a claim against the defendants for their portion of the commission. Instead, they chose to wait eight months before taking action, while continuing to remit the total gasoline receipts and accepting one-half of their commission from Wurster Oil. We conclude that the Chancellor's holding that, by continuing to remit the entire commission and accepting one-half of their commission from Wurster Oil, the Edwardses' accepted and ratified their contract with Wurster Oil, is not manifestly erroneous. As did the appellees in *Crabb,* the Edwardses had before them all facts material to acceptance or ratification at the time of their acceptance or ratification of the contract. They are, therefore, estopped from asserting their claim which arises from a provision within that contract.

AFFIRMED.

Case Questions:

1. Did the court consider it to be important that the store owners failed to act promptly to contest the amount of their compensation from the oil company?

2. Is this a case of acceptance and ratification of the contract after it was changed?

3. According to the court, when did the plaintiffs accept a counteroffer in this case?

4. If the storeowners wished to attack the validity of the agreement, what should they have done?

5. Is there some action that the storeowners could have taken during negotiations to avoid the ultimate outcome?

ACCEPTANCE BY AN AGENT

Can a third party accept for another? In most jurisdictions, the answer to this question is yes. If a person appoints an **agent** to act for him in certain matters, this person is vested with the same authority, at least to a certain extent, as the original person. This means that if an agent has expressly received authority to make or receive an offer, he or she can do so on behalf of the principal. As far as the law is concerned, an acceptance that has been communicated to the offeror's agent is as effective as an acceptance that was communicated to the offeror himself (see Exhibits 3-4 and 3-5).

agent: A person authorized by another person to act for him or her; a person entrusted with another's business.

Table 9. Case processing time from filing of complaint to final verdict or judgment for pairings of primary litigants in contract trials in state courts in the nation's 75 largest counties, 1996

Litigant pairs[a]	Number of contract cases	Number of months		
		Median	Minimum	Maximum
All contract trial cases[b]	4.008	19.1	0.5	145.0
Individual versus:				
Individual	713	18.8	0.5	145.0
Government	121	19.7	1.8	89.5
Business[c]	1,375	19.8	0.9	99.5
Hospital	39	19.4	10.1	71.8
Individual and nonindividual[d] versus:				
Individual	51	22.2	8.7	98.8
Government	4	32.3	18.2	39.6
Business[c]	154	19.9	4.8	74.7
Hospital	3	35.7	19.4	35.7
Nonindividual[d] versus:				
Individual	469	15.5	0.9	114.9
Government	43	15.5	0.9	50.4
Business[c]	1,017	19.6	1.4	93.2
Hospital	14	16.5	10.1	46.7

EXHIBIT 3-4: The time it takes for a contract case to reach the trial stage, nationwide.

Source: Contract Trials and Verdicts in Large Counties, 1996, Civil Justice Survey of State Courts, 1996, U.S. Department of Justice, p. 7.

✓ PARALEGAL CHECKLIST

When reviewing a contractual negotiation, do the following to confirm acceptance:

☐ Did the offeree actually accept?

☐ What physical actions did the offeree take to show acceptance?

☐ What facts prove/disprove that the offeree intended to enter into a contract?

☐ What witnesses can testify about offeree's intent (or lack thereof)?

☐ Did the offeree accept any benefits from the contract itself?

☐ Did the offeree act as though he/she were in a binding contractual relationship?

☐ If the offer was accepted, was it properly communicated?

☐ Were there any limitations or conditions placed on the acceptance by the offeror?

☐ If yes, what limitations were there?

☐ Did the offeror limit the manner/mode of acceptance?

☐ Did the offeree abide by these limitations?

- Did the offeree accept personally or use an intermediary?
- Were there any other limits on the offer, such as time limits?
- If yes, was the offer accepted within the prescribed time period?

EXHIBIT 3-5: Confirming acceptance.

Business Case File

Brenda Joy Bernstein, Attorney at Law

Brenda Joy Bernstein

Brenda Joy Bernstein is a former Assistant District Attorney in Atlanta, Georgia. She was a member of the child molestation prosecution team for years, but she eventually began thinking about leaving prosecution and opening up her own office.

"One of the reasons that I wanted to open my own firm was the chance for autonomy," she said. "I liked the idea that I only had to answer to myself. Once I made the decision to change from being a prosecutor to a private attorney, the first question I asked myself was, 'How will I get business?' I decided that I'd put myself on the court appointed list and that would at least generate some income while I got my practice going. I shared office space with another attorney, and that kept the expenses down. I wanted an office in downtown Atlanta because that's where I wanted to draw my clients.

"When I first got started, I contacted every person I knew to tell them that I was opening up a criminal defense firm. I took a lot of other attorneys out to lunch and had face-to-face meetings with lots of other people. I explained to the attorneys that I wasn't going to be coming in on their turf. If they were personal injury attorneys, I'd say, 'I'm going to specialize in criminal defense. If you have any clients who need that, I'd appreciate it if you would refer them to me. If I have any personal injury business, I'll send it your way.'"

Bernstein has represented some famous clients in cases that have received a great deal of media attention.

"I was fortunate because I got some great referrals early on. Several large firms sent their clients to me when they needed criminal work. I got a ton of business that way. Then, I got more business through word of mouth."

Contracts are a huge part of any law practice. When a client retains an attorney, they sign a contract setting out the attorney's obligations and the fee that the client will pay for those services. The attorney offers service in exchange for payment. The client manifests his or her acceptance by paying the fee.

Although many people don't think about a law office as a business, it has the same concerns as any other type of business. One such cost is advertising and finding new clients.

"Attorneys are really still hampered in how they can advertise," said Bernstein. "Even though a lot of the restrictions have been removed, attorneys who advertise are still seen as a suspect class. My best advertising came from satisfied clients and word of mouth."

One of the biggest surprises about opening up a law office was the interaction with the clients. "I always thought that a good result was the only thing that the client wanted, but that's not true. They want contact. I think that follow up with clients is crucial. You should always return client phone calls and keep the clients informed. I do it by phone. I'm on the phone all the time."

Bernstein has achieved the kind of success with her firm that other attorneys dream about. She has a beautiful office in downtown Atlanta, regularly appears on television, and can afford to indulge one of her lifelong passions: traveling. Her approach to the business of law has obviously paid huge dividends.

ETHICS FILE: How Ethical Rules Affect Attorneys and Paralegals

Attorneys are regulated by the state bar and often punished by the state's highest court. Depending on the state, an attorney can be investigated by the State Bar and sanctioned by the State Supreme Court (although the title may vary from state to state). There are different levels of punishments for attorney violators. The lowest form of punishment—usually reserved for technical infractions of ethical rules—is the private reprimand. An attorney is notified, usually by mail, that he or she has violated an ethical rule and is advised not to do so again. After this, the next level of punishment is the public reprimand. Here, an attorney's name and infraction are published so that everyone can read about the attorney's infraction. Other than causing embarrassment and loss of professional credibility, neither of these sanctions affects the attorney's right to practice law. This is not true for the remaining sanctions. Attorneys who commit more serious infractions, such as a criminal offense, are often suspended. A suspension can last for a relatively short period of time, or for several years, depending on the nature of the violation. The most severe punishment an attorney can receive is disbarment. An attorney who has been disbarred cannot practice law at all. Disbarments often are permanent—essentially stripping the lawyer of the right to practice his or her profession. The most common reason for an attorney to be disbarred is through embezzling client funds.

Paralegals are not directly supervised or regulated through the State Bar. Although they can be charged with the criminal offense of practicing law without a license, they do not face disbarment or other professional sanction. This does not mean, however, that paralegals should not concern themselves with ethical rules. On the contrary, paralegals should be highly attuned to the ethical rules, because their actions could result in sanctions against the attorneys with whom they work.

Chapter Summary:

Any contract involves a legally valid offer and an acceptance. Offer and acceptance show the parties' intent to contract with one another in what courts usually refer to as "meeting of the minds." In this chapter, we explored the legal concepts surrounding acceptance of a valid offer. An acceptance must first be communicated in an acceptable manner. If an offer is made in writing, an acceptance is normally also required in writing. An offer also can contain express language that limits exactly how an acceptance can be made. In this chapter, we have seen that the law governing acceptance of an offer can be complex. An offer can contain express limitations. For instance, an offer can expressly limit the manner in which the acceptance is communicated. An offer that states that it can only be accepted in writing must be accepted in that way or there is no binding contract. Offers also may contain other limitations on a person's ability to accept the offer. One of the most common limitations on offers deals with time. An offer may expire by its own terms, such as when the offer has an express deadline, or an offer may expire after a reasonable period of time. An acceptance that changes the terms or places conditions on the acceptance is usually interpreted to be a counter offer. A valid offer creates the power of acceptance in another person. The power of acceptance is the right to create a contract on a valid acceptance of an offer. Once an offer has been accepted, a person is no longer free to reject the offer. Under the law, when an offer has been accepted, a contract has been created. At that point, any attempt to modify the offer and the exceptions will be invalid. There also are some important court doctrines that govern the law of acceptance. Perhaps the most important, the Mailbox Rule, holds that when a person accepts an offer, and does so in writing by posting a letter to the person who made the offer, that acceptance is deemed to be valid the moment it is placed in the U.S. mail system. This is true even if the acceptance takes several days to actually reach the person who made the offer. Offers can be made and accepted by other parties, commonly referred to as agents. An agent may be vested with temporary authority, or have broad authority to enter into numerous types of contracts.

WEB SITES

Lex Mercatoria
www.lexmercatori.org
One of the original legal research sites; it is a compilation of international commercial law.

Pace Law School
http://www.law.pace.edu/
A law school site featuring information about becoming an attorney and the academic requirements for admission to law school.

Department of Commerce
http://www.commerce.gov/
Provides information and resources from the U.S. Department of Commerce.

Internet Legal Resource Guide
http://www.ilrg.com
Provides links for all aspects of legal practice.

Department of Business Regulations - Rhode Island
http://www.dbr.state.ri.us/

REVIEW QUESTIONS

1. What is an acceptance?
2. What is the Mailbox Rule? What are some of the exceptions to this rule?
3. What significance does it have to the transaction when the offeree changes the terms of the offer in his acceptance?
4. What is the legal significance of an offer that contains an express limitation about the mode of acceptance and the offeree chooses a different form of acceptance?
5. Are there legal limitations on a person's ability to accept an offer? If so, what are they?
6. Explain how the power of acceptance shifts between the parties during negotiations.
7. Why do the courts inquire about the sufficiency of acceptance?
8. Can an offer include alternative terms?
9. Why would it be legally valid for an offer to contain alternative terms?
10. Is it possible to accept a contract without speaking at all?
11. When an offer specifies a particular method of communication, and a person fails to use that form of communication, what effect does this have on a future contract?
12. Why does the Mailbox Rule continue to exist? Are there practical reasons for maintaining this rule?
13. What words are sufficient to indicate acceptance?
14. Why do courts require "unambiguous acceptance?"
15. What are the different levels of punishment that an attorney can receive for an ethical violation?
16. Explain the types of limitations that an offeror can place on the methods of accepting the offer.
17. Does an "open-ended" offer ever expire? Explain.
18. Why is the means used to communicate acceptance important in determining valid acceptance?
19. When, and under what circumstances, can an agent accept for another?
20. When is an offer to be considered "rejected?"

HANDS-ON ASSIGNMENT

Marcia is a waitress at a local restaurant that has several other locations throughout the city. One evening, the manager of her restaurant announces at an employee meeting that the company has started a new contest. "The waitress who sells the most beer over the next six months will win a Toyota." Marcia wants a new car desperately, and asks for additional details.

The manager tells her that if she wins, she will be responsible for paying the car taxes and associated costs, but she will definitely get a Toyota. For the next six months, Marcia works very hard and wins the contest. On the evening of the presentation, the manager blindfolds Marcia and leads her into the parking lot. When he wisks off the blindfold, Marcia sees a small Yoda doll, part of the Star Wars® action figures collection. The manager, laughing, says, "There you go, a toy Yoda!" Marcia gets very angry. Today, she has come to our firm and wants to know if she has a case. We must first decide if there was a contract. Has there been a valid offer and acceptance? Why or why not?

PRACTICAL APPLICATION

Review the *Long v. Allen* case provided in this chapter. What could the parties have done to make the issue of acceptance of the counteroffer clearer for all concerned?

HELP THIS BUSINESS

Miguel has decided that he is going to go into the home refurbishing business. He is going to purchase homes that are in need of repairs, make the repairs himself, and then resell the homes for what he hopes will be a substantial profit. He has had his eye on a particular house for some time. The house is just the down the street from Miguel's apartment. The grass is overgrown, the paint is peeling, and even the mailbox has fallen down. One day, Miguel knocks on the front door and when the owner appears, Miguel says, "I'd like to buy your house. What do you think of $30,000?"

The man shrugs. Miguel decides to push for an answer. "What do you think? I could take this place off your hands for $35,000. How about that?" When the man does not respond, Miguel says, "Okay, okay, I can see that you are a tough bargainer. I'll go $40,000 and that's it." At this point, the man opens the door and rubs his fingers together in a way that Miguel recognizes as asking for money. Miguel writes a check for $1,000 and says, "Okay, here's a down payment. I'll stop by on Monday and we can work out the details."

On Monday, Miguel checks with his bank and finds out that the man cashed the check. Miguel stops by the house and when the man appears, Miguel asks him about working out the moving details. "What details?" The man asks. "I never agreed to anything. You gave me $1,000 and I took it. I have no intention of selling my house."

Analyze Miguel's situation. Was there a valid offer and acceptance? If not, then why not? If yes, then why?

KEY TERMS

power of acceptance

agent

ENDNOTES

[1] *United States Hoffman Mach. Corp. v. Harris,* 167 SC 443, 166 SE 613 (1932).

[2] Restatement, Contracts 2d §56.

[3] *Federal Farm Mortg. Corp. v. Dixon,* 185 Ga 466, 195 SE 414 (1938).

[4] Restatement, Contracts 2d §69.

[5] *Long v. Allen,* 906 P.2d 754 (1995).

[6] *C.G. Schmidt, Inc. v. Tiedke,* 181 Wis 2d 316, 510 NW2d 756 (1993).

[7] *Edwards v. Wurster Oil Co., Inc.* 688 So.2d 772 (Miss., 1997).

 For additional resources, visit our Web site at www.westlegalstudies.com

CHAPTER 4

CONSIDERATION (BARGAINED FOR EXCHANGE)

Focus of this chapter: This chapter addresses the issue of consideration. One of the main requirements of any contract is that both parties incur some legal detriment or some benefit from the arrangement. Consideration is both a legal requirement for the formation of a contract and a prerequisite to enforcing a contract in the court system. As we explore the concept of consideration, we also explore the related issues of legal detriment and the court-created doctrines that were originally created to avoid injustice.

Chapter Objectives:
At the completion of this chapter, you should be able to:

- Define consideration and explain the importance of consideration in the formation of contracts
- Differentiate between a valid contract and a gratuitous promise
- Explain the concept of legal detriment
- Provide examples of consideration from typical contracts
- Differentiate between quid pro quo and consideration
- Explain why the courts generally do not inquire into the value of a contract's consideration
- Explain promissory estoppel
- Differentiate between promissory estoppel and waiver
- Analyze a case for consideration
- Demonstrate your understanding of this chapter's concepts by answering review questions and hypotheticals related to consideration

Introduction

In this chapter we examine one of the underlying legal requirements of most contracts: consideration. We will explore not only how consideration is defined but also the purpose that it serves in a contract. We begin by defining what consideration is.

What Is Consideration?

consideration: The basic reason for a contract; a person gives up something of value in exchange for receiving something of value through the contract.

Sidebar:
In order to be enforceable under the law, a contract must be supported by consideration.[4]

Sidebar:
Consideration has also been defined at "the reason or main cause for a person to make a contract."[5]

Often, the problem with the term **consideration** is not that it is difficult to define; the problem is that there are so many different definitions of this term. Consideration is often defined as "some right, interest, profit or benefit accruing to one party" or the loss, detriment, or responsibility assumed by a part to a contract.[1] Consideration also could be defined as "something given in exchange for the promise."[2] The Restatement of Contracts phrases it differently, referring to consideration as a performance or a return promise that is bargained for (see Exhibit 4-1). In essence, both parties are giving up something of value to obtain something of value. It is consideration that makes the promise enforceable. Consideration is also a requirement of a legally valid contract.[3] Consideration is one of the required principles that determines the development of a contract and is present in the contract when the parties intend an exchange.

Time after time, courts have defined consideration as, "Some right, interest, profit, or benefit accruing to one party, or some forbearance, detriment, loss,

---

(1) To constitute consideration, a performance or a return promise must be bargained for.

(2) A performance or return promise is bargained for if it is sought by the promisor in exchange for his promise and is given by the promisee in exchange for that promise.

(3) The performance may consist of

    (a) an act other than a promise, or
    (b) a forbearance, or
    (c) the creation, modification, or destruction of a legal relation.

(4) The performance or return promise may be given to the promisor or to some other person. It may be given by the promisee or by some other person.

EXHIBIT 4-1: Restatement definition of consideration.

Source: Restatement of Contracts, 2d §71.

or responsibility given, suffered, or undertaken by the other."[6] However, these various definitions do not actually explain what consideration is. A more concrete example might help.

HYPOTHETICAL 4-1   Natasha's New Business

Natasha has decided to begin a small catering business. She realizes that she will need occasional help with preparing and transporting the food. Michael knows that Natasha has plans to open a business and one day he approaches her and says, "If you need my help for a particular affair, just call me up and I'll come over. I'll even let you borrow my van."

Two weeks later, Natasha has a wedding for which she is the only caterer. It will be a large payday for Natasha and she calls Michael and says that she needs his help. Michael says that he cannot make it and that his van will not be available. Natasha becomes angry and decides to sue Michael.

Does she have a case?

Setting aside for a moment whether there was a valid offer and acceptance, there is no binding contract between Natasha and Michael for the simple reason that Michael's offer was a "gratuitous promise." There was no consideration. Michael's legal status did not change as a result of this supposed contract. He neither incurred any obligation, nor did he receive any benefit. At first glance, there is no enforceable contract between them. However, we will examine the concept of promissory estoppel later in this chapter that might come to Natasha's assistance.

The important aspect of consideration is that without it, the contract is considered void, and thus unenforceable.[7] When a party files suit to enforce a contract, one of the elements he must prove, in addition to offer and acceptance, is that there was consideration for the contract. Perhaps the best way to understand consideration is to inquire why it is required at all.

Why Is Consideration Required?

Consideration is required for the formation of a valid contract for the simple reason that it shows the parties' intent to be bound. When both parties exchange something of value, it clearly reveals their intent to create a contract. When one party to a contract neither incurs benefit nor detriment, it will be difficult to show that that party was serious about creating a contract. Courts in this country have been consistent in requiring consideration as a way of weeding out gratuitous promises from actual contracts. A one-sided promise does not put the other party in any different footing than he or she had prior to the promise. Gratuitous promises are not enforceable under the law because the party that receives this promise has not undertaken any legal obligation nor received any benefit.

By refusing to enforce gratuitous promises, the courts have forestalled numerous lawsuits. Generally, before a party can file suit to enforce a contract, both parties must have indicated their willingness to enter into a binding contract, and consideration is an indicator of that willingness.

TYPES OF CONSIDERATION

Consideration can consist of any of the following:

- A right
- A profit
- An interest
- A physical object
- A responsibility undertaken
- A legal detriment[9]

Generally, to qualify as consideration, the item exchanged must have some value. Although courts do not require that the item have much value, or even that the value of the consideration is commensurate with the value of the contract, something must be exchanged. This exchange can involve any of the situations presented in Exhibit 4-2.

Consideration can be based on the following scenarios:

Party A	Party B
Surrenders something of value	Obtains something of value
Does some action not legally required to do	Refrains from some action legally capable of doing
Takes on a responsibility	Transfers a responsibility

EXHIBIT 4-2: Consideration.

HYPOTHETICAL 4-2   From the Horse's Mouth

Ben is shopping for a house and finds the perfect one. It has all of the features that he wants. The home is listed "For Sale by Owner," so Ben approaches the owner and says that he wishes to purchase the home. Ben explains that he doesn't have much money just then, because he has been waiting for his first house to sell, but when it does, he will purchase the man's home. The owner wishes to create a contract stating this fact. Ben agrees. They draw up a contract and the man asks for some consideration for the contract. Ben again states that he doesn't have very much money, so the owner asks him to give him something of value to support the contract. The only thing that Ben has on hand is the bronze statuette of a horse's head. He offers it to the owner. The owner accepts it. Is this consideration?

Remember that consideration consists of anything of value. If the bronze statuette has value then it can be consideration for a contract. Although the common practice in situations like this is to offer cash, there is nothing prohibiting the parties from accepting some other form of consideration.

So far, we have limited the discussion of consideration to objects, but consideration can also be satisfied through actions. When a person assumes a legal **detriment**, this can also satisfy the requirement of a consideration.

When people incur legal detriment, it means that they are surrendering a right that they would ordinarily not be required to surrender. Incurring legal detriment can satisfy the requirement of consideration. Consider the scenario in Hypothetical 4-3.

detriment: The bargained for exchange in a contract, where the parties take on some responsibility that they are not legally obligated to undertake.

HYPOTHETICAL 4-3   Bad Habits

Aunt Mary is very rich and has been concerned about her nephew, Scott, for years. He drinks alcohol, gambles, and uses language that she thinks is inappropriate. One day, she calls Scott to her home and presents the following offer:

"Scott, if you give up your bad habits and start living like a true gentleman, I will leave you $100,000 in my will."

Scott immediately gives up drinking, gambling, and swearing. He gets a job and lives according to his Aunt Mary's dictates. Five years later, Aunt Mary dies and, when her executor reads her will, there is no provision for Scott. He is furious and sues her estate claiming that he had a valid contract with Aunt Mary and asking for an award of $100,000 from her will. The other beneficiaries to her will counter that there is no consideration to support the contract, and therefore it is unenforceable at law.

How does the judge rule?

Consideration not only takes the form of transfer of physical objects or cash, it also can take the form of legal detriment. When a person incurs legal detriment, it means that he did something he was not obligated to do, or refrained from doing something that he was legally able to do. In this case, Scott was legally able to drink and swear and live his life in what many would consider a disreputable, but not illegal, way. He refrained from doing those activities and so incurred legal detriment. By doing so, consideration was created for the oral contract he had with his aunt.

Suppose in Hypothetical 4-3 Aunt Mary asked Scott to refrain from doing something that he was not legally entitled to do in the first place. For instance, suppose that Scott is a convicted felon and is legally barred from holding public office. Aunt Mary approaches Scott and promises him $100,000 if he refrains from running for governor. Because Scott had no legal right to hold office, his acceptance of her offer did not change his legal status. He incurred no legal detriment; he suffered no loss. Therefore, there is no consideration.

A similar situation arises in the context of law enforcement. It is quite common for wanted felons to have reward amounts posted for their capture. Rewards often read, "$10,000 for information leading to the arrest and conviction of Mr. X." When Officer Smith arrests Mr. X, and Mr. X is later convicted, can Officer Smith claim the reward?

As we have seen in previous chapters, a reward is actually an offer. A person accepts the offer not by making a return promise but by taking action. In this case, Officer Smith has not only provided information, he has actually arrested Mr. X and, through Officer Smith's direct intervention, Mr. X has been convicted. This certainly seems to meet the conditions of the reward's offer. But there is one problem: consideration.

Officer Smith has a duty to arrest wanted felons like Mr. X. It is his job. When he arrests Mr. X, he has incurred no legal detriment; his legal status has not changed and therefore there is no consideration and thus no binding contract.

Because consideration can take the form of cash, objects or actions, courts are generally very liberal in finding consideration in a particular case. As a general rule, courts do not inquire into the actual value of consideration in a transaction, so long as some form of consideration exists. For instance, the courts will not invalidate a contract when the consideration given is of low value.[10] However, when the transfer of consideration is based on fraud, duress, or undue influence, courts can, and often do, intercede and invalidate the contract.[11] We discuss fraud and related issues in greater detail in a future chapter.

Proving Consideration

When the consideration for a contract is under dispute, the parties involved must devote time and energy in proving (or disproving) the existence of consideration. This raises the question: how does one prove consideration? Proof may come in the form of testimony and evidence, but it can also be established by certain presumptions.

When consideration is at issue, the party attempting to enforce the contract must present some evidence that there was valid consideration. This can come in the form of live testimony from the parties and witnesses to the contract about the negotiations and the rights/interests/property transferred to support the contract. Many times, the contract itself will recite the actual consideration (see Exhibit 4-3).

In many jurisdictions, there are legal presumptions that also may help to establish the existence of consideration. Written contracts, for example, are often presumed to have consideration, although the other party can rebut this presumption.[13] If the contract appears to lack consideration, then the party seeking to enforce it has the obligation of presenting proof that it

> . . . in consideration of one dollar ($1) paid . . .
>
> . . . in consideration of his continuing efforts on behalf of this company . . .
>
> . . . by acknowledgment of his tender of one thousand dollars ($1000), consideration paid . . .

EXHIBIT 4-3: Examples of consideration from actual contracts.

existed. If the party fails to do so, the court is authorized to rule that no consideration existed and that the contract is void.[14]

As a general rule, there is no requirement that consideration for a contract be recited or expressed in the writing. When it is not expressed, it can be implied or inferred from the contract terms.[15] The words "value received" usually create a presumption of valid consideration.[16]

Quid Pro Quo

The phrase **quid pro quo** is a Latin term that is usually translated as "something for something." It is used in common parlance to refer to any trade where something of value is traded for something else of value. In a typical retail purchase, for example, a buyer selects a shirt, goes to the cashier and presents cash, check, or credit card to pay for the purchase. The store is surrendering its goods to the purchaser in exchange for the money. The store's quid pro quo is the cash for the shirt; the customer's quid pro quo is the shirt for the cash.

quid pro quo: (Latin) "Something for something."[17]

Although quid pro quo sounds as though it is synonymous with consideration, there are some important differences. Quid pro quo is a general term; consideration is a specific, legal term. Quid pro quo can involve the exchange of legally valueless items, where consideration cannot.

The problem with a term such as quid pro quo is that many courts have used it as though it actually means "consideration." This has caused some confusion in legal circles and has not helped legal students clarify the issue. For our purposes, we will refrain from the use of the term quid pro quo for the very reason that it is too general. It does not adequately express the qualities and the requisites of consideration.

Inadequate or Insufficient Consideration

The interesting feature of consideration is that once a court determines that it exists, the court will generally stop any further inquiry at that point. Although consideration is a technical requirement of a contract, courts almost always refrain from determining the value of the consideration.

This paradoxical outlook is a direct result of the pragmatic nature of the court's role in determining contract disputes.

Generally, parties are free to negotiate any contract terms that they choose, as long as the contract does not involve fraud, duress, or undue influence over one party, or a contract that is void for public policy reasons. This means that parties are legally entitled to negotiate any terms agreeable to the parties, even if an outsider would consider the contract to be a "bad bargain" for one of them. This rule has been in existence of centuries: "It is commonplace, of course, that adult persons, suffering from no disabilities, have complete freedom of contract and that the courts will not inquire into the adequacy of the consideration. 'If a person chooses to make an extravagant [sic] promise for an inadequate consideration, it is his own affair.... It was long ago said that 'when a thing is to be done by the plaintiff, be it never so small, this is a sufficient consideration to ground an action.'"[18]

When evaluating a contract, a court is sometimes presented with two opposing requirements: on the one hand, a court must determine that a contract has consideration, but, on the other hand, the parties are free to negotiate whatever terms they wish (including what they determine to be adequate consideration).

The Restatement of Contracts offers very little to assist a researcher in clearing up the issue of adequate consideration. The Restatement offers the following: "Ordinarily courts do not inquire as to the adequacy of consideration, and this is particularly so when one or both of the values exchanged are uncertain or difficult to measure."

Because of this peculiarity in contract law, a court can rule that inadequate consideration is not considered insufficient consideration and therefore will not automatically void a contract.[20] However, the rule changes slightly when the consideration is considered to be "grossly" inadequate. In that situation, the Restatement of Contracts suggests that grossly inadequate consideration could be relevant to issues such as the party's mental state or the existence of fraud.

The reason for the courts' reluctance to inquire into the value of the consideration in a particular case is simple: they do not wish to put themselves in the position of acting as the final arbiters of value. After all, the parties are in the best position to negotiate the terms and to set the value on the contract; requiring a court to approve the consideration in each case would effectively grind business dealings to a halt. One court put it this way, "Where a party contracts for the performance of an act which will afford him pleasure, gratify his ambition, please his fancy, or express his appreciation of a service another has done him, his estimate of value should be left undisturbed, unless there is evidence of fraud."[22]

The practical result of this reluctance to assess the adequacy of consideration is that in most situations a contract will not be found to be unenforceable simply

Sidebar:
"It is competent for the parties to make whatever contracts they may please, so long as there is no fraud or deception or infringement of law. Hence the fact that the bargain is a hard one will not deprive it of validity."[19]

Sidebar:
Barring some determination of fraud, generally, the courts will not routinely inquire into the sufficiency of consideration.[21]

because the consideration for it seems paltry when compared to the obligations imposed on the parties through the contract. Generally, as long as the consideration has some value, that is enough to satisfy the courts[23] (see Exhibit 4-4).

If the requirement of consideration is met, there is no additional requirement of

(a) a gain, advantage, or benefit to the promisor or a loss, disadvantage, or detriment to the promisee; or

(b) equivalence in the values exchanged; or

(c) "mutually of obligation."

EXHIBIT 4-4: Adequacy of consideration.

Source: Restatement of Contracts, 2d §79.

Grossly Inadequate Consideration

Although courts will generally not inquire into the sufficiency of the consideration in a particular contract, there are exceptions to this rule. We have already seen that fraud, duress, or undue influence can invalidate consideration in a contract. Another exception is for grossly inadequate consideration seen in unconscionable contracts.

An unconscionable contract is one in which the terms or bargain is so obviously one-sided that the contract should be voided for public policy reasons. Examples of unconscionable contracts include installment loans in which the monthly payments quickly add up to far more than the original loan amount. Other examples include loans with exorbitant interest rates, or "take it or leave it" negotiations, in which one party has no power to alter terms.

In order to determine if consideration for a contract is unconscionable, or fails for other reasons, the courts will look for either of the following factors:

1. That fraud was exercised in inducing the execution of the contract, or
2. That the consideration was "so grossly inadequate as to shock the conscience, thus being tantamount to fraud."[27]

When consideration is at issue in a suit, the judge decides the issue, not the jury. Courts have consistently ruled that consideration is a question of law and thus falls within the province of the judge's powers.[28] For an example of grossly inadequate consideration leading to an unconscionable contract, see "The Case of the Disinherited Dutiful Son."

The Case of the Disinherited Dutiful Son[29]

McAMIS, Presiding Judge.

This is a suit to rescind and cancel for fraud, duress and lack of consideration a deed executed by Morgan Jones on June 16, 1955, conveying the remainder interest in his farm to eight children of his sister. Complainant is the only child of the grantor. Defendants are the grantees in the deed. The Chancellor after a hearing on oral testimony sustained the bill and defendants have appealed.

At the time of the execution of the deed the grantor was 85 years of age. After the death of his wife in 1954, and until his death in 1964 he lived alone on the farm but took his meals with complainant who lived with his wife and son on an adjoining farm. The undisputed proof shows that a normal, affectionate relationship always existed between the grantor and complainant and his family and that complainant was a dutiful son. In addition to providing his meals, complainant took his father in his car to town and wherever he wished to go.

The deed recites a consideration of one dollar and love and affection. It was withheld from registration and secreted by defendants for a period of nine years and placed of record three days after the grantor's death. Complainant and Mr. Hale, a neighbor and confidante of the grantor, were not aware of the execution of the deed until after the grantor's death. The bill was promptly filed following its registration.

Defendants state in their answer that the deed was withheld from registration at the request of the grantor but there is no proof to sustain this insistence. The proof shows that on June 16, 1955, the date of the deed, and for as much as 30 years theretofore all of the grantees lived in Michigan except the defendant Bessie Seal Irwin who died, without having testified, while this suit was pending. Mrs. Irwin lived in Claiborne County, Tennessee, and visited her uncle, the grantor, about once a month. The other grantees visited him about once each year.

The proof shows that Mrs. Irwin's husband drove the grantor to Knoxville where the deed was executed on a printed form filled in on a typewriter and acknowledged before Mary H. Montgomery, a Notary Public. The bill alleges that on the same date defendants procured the execution of a will devising to them the same property covered by the purported deed.

Defendants' answer admits the execution of the will. They failed to produce it in evidence or to call the Notary Public who acknowledged the deed or the witnesses to the will to testify in their behalf. The record is completely devoid of any explanation of this most unusual and innately irrational and unreasonable act. Why would a father with a dutiful son who was showing every consideration for his welfare and physical needs practically denude himself of his property and convey it without any consideration to his nephews and nieces for none of whom he entertained any peculiar affection so far as the record shows?

Other questions remain unanswered, such as the reason for taking the grantor from Morristown to Knoxville to have the deed and will executed and then withholding the deed from record for nine years. In the absence of an explanation there can arise only the inference that such secrecy was to further defendants' scheme to defraud the grantor of his property. Secrecy, unexplained, has frequently been considered the hallmark of fraud. The absence of consideration also raises a presumption of fraud or, as sometimes said, is a badge of fraud, and calls for proof to show that the conveyance was understandingly made.

'On a bill for recission [sic] because the consideration was grossly inadequate, the Court will inquire 1st, would a sane man, uninfluenced by some cause not explained, make such a contract; 2d, would the defendant if a fair man take such a contract; and 3d, if he would, ought a Court of Equity to permit him to do it.'

We think the circumstances, including the advanced age of the grantor, placed the burden upon defendants to prove the bona fides of the transaction or, at least, remove the suspicion.

It is said for defendants that since both Mr. and Mrs. Irwin died before the trial it was impossible for them to carry this burden. We cannot agree. The contemporaneously executed will withheld by defendants may have shed some light on the condition of the grantor and his intention in executing the deed. And, there must have been witnesses to the will whose names are known to defendants who, along with the Notary Public who took the acknowledgement to the deed, could have given valuable testimony about this transaction. In the absence of some explanation for not introducing these persons, we must assume their testimony would have been unfavorable to defendants. If Mr. Jones intended the deed to be a valid conveyance why did he think it necessary to make a will devising the same property? The will never offered in evidence may have explained this anomaly. Since it was withheld we must infer that the explanation would not have favored defendants.

For the reasons indicated we think the Chancellor reached the right result and it is unnecessary to consider each of the assignments separately in this opinion. The decree is in all respects affirmed at defendants' cost.

Case Questions:

1. Is it significant that the deed in this case was hidden away for nine years before it was recorded?

2. Does the court consider it to be significant that the deceased deeded his property to his nieces and nephews instead of his son?

3. Why does the court consider it to be important that the deceased was taken out of town to execute the deed in this case?

4. Why is the court so concerned about the secrecy inherent in the actions of the nieces and nephews in this case?

5. Why does the court place the burden of establishing the legitimacy of the transaction on the defendants?

Contracts "Under Seal"

In modern times, seals are rarely seen on any documents. However, in the past, a sealed document carried special significance under the law. For instance, under the common law, a contract under seal was presumed to have consideration and therefore no additional evidence or testimony about the consideration was required. Executing a contract under seal has become uncommon in many jurisdictions and its legal significance has diminished considerably in most parts of the United States.

Today, when a contract is executed under seal it is treated in exactly the same way as any other contract. The Uniform Commercial Code (discussed at length in later chapters) also does not apply the common law rules about seals to contracts.[30]

Sidebar:
These days, contracts under seal are considered mere formalities, lacking the legal significance they once carried.

Legal Doctrines that Affect Consideration

Now that we have addressed the topic of what consideration is and why it is required, we will address some court-created doctrines that affect the analysis of consideration in specific cases. One such doctrine that has tremendous importance in any discussion of consideration is promissory estoppel.

PROMISSORY ESTOPPEL

Before we discuss the doctrine of promissory estoppel, we will first address the issue of exactly what "estoppel" is and then build from that foundation to an understanding of promissory estoppel.

What Is Estoppel?

The term **estoppel** is an ancient legal premise and is firmly rooted in common sense. The basic idea behind estoppel is that when person A makes a statement that person B relies upon, A is prevented from denying the truth of his statement. Consider this example:

estoppel: When a person is barred by prior actions from claiming a right or a duty against another person who relied, in good faith, on those actions.

Theodora sees that Natasha has a vacant lot for sale and decides to buy. Because Theodora has very little cash, and is not able to obtain conventional financing from a bank, Natasha arranges for Theodora to make regular, monthly payments to her. However, Natasha refuses to give Theodora possession of the land until the final payment is made. Theodora makes regular payments to Natasha until the loan balance is paid off. When Theodora asks for a deed to the land, Natasha refuses, claiming that she never meant to sell the lot to Theodora in the first place, and that their original agreement was void. She also refuses to return Theodora's money, claiming that Theodora's regular monthly payments were simply a "gift."

Obviously, Natasha's actions are unfair. When Theodora brings suit against Natasha to enforce their contract, a ruling that would allow Natasha to keep both the land and the money would be unfair. That result would be an injustice to Theodora who has acted in good faith throughout. In such a situation, the court will most likely rule that Natasha is estopped from claiming that there was no contract because she has acted throughout the transaction as though the contract was valid and she has accepted payments from Theodora for the land.

Promissory Estoppel and Consideration

The doctrine of promissory estoppel developed from the general doctrine of estoppel. Under the theory of promissory estoppel, when Party B suffers some legal detriment as a result of the contract, Party A cannot claim that there was no consideration for the contract.

In essence, promissory estoppel acts as a substitute for consideration. Consider the next hypothetical.

HYPOTHETICAL 4-4   The Promising Partner's Promissory Estoppel

Ted, Frank, and Juan have been business partners for 20 years. Lately, Juan has been talking about how he would like to retire from business and spend more time with his grandchildren. Ted and Frank have been talking about changing the direction of the business, but each time they made a suggestion, Juan was not receptive. Now that Juan seems to be considering retirement, Ted and

Frank want to encourage him. They approach Juan and tell him that if he will retire from the partnership, they will arrange to increase his retirement package by 15% and pay his health and life insurance premiums for the remainder of his life. This offer is very attractive to Juan, who then decides to retire. However, once Juan has left the partnership, Ted and Frank refuse to pay Juan's health and life insurance premiums. When Juan complains, they state that their offer was gratuitous and therefore not supported by consideration.

Juan brings suit and alleges the doctrine of promissory estoppel. How does the court rule?

Answer: In this case, the court considers the statements of the partners and Juan's reliance on those statements in deciding to retire. The court rules that Juan relied on these statements to his detriment; therefore, the doctrine of promissory estoppel now prevents the partners from claiming that there was no consideration for the contract. The court rules that there is an enforceable contract and that Ted and Frank must pay Juan's insurance premiums for the remainder of John's life.[31]

Promissory estoppel is recognized not only in the Restatement of Contracts but also by nearly every jurisdiction in the United States.[32] Essentially, an action based on a promissory estoppel triggers a court's equity powers. When litigants ask a judge to use equity powers, they are requesting that the court force a party to take some action. In cases involving contract disputes, sometimes the litigants do not want a monetary award from the other party; they want the party to perform according to the contract terms. In the example provided in Hypothetical 4-4, Juan did not want the court to award him a sum of money. Instead, he wanted his former partners to be forced to live up to their promise to pay his insurance premiums. The court is authorized to enter such an order (and to enforce it) through its equity powers.

The Elements of Promissory Estoppel

Before the court will find promissory estoppel, three elements must exist. The court must find that (1) there was a clear and definite promise; (2) the promisor intended to induce reliance, and that reliance occurred; and (3) the only way to avoid injustice is to enforce the contract.[33]

Promissory estoppel requires first and foremost that a clear and definite promise existed. In the hypothetical situations we have discussed so far, whether they involved a promise to leave someone $100,000 in a will or to pay insurance premiums for life, these promises were specific and identifiable. Suppose, for example, that a person makes you the following promise, "If you don't get into any trouble this year, I'll do something nice for you."

Is this a clear and definite promise that could be used as the basis of promissory estoppel? The problem with this offer is that is too vague, both as to the request and how it will be rewarded. How would you go about performing under this contract? Failure to "get into trouble" could be construed in a wide variety of ways. The other problem is the second part of the clause: "I'll do something nice for you." This could mean almost anything from giving you a million dollars to refraining from punching you in the nose. As a result, there is no clear and definite promise and promissory estoppel will not rescue this "contract" from a failure of consideration.

The second element required for promissory estoppel is that the offeror intended to induce reliance in the other party and that this action actually occurred. When a person incurs no legal detriment as a result of a purported contract, there is no reliance and promissory estoppel will not supply consideration. A similar situation occurs when someone makes an offer in jest. The person does not actually intend for the person to take action on the basis of the jest and the second element of promissory estoppel will not be met.

The third element of promissory estoppel, that enforcing the contract is the only way to avoid injustice, is the least specific of the three elements. This third element gives a judge or jury wide latitude in deciding whether a specific contract should be enforced. Some argue that this third element is deliberately vague; it gives the judge or jury the ability to rectify unfair situations.

WAIVER

waiver: A voluntary and intentional abandonment or relinquishment of a known right, claim, or privilege.[36]

A concept that is frequently brought up in conjunction with promissory estoppel, waiver is actually an entirely different concept.[34] When a person gives a **waiver**, he or she surrenders a right, requirement, or obligation. For example, in many situations, a person can waive a technical requirement for a contract, including the presence of consideration.[35] Waiving a right is different from promissory estoppel in several important ways. First of all, when a person waives a right, she acknowledges that it exists and demonstrates this knowledge through some action, usually a writing, in which she spells out her awareness and her desire to surrender the right. By contrast, promissory estoppel is a court doctrine that prevents a party from denying the existence of a contract because of a person's actions.

> **Sidebar:**
> "Waiver is the voluntary surrender of a right where estoppel is the inhibition to assert it by reason of the mischief that has followed one's own fault."[37]

> **Sidebar:**
> Waiver can be proven through a party's actions, conduct, or the statements the party has made.

Waiver and promissory estoppel are usually discussed in conjunction with one another not because their legal elements are similar, but because their legal effect is virtually identical. In both situations, a contract that apparently lacks consideration is found to be enforceable. However, where promissory estoppel involves an examination of the actions of both parties, that is, their representations to one another, their actions based on those representations, and so on, waiver involves the actions of only one party (see Exhibit 4-5).

Promissory Estoppel	Waiver Promissory Estoppel
Arises even when there was no intention by the party to relinquish or change any existing right	Arises from the party's voluntary and intentional abandonment or relinquishment of a known right
Requires clear and distinct promise from one party to another	Requires no interaction with other party
Often implies injustice by one party to another	No injustice implied; action is voluntary by party

EXHIBIT 4-5: Comparing promissory estoppel to waiver promissory estoppel.

ACCORD AND SATISFACTION

Occasionally, parties change the terms of their contracts, or negotiate entirely new contracts based partly on a previously existing contract. In those cases, how is the analysis of consideration affected? Courts generally require consideration for all contracts, whether brand new or based on a prior transaction. Suppose for example, that X Company sends a letter to Mr. Jones stating that Mr. Jones owes them the sum of $2,000 for a service recently provided to him. Mr. Jones disputes this amount and tenders a check for $200 instead of $2,000. On the check, he writes the phrase, "accord and satisfaction." By writing this term on the check, Mr. Jones has stated that this is the total amount he will pay. If X Company cashes the check, it has agreed to that amount. Mr. Jones's check does not become the basis for a new contract, for instance, a monthly payment of $200 until the balance of $2,000 is paid off. Because there is no new consideration, there is no new contract, and if X Company tries to enforce the terms of this purported contract of $200 monthly payments by Mr. Jones, the suit will fail. Under the law of contracts, a new promise must be supported by new consideration.[38]

CONTRACTS FOR AN ILLEGAL PURPOSE

Just as we have seen in other contexts, a contract that contemplates an illegal purpose, such as a criminal act, will not become enforceable simply because it is supported by consideration.

In a similar vein, courts have consistently ruled that sexual favors cannot be the basis of consideration for a contract. Such a contract, and its underlying consideration, would be a violation of public policy, even if not an outright violation of a criminal statute. When a person is a party to a contract with an illegal purpose, and consideration has been paid, the person is free to repudiate the contract at any time and reclaim the money as long as the contract has not been executed.[39]

The Case of Consideration[40]

UHLENHOPP, Justice.

This appeal involves the enforceability of an employment agreement between a teacher and Parsons College. Ben L. Collins holds bachelor and Master of Arts degrees and a doctor of philosophy degree. He studied at Harvard University in addition and taught for a number of years. In the spring of 1966 he was a full professor with tenure at Wisconsin State University at Whitewater.

In March of 1966, Collins was invited to confer with Dr. W. B. Munson, vice president for academic affairs of Parsons College. Collins testified that the following transpired at that conference:

"Dr. Munson asked me to his office and told me he was prepared to offer me a contract for $25,000.00, that he would give me the rank of full professor and that I would be on full tenure." Further regarding the conference, Collins testified concerning salary increments: "Yes, he told me there would be annual increments of $1,000.00 per year until I reached $30,000.00 in 1971." The college introduced no evidence contradicting Collins' testimony about the conference. Munson tendered Collins a written contract for the first year incorporating the terms stated at the conference. Collins was to teach two trimesters in the academic year beginning October 1, 1966, at a salary of $25,000, with the academic rank of 'Professor of English and Humanities with tenure.' The contract covered the 1966–1967 school year and incorporated Parsons' faculty bylaws by reference. The last two paragraphs of the contract stated:

    4. You are hereby placed on tenure.

    5. You will receive annual increments of $1,000.00 to the level of $30,000.00 by 1971.

The faculty bylaws provided in part:

The service of a Faculty member on permanent tenure shall be terminated before retirement or his rank reduced only for just cause. Charges which may lead to the dismissal or reduction in rank of Faculty members with permanent tenure shall be made in writing through the Professional Problems Committee whose recommendation will be presented to a meeting of the tenured Faculty. (The parties do not make a point of the use of the expressions 'permanent tenure' in the bylaws and 'tenure' in the agreement, and we do not believe Munson was trying to trick Collins by using the words 'full tenure' rather than 'permanent tenure.' Other parts of the bylaws and the correspondence show 'tenure' and 'permanent tenure' used interchangeably.)

After considering the offer of the college, Collins accepted it and gave up his teaching position in Wisconsin. He signed the contract covering the first year and Munson signed it on behalf of the college. Collins taught during the 1966–1967 academic year pursuant to the contract. That year he was also appointed head of the English department.

In February 1967, Parsons tendered Collins a contract covering the 1967–1968 academic year, and he signed it. That contract also followed the original agreement. His rank was 'Professor of English and Humanities with tenure,' his salary was $26,000, and the contract again stated, 'You will receive annual increments of $1,000.00 to the level of $30,000.00 by 1971.'

In February 1968, however, Collins was tendered a different contract, to cover the following year. He was still to have the rank of 'Professor of English with tenure,' but at a salary of $15,000 with no provision for increment. The tendered contract also stated:

By accepting this contract, the Faculty member agrees that it shall constitute the only contract of employment with the College for the period set forth above and that he waives any rights or claims arising from any other contract of employment with the College, save and except any rights he may have to any unpaid salary or fringe benefits for service performed by him under any previous contract with the College.

The proposed salary of $15,000 was comparable to that then offered other professors. Collins did not sign this contract and in due course the college notified him that he would not be employed the following year. He desired to teach at the college under the original agreement, but in view of the action of the college he sought employment elsewhere. He secured a position at the University of North Dakota and taught there at a salary of $15,000 for the academic year commencing in the fall of 1968, $15,800 commencing in 1969, $16,400 commencing in 1970, and $16,700 commencing in 1971.

No one suggests that Collins did not perform his work properly at Parsons College or that the college had grounds to discharge him or to depart from the original agreement. No written charge was made against him before the tenured faculty, or before anyone else for that matter. In Collins' present action against the college, he asks as damages the difference between the amount he was promised by the college to 1971 and the amount he was able to earn elsewhere. The trial court tried the case by ordinary proceedings without a jury and held for the college. The controlling facts on liability are really uncontroverted. The dispute is over the legal conclusions to be drawn from the facts.

The parties argue a number of points, but we regard two principal issues to be decisive. First, what were the terms of the agreement? Second, was the agreement supported by consideration? The damage issue must also be considered.

I. Terms of Agreement. No one can gainsay that an agreement was made and that it was carried out by both sides for the first two years by executing and performing written contracts. What were the terms of the agreement?

The terms as to Collins' performance are clear. He was to teach, and he did so for two years. The terms as to performance by the college were clear as to the compensation it was to pay—$25,000 per year with annual increments to $30,000 in 1971. The college paid the promised compensation for two years. The term in controversy is the duration of the promised employment. Collins claims the college promised him a permanent position (at the stipulated salary and increments for the first five years), while the college contends the agreement was terminable by it at will. We think that two provisions of the agreement, taken together, demonstrate that the promise of the college was not terminable at will if Collins performed or was ready and willing to perform, as in fact he was. The first provision is the one calling for annual salary increments to 1971. This not only fixed

the amount of compensation; it also constituted some indication that the parties had in mind the employment would be ongoing, at least to 1971.

The second provision is the one granting Collins tenure. The term 'tenure' was employed at the original conference. In his pretrial deposition, Collins related the words of Munson thus: 'He said he didn't believe in beating around the bush, that he would offer me $25,000 to teach at Parsons. Then he said, 'Are you a full professor where you are?' I said, 'Yes.' He said, 'You are a full professor here.' He asked, 'Do you have tenure where you are?' I said, 'Yes.' He said, 'You have tenure here. Shall I draw up the contract?'' The term 'tenure' was also employed in the two written contracts carrying out the original agreement—'You are hereby placed on tenure' and 'Professor of English and Humanities with tenure.' The word tenure has come to have quite a definite meaning, especially in contracts of teachers in institutions of higher learning. But we need not base interpretation of this agreement on the meaning of tenure generally, for the faculty bylaws of the college specifically provided that the service of a tenured faculty member could be terminated only for just cause, on written charges before the tenured faculty. Collins was thus subject to removal only for cause—which is not involved here. We conclude that Collins had an agreement for a permanent position, and at a stated salary to 1971.

Collins did not waive his right of tenure by executing written contracts carrying out the original agreement in individual years. Moreover, in each of the two written contracts his right of tenure was affirmed.

But the college insists that it could terminate the employment at the end of any academic year because Collins had the right to do so. That he had such right cannot be doubted, and indeed he did consider other teaching positions from time to time. The college contends that the promises of parties must be mutually obligatory to make an agreement enforceable. This contention of the college brings us to the second principal issue, consideration.

II. Consideration. We have considerable doubt that an agreement for tenure such as this one requires mutuality in any event, As to duration of the employment. Tenured teachers in institutions of higher learning have permanent positions as spelled out in the bylaws of their institutions, just as civil servants have permanent positions as spelled out in statutes. Yet such teachers and servants are free to resign if they wish. But a different situation exists. As to compensation to be paid. This case presents both the duration and compensation aspects.

We do not place the decision, however, on the issue of whether mutuality is required in the case of tenured positions such as the present one. The contention of the college that mutuality of obligation is essential is not strictly an accurate statement of the law. Promises must be mutually obligatory if they constitute the only consideration for each other. But if a promise is supported by other consideration, it is enforceable although the promisee has the right to terminate his undertaking or indeed makes no promise at all, as in the case of unilateral contracts. Speaking for the court, Judge Evans stated the principle thus in Standard Oil Co. v. Veland, 207 Iowa 1340, 1343, 224 N.W. 467, 469: If the lack of mutuality amounts to a lack of consideration, then the contract is invalid. But mere lack of mutuality in and of itself does not render a contract invalid. If mutual promises be the mutual consideration of a contract, then each promise must be enforceable in order to render the other enforceable. Though consideration is essential to the validity of a contract, it is not essential that such consideration consist of a mutual promise. A promissory note for a consideration is valid, though no mutuality appear thereon. This is true of all unilateral contracts which are supported by a consideration.

The question before us, then, becomes one of consideration. Collins did not promise to serve permanently or even until 1971, and so we have no promise from him in exchange for the promise of the college to employ him permanently at a specified salary with increments to 1971. Did he provide other consideration?

Collins points to his surrender of his tenured position at Wisconsin State University to accept this position, to the knowledge of Parsons College. The evidence shows that he had good academic credentials as well as experience in teaching, and evidently the college believed he would be a valuable addition and would lend stature to its staff. The college appeared eager to get him and was aware that he was surrendering a secure position to accept its offer. Once Collins left Wisconsin, he lost his tenure there. Did his surrender of that position constitute consideration for the

agreement of Parsons College? Courts are divided on such a question, some holding yes and some no. This court has adverted to the question but does not appear to have decided it squarely. Some courts hold the surrender of employment to take a new job constitutes consideration if the new employer is aware that the employee is giving up the other position. Generally consideration may, of course, consist of a detriment to the promisee. Consideration need not move to the promisor. Restatement, of Contracts §75, Comment E ('It matters not from whom the consideration moves or to whom it goes.').

After considering the question, we think the better rule to be that an employee who gives up other employment to accept an offer of a permanent job provides independent consideration—at least, when as here the employment surrendered was itself permanent and the new employer is aware of the facts.

The result is that the college agreed to employ Collins permanently and at the salary and increments promised to 1971, and that Collins provided consideration for the agreement of the college.

No question can exist about the breach. The college did not go forward with the agreement after the second year but, instead, tendered a contract providing substantially reduced salary and requiring Collins to give up his existing contract rights. When he did not accept, he was not further employed.

III. Damages. The case was fully tried on liability and damages and no necessity exists to retry it. On remand, the district court is to consider the evidence on damages adduced at the original trial, find the amount of damages accordingly, and render judgment for Collins therefor, together with interest and costs.

Reversed and remanded with directions.

Case Questions:

1. What are the professor's contentions in this suit?
2. Did the college claim that the professor was not doing his work?
3. According to the court when and under what terms was the original contract created?
4. Was the college's employment contract one that could be terminated at will? Explain.
5. According to this court, must mutual obligations exist in a contract before consideration is created?

The Case of Crooked Consideration[41]

REECE, Judge.

Plaintiff, Julie Crocker, appeals the Summit County Court of Common Pleas judgment rendered in favor of defendant, Dennis Hood. This court affirms.

On December 13, 1989, Julie Crocker sent a letter through her attorney to Dennis Hood stating she had retained counsel to represent her in a lawsuit seeking damages for alleged sexual abuse committed against her by Hood. The letter indicated that if Hood did not agree to settle the matter by December 29, 1989, Crocker would sue Hood. On December 28, 1989, Hood conveyed his interest in residential/marital property to his wife by quitclaim deed. The land was an eleven-acre parcel located in the city of Tallmadge, Ohio. The deed indicated that Hood's wife, Shirley, paid $10 for the interest. After the conveyance, Hood continued to live on the land until five years later when he and his wife divorced. Crocker's lawsuit went to trial and she obtained a judgment in her favor. The amount awarded her was $150,000 in compensatory and $2,500,000 in punitive damages. This judgment remains unpaid.

On December 16, 1993, Crocker sued Hood. She alleged that Hood had fraudulently conveyed the land to his wife in order to avoid the judgment. She claimed that the conveyance rendered Hood insolvent, that the conveyance lacked adequate consideration, and that Hood transferred the land to Shirley with actual intent to defraud. The trial court heard the case without a jury and found that no evidence existed to show Hood had become insolvent as a result of the transfer. The trial court also found that sufficient evidence supported the conclusion that the conveyance occurred with fair consideration. Last, the trial court found that Crocker did not prove Hood actually intended to defraud her. Crocker now appeals from this judgment.

Crocker contends that the trial court mistakenly found that the conveyance was supported by adequate consideration.

Crocker also claimed that the conveyance was not supported by adequate consideration. She contends that Hood transferred the land for effectively nothing and therefore, his wife did not endure a legal detriment necessary to establish consideration.

R.C. 1336.03 defined "fair consideration" and provided:

"Fair consideration is given for property, or obligation:

"(A) When in exchange for such property, or obligation, as a fair equivalent therefor, and in good faith, property is conveyed or an antecedent debt is satisfied; or

"(B) When such property or obligation is received in good faith to secure a present advance or antecedent debt in amount not disproportionately small as compared with the value of the property or obligation obtained."

Generally, consideration necessary to support a contract may consist of either a detriment to the promisee or a benefit to the promisor. A detriment may consist of some forbearance, loss or responsibility given, suffered or undertaken by the promisee. Furthermore, any detriment, no matter how economically trifling, will support a promise. courts generally will not test the adequacy of consideration, an exception lies in cases of fraud. Because this is a fraud case, this court will examine whether the trial court's judgment as to the presence of adequate consideration was supported by sufficient evidence.

At trial, evidence indicated that Hood withdrew from his Sears, Roebuck pension and profit-sharing plan an amount of approximately $72,000. Shirley Hood testified that she believed that this money was destined to pay legal fees incurred in defending the sexual abuse lawsuit. She also testified that in 1989 she and Hood contemplated divorce and that she renounced her claims to any interest she may have in the pension and profit-sharing plan in exchange for obtaining the land when they divorced. Shirley also testified that she did not intend to divorce Hood until after the lawsuit was over. In addition, Shirley testified that a mortgage was taken on the property, which she signed as owner of the property. This apparently also went to pay for legal fees.

The trial court found that adequate consideration supported the conveyance. This court agrees because sufficient evidence existed to support the trial court's finding. Although the face of the deed indicated that Shirley paid only $10 for the land, her testimony also indicated that she endured other legal detriments, namely securing the mortgage and renouncing any claims to the amounts earned in the pension and profit-sharing plan during the marriage. Therefore, the trial court did not err in its judgment.

Accordingly, the second and third assignments of error are overruled.

In the first assignment of error, Crocker contends the trial court mistakenly found that Hood did not actually intend to fraudulently convey the land in violation of R.C. 1336.07, which stated:

"Every conveyance made and every obligation incurred with actual intent, as distinguished from intent presumed in law, to hinder, delay, or defraud either present or future creditors, is fraudulent as to both present or future creditors." 129 Ohio Laws 1008.

The Supreme Court of Ohio has recognized that it is difficult to prove actual intent to commit fraud under R.C. 1336.07. The court explained that "[d]ue to the difficulty in finding direct proof of fraud, courts of this state began long ago to look to inferences from the circumstances surrounding the transaction and the relationship of the parties involved." Such circumstances not only include the relationship of the parties, but also the lack of adequate consideration, a transfer completed under threat of litigation, insolvency as a result of the transfer, a reservation of

interest in the property by the debtor, and transfer of the debtor's entire estate. These circumstances are known as the badges of fraud. The plaintiff does not have to show evidence of all six badges of fraud. A court, however, must examine the totality of the circumstances to determine whether the plaintiff has established an inference of fraud necessary to shift the burden to the defendant to prove that fraud did not exist.

This court cannot say that the trial court's judgment was supported by insufficient evidence. At best, Crocker met only two badges of fraud. The record did not show any evidence of insolvency or a transfer of the entire estate. Moreover this court has determined that adequate consideration existed. Hood did not retain a legally cognizable interest in the estate. Consequently, Crocker only established that Shirley had a relationship with Hood and that a threat of litigation occurred. Based on the totality of these circumstances, this court cannot say that the trial court, given its superior vantage as the trier of fact, rendered an erroneous judgment.

Judgment accordingly.

Case Questions:

1. Was there consideration for the husband's transfer of property to his wife in this case?

2. What is the definition of consideration in Ohio?

3. What are the "badges of fraud" and what impact do they have on this decision?

4. Explain the rationale for the court's decision.

5. The court explains that it reviewed the case on the overall facts in reaching its decision. Does the court ignore any pertinent facts in reaching its decision?

✔ **PARALEGAL CHECKLIST**

Reviewing a contract for consideration:

☐ Have you read the contract thoroughly? (There is usually no requirement for a separate clause detailing consideration, so look for it)

☐ Is the contract required to be in writing by the Statute of Frauds? (Such contracts must also be supported by consideration)

☐ Are there any issues, such as consideration, which are listed to be decided "at a future time?" (Consideration must be present when the contract is created)

☐ Is the contract executed? (Consideration is usually not a question for executed contracts)

☐ Is the basis of consideration mere good will or natural affection? (Probably not valid consideration)

☐ Is the consideration certain and specific?

☐ Is the consideration "grossly inadequated"?

☐ Is there any indication of fraud, duress, or undue influence?

☐ Are there any issues regarding a party's age or mental ability to enter into a contract?

☐ Is the contract one that is required by statute, or legally obligated to be supported by a bond? (Consideration may not be required)

☐ Are there any actions by other party that later ratifies improprieties in the contract?

☐ Does promissory estoppel apply?

☐ Did either of the parties waive the requirement of consideration?

☐ Is the contract a new promise that requires new consideration?

EXHIBIT 1-5: Features that a contract should contain.

Business Case File

Mike Fulenwider, Entrepreneur

Mike Fulenwider

Mike Fulenwider has been in the restaurant business since he was 18 years old. "My father bought into a Kentucky Fried Chicken franchise in 1965. My father, my mother, and I all worked in it. We were completely blown away by the response; we couldn't make the chicken fast enough." His father plied the profits back into the business and before long, they'd opened up another KFC restaurant. Fulenwider went away to college, telling himself that he would never work in the restaurant business again. "The hours are long, you work nights, weekends, holidays. I was a fun loving college student going for an Engineering degree. When I got out, though, there were no jobs. My father had continued on with the business and I went back in with him, back into the food business."

Fulenwider eventually took over all of the stores, handling the books, payroll, and ordering supplies. "Wherever I happened to be, that's where the office was." Eventually, he acquired additional restaurants, including Burger King franchises, Subway Restaurants, Taco Bell, and Longhorn Steakhouse. "I began to realize that the real estate we placed these restaurants on was a real key to doing well. I started purchasing the lots, instead of renting them from others. That way, in fifteen to twenty years, you could pay off the mortgage on the restaurant, roll the equity forward, cut the overhead, basically improve your bottom line from the profits of the business."

Along the way to developing these many business ventures, Fulenwider has had to keep track of complicated real estate transactions, payroll taxes, Social Security employee payments, and a whole host of federal, state, and local legal issues. He formed Fulenwider Enterprises, Inc. to oversee these many businesses. As the company has grown, so has the number of employees. "We have over one thousand people working for us, now." That amount of employees prompted his decision to hire a Human Resources professional to oversee the company's employee policies. Besides employee issues, Fulenwider deals with legal issues nearly every day.

"We have labor law issues, mergers and acquisitions issues, you name it. When you have this kind of operation, there are always lots of details. You have real estate deals, contracts, acquisitions, assets, depreciation, accounting, and all kinds of other issues to deal with. If you serve liquor in your restaurants, for example, then you have Dram Shop liability to consider.

"I've noticed that the contracts we sign are always getting a little thicker. There are always more contingencies and other issues to consider. You have to think about landlord and tenant issues, fire and other insurance policies. We've been lucky. We've never been hit with any substantial litigation. We've had a few frivolous suits filed here and there, but that's about it."

Consideration as a contractual element features in all of his contracts. Without a showing that both parties have incurred some form of legal detriment, there would be no way for Fulenwider to enforce the many different contracts he has with other businesses and individuals.

(continued)

Fulenwider seems to thrive on the many business concerns he keeps under his control. His offices are a quiet hum of efficiency. He has many long-term plans, but there is one issue that he is currently giving a great deal of attention. "Right now, I'm concentrating on finding someone to replace me. I've told all of my top managers, find someone who could replace you. That's the only way that you'll free up additional time and resources to take on other projects."

ETHICS FILE: When Inadequate Consideration Indicates Other Problems

Although the courts make it a practice not to inquire into the sufficiency of consideration, disproportionate consideration can be an indication of other problems that could affect the validity of a contract. For instance, a person who is suffering from some type of mental impairment might also enter into a contract where the consideration is grossly inadequate. Consider the following scenario:

Uncle Joe, who is 88, recently entered into a contract to sell his home to a 22-year-old lady. The consideration for this transaction was only two dollars. Uncle Joe's home and surrounding lands are easily worth several hundred thousand dollars. As a legal professional, you should consider that the inadequate consideration is a symptom of a larger problem: Uncle Joe may no longer have capacity to handle his own affairs.

Chapter Summary:

Consideration is one of the basic elements of a contract. When a contract is supported by consideration, both parties have given up something of value in order to receive something of value. The thing of value may be property, cash, or an action. By requiring consideration in contracts, courts ensure that both parties are fully involved in a contractual relationship. Another way of establishing consideration is by showing that one party incurred legal detriment. Detriment refers to a situation in which a party gave up the right to do something that he or she was legally entitled to do, or took on an obligation he or she was not already obligated to assume. Consideration is sometimes referred to by the Latin term *quid pro quo*. Courts are generally reluctant to inquire into the sufficiency of the consideration for a contract, once consideration has been established. This is because courts do not wish to put themselves in the position of reviewing the terms of contracts negotiated between parties. Instead, the courts will generally find sufficient consideration to support a contract if the parties agree among themselves that the consideration had value.

WEB SITES

Jurist (University of Pittsburgh School of Law)
http://jurist.law.pitt.edu
Provides extensive information on a wide range of contract law topics, as well as other legal issues.

Duhaime's Online Legal Dictionary
http://www.duhaime.org
Provides an online legal dictionary.

Court TV
http://www.courttv.com/
A direct link to Court TV's home page.

Florida Attorney General
http://myfloridalegal.com/ag
Provides information about a wide range of consumer law issues.

REVIEW QUESTIONS

1. What is consideration?
2. Why is consideration a requirement of a valid contract?
3. How does consideration assist in making a contact enforceable?
4. Provide five examples of non-monetary consideration.
5. Explain the concept of legal detriment.
6. Explain two ways that consideration can be proven in an oral contract.
7. What is *quid pro quo* and how does it differ from consideration?
8. Is inadequate consideration the same thing as no consideration?
9. How does fraud affect the analysis of consideration in a contract?
10. Why are courts reluctant to inquire into the sufficiency of consideration in a particular contract?
11. What is an unconscionable contract?
12. How does an unconscionable contract differ from a contract that lacks adequate consideration?
13. Explain the court's reasoning in "The Case of the Disinherited Dutiful Son."
14. What is a contract "under seal?"
15. Explain promissory estoppel.
16. List and describe the elements of promissory estoppel. Why are these elements required? Which of the elements is often the hardest to prove?
17. What is a gratuitous promise?
18. Explain waiver.
19. How is waiver different from promissory estoppel?
20. Describe the legal doctrine of accord and satisfaction.

HANDS-ON ASSIGNMENT

Review your course syllabus and draft a contract based on its contents. You, as the student, are one party and your instructor is the other party. What are the terms of this contract? What will you, as the student, receive from the instructor? What will the instructor receive? What is the consideration for this contract?

PRACTICAL APPLICATION

Review your lease, car financing agreement, or any other contract you may have signed recently. What, exactly, is the consideration that supports this contract?

HELP THIS BUSINESS

How would you structure the college's agreement with the professor in "The Case of Consideration" so that the college would be protected?

KEY TERMS

consideration   estoppel

detriment   waiver

quid pro quo

ENDNOTES

[1] *Becker v. Colonial Life Ins. Co.*, 153 N.Y. App. Div. 382 (1912)

[2] *Phoenix Life Ins. Co. v. Raddin*, 120 U.S. 183 (1887).

[3] *Earl v. St. Louis University*, 875 S.W.2d 234, 91 Ed. Law Rep. 425 (1994).

[4] *Investment Properties v. Noburn*, 281 N.C. 191 (1972).

[5] *Oran's Dictionary of the Law*, Third Edition, Daniel Oran, West-Thomson Learning.

[6] *First Nat. Bank v. Marietta Mfg. Co.*, 151 W. Va. 636, 153 S.E.2d 172 (1967)

[7] *Green Co. v. Kelley*, 261 N.C. 166 (1964).

[8] *Smith v. Loos*, 78 N.M. 339 (1967)

[9] *Becker v. Colonial Life Ins. Co.*, 153 A. D. 382, 138 N.Y.S. 491 (1912).

[10] *United States v. United Shoe Machinery Co. of New Jersey*, 247 U.S. 32 (1918).

[11] *Smith v. Stevens*, 184 Ok. 4 (1938).

[12] *Smith v. Jack Pot Mining Co.* 109 Mont. 445, 97 P.2d 368 (1939).

[13] *Michaelian v. State Comp. Ins. Fund*, 50 Cal. App. 4th 2093 (1996).

[14] *Van Brunt v. Jackson*, 212 Kan. 621, 512 P.2d 517 (1973).

[15] *Horn v. Hansen*, 56 Minn. 43, 57 N.W. 315 (1893).

[16] *Finegan v. Prudential Ins. Co.*, 300 Mass. 147, 14 N.E.2d 172 (1938).

[17] *Oran's Dictionary of the Law*, Third Edition, Daniel Oran, West-Thomson Learning.

[18] *Mandel v. Liebman*, 100 N.E.2d 149 (1951)

[19] *Youssoupoff v. Widener*, 158 N.E. 64 (1927)

[20] *Mooney v. Green*, 4 Ohio App.3d 175, 446 N.E.2d 1135 (1982)

[21] *Hoffman La-Roche, Inc. v. Campbell*, 512 So.2d 725 (Ala. 1987).

[22] *Brown v. Golightly*, 106 S.C. 519, 91 S.E. 869 (1917)

[23] *Mencher v. Weiss*, 306 N.Y. 1 (1953).

[24] Am. Jur. 2d Contracts §135

[25] 17 Am. Jur. 2d Contracts §121 (2002)

[26] *F.N. Roberts Pest Control Co. v. McDonald*, 208 S.E.2d 13 (1974)

[27] *Cearley v. Cearley*, 331 S.W.2d 510 (1960)

[28] *Abrams v. Awotin*, 388 Ill. 42, 57 N.E.2d 464 (1944)

[29] *Jones v. Seal*, 409 S.W.2d 382 (1966)

[30] Am. Jur. 2d Contracts §116

[31] *Wickstrom v. Vern E. Alden Co.*, 240 N.E.2d 401 (1968)

[32] Restatement of Contracts §90

[33] *Olson v. Synergistic Technologies Business Systems, Inc.*, 628 N.W.2d 142 (2001)

[34] *Blake v. Irwin*, 913 S.W.2d (1996)

[35] *Greensburg Deposit Bank v. GGC-Goff Motors*, 851 S.W.2d 476 (1993).

[36] *Brown v. City of Pittsburgh*, 409 Pa. 357, 186 A.2d 399 (1962).

[37] *Sovereign Camp, Woodmen of the World v. Newsom*, 142 Ark. 132, 219 S.W. 759 (1920)

[38] Am. Jur. Contracts §173

[39] *Lund v. Cooper*, 159 Cal. App. 2d 349, 324 P.2d 62 (1958)

[40] *Collins v. Parsons College*, 203 N.W.2d 594 (1973)

[41] *Crocker v. Hood*, 113 Ohio App.3d 478, 681 N.E.2d 460 (1996)

 For additional resources, visit our Web site at
www.westlegalstudies.com

CHAPTER 5

MUTUAL ASSENT

> *Focus of this chapter:* This chapter focuses on the element of mutual assent that must be present in all contracts. Mutual assent refers to the voluntary and knowing undertaking of a contractual obligation. We will explore how mutual assent is formed, how it is determined from ambiguously worded contracts, and detail how it cannot be the product of force, duress, or fraud.

Chapter Objectives:

At the completion of this chapter, you should be able to:

- Define mutual assent
- Show how mutual assent is different from consent
- Explain how mistake can affect mutual assent
- Explain how the court system interprets contracts when the language concerning mutual assent is confusing or ambiguous
- Define fraud and how it affects the formation of a contract
- Explain the two types of fraud that can affect the formation of mutual assent
- Detail how an allegation of fraud should be alleged in pleadings
- Define duress, coercion, and undue influence
- Explain how mutual assent obtained through duress results in a voidable contract
- Define the concept of ratification

Introduction

One of the primary foundations of contract law is mutual assent. As we have seen in previous chapters, a contract is the result of an offer made by one party and accepted by another. The basic premise underlying the agreement is that both parties entered the agreement voluntarily. Parties should be free to enter into contracts, or to refuse to enter into contracts, as they see fit. Anything that constrains that power or compels agreement destroys this element of mutual assent. In this chapter, we will explore not only what mutual assent is but also how it can be overcome to create invalid and unenforceable contracts.

What Is Mutual Assent?

mutual assent: An offer and acceptance or other definite intention of both parties to make a valid contract.

Mutual assent is the term that we use to encompass not only the offer and the acceptance but also the understanding of the parties about what the contact contemplates. Mutual assent is not only necessary to the process of creating the contract but also to enforcing the terms of the agreement between the parties. When one party lacks mutual assent, there can be no enforceable contract. In this way, the term mutual assent covers several important principles: it refers not only to the process of making and accepting an offer, but also to the understanding and the rights of the parties to the contract. If a party has not entered into a contract by his own will, then he has not voluntarily undertaken the legal obligations of the contract, and therefore it is void.

MUTUAL ASSENT VERSUS CONSENT

consent: Voluntary and active agreement.

We have said that mutual assent is manifested by voluntary actions. Although this may sound similar to the concept of **consent**, mutual assent and consent are not the same thing. When a person consents, he or she is agreeing to a particular detail, such as time, place, or action. Mutual assent, by contrast, refers to the fact that a party voluntarily assumed the obligations, rights, and responsibilities under a contract and all that that entails.

MUTUAL ASSENT AND THE PARTIES' PREFERENCES

Mutual assent can be found in a contract even though the parties to the contract do not like the terms. A person can give grudging mutual assent to a contract and be just as bound by its terms as someone who enthusiastically embraces the terms of the contract.

Sidebar:
Mutual assent is often referred to as "meeting of the minds."

COMMON DESIGN OR PURPOSE

In order to have a valid contract, the parties to the contract must have a common design or purpose. Their understanding as to terms and the general approach to be used in the contract must be similar. In order to find mutual assent, the parties must agree to the same terms, the same obligations, and at the same time.

WHO WILL BE BOUND?

One of the essential elements of mutual assent is that the parties be in general agreement as to who will be bound by the contract. This means that the parties to the contract must be identifiable. Although many jurisdictions do not require that the parties' full legal names be used in a binding contract, the parties must be clearly identifiable or they will not be bound.

WHEN MUTUAL ASSENT IS ABSENT FROM A CONTRACT

When mutual assent is not present at the time that the contract is negotiated, this deficiency cannot be remedied by later negotiations. For instance, when a contract fails to set out who the parties are that will be bound by the contract and leaves this as a detail to be determined later, the contract is considered to be void.

This is not to say that every aspect of a contract must be established in order to have a binding contract. The foundations of a contract, such as offer, acceptance, consideration and mutual assent must be present, but other terms may be absent. In fact, a contract can be valid and contain blanks designed to be filled in at a later time. There is no requirement that a contract pin down every detail. However, mutual assent is not a petty detail. It is the bedrock of the contractual obligation of the parties and must, therefore, be established with certainty.

The language of the contract is essential to any determination of the rights and duties of the parties involved and to help answer the question, "Is there mutual assent?" To that end, the courts are usually the final interpreter of contract language. In the next section, we discuss how the courts go about interpreting the language of contracts.

Construing the Language of a Contract

Courts take a very liberal approach to interpreting contracts between parties. As a general rule, courts will attempt to enforce a contract and find a contract valid when the parties obviously intended to create one. However, when one party claims that he or she never intended to be bound by a contract, this raises the question of how to interpret the language of the contract when it was originally negotiated.

INTERPRETING MUTUAL ASSENT FROM A CONTRACT

Just because the parties later came into a disagreement about terms, sufficiency, or performance of the contract, this does not mean that there was no mutual assent at the time the contract was created. The courts will review the factual situation presented in each case and make a determination about mutual assent based on what the parties said and did and what the language of the contract itself stated.

The court is presented with an either/or situation when it comes to determining mutual assent. Either mutual assent was present, or it was not. If the court makes a determination that mutual assent existed, then the contract is enforceable and the court may next address the issue of assessing damages for breach of contract. If, by contrast, the court

Contract cases	4,850	31.0%
Fraud	668	4.3
Seller plaintiff	1,637	10.5
Buyer plaintiff	832	5.3
Mortgage foreclosure	65	0.4
Employment discrimination	311	2.0
Other employment dispute	309	2.0
Rental/lease	500	3.2
Tortious interference	236	1.5
Other contract	291	1.9

EXHIBIT 5-1: Types of contract cases litigated nationwide.

Source: *Civil Cases and Verdicts in Large Counties. Civil Justice Survey of State Courts,* 1996, p. 2. Bureau of Justice Statistics, U.S. Department of Justice.

determines that mutual assent was absent, then the contract is unenforceable and void.

INTERPRETING THE LANGUAGE OF A CONTRACT—GROUND RULES

When a court is called on to construe the language of a contract, there are some ground rules that will guide the court.

Rule #1. Words are given their normal and obvious meaning.

When the court reviews the terms of a contract, the words used by the parties are given their normal and common sense meaning. Consider the following contract:

"Southern Crushers, Inc. agrees to pay the sum of $1000 to Wally Webdesigner on the completion of its store Web page. Webdesigner agrees to create a quality Web site that will allow visitors to the site to post comments and send e-mail to the two owners of Southern Crushers, Inc., listed below. It will have Web graphics provided by Southern Crushers, Inc. The Web page must be to the satisfaction of Southern Crushers, Inc., before payment will be made."

Signed: Wally Webdesigner
Signed: Marvin Crusher
Signed: John Southern
Date: Today, This Month, This Year

If we construe this language in its normal way, the analysis leads to a simple conclusion: when the business owners are satisfied with the Web page designed by Wally, they will pay him $1000.

This appears to be a very straightforward contract. However, as we will see in later chapters, even a simply worded contract can spawn years of litigation. Is mutual assent present in this contract?

If we define mutual assent as a common agreement setting out a contractual obligation between two parties, then this contract qualifies. Notice that this contract is not bogged down in details. The question here is whether both parties voluntarily undertook a contractual obligation. Barring any additional evidence about some form of impropriety, the contract does appear to be voluntarily undertaken by all parties. There is mutual assent.

How does the court proceed when the contract language is ambiguous or difficult to understand? In this situation, the court will attempt to construe the language in its plainest and simplest meaning. Courts have a stated preference for construing a contract, even an ambiguous contract, to give it legal effect. Generally, contracts are not void because of a technical flaw. A misspelling, or an error in syntax, will not make a contract unenforceable. Contract law is based firmly in common sense and practicality.

Applying these basic ground rules means that, when given the choice between voiding the contract and creating a binding agreement between parties, courts invariably opt for the latter. Because the parties to a contract obviously intended to make some type of binding agreement to one another, the fact that their language in doing so is difficult to understand should not stand in the way of the fact that a binding contract was intended. This is especially true when one of the parties to the contract has already performed the contemplated action. In such a case, the courts will, more often than not, enforce the contract against the other party, rather than rule the contract is void for uncertainty.

We will return to our previous example:

Wally Webdesigner has created a standard business Web page. It has the graphics given to him by the owners of Southern Crushers, Inc. It also has a link that allows Web visitors to post comments at the bottom of the page and another link that permits Web visitors to send an e-mail directly to the owners. The Web page is operational and is similar to dozens of others that Wally has designed for area businesses. However, the owners refuse to pay Wally, saying that they are not "satisfied." When Wally asks for an explanation of what they are dissatisfied with, they are not specific. Wally presses for payment, but the owners refuse, saying that they never really intended to enter into a contract. Their intent, they claim, was simply to ask for a quote for Wally's services, not to have him actually complete a Web page.

Wally sues to enforce the contract. How does the judge rule?

The judge must review the wording of the contract and the other circumstances. Southern Crushers is claiming that no contract existed, that, in effect, there was never any mutual assent between the company and Wally. However, the judge can review the language of the contract and can clearly see that there was agreement in general terms about what Wally would do for Southern Crushers and the compensation that Southern Crushers would pay to Wally on satisfactory completion. The judge will doubtless rule that there was mutual assent between the parties at the time that the contract was signed and that Southern Crushers has violated the terms of the contract.

In discussing this scenario, we have seen another principle in use: timing.

The validity of a contract will be viewed based on the terms and expressions used at the moment that the contract was created, not by the subsequent actions of the parties. This leads directly to our second rule of interpretation.

Rule #2. The contract is evaluated at the time of its creation.

The parties' intentions are assessed at the moment that the contract is created, not by their later misgivings. Applying this rule to the scenario involving Wally and Southern Crushers, leads to one result: The fact that Southern Crushers, Inc., has some reservations about the contract after signing it does not invalidate their mutual assent at the time that they signed the contract.

Rule #3. The contract is interpreted to provide fairness to all parties, when possible.

Another ground rule followed by the courts is the requirement to pursue a fair and just remedy for the parties. As such, courts are often placed in the situation of choosing between alternate and conflicting clauses in a contract in order to create a valid and binding contract that is fair and just for both sides. The general rule is that a contract will not be void for uncertainty unless the court finds it impossible to interpret the intentions of the parties to create a binding legal agreement between them.

What if the parties interpret the language used in the contract in two different ways? In such a situation, courts will not rule that a contract is void for uncertainty simply because the subjective understanding of the parties about terms and conditions was different. In this case, mutual assent still exists. After all, the parties did intend to enter into a binding agreement. Their subjective understanding of various terms does not alter that situation. It may have a great deal to do with how the contract is enforced, but it does not affect the creation of the contract itself.

DEGREE OF CERTAINTY REQUIRED IN A CONTRACT

What degree of certainty or definiteness is required in a contract? Courts generally rule that the obligation of the parties must be reasonably certain and capable of being interpreted. Courts use a wide variety of tests in order to determine the degree of certainty in a contract. In some jurisdictions, courts require that the contract establish the parties' intentions. Other jurisdictions opt for a analysis that centers on the enforceability of the contract provisions. In those jurisdictions, courts will ask, "How do we enforce the provisions of this contract?" If there is no way to do so, then the contract may be voided for indefiniteness. By contrast, if, construing the words and phrases of the contract in their natural and common sense meaning, the contract can be enforced, then it is sufficiently definite. Some courts take a third approach: they ask, "What types of damages are available to a person who has breached this contract?" If no damages can be ascertained, the contract is void because it lacks sufficient definiteness.

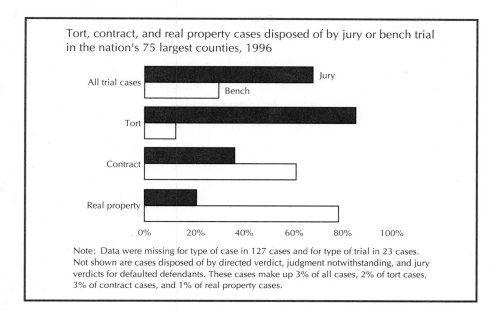

Tort, contract, and real property cases disposed of by jury or bench trial in the nation's 75 largest counties, 1996

Note: Data were missing for type of case in 127 cases and for type of trial in 23 cases. Not shown are cases disposed of by directed verdict, judgment notwithstanding, and jury verdicts for defaulted defendants. These cases make up 3% of all cases, 2% of tort cases, 3% of contract cases, and 1% of real property cases.

EXHIBIT 5-2: Tort, contract, and real property cases nationwide.

Source: *Civil Cases and Verdicts in Large Counties. Civil Justice Survey of State Courts*, 1996, p. 2. Bureau of Justice Statistics, U.S. Department of Justice.

A contract may be ruled sufficiently definite either because the terms expressed in the contract are specific enough to create a legally binding agreement between the parties or because the contract refers to some other document that clears up any ambiguities. Reference to another document is a common practice. Some jurisdictions approach this contract question from yet another viewpoint: they inquire whether the contract fixes a legal liability on both parties. If it does, then a valid contract exists. If it does not, then the contract is void for indefiniteness.

Sidebar:
When the terms of a contract are so ambiguous that the courts cannot ascertain the legal impact on the parties, the contract is void for uncertainty.

✓ PARALEGAL CHECKLIST

☐ Who is bound by the contract?

☐ Where is the contract to be performed?

☐ When are other services to be carried out?

☐ How is compensation to be paid?

If the answers to these questions are impossible to determine from the contract, it may be void for uncertainty.

EXHIBIT 5-3: Pinpointing the specifics of a contract.

Absolute Certainty Is Not Required

Absolute certainty is never a requirement for a contract. In fact, courts have consistently ruled that a reasonable certainty is the only requirement of a contract. This rule about reasonable certainty applies to the basic components of the contract: the offer, the acceptance, the manifestation of mutual assent and consideration. As long as these elements are present and capable of being understood, the basic components of a contract exist. The fact that some of the other details in the contract are not spelled out clearly, or are left to be determined at a later time will not void a contract for uncertainty.

When a court inquires into the specifics of a contract, it focuses on the point in time at which the contract was created. If the terms of the contract and the subsequent legal obligations of the parties are definite enough at the time of the contract is created, the contract is valid. A subsequent misunderstanding between the parties may raise a question about the extent of damages but will not affect the analysis that contract does, in fact, exist. When the object of the contract is uncertain, or the duties to be performed by a contracting party are indefinite, then there is no enforceable contract. One could argue, in such a scenario, that there was no mutual assent in the first place.

HYPOTHETICAL 5-1   The Cabin Contract

Juan contracts with Charles to build and maintain a set of tourist cabins on Charles's land. Their agreement states, in part, that once Juan has built the cabins, he will pay a specific amount of money to Charles every month for the use of these cabins to rent out to tourists. The contract also has a provision in it that states, "Charles agrees not to place any additional cabins on his property that will, in any way, compete with the tourist cabins." Is this contract void for uncertainty?

The first question we must ask ourselves in reviewing this contract is: does this create a legal, binding agreement between the parties? Put another way, is there mutual assent between these two parties? The contract certainly seems to be specific enough for us to determine the legal obligations between Juan and Charles. The question becomes, what about the provision dealing with competing cabins? Remember that the courts have a stated preference for finding that a contract exists when the parties obviously intended to create one. Following this philosophy, we could easily find a binding contract between Juan and Charles. The fact that we might find it difficult to determine what constitutes a "competing cabin" does not invalidate the entire agreement. For instance, if Charles builds a family cabin on some other part of his land, is this a violation of the contract? A judge might be called on to decide if Charles' new cabin is a competing cabin contemplated in the contract. In such a case, the judge would have to take into consideration whether Charles' new cabin competes with the cabins he is renting out to Juan. However, this judicial review does not invalidate the agreement reached between Juan and Charles in the first place. The court may have to interpret the contract language, but this interpretation does not affect the fact that a valid contract exists.

HYPOTHETICAL 5-2   Financing the Cabins

Now that Juan has an agreement with Charles to build cabins, Juan needs financing to construct them. He goes to a local bank, and applies for a $200,000 loan in order to construct the cabins and to build a road to the cabins from the highway. The loan officer is one of Juan's old friends. The loan officer looks over Juan's plans and says, "Sure, we can give you $200,000." Juan does not ask for any details about interest rates, repayment amounts, monthly payments, and so on. Instead, he leaves the bank, hires a general contractor, and begins making plans to build his cabins. Later, the bank turns down Juan's loan application. Juan sues for breach of contract. The bank counters that no contract ever existed, and shows that there were no specifics about the loan repayment terms. Is there a valid contract between Juan and the bank?

No. One of the problems that Juan faces in his claim that he had a valid contract with the bank is that he can provide no details of the extent of the legal obligation between himself and the bank. What are the specifics of the loan? How does Juan ask a court to enforce this agreement against the bank? If the court were to order the bank to specifically perform, what loan terms would the judge enforce against the bank?

Note: In the above scenario we have skipped over one important element: detrimental reliance. We have ignored the fact that Juan incurred legal expenses based on the loan officer's assurance that his loan would be approved. We explored the issue of detrimental reliance in the previous chapter. However, a brief word about it here should be stated. When a party incurs expenses or other detriment based on the assurance of the other party, courts will sometimes find that a contract exists, even though the contract terms are vague and indefinite. We have ignored the concept of detrimental reliance in this scenario.

Mistake

A contract can be voided for **mistake**. However, the term "mistake" has a particular meaning in contract law that is separate and distinct from the way that this term is used in everyday speech. The Restatement of Contracts defines mistake as, "A belief that is not in accordance with the facts."[1] That definition is not very helpful in building a solid understanding of this term as it relates to mutual assent. In the next few paragraphs, we will explore the concept of mistake in greater detail.

mistake: An unintentional error or act.

Mistake Is a Bilateral Act

When we are discussing contractual obligations, a "mistake" refers to an error shared by both sides of the contract. In this way, a mistake is a bilateral action. This is counter to how we use this word in other situations. A person might say, "I made a mistake," and from that statement we could infer that he or she did something wrong. In this scenario, the person's action is unilateral. For a plaintiff to take advantage of the legal defense of mistake, however, the plaintiff must show that both parties had a mistaken belief about the circumstances. Why would contract law impose this bilateral requirement?

The requirement of a bilateral mistake goes to the very heart of the question of contract formation. As we have seen in previous chapters, a contract is created out of the process of accepting a valid offer. Courts have consistently held to the position that judges are not the final arbiters of whether a contract is a good bargain. That is left to the parties. However, when it can be shown that both parties had a mistaken belief about a particular aspect of the contract, that mistake affects the very nature of their agreement. The rights and obligations that each has assumed were created by the agreement were not actually created; that may render the entire agreement void. However, when only one party claims mistake, that does not affect the agreement. Instead, that affects the details of how the contract will be enforced.

There is another, and far more practical, reason for requiring a mutual mistake before a contract will be voided. If this requirement did not exist, then persons who no longer wished to be bound by a contract would claim mistake as a way to get out of the contractual obligation. Courts would be flooded with lawsuits.

MISTAKE CONCERNS MATERIAL FACTS ONLY

material fact: A basic reason for a contract, without which it would not have been entered into.

There are other restrictions on the defense of mistake. One such restriction is that the mistake must concern a **material fact**. A material fact is a fact that is crucial to the parties' understanding of the transaction or a key point of negotiation. Put another way, a material fact is one that would either make or break the contract. Material facts are the pivotal issues in the contract, such as who will perform, what will be performed, and how much will the parties receive for this performance? An example of a nonmaterial fact might include the exact manner of performance, the manner of payment for the performance (cash versus check), etc. Read "The case of the Tenured Teacher" and ask yourself, "Does this case involve a mistake concerning a material fact?"

HYPOTHETICAL 5-3   The Case of the Tenured Teacher

Terry Teacher has been with the local college for over a year now. The college's policy is that all new teachers must serve a one-year probationary period. At the end of that one-year period, the teacher must either be given a contract for a tenured teaching position or be released. A tenured position is important to any teacher because it means that the teacher can only be fired for specific reasons: violation of school policy, commission of a crime, and so on. When a teacher is in a nontenured position, the teacher can be fired for any reason.

At Terry's meeting with the college president, vice president, and division dean, Terry is told that the college wishes to hire her as a full-time, tenured instructor. She is delighted. The college vice president hands Terry a document and asks her to sign it. When she asks about the wording, which includes the language, "voluntarily resigns," she is told that this is simply a formality. The vice president explains that she is resigning from her probationary period so that she can then accept full-time employment. Terry signs the form.

Several years later, Terry becomes an outspoken critic of the college administration. The new college president wants to fire Terry and casts around for some way to get around the tenured provision in her contract. The head of human resources produces the paper that Terry signed and sees that Terry actually signed a document stating that she had voluntarily resigned from any future tenured position. Apparently, Terry, the college president, the vice president, and the dean had all assumed that Terry was signing one document when she was actually signing another.

The new college president is delighted. He fires Terry the next day. Terry brings suit, alleging mistake. What is the result?

Terry's allegation is that there was a mistake. In order to prove mistake, Terry must show that at the time of the signing, there was a mutual mistake. Can Terry prove this? It certainly appears that Terry can. All of the people present at the signing believed, and will later testify, that they thought Terry had to sign the form in order to become a full-time faculty member. Terry will most likely prevail and be reinstated at the college.[2]

Sidebar:
One way to spot the material fact is to review the contract and ask, "Which of these facts, if deleted, would most likely have ended the contract negotiations?"

MISTAKE AND CONDITIONS PRECEDENT

When the parties predicate their contract on a specific fact and this fact is false, the contract can be voided for mistake. In such a situation, the specific fact is a **condition precedent** to the creation of contractual obligation between the parties.

condition precedent: A condition, fact, or occurrence that must occur before a contractual obligation is triggered.

HYPOTHETICAL 5-4   Grandmother's Surprise

Lila's grandmother had told her on numerous occasions that when she dies, she would leave Lila her house and property. Last week, Lila's grandmother died. Lila contacted a local builder and entered into a contract to renovate the entire structure. Today, Lila went to her grandmother's attorney so that she could hear the official terms of her grandmother's will. Lila was shocked to learn that her grandmother had left her entire estate, including her home, to a distant cousin. Lila now wants to void her contract with the builder on the grounds of mistake. Will she succeed?

In order to evaluate this scenario, we must first decide if this contract involves mistake. In this scenario, Lila's inheritance of her grandmother's mansion is a condition precedent. Both Lila and the builder assumed that Lila would receive the mansion through her grandmother's estate. Because she did not, this does qualify as a mutual mistake that can void the contract.

@@@

Sidebar:
When the parties are mistaken about one party's ability to perform, then a contract can be voided.

The fact that a particular event does not occur does not always void a contract. This is a situation where the wording of the contract is critical. If, for instance, the parties insert language in the contract that states that they realize that the occurrence is speculative they may still be contractually bound to one another. If, by contrast, the language is specific that the contract is conditional on the occurrence of a specific event, and that event fails to occur, the contract may be void after all.

WAIVING A CLAIM OF MISTAKE

A party can waive a claim of mistake by any of the following:

1. By failing to raise the claim within a reasonable period of time
2. By affirming the contract after learning of the mistake
3. By a contract provision that clearly states that the party was willing to take on the risk of mistake[3]

Although some of these factors are self-explanatory, the first deserves some additional discussion.

How Long Does a Plaintiff Have to Raise a Claim of Mistake?

A claim of mistake must be raised within a reasonable period of time. Courts have consistently refused to provide a set period of time. Instead, each case must be taken on its own merits. The courts will consider some or all of the following in deciding whether the plaintiff raised his or her claim of mistake within a reasonable period of time:

- At what point did the plaintiff learn of the mistake?
- The extent to which the plaintiff's delay resulted from justifiable reasons, such as reliance on the other contractual party or on a third party.
- Whether the mistake was the fault of either contracting party.
- Whether the delay in bringing the action was brought about by the plaintiff's own conduct.[4]

By Affirming the Contract After Learning of the Mistake

The parties are always free to affirm a contract after learning of the mistake. In such a case, they would simply agree to the new terms, accepting that the original contract terms were flawed.

By a Contract Provision Assuming the Risk

Finally, the parties are free to negotiate terms in the contract that specifically place the burden of the risk of mistakes on one or both parties. The parties essentially assume the risk of mistake as one of the potential pitfalls of doing business.

Fraud

When **fraud** is used to secure a party's mutual assent to a contract it is no mutual assent at all. Mutual assent is formed by the knowing and willing assumption of a contractual obligation. When that undertaking is based on trickery or deceit this acts to overcome a party's voluntary assumption of contractual obligation.

Fraud includes outright lying, as well as deceit, "confidence schemes," "scams," trickery, and any false claims that would induce a party to enter into a contract under a false impression of the facts. Fraud can occur when a person knowingly makes a false statement or when a person conceals or withholds a fact.

There is a general reluctance in the courts to inquire into particular contracts to see if they are wise and prudent business arrangements. However, this reluctance disappears when one party alleges fraud. When a person has been defrauded, his or her free will and consent have been overcome.

fraud: Any kind of trickery used to cheat another of money or property.

> **Sidebar:**
> There is a general rule that fraud voids all contracts. However, in practice, the rule is often modified: fraud makes a contract voidable.

Two Types of Fraud Involved in Contracts

In most jurisdictions, there are two types of fraud: fraud in the execution of a contract and fraud in the inducement of a contract. Defining the type of fraud in a specific case can have a profound impact on the outcome of litigation.

Fraud in the Execution of a Contract

Fraud in the execution of a contract, sometimes referred to as "fraud in the factum," occurs when one party is misled into entering into a contract with another. Examples of fraud in the execution could include substituting one paper for another when a party is signing or by tricking a party into signing a paper without realizing what he or she is signing.[5]

> **Sidebar:**
> "Fraud in the factum or execution renders the agreement void, whereas fraud in the treaty or inducement renders it merely voidable."[7]

Fraud in the Inducement

Fraud in the inducement occurs when a party agrees to enter into a contract, understands the rights and responsibilities of the contractual agreement, but has been induced into the agreement by false information provided prior to agreement.[6]

Fraud Creates a Voidable Contract

When fraud occurs during the creation of a contract, the contract is not automatically void, at least in the vast majority of jurisdictions. Instead, the contract is voidable at the election of the party who has been defrauded.[8]

Waiving the Right to Allege Fraud

Some jurisdictions follow a rule stating that if the party could have discovered the fraud through reasonable means, that is, reading the contract, and failed to do so, then the defense of fraud is no longer available.[9] The defense of fraud also may be waived in other circumstances. When the plaintiff discovers fraud and enters into a new agreement with the original party, the plaintiff has waived any claim of fraud for the original agreement. A plaintiff also may waive the right to claim fraud when he or she remains silent after discovering the fraud. In many cases, this silence is construed as acquiescence. Continuing with the contractual relationship after discovering fraud is also another way to waive any claim of fraud.[10]

Proving Fraud

In most jurisdictions, a party alleging fraud must prove the following:

a)   That the other party made a representation

b)   That this representation was about a material fact to the transaction

c)   That this representation was false

d)   That the party made this false representation with the intent of misleading the plaintiff into relying on the representation

e)   That the plaintiff did, in fact, rely on the representation

f)   That the plaintiff incurred damages from relying on this false representation[11]

Clear and Convincing Evidence Required to Prove Fraud

In a typical lawsuit, the plaintiff's burden of proof is **preponderance of the evidence**. However, most jurisdictions require that a plaintiff prove an allegation of fraud with **clear and convincing evidence**. This higher standard of proof is required because of several factors, including the fact that fraud is often a matter of interpretation.

FRAUD INVOLVES MATERIAL FACTS

Like mistake, an allegation of fraud is limited to dishonesty concerning material facts. However, there are specific types of statements that have routinely been classified as non-material. They include statements made by salespersons and opinions offered by others.

Sales Statements Are Usually Not Considered to Be Material Facts

We have all heard (or been subject to) a salesperson's pitch about a particular product. Statements such as, "this is the greatest product in the world," are routine in sales presentations. Such statements are not classified as material facts. Generally, sales exaggerations, or "puffing," is considered to be harmless as most people do not put much faith in such statements in the first place. However, there are times when a salesperson's statement can rise to the level of a material misrepresentation. Consider the next hypothetical.

preponderance of the evidence: The greater weight of evidence, not as to quantity but as to quality.

clear and convincing evidence: Proof that a particular set of allegations is likely true; it is a higher level of proof than preponderance of the evidence.

HYPOTHETICAL 5-5   "The Little Old Lady's Car"

Javier is desperate to make a sale this week. If he doesn't sell at least one car, his boss may fire him. Rhonda walks in and Javier immediately sees the possibility of a sale. Rhonda wants to look at a 10-year-old used car. She likes the color. When she asks about its history, Javier says, "Oh, it was owned by a little old lady who only drove it to church on Sunday. She was also an ace mechanic who treated this car with special love and attention. She did all the work on it herself. Look at that engine. You could eat off it." When Rhonda asks about whether the car has been in any accidents, Javier smiles and says, "Look at it. It's beautiful. Does it look like it's been in any accidents?"

Rhonda decides to buy the car. Later, she learns that the car has been in two prior accidents and that the three previous owners were all men who drove the car recklessly and never took care of it. Can Rhonda void the automobile sales contract on the grounds of fraud?

Answer: We must consider each of Javier's statements and then decide if any of them rose to the level of fraud. We have already established that in order for the plaintiff to prove fraud, the statement must involve a material fact. Do any of Javier's statements rise to the level of false statements of material facts?

Javier's statement about the previous owner—a "little old lady." This statement, even if misleading, does not seem to qualify as a material fact. Whether the previous owner was a little old lady or not would not appear to be the type of statement, standing alone, that rises to the level of inducing someone to purchase a car. Anyone who has purchased a used car has probably heard this statement and would be inclined to discount it.

Javier's statement that the old lady was an ace mechanic and kept the car in good repair—this statement very well could be a material fact because the condition of the car is a critical factor in the transaction.

Similarly, Javier's statement about the car never having been in a prior accident is also a material statement, for the same reasons as stated in point #2. However, Javier's didn't actually say that the car had never been in an accident. Does this make a difference? No. His statement clearly indicated that the car had never been in an accident, and certainly conveyed that impression, even if he didn't specifically say it.

Conclusion: Rhonda has a solid case for voiding the sales contract.

Opinions Are Usually Not Considered to Be Material Facts

Everyone has an opinion about something. A person's opinion about a particular situation usually does not rise to the level of a material fact. There are several obvious reasons for this rule. The first, and most obvious, is that an individual's opinion can be based on a wide variety of factors, most of which cannot be tested. Paraphrasing an old saying, a free opinion is worth what you pay for it. When a person offers an opinion and the plaintiff acts on that opinion to enter into a contractual obligation, the plaintiff usually has no grounds for a claim of fraud against the person who gave his opinion when the contract turns out to be a bad bargain. Opinions, and their effects on a contract, are explored in "The Case of the Sad Sharecropper."

The Case of the Sad Sharecropper[12]

McQUADE, Justice.

laintiffs commenced this action to recover from defendants' damages for violations of a farm lease. Defendants filed an answer to plaintiffs' complaint, and by cross-complaint sought damages which defendants contend they sustained by reason of plaintiffs' allegedly fraudulent representations in procuring the lease. Plaintiffs, on March 1, 1954, leased in writing to defendants three tracts of land. Defendants went into possession of the property on the day the lease was executed. Plaintiffs complain that defendants failed, neglected, and refused to comply with the terms of the lease for the year 1954 as follows: a. That upon 110 acres of tract no. 1 defendants failed to plant any of the crops agreed; that they failed to plant 35 acres in clover as agreed, but planted 17 acres of corn which was not watered sufficiently to mature the crop; that on 75 acres no crop was grown, and according to the crops to be grown on such area, the share plaintiffs would have received had a value of $3,860.41; b. That tract no. 2, consisting of 100 acres, was not planted and should have yielded a share to plaintiffs in the amount of $2,666.66; c. That upon tract no. 3 defendants failed to irrigate 35 acres of oats which should have yielded plaintiffs a share in the sum of $583 plus one-half the cost of the seed of $96; that defendants failed to plant early enough, and later to irrigate, 25 acres of corn which should have netted plaintiffs $1,250 if the land had been planted in potatoes and cared for properly, all according to the lease; d. That defendants allowed the premises to become overrun with weeds, which cost plaintiffs $240 to eradicate; e. That other damage to the property was in the sum of $164. Defendant C. D. Southwick went into possession about December 1, 1953, and Arthur J. Southwick went into possession on March 15, 1954. The defendants made proof under the cross-complaint that C. D. Southwick's entry onto the premises about December 1, 1953, was

pursuant to an oral agreement, and that the written lease was entered into April 14, 1954, and at that time and prior thereto plaintiffs made the following false statements and representations to the defendants and each of them: 1. That of the 900 acres, there were 400 acres ready for cultivation that were irrigable and tillable, fertile and productive; 2. That the ground tested 100 per cent fertility and germination; 3. That the ground had produced 75 to 100 bushels of grain per acre (tract no. 1, 50 to 60 bushels); 4. That the ground would grow 25 to 30 tons of sugar beets per acre; 5. That the ground would be leveled and prepared for irrigation for the 1954 growing season; 6. That plaintiffs would build a barn, farm shop, and suitable grain storage; 7. That plaintiffs were to build two houses for defendants and repair the roof on the small building then on the property. Defendants also alleged and proved that the land was arid desert land that contained alkali and salts which rendered the land incapable of producing good and marketable crops. Because of these alleged false and fraudulent representations, the defendants obtained a verdict on the cross-complaint and judgment for actual damages in the sum of $5,000. Frank Faria was not an experienced farmer, and had to rely upon others to acquaint him with farming methods, fertility of soil, and other information necessary to agricultural operations.

Before C. D. Southwick moved onto the premises he had been informed by Frank Faria that sulphuric acid was being applied to the land to counteract the alkaline condition of the soil. During the fore part of November, 1953, C. D. Southwick used a sprinkling system to apply the sulphuric acid as well as to water generally those new areas which were to be planted.

Carl Agenbroad, a neighbor who had extensive experience with 3,000 acres in the same area and was personally acquainted with the plaintiffs' land, testified that the farm generally contained new land which had not been cultivated, leveled, ditched, or cleared. To prepare this land for profitable cultivation, the evidence shows that the farm would have to be cleared, leveled, ditched, and farmed. This latter would require about 10 years of planned cultivation and the washing of alkali from the soil. To perform all of the requisite labor and furnish the machinery and supplies would require great sums of money which neither of the parties possessed. It was impossible for defendants under the terms of the lease to fulfill their covenants, and likewise it was impossible for plaintiffs to perform their covenants. As a result of financial strain, defendants went about the neighborhood doing custom work for hire, which plaintiffs complain resulted in inadequate irrigation of the crops planted.

Agenbroad testified that the Farias had a very poor farm, and at most only 80 of the 900 acres were capable of cultivation in 1954. He testified that a maximum of 30 acres in tract no. 1 could be cultivated to alfalfa, clover, or barley, and the balance of this land was alkaline, boggy, or not irrigable. According to the lease, a portion of this tract was to be irrigated with defendants' sprinkler system. The lease also called for the land to be planted to alfalfa, oats, clover, and grain.

Appellants' first assignment of error is:

'The Court erred in entering judgment upon the verdict and in denying plaintiffs' motion for new trial because the evidence fails to show that the claimed representations of the plaintiff Frank Faria were made with the intent to deceive.' Neither of the parties hereto possessed knowledge as to the fertility of the soil and how much of the land could be farmed. In addition to the evidence showing lack of deception on the part of plaintiff Frank Faria, it also shows that defendant Southwick assumed the land to be fertile and productive. In the case of Hammaker v. Schleigh, 157 Md. 652, 147 A. 790, 794, 65 A.L.R. 1285, that court succinctly stated the applicable rule: 'Where parties enter into a contract upon the common assumption that a particular and essential state of things exists with reference to a substantial subject-matter, the nonexistence of that state of things, through default of neither party, ends the liability and prevents the accrual of a duty dependent upon it.' Restatement of Contracts, volume 2, p. 847, states that with certain exceptions not applicable here 'a promise imposes no duty if performance of the promise is impossible because of facts existing when the promise is made of which the promisor neither knows nor has reason to know.' See also 12 Am. Jur., Contracts, sec. 131, p. 622.

In addition to the assumption that the land was fertile, the parties proceeded to draw up a lease for the planting of crops, part of which, according to the qualified witness Agenbroad, could not be raised upon the land, thereby making the performance of that portion of the lease impossible. 'Where parties make an agreement and are ignorant at the time that performance of the contract is impossible, there is no contract, if it appears on the construction of the agreement that it was intended to be conditional on the supposed possibility of performance.' 17 C.J.S. Contracts §462, p. 952.

Plaintiffs assert further error of the trial court in entering judgment on the verdict and in denying plaintiffs' motion for new trial because the claimed representations of fraud were not statements concerning past or existing facts but were merely statements of opinion, hope, or expectation. 'The question whether fraud may be based on false statements as to future profits and income may be influenced to a considerable extent by the present degree of certainty or uncertainty as to what the future will bring. 'Where the subject of the sale is a new business, so that there are few existing facts concerning its profits or prospects, the future is unusually speculative and it may well be held that representations concerning future profits involve too much guesswork to constitute actionable fraud, even in jurisdictions where a false opinion or false promise may constitute actionable fraud.' 27 A.L.R.2d 14. 'The above evidence with regard to loss of profits is insufficient to sustain the judgment in this regard.' O'Brien v. Best, 68 Idaho 348, 194 P.2d 608, 615. 'Prospective profits contemplated to be derived from a business which is not yet established but one merely in contemplation are too uncertain and speculative to form a basis for recovery.

There was no proof on the part of defendants to sustain the judgment for failure to build two houses, farm shop, grain storage, barn, use of pasture ground, and repair of a building. Because the contract upon which the parties rely was incapable of being performed through lack of knowledge of the parties, there is no foundation for the complaint nor for the cross-complaint. The judgment is reversed, and the trial court is directed to dismiss the complaint and the cross-complaint.

Costs to appellants.

Case Questions:

1. What allegations does the plaintiff make against the defendants in this case?
2. What are the allegations of false statements in this case?
3. Is this a case of mistake, as that term is defined in contract law?
4. How does the court define a statement of past or present material fact?
5. Explain the court's rationale for its holding in this case.

The Case of the Bothersome Brothers[13]

AMUNDSON, Justice.

Patrick and Michael Geraets appeal from a trial court judgment finding no enforceable contract on the sale of real property. We affirm.

FACTS

Patrick (Pat) and Michael (Mike) Geraets operated as a partnership known as "Geraets Brothers." Ernest and Ethel Halter owned land that the Geraets rented. Prior to the transaction in question, Ernest had always dealt with the partnership, Geraets Brothers, and not with either Pat or Mike individually.

On September 2, 1997, Mike Geraets and Ernest discussed the sale of Halters' land. A price of $750 per acre was agreed upon and the two decided to go to Ernest's attorney, Glen Eng, to draw up the necessary papers. On the way to Eng's office, Mike phoned Pat regarding the purchase of the land. Ernest was advised the brothers would be purchasing the land together.

When Ernest and Mike arrived at Eng's office, it was determined Mike and Pat were undecided as to the division of the land to be purchased. Attorney Eng advised the parties he would wait to draw up two offer and purchase agreements until the Geraets had decided how they wanted to split the land. A contract for deed would be drafted after the

purchase agreements were received back, along with a $500 down payment.

On September 19, 1997, Mike and Pat contacted Eng with the information on how they wanted to split the land. Eng drew up the purchase agreements and the Halters signed them. Eng subsequently sent out two separate offer and purchase agreements signed by the Halters to Mike Geraets.

Neither Eng nor the Halters received any word back until October 22, 1997. In the interim, Ernest frequently stopped by Eng's office to inquire whether he had received any response. On October 22, Ernest stopped at Pat's home to ask about the status of the agreements. Pat was not available, but Ernest spoke with Pat's wife. Pat's wife informed Ernest that Mike had injured his back and he was contemplating quitting farming. Furthermore, Pat and Mike were considering dissolving their partnership.

The following day, October 23, Ernest and Pat spoke on the telephone. Pat informed Ernest that Mike was no longer interested but he (Pat) would take the land himself. Pat testified Ernest replied that he would "just as soon deal with one person." Ernest testified the one person he had in mind was the Geraets Brothers. Following the phone conversation, the same day, Ernest went to visit Pat. Ernest testified he told Pat at that time he did not want to go through with the sale. Pat testified that Ernest had only mentioned he was unsure what he wanted to do with the land.

On October 28, at approximately 1:00 P.M., Ernest went to Pat's home and told him "the deal was off." Ernest also told Pat he was not going to sell the land for anything less than $1,000 per acre. Ernest then went to Eng's office to advise him he no longer wished to sell. That same day Eng sent two letters, one to Pat and one to Mike, stating that the Halters had withdrawn the offer.

At some point near the end of October, Mike decided to allow Pat to purchase all of the property and gave him a copy of his purchase agreement. Pat crossed out Mike's name and signed both agreements. On the morning of October 28, Pat placed both agreements in his mailbox at the end of the driveway.

On October 29, Eng received the signed purchase agreements and earnest money check from Pat. The Halters refused to sell.

Pat and Mike, brought an action seeking specific performance to compel the Halters to sell the land according to the agreements notwithstanding Mike's assignment to Pat. The trial court denied specific performance, finding no contract. Geraets appeal, raising the following issues:

Did the trial court err in holding that the "Offer and Purchase Agreement" documents that had been signed by the Halters were not contracts to sell, but only offers to sell?

If the signed "Offer and Purchase Agreement" documents were merely offers to sell, did the trial court err in holding that the Halters effectively revoked their offer prior to acceptance by the Geraets?

Whether there was an enforceable contract.

Under SDCL 53–1–2, the elements necessary for formation of a contract are:

(1) parties capable of contracting;
(2) their consent;
(3) a lawful object; and
(4) sufficient cause or consideration.

Parties must be identifiable. The trial court found the parties' initial negotiations did not constitute a contract because the critical element of who the buyer was had not been resolved. This information was later provided to attorney Eng and the purchase agreements were prepared for the parties to sign. The Halters signed the purchase agreements. The issue whether or not this was a final and complete agreement was contested at trial.

At trial, Mike Geraets testified: "I didn't know if I wanted to go through with the purchase at that time[.]" Pat testified, "when he [Ernest] called me I told him that Mike had hurt his back, and that we were wanting to buy the land, but we didn't know for sure who would take over that portion of Mike's[.]" The trial court reasoned: "If a contract had been reached, there's no discussion of who the buyer is, it's already bought. [I]f they have already reached a contract he [has] already bought, so he obviously did not believe that a contract had already been reached."

An agreement is the result of a mutual assent of two parties to certain terms, and, if it be clear that there is no consensus, what may have been written or said becomes immaterial. Consent is not mutual unless the parties all agree upon the same thing in the same sense. Ensuing negotiations evidence absence of intent that the purchase agreement constitutes a final and complete agreement.

While the Geraets contend the entire time they intended to purchase the land, their conduct showed otherwise. "Whether a contract is formed is judged objectively by the conduct of the parties, not by their subjective intent. The question is not what the party really meant, but what words and actions justified the other party to assume what was meant." The evidence showed a delay from September 19, 1997, when the purchase agreements were received, until October 28, 1997, when the agreements were finally signed and placed in the mail. During this time, the evidence showed the Geraets themselves were uncertain as to the future of their partnership and whether the land would be purchased and, if so, who would purchase it. When Ernest finally went to visit Pat to inquire on the status of the agreements, he was told by Pat's wife that Mike was contemplating quitting farming and the partnership would be dissolved.

Based upon the Geraets own testimony, the trial court determined on-going discussions between Pat and Mike manifested no assent to be bound to a final agreement. Although there are factual disputes, the trial court is in the best position to assess the credibility of witnesses, weigh the conflicting evidence and observe the witnesses and the evidence first hand. Upon review of the record, we find substantial evidence to support the conclusion of the trial court that no contract existed. Whenever an agreement has not passed beyond the condition of negotiation, "[a]nd, if it is left doubtful from all the evidence in the case whether a contract was concluded or not, equity will not grant specific relief."

We affirm.

Case Questions:

1. What are the central issues in this case?

2. Why does the court reach the conclusion that there was no mutual assent?

3. Did the delay on the part of the Geraets to close the deal contribute to the decision in this case? Explain.

4. What is the significance of the "on-going discussions" between the parties in this case?

5. What fact, if changed, would have altered the outcome of this case?

Duress, Coercion, and Undue Influence

It is one of the basic principles of contract law that persons cannot have contracts forced on them. A person undertakes a contract voluntarily. People are permitted to pick and choose the parties to whom they will be bound by contract. When one party uses duress, coercion or threats to obtain agreement by the other party to a contract, the contract is void. The simple reason is that the party who was coerced into signing the agreement did not do so of his or her own free will. The concept of mutual assent requires that parties act voluntarily and when force, threats or coercion are used free will is destroyed.

Because a contract cannot be the product of duress, coercion, or undue influence, we will explore each of these concepts in order to understand how they are defined.

DURESS

Duress is the application of unlawful force, or the threat of force, that causes a person to do something that he or she would not otherwise have done. When a person acts under duress he or she does not act voluntarily. Some jurisdictions define duress as any action that overcomes the will of another person and compels assent when the person really does not wish to give it.

In many ways, the techniques of duress rely on violence and the threat of violence.

What effect does a successful claim of duress have on the contractual agreement? The court will rule that the contract is void and unenforceable. The party who suffered the duress also may have additional claims against the person who caused the duress.

> **Sidebar:**
> The general rule followed by courts across the United States is that a person is presumed to know the contents of a contract that he or she has signed. Unless a person can show fraud, duress, coercion, or some other wrongful act, the party is bound by the terms of the contract.[14]

duress: Unlawful pressure on a person to do what he or she would not otherwise have done.

The difficulty in reviewing cases dealing with duress is that duress is difficult to define. Certainly a threat of physical violence would qualify as duress. But does duress continue to apply when the threat is simply verbal? Suppose that the threat is vague. Courts have been wrestling with the concept of duress for years.

When the parties can be shown to have exercised their own free will, and have acted with the deliberation, a claim of duress will almost always fail. The courts scrutinize claims of duress closely in order to avoid creating an automatic escape clause for person who later feels uneasy about his contractual obligations. The mere fact that a party has negotiated a contract and made a bad bargain does not automatically equate to a claim of dress.

Similarly, the fact that one of the parties later discovers an impropriety by the other party does not create duress at the time that the contract was created. Essentially, the court considers the time period surrounding the creation of a contract as a bubble. Only those events that bear directly on the creation of the contract at the time that the contract was created will be considered. Events that occur later generally will often be ignored as they relate to the creation of the contract.

Another complexity of contract of law dealing with duress is the question of what constitutes duress in the first place? Obviously, when one party threatens the other party with physical violence, that is duress. But just how far removed from physical violence must an action be before it is not considered to be duress? Suppose, for example, that the parties to the contract do not like one another. Is their mutual dislike sufficient ground for one party to claim duress in agreeing to the contract? Or, suppose that one party has an irrational belief that the other party is exerting some kind of control over him, a control that most people would not believe was a form of duress. Here, as in other situations, the reasonable person standard comes to the courts' rescue. Under the reasonable person standard, the party claiming duress must show that the force exerted was something that a reasonable, hypothetical person would agree was duress. Here, we approach the question from the objective, not the subjective. If a reasonable person would not believe that duress occurred, the claim will fail.

In some jurisdictions, courts have ruled that there is no duress when the party is free to consult with an attorney before entering into the agreement. Other jurisdictions limit the application of duress to situations involving direct threats of physical harm. In most jurisdictions, the fact that a party believed that signing the contract was the only way to avoid financial problems does not automatically qualify as duress. This is especially true when the other party did not cause the financial problems.

When courts consider a claim of duress, they are also permitted to take into account the level of the claimant's business experience. A seasoned veteran of business negotiations is held to a higher standard in a claim of duress than someone who has embarked on his or her first business enterprise.[15] It is also not considered to be duress when the bargaining power of one of the parties is considerably less than the other.[16]

Sidebar:
In the movie *The Godfather,* the following scene is described by a character: a member of organized crime points a gun at another man's head and tells him to sign a contract. This is clearly a case of duress. The man was frightened by the threat of physical violence into signing a contract he otherwise would not have signed.

Sidebar:
It is not duress when one party is in desperate financial straits and agrees to a contract when the other party is not responsible for that situation.[17]

Exercising a Legal Right Does Not Create a Claim of Duress

It is not duress to exercise a legal option. If a person threatens an appropriate legal action against another and the other person acts because of that threat, there can be no valid claim of duress. Consider Hypothetical 5-6.

HYPOTHETICAL 5-6   The Petting Zoo

Marvin has lived on the edge of town for years. One day he learns that Paul's Petting Zoos, Inc., plans on buying the lot next to Marvin and opening one of its "Touchy-Feely" Petting Zoos. Marvin does not like the idea. He knows that PPZ must apply for a zoning hearing and receive permission from the zoning board in order to put in the petting zoo. Marvin approaches the president of PPZ and makes the following offer:

"If you buy my house for $100,000, I won't oppose the zoning application hearing for your new petting zoo. If you don't, I'll fight it all the way to the Supreme Court." PPZ believes that this is a form of economic duress. Are they right?

Answer: No. Because Marvin had the right to oppose the zoning application, his threat to do so was not improper and does not form the basis of a claim of duress.[18]

Actions that are clearly duress

- Use of physical violence to compel a person's "agreement"
- Threat of physical violence

Actions that may be duress

- Threat of economic sanctions that would effectively crippled another's business
- Threat of groundless lawsuits

Actions that are not duress

- When the party agrees after consulting with an attorney[i]
- When the party enters into the agreement because of "hard times" not caused by the other party
- When a reasonable person would not believe that the other party's actions were duress

EXHIBIT 5-4: Duress.

[i] *St. Louis Park Invest. Co. v. R.L. Johnson Invest. Co.* 411 N.W. 2d 288 (Minn App., 1987).

COERCION

If duress has an element of physical threat, then **coercion** is the flip side: it is mental threat. When a person coerces another, he or she is still overcoming the other's will, just as in duress, but the pressures brought to bear are subtler than duress. Coercion can include blackmail and other psychological tactics. These ploys are designed to overcome the person's will through threats of humiliation, embarrassment, or some other form of mental duress. Examples of coercion include threatening to bring false criminal charges against a person or character assassination.

coercion: Compulsion or force; making a person act against free will.

UNDUE INFLUENCE

The third type of defense available to a person who claims that her will has been overcome is **undue influence**. If duress is a physical threat and coercion is a mental threat, then undue influence is a violation of trust. A defense of undue influence often comes about in situations where one person enjoys a position of trust with the plaintiff and then uses that position to deceive the plaintiff into entering a contract. Persons accused of undue influence are often caregivers or children who look after elderly parents. They use this position of trust and love to push the plaintiff into a contractual obligation she did not wish to undertake.

undue Influence: Abusing or misusing a position of trust to overcome a person's will, usually to the benefit of the person exerting the improper control.

A contract obtained through undue influence is voidable; in other words, the contract continues to have legal effect until the injured party raises a claim that mutual assent was improperly obtained.[19]

Ratification

The concept of **ratification** often comes into play when dealing with claims such as mistake, duress, or coercion. This doctrine is deceptively simple: a person may approve a previous improper action and make it valid. When this happens, the previously improper action is effectively waived. Ratification applies to voidable contracts. If a person enters into a contract under the influence of drugs, or when she is mentally incompetent, she has two options when she regains her full mental capabilities. She may either disaffirm the contract, making a voidable contract fully void, or she may ratify it, making a voidable contract valid. A person can effectively waive a claim of mistake or undue influence or any of a number of other improprieties by simply agreeing to be bound by the contract despite the impropriety. Consider Hypothetical 5-7.

ratification: Confirmation and acceptance of a previous act done by you or by another person.

HYPOTHETICAL 5-7　Charlie Childstar's Contract

Charlie Childstar is a famous actor. He is also 16 years old. One day, he enters into a contract with a Hollywood agent to represent him in an upcoming movie deal. The details of the representation agreement are straightforward: if the agent can present Charlie with an acceptable offer from a movie studio, the agent will receive 15% of Charlie's total remuneration from the deal. The agent works for months on the deal and then finally presents Charlie with a highly lucrative proposal. Charlie accepts. When the agent asks for his 15% fee, the agent learns that Charlie is only 16 years old. Charlie fully intends to pay the agent and waits until he is 18 years old to do so. Is this acceptable?

Answer: Yes. At the time that Charlie entered into the original agreement with the agent, he was not an adult and therefore the contract was voidable. It is voidable because Charlie can cancel the contract or not, as he decides. On his 18th birthday, when he is a legal adult, he can ratify the previous contract and carry through its provisions.

In many ways, ratification acts as a fix for a voidable contract. Voidable contracts, after all, have a specific problem but can continue to have legal effect until they are challenged.

RATIFICATION AND VOID CONTRACTS

<aside>
Sidebar:
Ratification changes a voidable contract into a valid contract.
</aside>

Throughout the discussion of ratification, we have consistently stated that a *voidable* contract can be ratified. When a contract is void, by contrast, it cannot be ratified. As far as the law is concerned, a void contract is no contract at all. Unlike a voidable contract, which may simply lack a vital element, a void contract has no legal effect. It cannot be ratified because there is nothing to ratify. In a similar vein, a contract that involves the commission of a crime cannot be ratified. Such an agreement is absolutely void and unenforceable.

<aside>
Sidebar:
The right to challenge a contract is lost when a party engages in any action that the law could characterize as ratification. [20]
</aside>

ACTIONS THAT QUALIFY AS RATIFICATION

A person ratifies a contract through action. The only way to successfully ratify a voidable contract is to wait until the legal impediment that made it voidable disappears. As we saw in Hypothetical 5-7, Charlie Childstar could ratify the contract with his agent, but he could only do so when he reached the age of 18. At that time, he could legally enter into a contract, which means that he could also ratify a previously voidable contract. When a contract is voidable because a person lacked mental capacity, or suffered from some other form of legal impediment, that legal problem must be removed before a successful ratification can occur. A person may ratify a voidable contract by a later agreement reaffirming her intent to be bound by its terms, continuing to receive benefit from the contract, or by failing to challenge the voidable contract within a reasonable period of time.

Later Agreement

A party can ratify a voidable contract by expressly affirming the contract, even though it is lacking some specific element. For instance, a party could actually make the following statement: "I acknowledge that the contract has some problems, but I agree to act as though everything with the contract is fine."

Continuing to Receive Benefit

Ratification also can occur through actions. A court may find that a party has ratified a contract even without a positive statement, where the party continues to receive benefit from the contract, or continues to act as though the contract is perfectly valid. In this situation, the court is essentially stating that by continuing to follow the contract, the party is ratifying it by implication.

Ratification by Delay

Finally, the courts may find that a party ratified a contract simply by failing to challenge it within a reasonable period of time. Once the party has learned of a contract condition that would legally permit her to rescind or cancel the contract and fails to do so, the courts will rule that this failure is a tacit agreement to the contract terms. In such a situation, the person's actions constitute ratification and may actually waive the right to challenge the contract.[21]

The Doctrine of Laches

The principle of waiving a right by not asserting it is an ancient one. It is the foundation of legislation such as statutes of limitation and the equitable principle of laches. The principle of **laches**, sometimes known as the Doctrine of Laches, is simple: when a party has a right and does not assert it, he or she will lose the right.

    The question in contract cases often centers on the question of how long a period is involved before a party loses the right to challenge a voidable contract. Courts have been vague on this point. Given the incredible variety of contracts, it is no wonder that courts have stayed away from applying a strict rule applicable to every contract. Instead, the courts have ruled that after a "reasonable period" of time, the aggrieved party loses her right to challenge the contract. Other courts have said that the aggrieved party must assert her right with "reasonable promptness." Although both of these terms are extremely vague, there is one clear guideline: sufficient time has elapsed when the both parties have continued to operate under the contract and the other party would be prejudiced by the plaintiff's contract challenge.[22]

laches: The legal doctrine that a delay (in pursuing or enforcing a claim or right) can be so long that the person against whom you are proceeding is unfairly hurt or prejudiced by the delay itself.

Sidebar:
Delay in asserting a right to challenge a contract may constitute ratification.

Ratification and Duress

An agreement obtained under duress also may be ratified at some later point in time. Although it would seem odd for a party who was originally forced into a contract to agree later to be bound by its terms, such things have happened. The rule here is straightforward: a contract obtained under duress can be ratified, but only when the conditions that created the duress are removed. Ratification obtained under duress is just as unlawful as obtaining mutual assent under duress.[23]

Business Case File

Southern Bella

Southern Bella is a boutique located in Asheville, North Carolina, which offers an eclectic blend of antiques, linens, and other accessories. It is owned by Ginger Frank and Carrie Westall. Neither has owned a business before and they have only been open for a year. As first-time business owners, they were presented with some unique business and legal challenges.

"Carrie and I worked together for several years as employees at (another business)," said Ginger Frank. "We used to talk a lot about one day getting our own store and what we'd love to have. We were just trying to figure out how we could get out of the mall. I said to Carrie, 'We don't want to spend another holiday at the mall, so what are we going to do?' We decided, first and foremost, that the location was key. We said that if we didn't find a location that we were in love with, it wouldn't be worth our effort.

"We just happened to be driving around one day and we saw a sign saying that they were redoing this building. We called and talked with the owner. We were the first people to lease space in this building. We signed a tentative lease, based upon our getting our information together."

What they did was to come up with a business plan. According to Carrie Westall, it was not very detailed. "Our original business plan was two pages long. At the time that we were pulling all this together, we were really flying by the seat of our pants. We just had to close our eyes and jump."

Ginger agreed. "We were very blind at that point. We came up with a short description to convey to other people the kind of store we had in mind. It boils down to 'Southern hospitality meets vintage charm.' We put together an informal business plan, then we had to get our finances together, go to market, get our business license, a commercial bank account, insurance, and stuff like that."

Along the way, they encountered a potentially devastating problem: construction delays. "One of the hard lessons I learned," said Ginger, "was not to

Ginger Frank (right) and Carrie Westall

take at face value what the contractors tell you. We quit our jobs thinking that we had only a short period of time to get ready. We gave up our income for about six months, waiting for them to finish the construction." The delay caused them to take a closer look at the terms of their lease. Carrie's mother works for a local attorney, and they took their lease to him for advice. "We wanted to know if there was some way that we could get back some of our rent because the building hadn't been finished in time," Carrie said. What they discovered was disappointing. "He told us that since there wasn't anything in the lease about it that the landlord wasn't under any obligation to return part of our rent."

Because Carrie and Ginger had not included a provision about construction delays, there was no agreement on this pivotal issue. In other words, there was no mutual assent on the point of when and under what circumstances, the premises would be ready for Southern Bella to move in.

Despite the delays, Southern Bella opened its doors in December and has been going strong ever since. They both agree that opening your own business can be daunting, but it also has its rewards. "I don't know," said Carrie, "if this is the stupidest thing we've ever done or the smartest. Depending on what time of the day you catch me, I'd give you a different answer."

ETHICS FILE: Creating a system to help avoid legal malpractice claims

One way of avoiding ethical problems, such as revealing confidential communications or missing important court deadlines, is to adopt systems and procedures that are used in all cases. For instance, many firms routinely conduct conflict-of-interest file checks on a regular basis. These conflict checks review all pending cases against recently retained cases to ensure that there are no conflicts of interest between the various clients. Obviously, an attorney cannot represent ABC Company in one action and a disgruntled ABC Company employee's action against the same company in another action. Such dual representation opens the door to a minefield of ethical problems. A conflicts check helps to eliminate this problem.

Other procedures used at firms include a docket system that is either computer-based or handwritten. Some legal malpractice insurers require such redundant backup systems. For instance, a firm might have a handwritten calendar that documents deadlines in all pending cases and a computer program that automatically notifies staff about pending deadlines.

When it comes to correspondence with clients, other systems may be used. All telephone calls either to or from the client are documented with a memo to the client file. All faxes are saved for future reference. The faxes themselves also should contain a warning, such as: "The information contained in the fax is confidential in nature and not intended to be read by anyone other than the recipient."

The widespread use of e-mail has created special ethical problems for attorneys and paralegals. Most people act as though e-mail is as confidential as a letter, despite court rulings to the contrary. E-mail can be read by anyone and communications with a client through this medium should be dealt with accordingly.

Chapter Summary:

Mutual assent is the product of the negotiations of the parties and reflects their understanding of the general terms and their intention of creating a binding, contractual agreement with one another. There are many situations that can adversely affect the creation of mutual assent. For instance, mutual assent can be destroyed when the parties can show mistake. Mistake is a bilateral act, in which both parties have an incorrect view of the facts or of the consequences of the contract. Mistake creates a voidable contract, but only when both parties have made it. Mistake by only one party does not affect the validity of the contract or the presence of mutual assent in a contract.

Mistake is not the only occurrence that will affect the validity of a contract. Contractual obligation cannot be the product of force or threats. When duress, coercion, or undue influence is employed against a party, the resulting mutual assent is invalid and the contract is not enforceable.

The various problems with mutual assent, including mistake and duress, can be repaired by when a party ratifies the contract. Ratification refers to a party's willingness to continue the contractual obligation after an acknowledgement of an initial problem. Even duress can be ratified, but only when the force or threat is no longer present.

WEB SITES

Federal Courts
http://www.uscourts.gov/
The home page for the U.S. federal court system.

California Law
http://www.leginfo.ca.gov
Provides a database for California law.

National Center for State Courts
http://www.ncsconline.org/
Information about state courts around the country.

U.S. Department of Justice
http://www.usdoj.gov/
Home page for the extensive resources of the U.S. Department of Justice.

REVIEW QUESTIONS

1. What is mutual assent?
2. How does mutual assent differ from consent?
3. What are the basic rules of construction that courts use to interpret ambiguous contracts?
4. What degree of certainty is required in contractual language when it pertains to mutual assent?
5. The text states "mistake is a bilateral act." What does that mean?
6. What is a condition precedent?
7. There are two types of fraud as they apply to mutual assent. What are they?
8. How can a party waive a claim of fraud?
9. What is the standard of proof required to prove fraud?
10. Why is an opinion generally not considered to be a fraudulent statement?
11. Provide an example of a sales statement that would not be classified as fraud.
12. Can mutual assent be obtained through force? Why or why not?
13. Explain duress.
14. How is duress different from coercion?

15. What is undue influence?
16. How is undue influence different from coercion and duress?
17. What is ratification?
18. Why would the courts ever develop the concept of ratification?
19. Is it possible to ratify a contract without doing so verbally or in writing?

HANDS-ON ASSIGNMENT

Review the contract in the chapter section entitled "Interpreting the Language of a Contract—Ground Rules." What changes can you make to Wally Webdesigner's contract that would help show mutual assent and avoid the type of problem Wally encountered in that example?

PRACTICAL APPLICATION

Contact the local government agency responsible for issuing business licenses and get specific details on how a person acquires one. What are the requirements for a business license? Are there different business licenses for different types of businesses? Why is the license necessary? How much does a license cost? Where would a person go to actually acquire the license?

HELP THIS BUSINESS

As you saw in the Business File section, one of the problems encountered by the owners of Southern Bella was construction delays. The store opening was delayed several months and, because of that, the owners were not able to sell any merchandise. To help you better understand the function of contracts, draft a provision for the business lease that would take this particular problem into account and provide some remedies or alternatives for Southern Bella and the landlord if the construction lasts much longer than originally anticipated.

KEY TERMS

mutual assent	clear and convincing evidence
consent	duress
mistake	coercion
material fact	undue influence
condition precedent	ratification
fraud	laches
preponderance of the evidence	

ENDNOTES

1. Restatement, Contracts 2d §151.

2. *Gould v. Board of Educ.* 81 NY2d 446, 599 N.Y.S.2d 787, 616 NE2d 142 (1993).

3. Restatement, Contracts 2d §154.

4. Restatement, Contracts 2d §381(3).

5. *Davis v. G N Mortgage Corp.*, 244 F. Supp. 2d 950 (N.D.Ill., 2003).

6. *Davis v. G N Mortgage Corp.*, 244 F. Supp. 2d 950 (N.D.Ill., 2003).

7. *In re Boggs' Estate*, 135 W. Va. 288, 63 SE2d 497 (1951).

8. *Commissioner of Banks v. Cosmopolitan Trust Co.*, 253 Mass. 205, 148 NE 609 (1925).

9. *Weis Builders, Inc. v. Kay S. Brown Living Trust*, 236 F. Supp. 2d 1197 (D.Colo., 2002).

10. Restatement, Contracts 2d §381(3).

11. *Porreco v. Porreco*, 811 A.2d 566 (2002).

12. *Faria v. Southwick*, 337 P.2d 374 (Idaho, 1959).

13. *Geraets v. Halter*, 588 N.W.2d 231 (S.D., 1999).

14. Am. Jur. Contracts §234.

15. See 25 Am. Jur. 2d, Duress and Undue Influence.

16. *Grubel v. Union Mut. Life Ins. Co.*, 54 App. Div. 2d 686, 387 NYS2d 442 (1976).

17. *French v. Shoemaker*, 81 U.S. 314, 20 L Ed 852 (1871).

18. *Grezaffi v. Smith*, 641 So. 2d 210 (La. App. 1st Cir, 1994).

19. *Loizos v. Mutual of Omaha Ins. Co.*, 229 Pa. Super. 552, 326 A2d 515 (1974).

20. Am. Jur. Contracts §549.

21. *Prince George's County v. Silverman*, 58 Md. App. 41, 472 A2d 104 (1984).

22. *McLean v. Clapp*, 141 U.S. 429, 12 S. Ct. 29, 35 L Ed 804 (1891).

23. 25 Am. Jur. 2d, Duress and Undue Influence §29.

 For additional resources, visit our Web site at www.westlegalstudies.com

CHAPTER 6

CAPACITY AND LEGALITY

Focus of this chapter: In this chapter, we examine the issue of capacity to contract. Capacity is one of the basic elements of a contract. When a person has capacity, he or she has the mental ability to know and appreciate the rights, duties, and obligations that come with entering into a contract. When a person lacks capacity, he or she is unable to create a binding, legal contract. We also will address the topic of third party beneficiary contracts, which create rights in persons who are not direct parties to the contract. Finally, we will explore the topic of legality of contracts and contracts that are void for public policy reasons.

Chapter Objectives:
At the completion of this chapter, you should be able to:

- Explain the concept of capacity
- Describe situations in which a person may suffer from legal incapacity to contract
- Explain why minors are not legally entitled to enter into contracts
- Define specific physical or mental problems that would indicate that a person lacks capacity
- Describe the function of authority in the creation of contracts
- Explain the basis of recovery for a third-party beneficiary contract
- Describe the various types of third-party beneficiary contracts
- Explain and provide examples of illegal contracts
- Define instances in which a contract would be void for public policy reasons
- Be able to draft a third-party beneficiary contract

Introduction

In this chapter, we explore the concepts of capacity and legality. In order to have a valid contract, all parties must be able to understand the nature and the obligations of the contract. Similarly, the contract itself must not be one that is either illegal or a violation of public policy. We will begin our discussion with capacity.

WHY IS CAPACITY IMPORTANT?

capacity: Ability to do something, such as the mental ability to make a rational decision.

Capacity, like mutual assent, consideration, and the other contractual elements we have explored in the past few chapters, is one of the foundations of a legally enforceable contract. If a plaintiff seeks to enforce a contract, he must prove that the defendant had legal capacity to enter into a contract. Without that proof, the plaintiff's case will fail.

Capacity is an essential element of a contract because it shows that a party understood the contractual obligation. Capacity has been defined as "intelligent assent" to a contract. A party must understand and knowingly undertake the obligations of a contract before the contract will be binding.

Interestingly enough, there are different levels of capacity required to create various legal documents. For instance, most legal authorities agree that the capacity required to make a contract is higher in degree than that required to make a will, or convey property by gift or deed. Contracts, after all, involve negotiations between parties who are dealing at "arm's length."

The requirement of consideration is part of a general philosophy running throughout our legal system: that a person must knowingly and voluntarily undertake an obligation.

Defining Capacity

What is capacity? As the definition above provides, capacity is a legal term that encompasses a person's ability to understand the rights and obligations of a contract. Without that understanding, there can be no valid contract.

Capacity refers to a party's ability to understand what is happening, the effect of what agreeing to a contract means, and the ability to exercise free will in making this choice. We explored mutual assent in the previous chapter. We saw that mutual assent that is the product of force, threats, or undue influence is legally insufficient to bind a person to a contract. The same could be said of capacity. Without a showing that the party understood what was happening, there can be no valid contract. Traditionally, a contract could be voided where a party was declared legally insane. However, there are many other circumstances that can create legal incapacity.

Capacity is not the same thing as wise choice. A person can exercise poor judgment, enter into a contract that is disadvantageous, or even make a bad bargain, and still have full, legal capacity to contract. As we have seen in other chapters, courts are reluctant to inquire into the wisdom of the particular contract terms. Simply because a person has made a bad bargain does not mean that the person lacks the mental capacity to enter into a contract. Capacity is something more: It shows that the party knew and understood what he was doing, and voluntarily undertook a contractual obligation. The specifics of the bargain can come into play when there is an allegation of lack of capacity. However, a bad bargain, standing alone, will not be determinative. If the plaintiff is attempting to show that one of the parties lacked capacity, he must show something beyond poor judgment. Proof of lack of capacity must involve some facts that would show that the party did not know or understand what he was doing.

Capacity is defined differently depending on the area of law. For instance, a person who is drafting a will must have capacity but, in this case, capacity simply means that the person had a sound mind and was able to make dispositions of his property. However, when we are discussing contracts, the standard for capacity is higher. Here, a person must know and voluntarily undertake the rights and responsibilities of a contract (see Exhibit 6-1).

Sidebar:
There are jurisdictions in which the test for capacity to enter into a contract and the test for capacity to make a testamentary gift are the same, but most follow a scheme that requires a higher degree of capacity for contractual obligations.

"No one can be bound by contract who has not legal capacity to incur at least voidable contractual duties. Capacity to contract may be partial and its existence in respect of a particular transaction may depend upon the nature of the transaction or upon other circumstances."[i]

EXHIBIT 6-1: Restatement position of capacity.

---

[i] Restatement of Contracts, Second §12(1).

A Short History of Capacity

Before a more enlightened approach to law in general and contractual obligations in particular, certain classes of people were absolutely barred from entering into contracts. For instance, when the United States still allowed slavery, a slave was prohibited from entering into a contract. Similarly, married women, minors, and the insane also were barred from any contractual obligation. Some of these categories, such as minors and legally insane persons, continue to face contractual limitations, whereas others, such as married women, have had legal impediments removed.

Contract law as a legal topic ranked very low in most law school curricula for centuries. However, in the 1800s, there was a tremendous growth in this topic, brought about by the Industrial Revolution and the thousands of contracts (and contract enforcement actions) it brought about. Commerce, industry, and shipping became the lifeblood of business in the United States and Great Britain and all of these areas require safe and secure contractual

Sidebar:
Before the 1800s, married women in the United States had no individual power to enter into a contract.

obligations to keep the engine of business running. Along with this rapid growth in business, there was a strong push to enfranchise members of society who had previously been denied the right to contract. It is no coincidence that many of the important issues in contract law were developed in the late 1800s and early 1900s.[1] Among these long-settled topics is the issue of legal competency.

WHO MAY ENTER INTO A CONTRACT?

It should be obvious that a contract requires at least two parties, both of whom have legal capacity.

Natural Persons

Any person who is not disqualified for some reason can enter into a contract, provided that he or she has legal capacity. A person may be disqualified on the basis of age, mental impairment, or other reason. We will explore each of these reasons later in this chapter.

Artificial Persons

Corporations, and some other forms of business entities, are considered to be **artificial persons**. They can bargain, negotiate, and enter into contracts. Artificial persons have capacity.

Legal Competency

To say that a person is legally competent is to say that she has the ability to know, understand, and voluntarily engage in actions that can affect her interests. Some categories of individuals are automatically considered to lack legal capacity. Individuals can have their legal competency attacked on the basis of their physical or mental condition.

AGE OR INFIRMITY

The legal protections centering on the age of the individual were specifically designed to assist the most vulnerable members of our society: children.

Infants or Minors

When a person's age is below a certain level, the law presumes that he or she lacks capacity to contract. This age varies from state to state, but is usually either 18 or 21 years old. Persons under this age lack the capacity to enter into a contract. If a person who qualifies as a **minor** or an "infant" actually does enter into a contract, that contract is usually classified as voidable. The person's age is a contractual impediment that gives the child the right to cancel the contract. However, age is one of those deficiencies

Sidebar:
Generally speaking, husbands and wives are barred from contracting with one another. The reason for this is that, under the law, a married couple is considered to be a single entity. Because the contract requires at least two separate entities, a contract between a husband and wife is not enforceable.

artificial person: An entity or "thing," especially a corporation, that the law gives some of the legal rights and duties of a person.

minor: A person who is under the age of full legal rights and duties.

that can be nullified by ratification. For example, when the child reaches adulthood, he or she can simply ratify the contract and turn a voidable contract into a fully valid contract.

Advanced Age

Although there is a specific age that a person must attain before he will be able to enter into a contract, there is no age limit on the other end of life: old age. No state, for instance, has a rule stating that a person above a specific age is presumed to be legally incompetent to enter into a contract. Such a rule would be silly. Many people remain vital, energetic, and mentally sharp well into old age. However, it is also true that as people age, some suffer from age-related illnesses, including senile dementia, Alzheimer's disease, and other conditions that affect their ability to know and understand their actions.

A person's age is one of the factors that a court may take into account when it assesses a person's capacity. Old age, like physical infirmity or low intelligence, is an important factor in the court's determination, but by no means the only yardstick the court uses. The rule followed by all jurisdictions is that an elderly person lacks capacity only when his or her mental or physical problems impair the person's ability to understand the nature, terms, and obligations of the contract.

In this era of sweeping changes in medical treatments, terms such as "senile dementia" or "imbecility" are giving way to diagnoses of specific illnesses, such as Alzheimer's disease and other conditions that manifest themselves in mental and physical problems. With the recognition that advanced age does not always result in senility, the rules concerning the elderly and their ability to contract will undoubtedly grow even more liberalized.

ETHICS FILE: The Duty to an Incapacitated Client

A legal professional's duty to a client does not disappear when the client is declared to be mentally incompetent or when other situations incapacitate the client. In fact, because legal professionals have an obligation to act in the best interests of their clients, one could argue that the ethical obligation increases to a client who is no longer able to handle his or her affairs. There is also a period between detecting the incapacity and a court's declaration of incapacity (and the appointment of a guardian or other to handle that person's affairs). Legal professionals should be especially vigilant during this period to make sure that the client's interests are protected, not only from unscrupulous business associates, but also from friends or family who might take advantage of the person's incapacity.

A Case of Capacity?[2]

CUTTER, Justice.

In 1951, the Dowling Block, 'a 100% location' in the business section of Malden, as owned by Jewell A. Dowling, except for a portion (Lot A) owned by Dowling as trustee of a trust under his father's will. On June 14, 1951, when Dowling was nearly seventy-five, he executed as trustee and individually a lease to F. N. Joslin Company (Joslin) of the whole block for a term of fifty years at an annual net rental of $35,000. The lessee could terminate the lease unless by July 1, 1952, a Probate Court decree should establish Dowling's authority to lease Lot A. On June 8, 1954, Mr. Meserve, an attorney, was appointed Massachusetts conservator of Dowling's property. On November 26, 1954, he filed a bill in equity against Jordan Marsh Company (Jordan), with which Joslin had been consolidated, to obtain rescission of the lease and other relief on the ground that on June 14, 1951, Dowling was 'mentally incompetent.' After Dowling's death in 1955, Mr. Meserve as special administrator was substituted as plaintiff.

The case was tried together with a bill in equity brought by Dowling's two successors (the successor trustees) as trustees seeking rescission of the lease and reconveyance of Lot A to the trustees. Lot A had been conveyed by Dowling as trustee to himself individually on February 21, 1952, by a deed reciting that the consideration was $202,000 'paid.' The trial judge found that in June, 1951, Dowling 'had the mental capacity to make that particular lease; that he knew and understood [its] contents and was satisfied with it; that he had the mental capacity to negotiate with respect to the lease and to take care of his personal interests and to get what he wanted; that no one took advantage of him; and that there was no undue influence, imposition, or misrepresentation.' In the case brought by the successor trustees, the judge found that 'Dowling was guilty of a breach of trust in paying for Lot A with his personal note that neither Jordan and Joslin nor their attorneys knew of this breach of trust,' but that 'they relied on the

statement in the deed that' the $202,000 was paid by Dowling. The judge also found that on June 14, 1951, 'the net rental value of Lot A was' $8,000 a year. Mr. Meserve has appealed from a final decree dismissing his bill. A final decree was entered upon the successor trustees' bill directing the reconveyance of Lot A to them and awarding them their share of the rent accrued from Dowling's death to January 1, 1959, with interest. It further directed that $8,000 per year, in quarterly installments, be paid from and after January 1, 1959, to the successor trustees from the rent under the lease, which was not set aside by the decree. From this decree also Mr. Meserve has appealed. The successor trustees have waived their appeal. The evidence is reported. The scope of our review is that stated in Lowell Bar Ass'n v. Loeb, 315 Mass. 176, 178, 52 N.E.2d 27.

1. The rule as to avoiding transactions because of mental incapacity was stated in Reed v. Mattapan Deposit & Trust Co., 198 Mass. 306, 314, 84 N.E. 469, 471, as follows: '[T]he true test is, was the party whose contract it is sought to avoid, in such a state of insanity at the time as to render him incapable of transacting the business? When this fact is established the contract is voidable and it is no defense that the other party acted fairly and without knowledge of his unsoundness, or of any circumstances which ought to have put him upon inquiry.' In Sutcliffe v. Heatley, 232 Mass. 231, 232–233, 122 N.E. 317, 318, this court set aside the transaction of an alleged incompetent, saying, 'If she could not understand the nature and quality of the transaction or grasp its significance, then it was not the act of a person of sound mind. There may be intellectual weakness not amounting to lack of power to comprehend. But an inability to realize the true purport of the matter in hand is equivalent to mental incapacity.'

2. Mr. Meserve argues that Dowling's incapacity is shown by the 'shocking inadequacy of the considera-

tion received by Dowling under the lease,' by his ineffective efforts at negotiation, by his conduct of other transactions, by medical testimony, and by Dowling's personal and medical history. The evidence has been examined to determine whether the judge's findings were plainly wrong and his conclusions improper, giving them due weight. In 1934, Dowling was in a hospital because of a spontaneous subarachnoid hemorrhage. In 1940, when he was sixty-four, he suffered a cerebral accident and was hospitalized for twenty-one days. He recovered gradually although, after 1940, he suffered from paralysis of the right side, walked with difficulty, and needed assistance. He showed from then on symptoms of arteriosclerosis and high blood pressure. He became more intensely stubborn, opinionated, and quick tempered. Although he could carry on conversations intelligibly, he became repetitive and talkative, and sometimes forgetful, particularly about recent events. He 'was not as sharp in the years around 1948 to 1952—as he previously had been. He had changed in his dress, in his habits, which a man of normal mental capacity would not do,' in the opinion of his family physician. He continued, however, to participate to some extent in managing certain properties, with the assistance of employees, even during and after the period of the lease negotiations. As the judge found, prior 'to 1940, Dowling was a neat dresser. A few years later he became careless in his dress. He was physically unable to control his bladder, and he began wearing khaki pants which were frequently stained. On some occasions he [relieved himself] in a public street alongside of his car and on several occasions in a chair.'

Dowling's mental deterioration became sufficiently pronounced in 1954 to require the appointment of a receiver of his Florida property and a conservator in Massachusetts. The first time, however, that a physician, who saw him frequently, made a notation that Dowling had 'slipped mentally' was October, 1952. The testimony of two qualified medical expert witnesses revealed conflicting opinions about his mental condition in 1951. The whole testimony thus presented the issue of fact whether Dowling had so deteriorated by June 14, 1951, as to render him incapable of understanding 'the nature and quality of the transaction' in contrast with 'intellectual weakness not amounting to lack of power to comprehend.'

The judge found that 'Dowling was a wealthy man and a liberal spender. He spent considerable money in maintaining two boats. He had no one dependent upon him. He never had any children. In 1951, his wife owned' assets worth more than $147,000, and had a personal income from securities, before taxes, of $11,521. In addition to the Malden property, Dowling owned real estate in Miami (gross rental, $53,000) and in Allston (gross rental, $28,000). These findings were justified, but there was also evidence the Dowling maintained the two boats, one at least in bad shape, principally because it gave him 'pleasure to see them tied up at the dock.'

After making the 1951 lease he had to borrow $30,000 from a bank. Some of his real estate was substantially mortgaged. His liquid cash position was poor. His expenditures rose and his income after taxes declined. By the end of 1952 he had also borrowed $20,457.65 from Mrs. Dowling and owed $22,626.91 in delinquent taxes. Mrs. Dowling thought her husband was 'in an awful condition' and 'was complaining bitterly that he should have a conservator,' but the evidence indicated that he and Mrs. Dowling had led a somewhat unhappy relationship for a considerable period. She was declared incompetent herself later.

On June 8, 1951, Dowling, Gilman, Puckett, Brett, and a representative of Jordan conferred in Malden. Puckett said he was interested only in major construction, that 'several hundred thousand dollars of new fixtures and equipment would be required and that the lease would have to be for a long term. Dowling said he didn't have money for major construction and wouldn't put any money in at his age' and 'wouldn't sell because of the capital gain tax.' He also said 'he would like to be free from dealing with a number of tenants and would like Joslin to take over the whole block.'

An appraisal of the property ($1,300,000) 'was discussed and Puckett said that it was too high and that a return ought to be considered on a basis of a million dollar appraisal. He offered a 2 1/2% net rent and then 3%. Gilman advised Dowling not to take it.

Puckett asked Dowling if he would take $35,000 net rent and Dowling said he would consider it. The next day Dowling telephoned Brett that he would take $35,000. Dowling understood that net rental meant that the lessee would pay taxes [other than his own income taxes] and all other charges except interest and principal on the mortgage.' The 'trust property was discussed. Puckett said that the title would have to be worked out to the satisfaction of the [lessee's] lawyers or the deal would be off.' The lessee's attorneys, with assistance from Mr. Plummer, attorney for the Malden Savings Bank, drafted the lease. This was executed on June 14. The savings bank reduced the mortgage interest to 3 1/2% and subordinated its mortgage to the lease.

The judge found the 'fair market value of the' block just prior to the lease was about $1,000,000. Prior to the lease the trend of Joslin's 'business was downward and had fallen off.' The net income of the block just prior to June, 1951, 'before depreciation and interest on the mortgage, was about $82,000.'

The following evidence seems of significance. Gilman participated in the 1951 lease situation, without compensation from Allied or Dowling, the mortgagee' and also 'assisting Dowling wherein [he] could.' Neither Gilman nor Dowling consulted one Nessen who had been doing most of the work of management prior to the lease. Nessen ceased to work for Dowling when he learned of the lease. Allied, during the negotiations, was represented by Boston counsel. Dowling was not represented by any lawyer, except that Mr. Plummer, counsel for the savings bank, was called in after the negotiations had been completed to assist in drafting the lease, to straighten out the situation with respect to Lot A, and to draw wills for Dowling and his wife. So far as Mr. Plummer was 'concerned the [lease] terms were all settled, and [he] was told what they were.' He never got around to sending a bill to Dowling. There was seriously conflicting evidence about how accurately Dowling understood the terms of the lease. The judge obviously did not believe some of this testimony. Those present at the negotiations thought Dowling knew what he wanted and that he understood what was being discussed, although

Mr. Plummer noticed Dowling's physical weakness and thought that he tended to tire easily and to get off the subject in hand.

The deal, as the trial judge found, resulted in a serious reduction in Dowling's income before income taxes. Dowling, however, had no assurance that, if he did not make the lease, Joslin would continue in the premises. He did not want to rehabilitate the 'terribly run-down physical plant' himself. Even if the lease did not require Joslin to make the expenditures, he had every reason to suppose that enlightened self-interest would force these permanent improvements. He wanted to be relieved of management problems. He was old and sick and his wife was his only close relative. She had some independent means. Doubtless, although this does not appear to have been discussed, the reduction in Dowling's income was accompanied by a substantial reduction in his later Federal income taxes, so that the whole burden of the reduction of his gross income did not fall on him.

Because of the risks of inflation, many owners would have sought either periodic upward readjustments of rent or some percentage rent provision. Dowling, of course, had little incentive to look at the matter from a long range viewpoint. He had, however, no competent advice in negotiating, other than casual help from Gilman, admittedly primarily interested from the standpoint of the savings bank. The case thus is not one where a person of possibly impaired talents has been represented by competent, independent counsel. Mr. Plummer assumed no responsibility for the lease terms.

We have viewed the rent as low and as probably providing an inadequate return on the fair market value of the property. This value, on widely varying appraisals, the judge was justified in finding to be about $1,000,000. Dowling also certainly left himself unprotected (except possibly by oral assurances) from a substantial increase in the interest payable under an overdue mortgage. Such an increase would have reduced or eliminated his share of the rent. This record shows no such increase. Despite various circumstances unfavorable to Dowling's trading position, we assume that a better negotiator could have won a more favorable lease and that

Dowling himself would have done better advised by a competent, independent lawyer, real estate man, or accountant. The record, however, does not convince us that the trial judge was wrong, on evidence largely oral, in his conclusion that Dowling 'had the mental capacity to make that particular lease, understood what he was to get and was satisfied with it.' Giving due weight to the findings of the judge, we do not reach a different conclusion.

The judge was justified in concluding that 'there was no undue influence, imposition, or misrepresentation.' Undoubtedly, Puckett was trying to get the best lease he could and Gilman was interested in protecting his bank's mortgage position. The facts, however, are that Joslin made an offer to Dowling, which he had the capacity to understand, that the Joslin representatives advanced fairly the trading points they had, and that Dowling weighed them and accepted the offer.

Dowling undoubtedly handled other matters ineptly and foolishly during this period. He dealt with business papers sent to him in Florida in dilatory fashion. Some of his business actions seem, at the least, careless. All these matters have been considered.

Each of the final decrees is affirmed.

So ordered.

Case Questions:

1. Why did the plaintiff seek to rescind the lease in this case?

2. What was the trial judge's ruling about Dowling's mental capacity?

3. What is the rule about avoiding transactions on the basis of mental incapacity?

4. Is it a defense that the other party acted properly and in good faith in dealing with a person who has no legal capacity?

5. What were the alleged symptoms of Dowling's incapacity?

The Case of Questionable Collateral[3]

SNYDER, Judge.

The issues in this case arise out of a loan made by Union State Bank of Wautoma to Kathy Hauer. The Bank appeals from a judgment which (1) voided the loan on the grounds that Hauer lacked the mental capacity to enter into the loan and (2) required the Bank to return Hauer's collateral. Because we conclude that there is evidence in the record to support the jury's findings that Hauer was mentally incompetent at the time of the loan and that the Bank failed to act in good faith in granting the loan, we affirm.

In order to place the loan in context, we must first set forth the relevant events giving rise to the loan. The following facts are taken from court documents and undisputed testimony at trial.

In 1987, Hauer suffered a brain injury in a motorcycle accident. She was subsequently adjudicated to be incompetent, resulting in a guardian being appointed by the court. On September 20, 1988, Hauer's guardianship was terminated based upon a letter from her treating physician, Kenneth Viste. Viste opined that Hauer had recovered to the point where she had ongoing memory, showed good judgment, was reasonable in her goals and plans and could manage her own affairs. Her monthly income after the accident was $900, which consisted of social security disability and interest income from a mutual fund worth approximately $80,000.

On October 18, 1988, the Bank loaned Ben Eilbes $7600 to start a small business. In December, Eilbes requested but was denied an additional $2000 loan from the Bank. By June of 1989, Eilbes was in default on the loan. Around this time, Eilbes met Hauer through her daughter, who told Eilbes about the existence of Hauer's mutual fund. Eilbes subsequently discussed his business with Hauer on several occasions and Hauer expressed an interest in becoming an investor in the business. Because Hauer could only sell her stocks at certain times, Eilbes suggested that she take out a short-term loan using the stocks as collateral. Eilbes told Hauer that if she loaned him money, he would give her a job, pay her interest on the loan and pay the loan when it came due. Hauer agreed.

Eilbes then contacted Richard Schroeder, assistant vice president of the Bank, and told Schroeder that Hauer wanted to invest in his business but that she needed short-term financing and could provide adequate collateral. Eilbes told Schroeder that he would use the money invested by Hauer in part to either bring the payments current on his defaulted loan or pay the loan off in full. Schroeder then called Hauer's stockbroker and financial consultant, Stephen Landolt, in an effort to verify the existence of Hauer's fund. Landolt told Schroeder that Hauer needed the interest income to live on and that he wished the Bank would not use it as collateral for a loan. Schroeder also conceded that it was possible that Landolt told him that Hauer was suffering from brain damage, but did not specifically recall that part of their conversation.

At some later date Eilbes met personally with Schroeder in order to further discuss the potential loan to Hauer, after which Schroeder indicated that the Bank would be willing to loan Hauer $30,000. Schroeder gave Eilbes a loan application to give to Hauer to fill out. On October 26, 1989, Hauer and Eilbes went to the Bank to meet with Schroeder and sign the necessary paperwork. Prior to this date, Schroeder had not spoken to or met with Hauer. During this meeting Schroeder explained the terms of the loan to Hauer—that she would sign a consumer single-payment note due in six months and give the Bank a security interest in her mutual fund as collateral. Schroeder did not notice anything that

would cause him to believe that Hauer did not understand the loan transaction.

On April 26, 1990, the date the loan matured, Hauer filed suit against the Bank and Eilbes. Hauer alleged the following specific causes of action: (1) the Bank knew or should have known that she lacked the mental capacity to understand the loan, (2) the Bank intentionally misrepresented, negligently misrepresented, or misrepresented the circumstances surrounding the loan on which she relied, and (3) the Bank breached a fiduciary duty owed to her.

On January 7, 1992, the Bank moved for summary judgment on the grounds that Hauer failed to state any claim for which relief could be granted. The trial court granted summary judgment in part by dismissing Hauer's misrepresentation claims. However, the court held that the pleadings stated the following causes of action which required factual determinations: (1) Hauer lacked the mental capacity to enter into the loan agreement and the Bank knew or should have known about her condition, (2) the Bank breached its duty of good faith and fair dealing under § 401.203, Stats., and (3) the Bank had a fiduciary duty to Hauer and breached that duty.

Prior to trial and over the Bank's objection, Hauer dismissed Eilbes because he appeared to be judgment proof and was filing bankruptcy. A twelve-person jury subsequently found that Hauer lacked the mental capacity to enter into the loan and that the Bank failed to act in good faith toward Hauer in the loan transaction. The trial court denied the Bank's motions after verdict and entered judgment voiding the loan contract, dismissing the Bank's counterclaim and ordering the Bank to return Hauer's collateral. The Bank appeals.

Over the Bank's objection, the jury was presented with the following special verdict question: Did the plaintiff, Kathy Hauer, lack the mental capacity to enter into the loan transaction at the time of that transaction? The jury answered this question, "Yes." In denying the Bank's motions after verdict, the trial court held that based on this finding, the note and security agreement were "void or voidable." Further, the court ruled that Hauer was not liable for repayment of the $30,000 loan because she no longer possessed the funds.

The Bank in its motions after verdict and on appeal argues that the jury's verdict as to mental incompetency is invalid. The Bank contends that the evidence does not support the jury's verdict.

The law presumes that every adult person is fully competent until satisfactory proof to the contrary is presented. The burden of proof is on the person seeking to void the act. The test for determining competency is whether the person involved had sufficient mental ability to know what he or she was doing and the nature and consequences of the transaction. Almost any conduct may be relevant, as may lay opinions, expert opinions and prior and subsequent adjudications of incompetency.

Our review of the record reveals that there is credible evidence which the jury could have relied on in reaching its verdict. First, it is undisputed that Hauer was under court-appointed guardianship approximately one year before the loan transaction. Second, Hauer's testimony indicates a complete lack of understanding of the nature and consequences of the transaction. Third, Hauer's psychological expert, Charles Barnes, testified that when he treated her in 1987, Hauer was "very deficient in her cognitive abilities, her abilities to remember and to read, write and spell ... she was very malleable, gullible, people could convince her of almost anything." Barnes further testified that because Hauer's condition had not changed in any significant way by 1990 when he next evaluated her, she was "incompetent and ... unable to make reasoned decisions" on the date she made the loan.

The Bank argues that Barnes's testimony was irrelevant and erroneously admitted because Viste, Hauer's treating neurologist, informed the court that in his opinion Hauer was no longer in need of a guardian and could manage her own affairs a year prior to the loan. The Bank contends that Hauer should be judicially estopped from asserting incompetence at the time of the loan after convincing the court the previous year that she was competent. However, competency must be determined on the date the instrument was executed. Over the Bank's objection, a portion of Viste's deposition was read at trial, where Viste concluded that based on Barnes's opinion, he had erred in finding that Hauer was competent and no longer in need of a guardian in 1988.

The Bank further points out that both Eilbes and Schroeder testified that Hauer was much different at trial than she was on the day the loan was executed. Nevertheless, the weight and credibility of the evidence are for the jury to decide, not this court. The jury apparently gave more credence to Hauer's and Barnes's testimony than Schroeder's testimony and Viste's 1988 opinion. In sum, while we agree that there is evidence which the jury could have relied on to find that Hauer was competent, we must accept the inference that favors the jury's verdict when the evidence permits more than one inference.

Having concluded that Hauer stated a claim for relief and that sufficient credible evidence was presented to sustain the jury's verdict, we now turn to the unresolved problem regarding the rights and responsibilities of the parties relative to the disposition of the consideration exchanged in the loan transaction. We must decide the legal question of whether Hauer may recover her collateral without liability for the loan proceeds.

Postverdict, the trial court ruled that Hauer's action to void the contract required the Bank to return her collateral and Hauer to return any loan proceeds in her possession. However, it is undisputed that Hauer loaned the entire $30,000 to Eilbes and that the money had long since disappeared. On appeal, the Bank contends that equity dictates that the proper remedy upon voiding the loan transaction is to return the parties to their preloan status—the Bank must return Hauer's stocks and Hauer must be held liable to the Bank for $30,000.

The trial court offered two explanations for voiding the contract but not holding Hauer liable for repayment of the loan: (1) the law and policy of the "infancy doctrine" and (2) the jury's finding that the Bank failed to act in good faith. We will address each in turn.

A. INFANCY DOCTRINE

In *Halbman*, our supreme court held that a minor who disaffirms a contract may recover the purchase price without liability for use, depreciation or other diminution in value. As a general rule, a minor who disaffirms a contract is expected to return as much of the consideration as remains in the minor's possession. However, the minor's right to disaffirm is permitted even where the minor cannot return the property. The trial court ruled that the infancy doctrine was analogous and applies when the voidness arises from mental incapacity to contract. We disagree.

The purpose of the infancy doctrine is to protect "minors from foolishly squandering their wealth through improvident contracts with crafty adults who would take advantage of them in the marketplace." The common law has long recognized this policy to protect minors. However, "[a] contract made by a person who is mentally incompetent requires the reconciliation of two conflicting policies: the protection of justifiable expectations and of the security of transactions, and the protection of persons unable to protect themselves against imposition."

The trial court's analogy fails given the fact that the two types of incapacity are essentially dissimilar. "An infant is often mentally competent in fact to understand the force of his bargain, but it is the policy of the law to protect the minor. By contrast, the adult mental incompetent may be subject to varying degrees of infirmity or mental illness, not all equally incapacitating." This difference in part accounts for the majority of jurisdictions holding that absent fraud or knowledge of the incapacity by the other contracting party, the contractual act of an incompetent is voidable by the incompetent only if avoidance accords with equitable principles. Accordingly, we conclude that the infancy doctrine does not apply to cases of mental incompetence.

B. GOOD FAITH

The jury was presented with the following special verdict question: "Did the defendant, Union State Bank of Wautoma, fail to act in good faith toward [Hauer] in the loan transaction?" The jury answered that question, "Yes." In denying the Bank's motions after verdict, the court concluded that even if the infancy doctrine did not apply, the jury's finding that the Bank failed to act in good faith in the loan transaction distinguished this case from the "general rule" providing that the person seeking relief from a contract must return the consideration paid. We agree.

Section 401.203, Stats., is a general provision of Wisconsin's Uniform Commercial Code. According to § 401.203, "[e]very contract or duty within [the Uniform Commercial Code] imposes an obligation of good faith in its *performance or enforcement*." (Emphasis added.) However, at issue in this case is the Bank's good faith in the *formation* of the contract with Hauer. Because the general requirement of good faith under this section applies only to the performance or enforcement of a contract, it does not impose a duty of good faith in the negotiation and formation of contracts.

The Uniform Commercial Code defines good faith as honesty in fact. Beyond that ... good faith is another way to describe the effort to devise terms to fill contractual gaps. As a method to fill gaps, it has little to do with the formation of contracts....

Wisconsin common law, like other states, reads the duty of good faith into every contract. The great weight of authority from other jurisdictions provides that the unadjudicated mental incompetence of one of the parties is not a sufficient reason for setting aside an executed contract if the parties cannot be restored to their original positions, provided that the contract was made in good faith, for a fair consideration and without knowledge of the incompetence.

Stated differently, if the contract is made on fair terms and the other party has no reason to know of the incompetency, the contract ceases to be voidable where performance in whole or in part changes the situation such that the parties cannot be restored to their previous positions. If, on the other hand, the other party knew of the incompetency or took unfair advantage of the incompetent, consideration dissipated without benefit to the incompetent need not be restored.

Whether the Bank knew or had reason to know that Hauer was incompetent is a question of fact for the jury to decide. Inexplicably, the Bank neither requested a special verdict question regarding its knowledge nor objected to the form of the special verdict on the grounds that it lacked a question pertaining to knowledge. This is true despite the fact that *Hauer* in her proposed special verdict submitted a question regarding the Bank's knowledge, and that the trial court concluded at the summary judgment stage that there was a dispute of material fact as to whether the Bank had knowledge of Hauer's incompetence.

The Bank argues that it does not have an affirmative duty to inquire into the mental capacity of a loan applicant to evaluate his or her capacity to understand a proposed transaction. We agree. However, a contracting party exposes itself to a voidable contract where it is put on notice or given a reason to suspect the other party's incompetence such as would indicate to a reasonably prudent person that inquiry should be made of the party's mental condition. As the trial court aptly stated: "I did not say there's any duty to make an investigation, but the bank takes a risk the contract will be . . . voidable if they know of facts which support the claim of inability to contract."

The last question we must address is whether there was any credible evidence to sustain the jury's verdict that the Bank failed to act in good faith. If there is, we are bound to sustain the jury's verdict. The Bank contends that "[t]he record is devoid of any evidence that the Bank had knowledge of any facts which created a suspicion that it should not enter the loan." We agree with the trial court's summary that there is evidence in the record "that there were flags up that would prompt a reasonable banker to move more slowly and more carefully in the transaction."

For example, the Bank knew that Eilbes was in default of his loan at the Bank. Eilbes approached the Bank and laid all the groundwork for a loan to be given to a third-party investor, Hauer, whom the Bank did not know. Eilbes told Schroeder that he would make his defaulted loan current or pay it off entirely with Hauer's investment. Schroeder testified that upon investigating the matter initially, Hauer's stockbroker told him not to use Hauer's fund as collateral because she needed the fund to live on and Hauer could not afford to lose the fund. He further testified that it was possible that the stockbroker told him that Hauer suffered a brain injury. In addition, Hauer's banking expert opined that the Bank should not have made the loan. Accordingly, we conclude that the evidence and reasonable inferences that can be drawn from the evidence support the jury's conclusion that the Bank failed to act in good faith.

Case Questions:

1. Explain why Hauer was held to be incompetent in this case but had been held to be competent a year before signing the loan.

2. What is the Uniform Commercial Code's definition of good faith?

3. According to the court, how did the bank act in bad faith in this case?

4. What are some of the facts that indicated the bank's bad faith?

5. Is this a case in which the appellate courts are bending the rules to obtain a result that favors a particular plaintiff? Explain your answer.

Physical Infirmity

When a person suffers from some form of physical infirmity that does not affect his or her mental abilities, the physical condition is irrelevant to capacity. A disabled person who has the mental capacity to contract may do so, regardless of the disability. The court's only test in this situation is the person's intelligence and ability to understand the contractual obligation. If that is present, other considerations are meaningless.[4]

Although a person can suffer from a severe disabling condition and still enter into a contract, it is also true that the person's physical condition could affect capacity. A person may be in such severe pain, or under the influence of drugs, that his capacity will be affected.

Similarly, a person's lower than average intelligence does not disqualify him from entering into a contract.[5] See Exhibit 6-2 for other conditions that will not automatically result in a finding that the person lacks capacity.

A person may still have legal capacity despite.

- unusual or even paranoid beliefs
- lower than average intelligence
- eccentric beliefs
- unusual religious beliefs
- loss of memory
- chronic fatigue
- irrationality on certain topics
- routinely exercising poor judgment

EXHIBIT 6-2: Legal capacity.

GUARDIANSHIP

When a person has been declared mentally incompetent, it is common for a court to appoint a **guardian** to represent that person. When a person is a guardian for another, it means that the guardian has control over the incompetent person's affairs. In such a situation, the incompetent person (the ward) is barred from conducting any of his or her own affairs. All transactions must be handled through the guardianship.[6]

When a person enters into a contact with a person for whom the court has appointed a guardian, the contract is void, even if the person did not know of the guardianship. The courts will usually rescind the contract and attempt to put the parties back in the position they were in before the contract was negotiated. However, when that is impossible, the person who provided a necessary service to the ward, such as food or medical treatment, will be entitled to compensation. When the contract does not embrace "necessaries" such as food and medical treatment, the person may not be entitled to any compensation. Contracts entered into by the ward cannot, for example, be ratified by the ward's actions. This would effectively give the ward power to negotiate contracts indirectly, thus avoiding the reason for creating the guardianship in the first place.

Partial versus Total Incapacity

Some physical or mental problems can result in a finding of partial incapacity. In such situations, a person may still undertake a contractual obligation. However, the contract may receive greater scrutiny for such claims as mistake, duress, or undue influence, as discussed in the previous chapter. When a person is totally incapacitated, he or she cannot make a contract. Instead, the person's guardian has that power.

MENTAL INCOMPETENCE OR MENTAL ILLNESS

When a person is of lower than average intelligence, or suffers from some form of mental illness less than legal insanity, this person is still entitled to enter into a contract. Such people have capacity. However, the degree of their impairment may become significant when the other party seeks to enforce the contract through the court system. If the court finds that the person is so impaired that he or she cannot understand the consequences, the rights or the obligations of the contract, then the court may rule that this person lacks capacity.

One of the problems encountered by those who wish to enforce a contract against a person who has been held to be mentally incompetent is that some people who suffer from severe mental illness do not appear to be insane. They may appear quite lucid, at times, and a person negotiating with such a person might have no way of suspecting that the person is mentally impaired. A party may negotiate in good faith with another party and not realize that the other party is mentally incompetent. In such situations, courts often use their equity powers to nullify the contract, on the basis that the wisest course to take in such cases is to put all parties back into their original positions rather than attempting to enforce a contract against a person who has been declared to be mentally incompetent. As we will see in future chapters, placing the parties back in their original position may not always be possible. In such situations, the party who has provided service or mentally incompetent person may be entitled to some form of compensation less than actual performance of a contract.

Jurisdictions approach the issue of contracts with the legally insane in different ways. For instance, some jurisdictions follow the rule that such a contract is immediately void, while other jurisdictions state that the contract is simply voidable.[8] However, in situations in which the person has been adjudicated legally insane, most jurisdictions follow the rule that such a contract is absolutely void.[9]

Mental incompetence is not an absolute. There are degrees of insanity. Courts are free to consider the degree of a person's impairment in deciding whether or not he had capacity. If the person is incapable of understanding the terms and conditions of the contract, then the court will rule that he lacks capacity and the contract is void. However, where the person has some degree of understanding, the contract may simply be voidable and a court may subsequently rule that it is valid (see Exhibit 6-3).

- Infancy
- Mental illness of incompetence
- Intoxication
- Where a guardian has been appointed

EXHIBIT 6-3: Conditions that render a party incompetent to enter into a contract.

HYPOTHETICAL 6-1   Depression

Stan has been depressed for some time. His depression manifests itself in periods of indifference and self-destructive behavior. During one such spell of depression, he advertises his car for sale, listing a price that is less than half of its value. Sylvia sees the ad and immediately contacts Stan. She offered $100 less than the price in his ad and Stan replies, "Whatever." She shows up later that day with the money in hand. Stan has prepared the title. Sylvia tenders the money and asks for the car keys and the title to the car. At this point, is there a valid contract? Put another way, do Stan's actions indicate a lack of capacity?

Answer: In almost any jurisdiction the answer would be no. Depression is not considered to be a mental illness that affects a person's capacity, at least in the more typical manifestations of the disease. The contract may not be advantageous to Stan, but neither that fact nor the fact that he has been diagnosed with depression will affect his legal capacity to enter into a contract. [10]

The Other Party's Good Faith

Suppose that A is legally insane and enters into a contract with B who has no knowledge of A's mental illness. B acts properly in the transaction and never has any indication that A is mentally ill. When A's condition comes to light, B does not wish for the contract to be voided. B counters that regardless of A's condition, this contract is actually beneficial to both parties and no improprieties have occurred. Is there a "good faith" exception in this scenario?

No. The contract is void and B's proper behavior and lack of knowledge about A's condition will not create a valid contract under these circumstances. If this rule sounds like a harsh application of the law, consider the scenario from a different perspective. Suppose that B has not acted properly, but still wishes to enforce the contract? In either case, A's incapacity is still present. By ruling that such a contract is void, the courts have effectively prevented such "indirect contracts" and protected individuals who are incapable of protecting themselves. This sometimes results in an adverse ruling for a person who has dealt with another on fair and equitable terms, but placed in this situation, the court's reasoning is simple: of the two, who should receive more protection, the person already adjudicated incapable of protecting himself or a sane person who can make other arrangements? Faced with such a choice, the decision seems clear.[11]

INTOXICATION

Just as a contract entered into with a minor, mentally incompetent person, or someone suffering from Alzheimer's disease is voidable, so, too, is a contract entered into with an intoxicated person. No one would argue that people who are acting under the influence of alcohol or some other drug are not in their right mind. In this way, intoxication resembles a form of insanity. Although there are jurisdictions in which such contracts are absolutely void, most opt for a middle ground and merely rule that the contract is voidable. When the intoxicated person regains his sobriety, the contract could be ratified or challenged as unenforceable.

Authority

We discuss **authority** in this chapter, even though it is more properly considered as part of a discussion of agency, because it is the perception of a person's power to contract versus the reality that we explore in this chapter. When we say the person has authority to enter into a contract it simply means that he or she has legal capacity and has no legal impediment to becoming a party to a contract. Authority comes in two forms: apparent authority an actual authority.

authority: Permission to act; power to act.

APPARENT AUTHORITY

Apparent authority deals with the perception of the parties involved in the transaction. If it appears that a person has the authority to make certain commitments in a contract, or to act for another, and the principal does not negate this perception, then the person has authority, even though it was never officially conferred upon him.

ACTUAL AUTHORITY

In contrast, actual authority refers to the legally vested rights in a party that allows him to engage in a contract. When a person has actual authority it is usually vested in him through some overt action by another. For example, when a person acts as an agent for another, the agency relationship usually spells out in detail the authority of the agent to act for the principal. The limit of this authority is the person's actual authority. Issues surrounding authority often rear their heads when we discuss third-party contracts.

> **Sidebar:**
> A person may become obligated in a contract through the actions of his or her agent, but in this situation, the agent is acting with the authority of the person and this authority includes the right to obligate the principal in a contract.

Third-Party Contracts

As we have already seen in this chapter, a contract requires at least two separate entities. These parties have rights that derive from the negotiated terms of the contract that allow them, among other things, to bring a legal action to enforce the terms. There are situations, however, when a person who is not a party to a contract is allowed to bring an action to enforce it. Such persons are termed "third parties" because they are not directly involved in the contract itself. This right stems not from their involvement in the contract but from the fact that they derive some benefit from the contract between the other parties.

The right of a third party to sue on his or her own behalf even though not actually a party to the contract was originally created as an exception to a general rule of contracts. The general rule was that only parties to the contract could seek to enforce it. Permitting recovery for third parties who benefited from the contract was originally seen as a radical, but necessary exception to this rule. However, the exception is now recognized in nearly all jurisdictions and third-party actions have become so common that these actions are considered to be routine.[12]

What is the theory that justifies a third party's action to enforce a contract to which he or she is not a party? This simple question has generated a mountain of judicial opinions. Is the third party really the beneficiary of a trust created by the parties to the contract? Is the third party an "implied party" to the contract and therefore has the same legal recourse as an actual party? Most jurisdictions avoid the question by taking a more pragmatic approach: allowing a suit by a third party is often the only practical way for the third party to protect his or her rights. In the next few sections, we will examine specific types of third party beneficiaries and how their rights are created. For an example of a third-party beneficiary contract, see Exhibit 6-4. See also Exhibit 6-5.

CREDITOR BENEFICIARIES

Creditor **beneficiaries** are created when a contract's provisions include a promise to satisfy an outstanding debt. Like all third-party contracts, the rights of the third party arise from an interpretation of the language of the contract and the facts surrounding its creation.

Some jurisdictions have wrestled with the concept of third-party creditors and how such a right can be enforced. In some jurisdictions, for example, there is a rule stating that the third-party creditor must be in privity with one of the parties or that the creditor provided some form of consideration for the commitment expressed in the contract to repay the creditor. However, the general rule in most jurisdictions is to allow third-party creditor rights without either privity or consideration requirements.

Sidebar:
The rule that permits a third party to bring an action to enforce a contract to which he or she is not a party is also referred to as the "third party beneficiary doctrine."

Sidebar:
Your state may have codified the third-party beneficiary rule. You should review your statutes to determine if third-party beneficiary actions are authorized by statute.

Sidebar:
Third-party contracts are strictly construed by the courts.

beneficiary: Anyone who benefits from something or who is treated as the real owner of something for tax or other purposes.

Sidebar:
One way of determining whether a third party qualifies as a creditor-beneficiary is by reviewing the contract language. If it is clear that the promise to the creditor is not a gift and the promise is designed to satisfy the debt.[13]

This agreement, made on the 2nd day of May, 2003, by and between Rubar Stamping Company of Boston, Massachusetts, hereinafter referred to as "Rubar" and Deborah Bolstridge, Inc., of Asheville, North Carolina, hereinafter referred to as DB Inc., made in consideration of value given, mutual promises exchanged and specific stipulations set out below, sets out the following:

I.   This is a third-party beneficiary contract. The purposes of this contract is to create a right in the individual named in paragraph IV is to receive specific sums as a result of a binding, legal, and mutually-agreed upon contract between the parties listed herein.

II.   DB Inc. hereby agrees to sell to Rubar original artwork, created by DB Inc., and rendered in a negative rubber stamp mold medium ("molds") a series of 23 individual molds depicting various scenes of a "Day in the Country" theme. These molds will be in production-ready medium, no smaller than 2 inches by 2 inches and no larger than five inches by five inches. DB Inc. will prepare said molds using appropriate techniques.

III.   The molds prepared by DB Inc. will be to the satisfaction of Rubar's production guidelines. (See Attachment A.)

IV.   With the delivery of said molds and acceptance by Rubar, Rubar agrees to pay the sum of $1150 per acceptable mold to John Doe, 210 Maple Drive, Asheville, North Carolina, in consideration of and for outstanding debts owed by DB Inc. to said John Doe. For purposes of this contract, Mr. Doe is a third-party beneficiary, as that term is defined under the laws of North Carolina and Massachusetts.

V.   This contract constitutes the entire agreement between the parties and contains all of the provisions of said agreement between the parties. No statements, promises or inducements made by any party or agent of any party that are not contained in this written contract shall be valid or binding. This contract may not be enlarged, modified, or altered except in writing signed by all the parties and indorsed on this agreement.

Executed on the 2nd day of May, 2003, in the town of Asheville, North Carolina by the following.

(Signature)	(Signature)
Felix Rubar	Alice Rubar
President & Chief Executive Officer	Vice President/Secretary
Rubar Stamping Company of Boston,	Rubar Stamping Company
Massachusetts	of Boston, Massachusetts
(Signature)	(Signature)
Deborah Bolstridge	Betsy Bolstridge
President	Secretary
Deborah Bolstridge, Incorporated	Deborah Bolstridge, Incorporated

EXHIBIT 6-4: Third-party beneficiary contract.

✓ PARALEGAL CHECKLIST

- ☐ Results from the parties' clear intention to benefit a person/entity who is not actually a party to the contract
- ☐ Contains language unambiguously stating that the third party will be a beneficiary of the contract
- ☐ Does not simply create a potential right in a third party to benefit
- ☐ Does not contain a clause or provisions specifically stating that it is not intended to benefit other parties (although the absence of this clause is not conclusive of the opposite scenario)

EXHIBIT 6-5: A third-party contract.

DONEE-BENEFICIARY

Determining if someone is donee-beneficary again requires close review of the contract provisions. In most jurisdictions, a donee-beneficary is created by contract provisions that show a clear intention by the parties to make a gift to a third party.[14]

Sidebar:
Before the court will enforce a third-party contract, the language contained in it must be specific and unambiguous. The contract must clearly state the intention to create a right or confer some benefit on a person who is not a party to the contract.[15]

ASSIGNEE-BENEFICIARY

An assignee-beneficiary is a person or entity who eventually will be granted a specific right under the contract, such as a person who will eventually become a party to the contract. The assignee has the right to enforce provisions of the contract even before the assignment occurs.

HYPOTHETICAL 6-2 Out of Luck Lottery

Maria buys a lottery ticket every week. The lottery is legal in her state and is administered through contracts between the state lottery commission and various convenience and liquor stores around the state. The way the lottery works in Maria's state is that she can punch in a 10-digit number on a machine in a local convenience store. Last week, Maria attempted to punch her number into the machine, but the machine was malfunctioning. Instead of generating a ticket with Maria's number on it, the machine produced a ticket with an entirely different number. Apparently, when the machine malfunctions, it generates random numbers. Maria took her ticket home and dutifully watched the weekly broadcast where the lottery winners were announced. She was shocked to learn that the number that she had wanted to punch into the machine turned out to be the winning number. Unfortunately, her ticket contains the randomly generated number. Maria wants to bring suit to enforce a third-party contract. Her theory is that she is a third-party beneficiary in the contract between the state lottery commission and the local convenience store where she always buys her ticket. Will Maria succeed on her claim as a third-party beneficiary?

Answer: Maria has certainly come up with a novel approach to third-party beneficiary contracts. However, it is important to review the original contract and to examine the reasons for its creation. In the states that have created a state lottery, almost all of them have done so as a way of generating income for the state educational system. Certainly, the educational system is a third-party beneficiary of these contracts, but is Maria? She is a person who likes to gamble and to try her luck at winning millions of dollars. She is not a third-party beneficiary. Does she fall into any other third-party category? She does not qualify as a third-party creditor, donee, or assignee. Maria has no cause of action against either the convenience store or the state lottery commission as a third-party beneficiary. [16]

Legal Subject of Contract

In order for a contract to be valid and enforceable, it must not only contain all of the foundational elements, such as mutual assent, consideration, and capacity of the parties, but also avoid some other issues. One such issue concerns the legality of the subject matter. A contract is void when the subject of the contract is illegal, such as a contract to engage in illegal activity or for an illegal purpose (see Exhibit 6-6).

A contract is void for legality when:

- it concerns the violation of a statute
- it violates common law
- it violate the laws of another country

EXHIBIT 6-6: Examples of contracts for illegal purposes.

CONTRACTS THAT ARE ILLEGAL BECAUSE OF SUBJECT

Contracts that involve illegal actions are void for a very simple reason. If this were not so, then a party seeking to enforce the contract could bring an action through the court system and request that a judge rule on the contract. This would place a judge in a bizarre and ironic position. He or she would be forced to enter an order compelling a party to obey the terms of the contract and violate the law.

Interestingly enough, a court is not permitted to declare that a certain contract is illegal unless the subject matter has actually been declared so by the legislature. A judge cannot, for example, attempt to create a new category of illegal contracts simply because he or she does not like the subject of the contract.

Suppose that one party realizes that the other party intends to use the contract for an illegal purpose, even though the contract itself does not contemplate an illegal activity? Jurisdictions are split between those that label such a contract as illegal and those that do not. Consider Hypothetical 6-3.

HYPOTHETICAL 6-3   Manny the Money Launderer

Carl has recently negotiated a contract with an acquaintance named Manny. Carl is in the business of selling new and used appliances. Manny wishes to purchase a large number of washing machines, dryers, refrigerators, and other large appliances. Carl is delighted. Manny has some unusual stipulations, however. For one thing, Manny insists on paying cash for all transactions. Manny does not wish his name to appear on any of the purchase orders or any other documents, except for the actual contract. Manny also wants to pick up his appliance orders at night and drive them immediately to a local airport, where they will be shipped to South America.

Although Carl is in desperate need of money and the contract with Manny would make him rich, he has some reservations. He suspects that Manny might be using drug money to purchase the appliances and, by shipping them to South America, he could either be laundering the money or using it to conceal drugs or money. Is the contract between Carl and Manny illegal?

At this point, the answer would be no. Carl has no direct knowledge of impropriety and has only his suspicions about the source of Manny's money. Mere suspicion of illegal activity does not rise to the level of a contract for an illegal purpose. However, Carl may wish to seriously consider his options, and may wish to ask some additional questions before he gets more deeply involved in this transaction.

There is no such split of opinion, however, when the contract involves a serious or heinous crime, such as murder. In such a situation, the contract is illegal and unenforceable in all situations, regardless of what either party knew or suspected.

CONTRACTS THAT ARE UNENFORCEABLE BECAUSE OF PUBLIC POLICY

As we have seen, a court may be limited in its ability to declare that a specific contract is illegal, but the category of "void for public policy reasons" is so broad that it more than makes up for it. The general rule followed in all jurisdictions is that any contract that violates public policy is void and unenforceable. When a contract requires the surrender of a fundamental right of a citizen, such as the right to enter into any contracts, this would be considered a violation of public policy and renders the contract void. There is no requirement that the subject of the contract actually be illegal, or that it involve a violation of criminal or civil codes, or even of common law. For a list of public policy reasons to void a contract, see Exhibit 6-7.

Sidebar:
A court can refuse to enforce a contract even where the parties have failed to allege that it is a violation of public policy.

Contracts to:

- Bribe government officials
- Bribe or otherwise influence the testimony of a witness in a civil and/or criminal proceeding
- Encourage one person to sue another
- Conceal or destroy evidence
- Rig the bidding at foreclosure sales or auctions
- Prevent a person from ever marrying anyone
- Prevent a person from engaging in any type of commerce
- Encourage one person to abandon his or her duty to another

EXHIBIT 6-7: Contracts violations of public policy.

Business Case File

The Scrapbook Company

Holly Ashby, owner and operator.

The Scrapbook Company is a store that provides a wealth of accessories to people who wish to make their own scrapbooks. It is owned and operated by Holly Ashby. Holly has a large inventory and is constantly ordering new and improved products to keep customers satisfied. She is an energetic and lively woman who obviously loves what she does.

Holly used to work in the store, but when the owner announced that she was thinking of selling, Holly decided to try to purchase it herself. Her parents helped her with the financing, and she purchased the store several years ago.

"I knew I could run the store no problem, because I've worked here for several years. I could manage the store and handle the inventory, so I was pretty confident about running the business. There is a big difference between managing a store and owning it. As a manager, you try to make sure that everything is good, but if business suffers on any particular day, it doesn't particularly worry you. But when you're the owner, you worry about that all the time. You worry about what's doing well and what isn't and what you can do to help improve business. If it doesn't go well, I have no one to blame but myself.

"One of the problems with running your own business is that you have a certain way of doing things. If I'm not here, no one else knows how to do it. I should have some redundancy built into the system, so that someone else can come in and take over for me at a moment's notice. Last week, for instance, my grandmother died, and it was hard to get anyone else in here to cover the store while I went to the funeral. If they can't run the computer, they can't run store. I got sick this winter, and when there wasn't anyone in the store, I just laid on the floor. I don't have anybody to come in for me when I'm sick. You are definitely tied down to the store. I have to be here when it opens and I have to stay here until it closes."

Because she runs the business herself, another concern for Holly is what would happen to the business in the event she was no longer able to conduct it. What if Holly was suddenly incapacitated? Who would negotiate contracts with others if Holley should no longer have the mental or physical capacity to do so? Spurred by these concerns, Holly formed a corporation, which shifted the concern about capacity from her as an individual to the capacity of the corporation. That way, she can concentrate on her personal relationships with her customers.

"Your personality is very important. You can have the best store in the world, but if your customers don't like you, they won't be coming back. A lot of times you have to watch what you say. You've just got to keep customers happy. Sometimes, you have to pretend to be happy.

"I love what I do. I love paying the bills. I love ordering new inventory. I love the store, but sometimes I don't love working 65 hours a week. Retail isn't for everyone. I happen to love it, but you have to find something that you're comfortable with."

(continued)

"I'd never work in an office. I can't keep paperwork straight, and I get bored easily. My systems work for me, but they are very unorganized. My mother is a very organized person, and my system drives her crazy."

Holly raises some very good points about the concerns that business people have when dealing with legal problems. Time is a precious commodity when you run your own business. When working with a businessperson who has a legal problem, you should realize that he or she does not have the time or the resources for a lengthy lawsuit. They need answers, and they need them fast. The sooner that your firm can provide those answers, the more likely they are likely to return for additional legal help.

Chapter Summary:

Capacity is a legal requirement of a contract. In order to have a binding contract, both parties to it must have legal capacity. Legal capacity is defined as the ability to know and understand the consequences of entering into a contract. There are people who lack capacity for specific reasons. Persons who have been declared to be insane lack the capacity to enter into a contract. In addition, a person may lack capacity because he or she has not reached legal adulthood. Contracts also may be voided where a person is acting under the influence of alcohol or other drugs at the time that the contract is created.

Both natural persons and artificial persons (corporations, etc.) may enter into a contract. When a contract is created to benefit a person who is not actually a party, this is referred to as a third-party beneficiary contract. A third party, under these circumstances, may have the right to bring action to enforce the contract. Contracts must not only meet the requirement of capacity, but they also must have a legal subject. A contract that contemplates the commission of a crime is a void contract and will not be enforced through the court system. Finally, a contract also may be unenforceable because of public policy reasons.

WEB SITES

The Virtual Chase (Online Legal Research)
http://www.virtualchase.com/
An online legal research link.

Georgia State University–College of Law
http://gsulaw.gsu.edu/metaindex/
A more or less complete listing of online legal research sites.

The White House
http://www.whitehouse.gov/
Provides access to the White House Web site.

U.S. District Court for Eastern District of Texas
http://www.txed.uscourts.gov/
Provides local rules, cases, telephone numbers, and a wealth of other information for the federal court system.

REVIEW QUESTIONS

1. The text mentions that contracts between husbands and wives are generally not enforceable. What about prenuptial agreements? Aren't these valid contracts? Explain your answer.

2. Why do the courts impose the requirement of capacity in creating a contract?

3. Define legal capacity to contract.

4. How is a person's capacity to contract affected by advanced age?

5. What is a third-party beneficiary contract?

6. What are some examples of contracts that have an illegal subject?

7. When would a contract be considered to be void for public policy reasons?

8. What are some examples of public policy reasons that would void a contract?

9. Why is a minor only able to create a voidable contract?

10. Why is the standard for capacity to create a will different from the standard to create a contract?

11. When a person enters into a bad bargain, why is this not an example of lack of capacity?

12. Explain why the court did not rule that the elderly man in "A Case of Capacity?" was mentally incompetent.

13. Explain how you would avoid breaching a client's confidentiality.

14. Can a physical impairment result in mental incompetence? Explain.

15. What effect did the Industrial Revolution have on contract law?

16. Why would a person of lower than average intelligence still possess legal capacity?

17. Why is a person unable to enter into a contract when a guardian has been appointed to represent him or her?

18. What is the difference in terms of legal capacity to contract between a person who has partial capacity compared to a person who is totally incapacitated?

19. Does everyone who suffers from mental illness automatically lack capacity? Why or why not?

20. How do contracts that are void for legality differ from contracts that are void for public policy?

HANDS-ON ASSIGNMENT

Draft a contract that gives you authority to carry out a transaction for a friend. The transaction involves the purchase of an automobile. Your friend has authorized you to spend up $1500 and no more. Your friend also wants the title to be transferred to him or her on the 2nd day of next month.

PRACTICAL APPLICATION

Review your state's law on incapacity. What types of mental conditions are prima facie evidence of legal incapacity to contract?

What is the minimum age that a person in your state must achieve before he or she can be legally bound by a contract? Does your state have a rule concerning "emancipated adults"? What are emancipated adults?

HELP THIS BUSINESS

Suppose that Holly Ashby of the Scrapbook Company has recently entered into a contract with a manufacturer of high-quality, rubber stamps that depict water birds. The stamps are created and manufactured by a man named Walter Byrd. The terms of the contract provide that when the manufacturer, Water Bird Stamps, a sole proprietorship delivers 100 rubber stamps with a water fowl theme, Holly will pay, within 10 days of delivery, $2.50 per stamp. Holly has a concern, however. In her negotiations with Walter Byrd, Holly has noticed that he tends to talk to himself and sometimes with other people who are not actually in the room. After her last meeting with Walter, Walter's wife took her aside and told her that there is a possibility of Walter being involuntarily committed to a state mental hospital. Holly wants the rubber stamps very much because there is nothing else like them on the market, but she wants a contract that will protect her rights and the uniqueness of Walter's manufactured stamps should something happen to him.

Draft a contract setting out these basic details and include a provision that answers Holly's concerns.

KEY TERMS

capacity	guardian
artificial person	authority
minor	beneficiary

ENDNOTES

1   *A History of American Law*, Lawrence Friedman, Simon and Schuster New York, 1973, p. 244.

2. *Meserve v. Jordan Marsh Co.*, 165 N.E.2d 905 (Mass. 1960).

3   *Hauer v. Union State Bank of Wautoma*, 192 Wis.2d 576, 532 N.W.2d 456 (1995).

4   *Uribe v. Olson*, 42 Or. App. 647, 601 P.2d 818 (1979).

5   *Wilson v. Findley*, 223 Iowa 1281, 275 N.W. 47 (1937).

6   *Grayson v. Linton*, 63 Idaho 695, 125 P.2d 318 (1942).

7   *Matter of Guardianship of Hedin*, 528 N.W.2d 567 (Iowa, 1995).

8   *Handley v. Handley*, 172 Kan. 659, 243 P.2d 204 (1952).

9   CJS Contracts §145.

10 *Willgerodt on Behalf of Majority Peoples' Fund for the 21st Century, Inc v. Hohri*, 953 F. Supp. 557 (S.D.N.Y. 1997); CJS Contracts §141.

11 *Meserve v. Jordan Marsh Co.*, 340 Mass. 660, 165 N.E.2d 905 (1960).

12 *Kansas City N.O. Nelson Co. v. Mid-Western Constr. Co.*, 782 S.W.2d 672 (Mo. App.).

13 *Hartman Ranch Co. v. Associated Oil Co.*, 10 Cal. 2d 232, 73 P2d 1163 (1937).

14 Am. Jur. Contracts §452.

15 *Don Rose Oil Co., Inc. v. Lindsley*, 160 Cal. App. 3d 752, 206 Cal Rptr 670 (1984).

16 *Brown v. California State Lottery Com.*, 232 Cal. App. 3d 1335, 284 Cal Rptr 108, 91 (1991)

 For additional resources, visit our Web site at www.westlegalstudies.com

CHAPTER 7

PUTTING IT IN WRITING

Focus of this chapter: This chapter develops the importance of written contract provisions. The statute of frauds is examined in detail. This chapter lays the foundation for subsequent chapters in which we will explore contract clauses and provisions. We will also examine the purpose of the Statute of Frauds and how this ancient legal doctrine continues to have relevance today.

Chapter Objectives:
At the completion of this chapter, you should be able to:

- Explain the historical development of the Statute of Frauds
- Describe the various types of contracts that are required to be in writing under the Statute of Frauds
- Explain why certain contracts, even those not covered by the Statute of Frauds, are usually put into writing
- Explain the types of concerns raised when putting an agreement into written form
- Explain the exception to the Statute of Frauds known as "partial performance"
- Describe other exceptions to the application of the Statute of Frauds
- Explain how the UCC has modified the Statute of Frauds
- Explain how courts calculate time periods under the Statute of Frauds
- Define the significance of a "memorandum of contract" under the Statute of Frauds
- Describe the wide variety of writings that satisfy the Statute of Frauds

Introduction to Written Contracts

So far, our discussions about contract law have made no clear distinction between oral contracts and written contracts. The reason for this is that basic contract law uses a similar approach regardless of whether the contract is a 100-page contract or a simple handshake agreement. However, the vast majority of business contracts are in some form of writing. Writing down the terms of an agreement is simple common sense. When the parties memorialize their agreement, they can avoid any potential misunderstandings and iron out certain details that might be left vague with a simple verbal agreement. There is another reason to put a contract into writing: the law may require it. There are certain categories of contracts that must be in writing. In the first part of this chapter, we will explore these various categories of contracts and explain the function of the Statute of Frauds. Later, we will explore specific examples of contract provisions to lay the foundation for future chapters where we examine contract clause provisions in much greater detail.

The Statute of Frauds

Statute of Frauds: Any of various states' law, modeled after an old English law, that require many types of contracts to be signed and in writing to be enforceable in court.

The **Statute of Frauds** is an ancient legal doctrine that requires certain forms of contracts to be in writing before they will be enforceable. Under the Statute of Frauds, as it was first enacted in England, when a contract involves a specific category of agreement, some form of writing was required. If the contact were not in writing, then it was considered to be a void agreement.

The Statute of Frauds would more properly be known as the Statute against Frauds. The purpose of the statute, as originally enacted by the British Parliament, was to prevent fraud. There are certain categories of transactions between individuals that can have profound impact on a person's finances. Given the fact that some of these transactions were open to fraud, the British Parliament created a statute that required contracts to be in writing so that anyone could read their provisions and understand the consequences of the contract. In addition, the statute also required that the person "to be charged" with a duty under a contract must sign his or her name to the document. Being "charged" under a contract meant to take on a duty and assuming this duty had to be done in writing.

A Short History of the Statute of Frauds in America

Most states adopted the original English statute verbatim and have made very few changes to it since. However, there is one important exception, found in the provisions of the Uniform Commercial Code (UCC), which created its own version of the Statute of Frauds. We will discuss the UCC in a later chapter.

Sidebar:
You should always review your state's Statute of Frauds when dealing with any contract that falls into the category discussed in the text.

Because most states adopted the Statute of Frauds as it was originally created, we will discuss the Statute of Frauds throughout this chapter as though each state's statute is identical to that of every other state. However, you should keep in mind that there may be some variations (see Exhibit 7-1).

N.Y. GEN. OBLIG. §5-701

§5-701. Agreements required to be in writing

a. Every agreement, promise or undertaking is void, unless it or some note or memorandum thereof be in writing, and subscribed by the party to be charged therewith, or by his lawful agent, if such agreement, promise or undertaking:

1. By its terms is not to be performed within one year from the making thereof or the performance of which is not to be completed before the end of a lifetime;

2. Is a special promise to answer for the debt, default or miscarriage of another person;

3. Is made in consideration of marriage, except mutual promises to marry;

[4. Repealed]

5. Is a subsequent or new promise to pay a debt discharged in bankruptcy;

6. Notwithstanding section 2-201 of the Uniform Commercial Code, if the goods be sold at public auction, and the auctioneer at the time of the sale, enters in a sale book, a memorandum specifying the nature and price of the property sold, the terms of the sale, the name of the purchaser, and the name of the person on whose account the sale was made, such memorandum is equivalent in effect to a note of the contract or sale, subscribed by the party to be charged therewith;

[7, 8. Repealed]

9. Is a contract to assign or an assignment, with or without consideration to the promisor, of a life or health or accident insurance policy, or a promise, with or without consideration to the promisor, to name a beneficiary of any such policy. This provision shall not apply to a policy of industrial life or health or accident insurance.

EXHIBIT 7-1: New York's Statute of Frauds *(continued)*.

> 10. Is a contract to pay compensation for services rendered in negotiating a loan, or in negotiating the purchase, sale, exchange, renting or leasing of any real estate or interest therein, or of a business opportunity, business, its good will, inventory, fixtures or an interest therein, including a majority of the voting stock interest in a corporation and including the creating of a partnership interest. "Negotiating" includes procuring an introduction to a party to the transaction or assisting in the negotiation or consummation of the transaction. This provision shall apply to a contract implied in fact or in law to pay reasonable compensation but shall not apply to a contract to pay compensation to an auctioneer, an attorney at law, or a duly licensed real estate broker or real estate salesman.

EXHIBIT 7-1: New York's Statute of Frauds *(continued)*.

Sidebar:
Courts have consistently held that the legislature has no power to interfere with the right to contract, but it can put restrictions on how this right is exercised. The right to enter into contracts is guaranteed under the U.S. Constitution, but the legislature can enact specific restrictions on this right, such as requiring some contracts to be in writing.

Sidebar:
The original English statute was named, "An Act for the Prevention of Frauds and Perjuries."[4]

Sidebar:
Interestingly enough, the country that developed the Statute of Frauds repealed it in 1954. English jurists considered it a "technicality" that often stood in the way of justice.[5]

CATEGORIES OF TRANSACTIONS THAT FALL UNDER THE STATUTE OF FRAUDS

Simply because a contract is required to be in writing under the Statute of Frauds does not mean that all aspects of the parties' negotiations must be in writing. It simply means that the final product, that is, their agreement, must be in writing.

The Statute of Frauds covers the following types of transactions:

1. Contracts involving testamentary transactions (wills, etc.)
2. Contracts to answer for the debt of another
3. Contracts in anticipation of marriage (prenuptial/antenuptial agreements)
4. Contracts for the sale of land
5. Contracts that cannot be performed within one year of the date of their creation[1]
6. Contracts for the sale of goods exceeding $500 in value[2]
7. Contracts for the sale of securities (stocks, bonds)[3]

Numbers 6 and 7 have been absorbed into the Uniform Commercial Code provisions adopted by all states. We will discuss this aspect later in the chapter.

Contracts Involving Testamentary Transactions (Wills, Etc.)

When a person makes disposition of his or her property through a will, the law requires that the will be in writing. Like so many of the rules regarding the Statute of Frauds, the reason is simple: it avoids a minefield of contentions among the surviving heirs. By requiring that the testator write down his or her desires about dispositions of property many of the questions about the testator's intent are resolved. When a testator wishes to make disposition of real estate, this is required to be in writing not only because it involves a testamentary transaction but also because transfers of interest in real estate are required to be in writing, as well.

The interesting point about testamentary writings is that the rules applying them are very liberal. Wills have been typed, handwritten, even scrawled on scrap pieces of paper. As long as they satisfy the general requirements of a will, courts will enforce the testator's wishes.

Contract to Answer for the Debt of Another

The Statute of Frauds requires that when one person agrees to pay the debt owed by another this agreement must be in writing. Voluntarily assuming another person's debt is a significant legal transaction and will place this person in the position of paying off the entire balance owed by another. This, like so many other instances covered by the Statute of Frauds, is not a step to be taken lightly.

One of the primary reasons for specifying a written agreement in this situation is to prevent a third party from being deceived into assuming another person's debts. In most states, the agreement must not only be in writing, but must be signed by the third party who is undertaking this burden.

Contracts in Anticipation of Marriage (Prenuptial/Antenuptial Agreements)

When two people are contemplating marriage and enter into an agreement about how their marital estate will be divided in the event of divorce, this agreement is covered by the Statute of Frauds and must, therefore, be in writing. Commonly referred to as **prenuptial** or **antenuptial** agreements, these agreements are used in situations where one spouse brings considerable assets to the marriage and his or her family wishes to keep those assets in the original family, rather than have them divided up through a divorce proceeding.

prenuptial/antenuptial agreement: A contract between persons about to marry. It usually concerns the way that property will be handled during the marriage, the way it will be divided in case of divorce, and the limits on spousal support obligations.

Prenuptial agreements must be made prior to marriage. They have no effect if they are drawn up after marriage. Once a husband and wife have married, as far as the law is concerned, they are considered to be a single entity. As we have seen in other contexts, married couples cannot contract with each other.

The other reason to require prenuptial agreements to be in writing is a practical consideration. When parties later decide to end the marriage the relationship between them is at best strained if not openly antagonistic. To require persons in this situation to testify truthfully about an agreement to limit recovery from the marital estate would be ridiculous. In addition to that, an oral agreement, made years or even decades before is open to considerable interpretation. A written agreement, made before marriage, does away with most of these problems.

Live-in Lovers

In recent years, many states have amended their Statute of Frauds to include agreements between persons who cohabit but do not marry. In many such cases, the parties may have entered into an oral agreement about the disposition of their property if they should choose to split up. Contesting these oral agreements presented all of the same difficulties as outlined in the previous paragraph. In order to avoid these problems, many states simply added cohabitation agreements as a form of contract required by the Statute of Frauds.[6]

Contracts for the Sale of Land

Requiring a writing in real estate transactions may have been one of the primary reasons for the creation of the original Statute of Frauds. The sale of real estate, especially personal residences, remains one of the biggest financial transactions most people will ever be involved in and the potential for fraud is as real today, as it was three centuries ago.

Why should real estate transactions enjoy such a special status under the law? There are a wide variety of reasons. First of all, land was the primary source of wealth in ancient England. (The British Royal family continues to be the wealthiest landholding family in the world). Because of the wealth and status derived from land possession, many people wished to acquire land, often without regard to the legality of the transactions. Requiring real estate transactions to be in writing helped avoid a practice of one person usurping another's ownership in land through fraud or trickery. However, there is another reason to require real estate transactions to be in writing: the writings themselves can be collected in the public records.

By requiring a written system of real estate transactions, the Statute of Frauds fostered an entire governmental industry. Land record offices, deed rooms, and public records all owe their existence in some measure to the original Statute of Frauds. Almost all states have some form of deed or land office that is responsible for storing deeds, contracts, and other real estate transactions.

The role of the Statute of Frauds in real estate transactions may account for the continued vitality of this rule well into the 21st century. When a person purchases real estate, the deed that proves this event is recorded at the local courthouse. Anyone can go there and see a copy of it. This creates an open and transparent system for transferring interests in real estate. This system gives creditors, family members, and the government the right to discover who owns or does not own certain parcels of land. It promotes honesty and fair dealing and ensures that tracts of land will not remain vacant and unused simply because no one knows the status of the property (see Exhibit 7-2).

Contracts That Cannot Be Performed within One Year of the Date of Their Creation

All states have a provision of their Statute of Frauds that requires any agreement that cannot, by its own terms, be performed within a year to be in

- Sales of real property
- Leases of real property for a term greater than one year
- Restrictive covenants on the use of the property
- Contracts for the sale of real estate
- Mortgages
- Liens

EXHIBIT 7-2: Real estate transactions that must be in writing under the statute of frauds.

Source: *Avey v. Via*, 225 Ky. 155, 7 S.W.2d 1057 (1928).

writing. In most jurisdictions, an oral contract for a term greater than a year is void and cannot be enforced through the court system.

Calculating Time Periods under the Statute of Frauds

This rule raises some interesting legal and evidentiary issues. For instance, what qualifies as the date of "creation" of the contract and how do the courts calculate the time periods involved?

For purposes of the Statute of Frauds, the "creation" of a contract refers to the day on which the agreement was made. This means the precise date when all of the elements of a contract were brought together: offer–acceptance, consideration, mutual assent, and so on. It does not refer to the negotiations and counteroffers leading up to the formation of the contract.

The time period runs from the date of the agreement, not the date that actual performance of the contract begins. Suppose, for example, that a contract states that it will run from May 1 of this year and will expire on April 30 of next year. Would such a contract need to be in writing under the Statute of Frauds?

Most courts would rule that it would not. The reason is that the courts calculate a year using the following system: the date that the contract is created is not counted. Instead, the following day is the first full day of the contract. A year is then calculated based on that date. The year expires on the same date the following year, at the conclusion of the day (midnight), unless some other time is expressly provided.

> **Sidebar:**
> To calculate a year under the Statute of Frauds, begin with the first full day following the date that the contract was created and end with the one-year anniversary of that date (see Exhibit 7-3).

WHAT TYPE OF WRITING SATISFIES THE STATUTE OF FRAUDS?

So far, we have consistently referred to specific categories of contracts that must be in "writing." However, what type of writing will satisfy the Statute of Frauds? Will any type of writing suffice, or must the writing be a formal, typed contract?

> The one-year rule under the Statute of Frauds covers all of the following arrangements:
>
> - An agreement to extend credit to a customer for a period of up to two years
>
> - An oral agreement to extend credit to a lender to make regular, annual purchases for the next five years
>
> - An agreement to buy farm land on an "installment contract" for ten years

EXHIBIT 7-3: The one-year rule.

Source: *Shaughnessy v. Eidsmo*, 222 Minn. 141, 23 N.W.2d 362 (1946).

The simple, and somewhat misleading, answer is to say that a contract covered by the Statute of Frauds must meet the Statute's requirements. But that doesn't really answer the question. What are those requirements?

Under the Statute of Frauds a "writing" must identify the following elements:

- The Parties
- The Property
- The Consideration
- The Promises
- The Time and Manner of Performance[8]

HYPOTHETICAL 7-1   The Reality TV Show and the Statute of Frauds

Last year, Rich and Annabelle were both contestants on a reality show called *The Best Man*. The premise of the show is that one woman, in this case Annabelle, has 25 suitors and then, through interviews, group dates, and one-on-one meetings slowly winnows the field down to one man. Annabelle chose Rich and he proposed to her on national television. However, Annabelle is also the heiress to a multibillion dollar automobile tire business and her family insisted that she sign a prenuptial agreement before marrying Rich.

As a way to spite her parents, Annabelle wrote the following on the wedding dress presented to her by the producers of the television show:

"Rich, you agree that you won't claim any of my (Annabelle's) family's money if we get divorced or if I die."

She signed it and, again on national television, Rich also signed it.

Seven weeks later, when the couple is going through divorce, Rich contests the wedding gown contract by claiming that it fails to abide by the terms of the Statute of Frauds. Is he right?

Answer: If this unusual writing is a prenuptial agreement, then it must satisfy the elements of the Statute of Frauds. Does it?

Does it identify the parties? The writing on the dress certainly identifies the parties to the purported contract. It identifies both Rich and Annabelle and also includes their signature.

Does it identify the property? The writing specifically mentions Annabelle's family money and would, at least arguably, satisfy that element.

Does it identify the consideration? The consideration here is presumed. Rich is giving up something of value (any claim on Annabelle's estate) in exchange for something of value (marrying Annabelle). Consideration would appear to be satisfied.

Is it specific about the promise? Again, the answer seems to be yes. Rich is agreeing to waive any rights he would normally have to Annabelle's estate.

Does is satisfy the elements of time and manner of performance? Although we have some potential problems here, again the answer appears to be yes. Rich is waiving his rights in the event of divorcing Annabelle or in the event of her death. Both are specific events.

Although Annabelle created the written contract on her wedding dress out of spite, it appears to be an agreement that meets all of the requirements of the Statute of Frauds.

No Particular Contract Form Is Required

Under the Statute of Frauds, there is no requirement that a specific type of contract form be used. A memorandum of agreement setting out the above elements would satisfy the Statute. There is no requirement, for instance, that a professionally printed contract must be used, or that the contract be notarized or contain specific language, such as "party of the first part."

As long as the writing records the details of the actual transaction, it will satisfy the Statute of Frauds. Because of this, contracts can be created under very unconventional circumstances and using unusual terms (see Exhibit 7-4 on the following page).

A **memorandum of contract** may be sufficient under the Statute of Frauds even though the parties did not prepare it with the Statute in mind. However, both parties must sign the memorandum. A memorandum of contract is simply a printed memorandum that notes the important details of the contract. It is often used to draft the later, official contract.

Preparing the Writing

There is no requirement that ink be used to prepare the contract or the memorandum of contract. A contract written in pencil is sufficient.[9] No special paper is required. A fully legal and binding contract can be written on any type of paper, even a scratch pad.[10] The writing also

Sidebar:
Most states define "written" or "writing" as printing, typewriting, or any other intentional reduction to tangible form.

memorandum of contract: A writing that proves the existence of a contract.

Sidebar:
Contracts that satisfy the Statute of Frauds have been written on scraps of paper and even on T-shirts.

In his short story, "The Man Who Would be King," Kipling's two protagonists, "Peachey" Carnehan and Danny Dravot resolve to make themselves kings of distant (and fictitious) Kafiristan. Although Kipling was probably not concerned with the Statute of Frauds when he wrote his story, the contract does pass muster as a legally binding, if unconventional, document.

> *"This Contract between me and you persuing witnesseth in the name of God—Amen and so forth."*
>
> *(One) That me and you will settle this matter together; i.e., to be Kings of Kafiristan.*
>
> *(Two) That you and me will not, while this matter is being settled, look at any Liquor, nor any Woman black, white, or brown, so as to get mixed up with one or the other harmful.*
>
> *(Three) That we conduct ourselves with Dignity and Discretion, and if one of us gets into trouble the other will stay by him.*
>
> *Signed by you and me this day,*
>
> *Peachey Taliaferro Carnehan*
>
> *Daniel Dravot*
>
> *Both Gentlemen at Large*

EXHIBIT 7-4: Rudyard Kipling and the Statute of Frauds.

Source: *Collected Stories*, Rudyard Kipling, Knopf (October, 1994).

may be contained in a letter, telegram, or fax. The terms of the contract can be contained in several different documents.[11] However, they must cross-reference each other. (See the Appendix for an example of a contract that was created with the Statute of Frauds in mind. See also Exhibit 7-5.)

WORDING REQUIRED UNDER THE STATUTE OF FRAUDS

Courts have been very liberal in interpreting the language required to create a binding contract under the Statute of Frauds. They have consistently ruled that no particular language is required. For instance, there is no requirement of "legalese" in a contract. *Legalese* is the term used to describe the confusing, legalistic terms often found in contracts and other legal documents. For example, there is no requirement that a contract use the terms "promisor/promisee," "consideration," or "detriment." The final decision on

- Letters
- Faxes
- Checks
- Deeds
- Public Records
- Legal Pleadings
- Receipts
- Payroll Stubs

EXHIBIT 7-5: Other types of documents that will satisfy the statute of frauds.

Source: *Meyer v. Redmond,* 205 N.Y. 478, 98 N.E. 906 (1912).

the legality of the contract and the terms used is left to the judge who is asked to enforce it.[12]

Signature of the Parties

The best practice is to have both parties sign a contract. This is also the standard set out in the Statute of Frauds. Before a contract can be enforced against a party, that party must have signed it. This rule is modified under contracts governed by the UCC.[13]

Is Delivery of the Writing Required?

One interesting point about the Statute of Frauds concerns what happens when the writing is complete. Must both parties receive a copy of the contract before it is binding? In a typical real estate transaction, for instance, all states have a requirement that the deed must not only be signed by the seller but also that the deed be delivered to the buyer. Delivery means physically handing the writing to the other party.

There is no delivery requirement under the Statute of Frauds. A contract is fully legal even if the other party does not receive a copy of it. There are some jurisdictions that do require delivery in certain commercial transactions under the UCC.[14] We will discuss those transactions in the next chapter.

An Exception to the Statute of Frauds: Partial Performance

The purpose of the Statute of Frauds is to prevent fraud and injustice to the contract parties. To that end, the Statute of Frauds will not be employed to bring about an unjust result. Suppose, for example, that one party, in full knowledge that a particular contract should be in writing under the Statute of Frauds negotiates an oral contract with another. Then, after the second party has performed under the contract terms, the first party refuses to comply, stating that the Statute of Frauds makes the contract illegal. Although this is technically correct, the courts have created an exception to the Statute of Frauds for this specific situation. This doctrine is referred to as **partial performance.**

partial performance: Carrying out some, but not all, of a contract, or doing something in reliance on another's promise.

Partial performance is a theory that allows the court to override the Statute of Frauds when justice requires it. Using a court's equity powers, a judge can rule that because one party partially performed under a contract that was technically void under the Statute of Frauds, the contract will be considered valid and enforceable.[15] Courts have broad powers to enforce the true purpose of the Statute of Frauds.

ALLEGING THE STATUTE OF FRAUDS IN PLEADINGS

When a contract is in dispute, the plaintiff must prove that the writing is a transaction that is covered by the statute. It is one of the essential elements of the plaintiff's case and must be proven at trial. The plaintiff must prove not only that the contract falls under the Statute of Frauds but also that the contract is in writing.

The Statute of Frauds is a defense and can be pleaded by the defendant in his or her answer.[16] However, it cannot be raised as a defense to a contract that has already been executed. The Statute of Frauds is only a defense to executory, not executed, contracts.[17] When a contract has been completed, there are no issues about formation to be litigated and questions about the Statute of Frauds are essentially moot.

Although the Statute of Frauds can invalidate a contract, it does not affect related claims that derive from the contract, such as claims of fraud, undue influence, and so on.[18] A party can still bring a suit for fraud, or other irregularity, even though the Statute of Frauds was not properly followed. The Statute of Frauds can only be invoked as a defense by a party to the contract, not by third parties.[19]

HYPOTHETICAL 7-2   The Book Deal

Vague Books Production Company is in the business of creating new authors. For a stated price, Vague Books will create a book on business law that appears to be written by the client. The client's name will appear on the front cover of the book and on the title page of the book, even though the text was actually written by a member of the Vague Books staff. The price for this service is 14 monthly installment payments of $400.

Sasha wants to be an author but doesn't have the time to actually write. She contacts Vague Books and creates an oral contract for the service. She receives her textbook, complete with her name on the front cover and on the title page. She proudly displays it in her home and shows it off to friends. A local, unpublished author becomes irate about the arrangement and brings suit alleging that Sasha's arrangement violates the Statute of Frauds. How does the court rule?

Answer: Sidestepping the issue of whether or not the author had a legal basis to complain about the arrangement, the fact that it violated the Statute of Frauds is no longer an issue. The arrangement has been completed, to the satisfaction of both parties and because the author was not a party to the contract, he could not challenge it on the basis of a violation of the Statute of Frauds.

Sidebar:
The Statute of Frauds will not be used to perpetrate fraud.[20]

The Statute of Frauds under the UCC

With the adoption of the Uniform Commercial Code in all states (in more or less complete form), the Statute of Frauds underwent a significant change. Before the adoption of the UCC, states had at least seven types of contracts to which the Statute of Frauds applied. However, the UCC has specific provisions regarding contracts that must be in writing and at least two now fall under the jurisdiction of the UCC provisions. These two are:

1. When the contract involves the sale of goods for the price of $500 or more, or

2. Contracts for the sale of securities (stocks, security agreements, bonds and other personal property not already covered in other sections)

Under the provisions of the UCC, in order to enforce a contract in either category, it must be in writing and signed by the parties involved.

Under the UCC's Statute of Frauds, a minor error will not void a contract. For instance, when a contract incorrectly states a term, it will not be voided. Instead, the parties will be given latitude to clear up discrepancies. The UCC has a very liberal approach to the whole issue of what constitutes a writing and what will satisfy its own version of the Statute of Frauds (see Exhibit 7-6).

The UCC requires a written contract for the following situations:

- A contract for the sale of goods for the price of $500 or more[i]

- A contract for the sale of securities[ii]

- A contract for the sale of personal property not otherwise covered[iii]

EXHIBIT 7-6: The statute of frauds under the Uniform Commercial Code.

[i] Uniform Commercial Code §2-201.
[ii] Uniform Commercial Code §8-319.
[iii] Uniform Commercial Code §1-206; Restatement of Contracts §110.

The UCC's approach to the Statute of Frauds is usually seen as a modification and an update on the entire concept of how and under what circumstances one party might defraud another. As such, the UCC's approach is not as extensive as the original Statute of Frauds.[21] The original Statute of Frauds was created to control a whole host of potential abuses. The UCC only focuses on sales and giving security for loans.

Exceptions to the UCC's Rule on the Statute of Frauds

Just as we saw with the rule of partial performance under the Statute of Frauds, there are situations in which the UCC creates an exception to its own version of the Statute of Frauds. The writing requirement can be circumvented in three instances:

- A writing is not required for specially manufactured goods, or
- When a party admits in a court that an oral contract existed, or
- If the goods have been delivered, paid for and accepted.[22]

The UCC does not require a written requirement when the parties have entered into an agreement to produce specific or unique goods. A party's admission that an oral contract existed is sufficient evidence to overcome the original requirement that the contract must be in writing. After all, if the party admits that there was a contract, the issue about a contract's existence is no longer pertinent. When goods have been delivered, paid for, and accepted, the UCC also ceases to require written contracts. In this situation, the contract is executed and, like the original Statute of Frauds, the existence of the contract is now a moot point.

Concerns with Written Contracts

Attorneys are the people usually selected to draft contracts. Many times, you, as the legal assistant, may be called on to research a particular provision of that written contract to ensure that it is legally valid. Exhibit 7-7 provides a checklist of items to consider when drafting a contract that is covered by the Statute of Frauds.

✓ PARALEGAL CHECKLIST

- ☐ Are the parties named in the contract?
- ☐ Are the parties' addresses provided?
- ☐ What is the consideration?
- ☐ What are the precise duties of each party?
- ☐ What obligations are the parties assuming?
- ☐ How long will the contract run (don't forget the Statute of Frauds)?
- ☐ Is the contract dated?

EXHIBIT 7-7: Drafting a contract under the Statute of Frauds.

Source: Am. Jur. Contracts §17.

SPECIAL CLAUSES IN CONTRACTS

We deal with specific contract clauses later in this text, but a word about them here is also appropriate. The rule followed in all jurisdictions is that any ambiguities in the contract are construed against the party who created them. This also holds when the party's attorney drafted the contract. In order to avoid ambiguities in contracts, the following should be considered:

- Does the clause clearly explain its purpose?
- Is the clause precise about:
  - Time for payment?
  - Amount to be paid?
  - Conditions that must be met before payment will be made?
- What is considered to be a breach of the contract?
- Is a party required to give notice that a particular contract clause has been breached?
- Is the contract precise about who is to be paid?
- Is the contract precise about where payment is to be made?
- Is the contract precise about the form of payment (cash, personal check, certified funds, etc.)?[23]

STATUTE OF FRAUDS CONSIDERATIONS IN DRAFTING CONTRACTS

Because the majority of this chapter is spent discussing the concept of the Statute of Frauds, we will focus on this topic as it relates to the Statute. The first, and most obvious, question that should be asked before drafting a contract is: Does the Statute of Frauds apply?

If the Statute of Frauds applies, then the contract must be in writing. Although putting any contract into writing is usually a good idea, if the contract falls within the list of required contracts, then it will not be enforceable unless it is in writing.

Once a determination has been made about the applicability of the Statute of Frauds, the next concern is to ensure that the written contract meets the requirements of the Statute. Exhibit 7-8 contains a list of items to double-check when drafting a contract covered by the Statute of Frauds.

INTERNAL INCONSISTENCIES IN A CONTRACT

What happens when a contract has internal inconsistencies? Consider the following hypothetical.

HYPOTHETICAL 7-3   The Confusing Contract

Hal and David have decided to enter into a contract with one another. David is a landlord and owns several pieces of commercial property. Hal wishes to rent one of these properties in order to open a health food store. They negotiated a lease for a five-year period. David types up the agreement during a meeting that he has with Hal. David prints off what he believes is the finished contract and hands it to Hal for signature. Later, Hal takes out a pencil and writes in some additional language changing some of the terms. One change, appearing on page 2 of the document, is a provision that states that the contract term is for a four-year period. This is in direct conflict with the typewritten provisions on page 1, where they negotiated a term of five years. Later, when David sues Hal to enforce the provisions of the lease, the court is presented with a problem: Which provision is controlling? Does the judge enforce the typewritten portion of the lease or the handwritten portion?

Answer: The judge will enforce the typewritten portion of the lease. Most jurisdictions follow a rule that guides judges in this context. When there are conflicting provisions in a contract and one is typed and the other is handwritten, enforce the typed provision.

☐ Which document(s) contains the agreed-on terms of the contracts?

☐ Which document(s) will be designated mere correspondence or preliminary negotiations and will not be considered to be the actual contract?

☐ Is the contract governed by the UCC? (If so, then that Code's rules must be followed about written contracts?

☐ Does it identify the parties?

☐ Is it signed by all parties?

☐ Is the consideration for the contract clearly stated?

☐ Is the contract specific about the parties' promises?

☐ Is the contract specific about the time and manner of performance under the contract?

EXHIBIT 7-8: Double-checking a contract under the Statute of Frauds.

Why would the rule set out in Hypothetical 7-3 exist? First of all, the typed portion of the contract is what was produced when both parties were present and, if there had been some disagreement about the terms, presumably it would have been cleared up on the spot. There is also a practical concern here. Typed words are easier to read than handwritten words. There are individuals in the world whose handwriting is so poor that it is almost indecipherable. Faced with two possible clauses, one in typed print and the other garbled handwriting, the courts usually opt for the former.[24]

The Statute of Frauds and Real Estate Transactions

As we have seen, almost all types of real estate conveyances require a writing to be enforceable under the Statute of Frauds. There is a wide variety of real estate contracts, from listing agreements to offer to purchase contracts. Each has its own peculiar challenges under the Statute of Frauds.

LISTING AGREEMENTS

Listing agreements are the contract between a real estate broker and the seller. This contract sets out the duties of the broker to advertise the house for sale and use reasonable efforts to produce a buyer who is ready, willing, and able to purchase the home. In exchange for providing this service, the broker will be paid a commission based on a percentage of the sale price. There are several different types of listing agreements, but they all provide this basic arrangement.

OFFER OF PURCHASE AND CONTRACT

When the broker produces a buyer, the seller and buyer enter into an offer of purchase and contract for the sale of the home. This contract sets out the negotiated details between the buyer and seller, including:

- The sale price
- The date for the closing
- The purchase of any items of personal property inside the home (such as drapes, window treatments, or appliances)
- The conditions on which the sale is predicated, such as obtaining sufficient financing to purchase the home and a passing report on the structure by a building inspector
- Particular contract clause provisions, such as "time is of the essence"

Time Is of the Essence Contract Clause

When an offer of purchase and contract contains a "time is of the essence" clause, this means that the parties have negotiated a specific date for the closing. If the closing does not occur on that date, then the contract is voided and the parties are no longer bound to conclude the transaction. A party might insist on this provision if there is another sale that must be completed (such as the buyer's current home) before the transaction can be completed.

Sidebar:
The most common type of listing agreement is the Multiple Listing. Under this arrangement, the broker who contracts with the seller advertises that he or she will share the commission with any other broker who produces a buyer. It is essentially an offer to share the commission and greatly improves the chance that the house will be sold.

The Case of the Hostile Hay Haulers[25]
OPINION
MOWBRAY, Justice

This case centers about the enforceability of an oral agreement to purchase 1500 tons of hay. The principal issue presented for our determination is whether the periodic accountings prepared by the seller and sent to the buyer covering the sale of the hay constituted confirming memoranda within the provisions of NRS 104.2201(2) of the Uniform Commercial Code and, if so, whether the seller sent them within a reasonable time as required by that statute so that the oral agreement is not barred by the statute of frauds. The district judge ruled that the mandates of NRS 104.2201(2) had been satisfied, and he upheld the validity of the agreement.

We agree, and we affirm the judgment of the lower court.

1. THE FACTS

Appellant J. L. Azevedo is a rancher who buys and sells hay. He is licensed to do so, and he is bonded by appellant United States Fidelity and Guaranty Company. Respondent Bolton F. Minister operates the Minister Ranch near Yerington, Nevada, where he raises and sells large quantities of hay. In early November 1967, Azevedo approached Minister for the purpose of buying hay. Terms were discussed. Several days later an agreement was reached by telephone. Both parties acknowledge that Azevedo agreed to purchase hay from Minister at a price of $26.50 per ton for the first and second cuttings and $28 per ton for the third cutting and that the parties opened an escrow account in a Yerington bank in Minister's favor, where Azevedo agreed to deposit sufficient funds to cover the cost of the hay as he hauled it from the Minister Ranch. The parties are in dispute as to the total quantity of hay Azevedo agreed to purchase. Minister claims Azevedo contracted to purchase 1,500 tons. Azevedo maintains that they never had an agreement as to quantity.

Soon after this telephone conversation, Azevedo deposited $20,000 in the designated escrow account and began hauling hay from the Minister Ranch. As Azevedo hauled the hay, Minister furnished him with periodic accountings, commencing December 4, which specified the dates the hay was hauled, names of the truckers, bale count, and weight. This arrangement was satisfactory to the parties, and it continued until the latter part of March 1968, when Minister loaded only two of four trucks sent by Azevedo for hay, because the funds on deposit in the escrow account were insufficient to cover all four loads. Azevedo then refused to buy any more hay, and Minister commenced this action in district court.

2. THE STATUTE OF FRAUDS

The determination of the legal issues presented for our consideration will turn on our interpretation of NRS 104.2201(2) of the Uniform Commercial Code. Since the enactment of the Uniform Commercial Code, sweeping changes have been effectuated in the law of commercial transactions. NRS 104.2201 provides:

'1. Except as otherwise provided in this section a contract for the sale of goods for the price of $500 or more is not enforcible (sic) by way of action or defense unless there is some writing sufficient to indicate that a contract for sale has been made between the parties and signed by the party against whom enforcement is sought or by his authorized agent or broker. A writing is not insufficient because it omits or incorrectly states a term agreed upon but the contract is not enforcible (sic) under this subsection beyond the quantity of goods shown in such writing.

'2. Between merchants if within a reasonable time a writing in confirmation of the contract and sufficient against the sender is received and the party receiving it has reason to know its contents, it satisfies the requirements of subsection 1 against such party unless written notice of objection to its contents is given within 10 days after it is received.

'3. A contract which does not satisfy the requirements of subsection 1 but which is valid in other respects is enforcible (sic):

'(a) If the goods are to be specially manufactured for the buyer and are not suitable for sale to others in the ordinary course of the seller's business and the seller, before notice of repudiation is received and under circumstances which reasonably indicate that the goods are for the buyer, has made either a substantial beginning of their manufacture or commitments for their procurement; or

'(b) If the party against whom enforcement is sought admits in his pleading, testimony or otherwise in court that a contract for sale was made, but the contract is not enforcible (sic) under this provision beyond the quantity of goods admitted; or

'(c) With respect to goods for which payment has been made and accepted or which have been received and accepted (NRS 104.2606).'

As with all codifications, it was impossible for the Uniform Commercial Code to encompass every conceivable factual situation. Realizing this limitation, its drafters couched much of the language of the text and comments in broad generalities, leaving many problems to be answered by future litigation. The development of the action of assumpsit in the fourteenth century gave rise to the enforceability of the oral promise. Although parties to an action could not be witnesses, the alleged promise could be enforced on the strength of oral testimony of others not concerned with the litigation. Because of this practice, a party could readily suborn perjured testimony, resulting in marked injustice to innocent parties who were held legally obligated to promises they had never made. The statute of frauds was enacted to preclude this practice. The passage of the statute did not eliminate the problem, but rather, has precipitated a controversy as to the relative merits of the statute. Those favoring the statute of frauds insist that it prevents fraud by prohibiting the introduction of perjured testimony. They also suggest that it deters hasty action, in that the formality of a writing will prevent a person from obligating himself without a full appreciation of the nature of his acts.

Moreover, it is said, since business customs almost entirely conform to the mandates of the statute, an abolition of the statute would seriously disrupt such affairs.

On the other hand, in England the statute of frauds has been repealed. The English base their position upon the reasoning that the assertion of the technical defense of the statute aids a person in breaking a contract and effects immeasurable harm upon those who have meritorious claims. It is further maintained by the advocates of the English position that the rationale for the necessity of the statute has been vitiated, because parties engaged in litigation today may testify as witnesses and readily defend against perjured testimony.

The Uniform Commercial Code, however, has attempted to strike a balance between the two positions by seeking to limit the defense of the statute to only those cases where there is a definite possibility of fraud. It is in the light of this historical background that we turn to consider whether the oral agreement of the parties in this case is barred by the statute of frauds.

There is no question that the Azevedo-Minister agreement was oral and that its enforceability is governed by NRS 104.2201(2), supra. The sale of hay is included within the definition of the sale of 'goods' as defined by NRS 104.2105(1) and NRS 104.2107(2), which when read together provide that the sale of 'growing crops,' when they are to be 'severed by the buyer or by the seller,' constitutes the sale of goods within the definition of that expression in the Uniform Commercial Code. The parties agree that they are 'merchants' within the meaning of that term as defined in the Code.

It is also true that the statute of frauds is no defense to that portion of the contract that has been performed under the provisions of NRS 104.2201(3) (c), supra, which makes enforceable an oral contract '(w)ith respect to goods...which have been received and accepted.' The legal issues are, therefore, (1) whether Minister's accountings constituted confirming memoranda within the standards of NRS 104.2201(2) and, if so, (2) whether Minister sent them within a reasonable time as required by the statute.

3. THE CONFIRMING MEMORANDA

(a) The accounting of January 21, 1968.

In addition to the data set forth in the periodic accountings covering the dates on which hay was hauled, the names of the truckers, and the bale counts and weights, Minister added the following statement in his January 21 accounting to Azevedo:

'From your original deposit of $20,000.00 there is now a balance of $1819.76. At this time there remains (sic) approximately 16,600 bales of hay yet to be hauled on your purchase, about 9200 of which are first crop, 7400 of which are second crop.

'We would appreciate hearing when you plan to haul the balance of the hay. Also please make a deposit to cover the hay, sufficient in amount to pay for the hay you will be currently hauling. At this time you have only about $2.25 deposit per ton on the remaining balance of the hay, and we cannot permit a lower deposit per ton and still consider the hay as being sold.' (Emphasis added.) Azevedo did not challenge or reply to Minister's accountancy of January 21. Rather, he deposited an additional $3,000 in the escrow account and continued hauling hay.

(b) The accounting of February 22, 1968.

In the regular accounting of February 22, Minister added the following:

'Balance of deposit on approximately 14000 bales remaining to be hauled—$1635.26.' Azevedo did not challenge or reply to the February 22 accounting. It is these two accountings that the district judge found constituted confirming memoranda within the meaning of NRS 104.2201(2). There is little authority articulating the meaning of a confirming memorandum as used in the Code. The official Comment, Uniform Laws Annotated, Uniform Commercial Code s 2-201 1968), states at 90, 91:

'Only three definite and invariable requirements as to the (confirming) memorandum are made by this subsection. First, it must evidence a contract for the sale of goods; second, it must be 'signed,' a word which includes any authentication which identifies the party to be charged; and third, it must specify a quantity.'

The parties concede that the memoranda were 'signed' within the meaning of the statute, but appellant Azevedo urges that neither memorandum confirms the existence of an oral contract.

While s 2-201(2) of the Code is entirely new in the commercial law field, its only effect is to eliminate the defense of the statute of frauds. The party alleging the contract still has the burden of proving that an oral contract was entered into before the written confirmation. The purpose of the subsection of the Code is to rectify an abuse that had developed in the law of commerce. The custom arose among business people of confirming oral contracts by sending a letter of confirmation. This letter was binding as a memorandum on the sender, but not on the recipient, because he had not signed it. The abuse was that the recipient, not being bound, could perform or not, according to his whim and the market, whereas the seller had to perform. Obviously, under these circumstances, sending any confirming memorandum was a dangerous practice. Subsection (2) of Section 2-201 of the Code cures the abuse by holding a recipient bound unless he communicates his objection within 10 days.

Appellant urges that the January and February accountings do not meet the standards of the subsection because neither memorandum makes reference to any oral agreement between the parties. A fair reading of the memoranda shows otherwise. The January memorandum states that, 'At this time there remains (sic) approximately 16,600 bales of hay yet to be hauled on your purchase', and, further, that, 'We (Minister) would appreciate hearing when you plan to haul the balance of the hay.' Although neither the January nor the February memorandum refers to the previous November agreement by telephone, the language clearly demonstrates that the referred-to agreement between the parties was not an in futuro arrangement, but a pre-existing agreement between Azevedo and Minister. As the court said in Harry Rubin & Sons, Inc. v. Consolidated Pipe Co., 396 Pa. 506, 153 A.2d 472, 476 (1959), in ruling on a case involving subsection (2) of section 2-201:

'Under the statute of frauds as revised in the Code(,) 'All that is required is that the writing afford a basis for believing that the offered oral evidence rests on a real transaction." (Footnote omitted.)

The district judge found that it did so in the instant case, and the record supports his finding.

4. THE 'REASONABLE TIME' FACTOR

Subsection 2 of NRS 104.2201 provides that the confirming memorandum must be sent within a reasonable time after the oral contract is made. Appellant argues that the delay of 10 weeks (November 9 to January 21) as a matter of law is an unreasonable time. We do not agree. What is reasonable must be decided by the trier of the facts under all the circumstances of the case under consideration. Subsection 2 of NRS 104.1204 provides:

'What is a reasonable time for taking any action depends on the nature, purpose and circumstances of such action.'

In this case, the parties commenced performance of their oral agreement almost immediately after it was made in early November. Azevedo deposited $20,000 in the designated escrow account and began hauling hay. Minister commenced sending his periodic accounting reports to Azevedo on December 14. It is true that the accounting containing the confirming memorandum was not sent until January 21. It was at that time that Azevedo's deposit of $20,000 was nearing depletion. Minister so advised Azevedo in the January memorandum. Azevedo responded by making an additional deposit. He did not object to the memorandum, and he continued to haul the hay until the latter part of March. Under 'the nature, purpose and circumstances' of the case, we agree with the district judge that the delay was not unreasonable.

The judgment is affirmed.

Case Questions:

1. Explain the impact of the Statute of Frauds on this case.

2. What is the impact of the Uniform Commercial Code on the Statute of Frauds in this case?

3. When a contract fails to satisfy the provision of the Statute of Frauds, what does the court say about the contract's enforceability under other circumstances?

4. According to the court, why did the English legal system abolish the Statute of Frauds?

5. Was there a confirming memorandum of the contract in this case?

ETHICS FILE: Avoiding Legalese

One important consideration that all legal professionals face when they draft contracts is to avoid overly complicated verbiage in creating contract provisions. There is a natural tendency to use legal-sounding phrases, such as, "Party of the first part," and "heretofore." However, these phrases rarely contribute to the main goal of a contract: to spell out the agreement between the parties in such a way that everyone can understand what the agreement is. These legal phrases are often referred to as "legalese." In many ways it is more difficult to draft a contract using simple language than it is to rely on outmoded and often misunderstood legal phrases. Brevity and clarity are the goals of legal professionals and legalese doesn't achieve either.

The Case of the Unsigned Credit Agreement[26]

Opinion by Judge DAVIDSON.

In this action for breach of a sales agreement, plaintiffs, Univex International, Inc., and CPC, Inc., now known as Data Packaging Corporation, appeal from the summary judgment entered in favor of defendant, Orix Credit Alliance, Inc. (Orix). We affirm.

In 1989, Communications Packaging Corporation, Media Packaging, Inc., Mary E. Rose, and Robert D. Rose (debtors) gave Orix a security interest in certain items of equipment as collateral for a loan. In January 1991, debtors defaulted on the loan.

Plaintiffs, debtors, and Orix then commenced negotiations towards a voluntary foreclosure which would be followed by a purchase of the equipment by plaintiffs. In the course of the negotiations, certain necessary documents, including a bill of sale, a promissory note, and a security agreement, were drafted and sent as a package to plaintiffs' attorney. None of these documents was ever signed.

On March 4, 1991, plaintiffs' attorney sent Orix a note outlining plaintiffs' proposed changes to the document package. At or near the same time, debtors informed Orix that they were not going to agree to a voluntary foreclosure, and shortly thereafter, debtors procured a buyer who purchased Orix's security interest for the amount outstanding on the loan.

Plaintiffs then initiated this action against debtors and Orix. Debtors were dismissed from the action by stipulation and Orix moved for summary judgment on plaintiffs' claims against it for breach of contract and promissory estoppel. The trial court granted the motion on the grounds that the lack of a signed contract precluded both claims pursuant to the Colorado Uniform Commercial Code version of the statute of frauds, Plaintiffs appeal, contending that this was a sale of goods between merchants which required only a confirming memorandum under the Colorado Uniform Commercial Code. Alternatively, they argue that the trial court erred in determining that, because of §4-2-201, plaintiffs' reliance upon an oral promise for the sale of the equipment was unreasonable as a matter of law.

I

Orix contends, as it did in the trial court, that §38-10-124, C.R.S. (1994 Cum.Supp.) requires all credit agreements to be in writing and precludes finding implied credit agreements under any circumstances, including those which would otherwise support promissory estoppel. Plaintiffs argue that this contention was not properly raised and should not be considered on appeal. We disagree that this contention is not properly before us. Furthermore, because we find that §38-10-124 is dispositive, we affirm the trial court's judgment.

According to §38-10-124(2), C.R.S. (1994 Cum. Supp.):

Notwithstanding any statutory or case law to the contrary, including but not limited to section 38-10-112, no debtor or creditor may file or maintain an action or a claim relating to a credit agreement involving a principal amount in excess of twenty-five thousand dollars unless the credit agreement is in writing and is signed by the party against whom enforcement is sought.

"Credit agreement" is defined by §38-10-124(1)(a), C.R.S. (1994 Cum.Supp.) as:

(I) A contract, promise, undertaking, offer, or commitment to lend, borrow, repay, or forbear repayment of money, to otherwise extend or receive credit, or to make any other financial accommodation;

(II) Any amendment of, cancellation of, waiver of, or substitution for any or all of the terms or provisions of any of the credit agreements defined in subparagraphs (I) and (III) of this paragraph (a); and

(III) Any representations and warranties made or omissions in connection with the negotiation, execution, administration, or performance of, or collection of sums due under, any of the credit agreements defined in subparagraphs (I) and (II) of this paragraph (a).

Under this broad definition, the alleged contract here is a credit agreement. It provides for financing by Orix in excess of $25,000. Orix is a financial institution and, therefore, a "creditor" as defined by §38-10- 124(1)(b), C.R.S. (1994 Cum.Supp.).

Plaintiffs argue that, notwithstanding the broad definition of credit agreement, §38-10-124 is not applicable because they only seek to enforce that portion of the alleged agreement which relates to the sale of the equipment and do not seek to enforce that portion of the agreement that provides for financing. We are not persuaded.

Section 38-10-124 applies to any agreement to extend credit, regardless of the context in which the agreement was formed, and bars any action or claim relating to a credit agreement, regardless of whether the action is based upon a breach of contract or on some other theory of recovery. Therefore, plaintiffs may not transform this somewhat complex financial transaction into a simple cash purchase by selecting certain portions that they wish to enforce and disregarding the remainder of the agreement.

Plaintiffs also argue that a material issue of fact remains as to whether, taking several documents together, Orix had sufficiently "subscribed" the agreement so as to fulfill the signing requirement pursuant to judicial interpretation of the statute of frauds. Again, we disagree.

Plaintiffs rely upon authority interpreting the statute of frauds as codified at §38-10-112, C.R.S. (1982 Repl.Vol. 16). Section 38-10-124 specifically provides, that in the case of a credit agreement, it, and not §38-10-112, controls.

Section 38-10-124(2) requires a signature. No signature by Orix was ever obtained on any of the documents which comprise the agreement plaintiffs seek to enforce.

A correct result will be upheld on review, even if the reason for the trial court's ruling was wrong. *Norwest Bank Lakewood v. GCC Partnership, supra; Cole v. Hotz,* 758 P.2d 679 (Colo.App.1987). Because plaintiffs' claims are precluded by §38-10-124, we affirm the judgment without considering plaintiffs' other contentions.

The judgment is affirmed.

Case Questions:

1. According to this court, is the transaction in this case covered by the statute of frauds (as it is presented under the Uniform Commercial Code)?

2. Explain what is meant by a "credit agreement" in this case.

3. What are the reasons given for the court's ruling in this case?

4. Why isn't this considered to be a simple sale of equipment, rather than a transaction that falls under the jurisdiction of the statute of frauds?

5. What are the requirements of a credit agreement under the statute of frauds?

Business Case File

Stock Properties

Barry Stock

Barry Stock has been a realtor for 26 years. He currently specializes in commercial and industrial properties, but he has worked all aspects of real estate. "I was a residential agent for over 18 years. My mother was a real estate agent, one of the first women realtors in this area. I got my real estate license two weeks before I graduated from high school and I've been an agent ever since.

"Real estate is a people business. There's nothing like the feeling you get when you help a young couple buy their first home." Stock moved out of residential properties a few years ago for the challenges of commercial property. "With commercial property, you have a different set of demands. The people you work with are more sophisticated; they are usually pretty savvy investors. A side benefit was that I got away from some of the avalanche of paperwork that is involved in residential transactions."

The primary reason for all this paperwork is the Statute of Frauds. As we have seen in this chapter, nearly every type of real estate transaction must be in writing under the Statute of Frauds before it is enforceable.

Stock deals with the law in some capacity every day. "When you first meet with a client, there are agency disclosure forms that you have to go over. Later, you'll have to go through the Offer of Purchase contract and other legal documents. If you're working with a seller, you'll sign a Listing Agreement that gives you permission to try to sell his property."

There are potential legal minefields to deal with, as well. For one thing, there are conflicts of interest to avoid. "Let's say that I'm a seller's agent and a buyer asks me what he should offer on the house? I can't go against my client, the seller, by telling the buyer confidential information. On the other hand, I don't want to waste everyone's time. I'm obligated to say that they should offer the listing price. However, when I'm working as a buyer's agent, I'm free to make suggestions about price. It depends on my role. My motto is: put service first, and the dollars will follow."

Although the real estate business has become paper-intensive, it wasn't always so. "My mom once wrote a legal and binding offer of purchase contract on the back of one of her business cards. All the details were there: who, what, when and how much. The parties signed the card on a Tuesday and closed on Friday. That would be impossible today. Those days are gone forever." Stock continues to run a successful real estate business by concentrating on the fundamentals of customer service and fair dealing.

Chapter Summary:

The Statute of Frauds was originally developed in England in 1677. Part of the motivation for its creation was to avoid fraud by requiring specific types of contracts to be put into writing before they could be enforced through the court system. The Statute of Frauds was later adopted by all of the states in the United States. The specific categories of contracts that are required to be in writing under the states' Statute of Frauds include contracts involving testamentary transactions, contracts to answer for the debt of another, contracts in anticipation of marriage, contracts for the sale of land, and contracts that cannot be performed within one year of the date of their creation. Originally, two other types of contracts were required to be in writing under the Statute of Frauds: contracts for the sale of goods exceeding $500 in value and contracts for the sale of securities. However, with the adoption of the Uniform Commercial Code by the states, these two categories of transactions are now covered by UCC rules.

Under the Statute of Frauds no particular form of writing is mandated. Instead, the Statute merely requires a writing, setting out the details of the transaction be prepared. This writing must contain the specifics of the agreement between the parties and must be signed. The Statute of Frauds is a technical requirement that can be waived under certain conditions. For instance, if justice requires that an otherwise invalid contract be considered valid, then the Statute of Frauds will not be enforced. A typical example of this is when one party partially performs under the contract, despite the fact that it is not in writing.

The UCC created its own version of the Statute of Frauds and is similar in many ways to the traditional Statute of Frauds. Great care should be taken when drafting a contract that is covered by the Statute of Frauds. Such contracts should include specifics about the parties, the duties to be performed, and the manner of payment, among other things.

WEB SITES

Yahoo Directory
http://dir.yahoo.com
Provides a list of online legal research sites.

Expert law.com
http://www.expertlaw.com
Expert witness and litigation support, as well as interesting and informative articles on the Statute of Frauds.

New Jersey Law Review Commission
http://www.lawrev.state.nj.us
This commission recently reviewed the applicability and usefulness of the Statute of Frauds and has published an extensive report about it on this site.

REVIEW QUESTIONS

1. Why was the Statute of Frauds enacted?
2. List and explain each of the five categories of contracts that must be in writing under the modern Statute of Frauds.
3. Is the Statute of Frauds still necessary? Create one argument for the continued existence of the Statute of Frauds and another against it.
4. Explain how the Statute of Frauds applies to live-in lovers or persons who cohabit with another.
5. Explain how a year is calculated under the Statute of Frauds.
6. Why is there no requirement of particular types of words that must be used in order to create a legally sufficient contract under Statute of Frauds?
7. Why is the signature of the party against whom the contract will be enforced required on a contract covered by the Statute of Frauds?
8. Explain partial performance under the Statute of Frauds.
9. What are some important considerations when alleging a violation of the Statute of Frauds in a complaint?
10. Is the Statute of Frauds a defense? How?
11. How has the UCC modified the Statute of Frauds?
12. What are the two most common types of contracts that are required to be in writing under the UCC?
13. How do the courts resolve internal inconsistencies in a contract?
14. What is the rule about changes to a contract made in typed print versus handwritten print?
15. Why should a paralegal avoid a claim of unauthorized practice of law?
16. What are some of the methods that a paralegal can use to avoid such a claim?
17. In the 1600s, most people were illiterate. Why would a statute require that a contract be in writing if most people couldn't read it?
18. Why is it important that land transactions have "transparency"?
19. Why is it important for a business owner to have a will?
20. Why did Azevedo lose in "The Case of the Hostile Hay Haulers?"

HANDS-ON ASSIGNMENT

Belinda Buyer wishes to purchase a car from Marcus Merchant. The car is a 2002 Micro Allevia. The purchase price is $1,200. The parties have negotiated the following terms: Belinda will pay 36 monthly payments of $55.55 to Marcus. When Belinda has tendered the final payment, Marcus will deliver to her the title on the automobile, free and clear of any other liens. Belinda will possess the car during the time that she is making the payments, but Marcus will have a security interest in the car. If Belinda fails to make regular payments, Marcus can repossess the car. Draft a contract, based on these facts that complied with the Statute of Frauds. Include any additional contract clauses that you believe would be appropriate.

PRACTICAL APPLICATION

Is an oral prenuptial contract made valid by the marriage of the parties? Put another way, is marriage "partial performance" that would validate an otherwise invalid contract?

Review an apartment lease, contract for sale of real property, or a sales agreement for the purchase of an automobile. What provisions in this contract are there specifically because of the Statute of Frauds? Identify each and explain their function.

HELP THIS BUSINESS

Suppose that Jill McFarlane of Fiction Addiction wants to embark on a new sideline in her business: she wants to sell rare, first edition books. These books range in value from a minimum of $500 to a maximum of $5,000. Locate a sample contract that she can use to sell such books that also will satisfy the Statute of Frauds. Modify the sample contract to meet Jill's needs.

KEY TERMS

Statute of Frauds

prenuptial/antenuptial agreement

memorandum of contract

partial performance

ENDNOTES

[1] Restatement Second, Contracts §110(1).

[2] UCC §2-201.

[3] UCC §8-319.

[4] Am. Jur Statute of Frauds §1.

[5] *Azevedo v. Minister*, 86 Nev. 576, 471 P.2d 661 (1970).

[6] *In re Estate of Palmen*, 588 N.W.2d 493 (Minn. 1999).

[7] 29 Charles II c. 3, §4.

[8] *MacKnight v. Pansey*, 122 R.I. 774, 412 A.2d 236 (1980).

[9] *Reed v. Roark*, 14 Tex. 329 (1855).

[10] UCC. §2-201, Official Code Comment 1.

[11] *Rose v. Lang,* 85 N.C. App. 690, 355 S.E. 2d 795 (1987).

[12] *Commercial Credit Corp. v. Marden,* 155 Or. 29, 62 P.2d 573 (1936).

[13] *Neujahr v. Producers Com'n Ass'n,* 838 F.2d 1003 (8th Cir. 1988).

[14] *Louisville Trust Co. v. National Bank of Kentucky,* 3 F. Supp. 909 (W.D. Ky. 1932).

[15] *Scurry v. Edwards,* 232 S.C. 53, 100 S.E.2d 812 (1957).

[16] *Herring v. Volume Merchandise,* Inc., 249 N.C. 221, 106 S.E. 2d 197 (1958).

[17] *Willis v. Willis,* 242 N.C. 597, 89 S.E. 2d 152 (1954).

[18] *Kent v. Humphries,* 303 N.C. 675, 281 S.E. 2d 43 (1981).

[19] *Davis v. Lovick,* 226 N.C. 252, 37 S.E. 2d 680 (1946).

[20] *Johnson v. Noles,* 224 N.C. 542, 31 S.E. 2d 637 (1944).

[21] *Azevedo v. Minister,* 86 Nev. 576, 471 P.2d 661 (1970).

[22] UCC §2-201 (3).

[23] Am. Jur. Contracts §475.

[24] Am. Jur. Contracts §395.

[25] *Azevedo v. Minister,* 86 Nev. 576, 471 P.2d 661 (1970).

[26] *Univex Intern., Inc. v. Orix Credit Alliance, Inc.,* 902 P.2d 877 (Colo. App., 1995).

 For additional resources, visit our Web site at www.westlegalstudies.com

CHAPTER 8

CONTRACT CLAUSES

▌ **Focus of this chapter:** In this chapter we explore contract clauses, including contract conditions, exceptions, and the ways that courts interpret these various provisions. Particular attention is paid to contract conditions, such as express, implied, and subsequent conditions.

Chapter Objectives:
At the completion of this chapter, you should be able to:

■ Explain the function of contract conditions

■ Explain the difference between an express and an implied contract

■ Provide examples of contracts with conditions subsequent

■ Draft a contract with a condition precedent

■ Be able to explain how the courts interpret ambiguous language in a contract

■ Describe the role of contract exceptions

■ Distinguish between specific contract clauses

■ Explain the function of the "time is of the essence" contract clause

■ Describe the purpose of a noncompete clause

■ Distinguish between promises and conditions in a contract

Introduction to Contract Clauses

In this chapter, we will explore various types of contract clauses. A contract **clause** is simply a statement contained in a contract. A clause can be as mundane as a signature line, or as crucial as limiting one party's right to sue. A consideration of all types of contract clauses is far too large a topic to cover in a single chapter. Instead, we will focus on specific types of clauses, paying special attention to the ones that you, as a legal professional, are

clause: A statement or sentence that is part of a legal document such as a contract, a will or a legal pleading.

most likely to encounter, and describing the process used by the court system to interpret these various types of contract provisions.

Arguably the most important, at least in terms of litigation, are contract clauses containing conditions.

Conditions

condition: A future uncertain event that creates or destroys rights and obligations.

A **condition** is a contract clause that modifies the basic agreement between the parties. A condition makes the contract contingent on some event or act. Although conditions can be complex, at their simplest formulation, they can be expressed as, "If you do this, I'll do that." Conditions that rely on an event instead of an action can be expressed as, "If this happens, then I'll do that." There are many different types of conditions, including implied, express, conditions precedent, and conditions subsequent.

It is perfectly legal—and very common—for a contract to contain conditions. The reasons for inserting conditions into contracts are almost limitless. A condition can either modify or rescind the contract. A condition can be based on a certain action, either of the parties themselves or some other outside action. Consider Hypothetical 8-1.

HYPOTHETICAL 8-1   Their First House Purchase

Sandy and Ramon Cortez have been married for a year. They would like to buy a home. Neither of them has ever owned a home before, so they have purchased books on the subject and they have made an appointment with a real estate agent. The books that they've bought tell them that financing is a crucial issue for homebuyers. After all, who has enough cash on hand to purchase a house outright? The real estate agent takes them around to look at various houses that are currently on the market. They immediately fall in love with the third house that they see that first day. The sale price is listed as $100,000. Sandy and Ramon think that they qualify for a mortgage, but they aren't sure. The real estate agent tells them that they should put in an Offer of Purchase on the house. An offer of purchase is exactly what it sounds like; Sandy and Ramon are offering to purchase the home for a specified amount. Their offer is $95,000. However, when they finish working up the offer, Ramon has some concerns. What happens if they can't get financing?

There is a standard clause in an Offer of Purchase contract that makes the contract conditional on obtaining financing. The actual clause reads, "The Buyer must be able to obtain a firm commitment on or before (date), effective through the date of closing, for a purchase mortgage loan in the principal amount of $95,000 for a term of 30 year(s), at an interest rate not to exceed 9% per annum, with mortgage loan discount points not to exceed 2% of the loan amount. Buyer agrees to use his best efforts to secure such commitment and to advise Seller immediately upon receipt of the lender's decision."

Will this condition protect Sandy and Ramon if they are unable to secure a loan?

Answer: Yes. This is an example of a typical condition. As we have already said, a condition can modify, limit, or even cancel a contract. In this hypothetical, if they the use their "best efforts" to obtain financing and are unsuccessful by the date indicated, then the contract is rescinded. Of course, this leaves a couple of issues unresolved, such as what constitutes "best efforts." (It also oversimplifies the math surrounding a real estate transaction.)

Simply because a contract is conditional does not make it unenforceable. Later, we will discuss how courts approach the analysis of a conditional contract. However, these contracts are perfectly legal and are in use every day across the planet.

A condition can be based on the happening of an event. In Hypothetical 8-1, the condition was based on the Cortez family being able to obtain financing to purchase their first home. However, conditions also can be based on a specific event not happening.

HYPOTHETICAL 8-2   The House Inspection

Sandy and Ramon have obtained financing to purchase their home. They are ecstatic. During their interview with the bank loan officer, she mentioned something about a house inspection. Neither Sandy nor Ramon had paid much attention to that clause in the Offer of Purchase Contract. That clause reads, "Buyer shall have the option to have the home inspected by a reputable inspector or contractor, at Buyer's expense. Such inspection must be completed in sufficient time before closing to permit any repairs to be completed by closing."

The housing inspector finds nothing wrong with the house. Does this event affect the sale of the house?

Answer: No. In this case, the condition was based on something not occurring, such as a report of a structural or other problem with the home. When the inspector fails to find anything wrong with the house, this condition is satisfied.

Conditions do not create rights; they limit them. It is important to note, however, that a condition may alter a right or a duty under a contract, but conditions do not affect the existence of the contract itself. In order for a condition to be legally effective, the underlying contract must meet all of the requirements that we have discussed in previous chapters. A condition that purports to affect mutual assent, for instance, is not actually a condition at all. Because mutual assent is a necessary requirement for a valid contract, any language that eliminates that requirement destroys the validity of the contract itself.[1]

DISTINGUISHING CONDITIONS FROM PROMISES

A condition is different from a promise. A condition modifies, alters, or even rescinds the agreement. A promise is the party's pledge to be bound by the contractual agreement.

When the language in a contract is misleading or ambiguous, the courts will construe the language in such a way as to find a promise, not a condition. The reason for this rule has to do with the type of remedy available. If the court finds a condition, the contract may be canceled, while if the court finds a promise, the parties may seek damages for breach (see Exhibit 8-1).

I promise to pay you $2,000 for your car.
(Contract with no condition)

I promise to pay you $2,000 for your car, if a mechanic certifies that it has no major mechanical problems.
(Contract with a condition)

EXHIBIT 8-1: Distinguishing promises from conditions.

What occasionally happens is that when people review the language of a contract they will see language that seems to indicate a condition when what they are actually reading is a promise. Here is an example:

I promise to pay you $2,000 if you sell your car to me.

The "if" in the above sentence seems to indicate a condition. We all associate that word with some conditional event. "If" suggests, "If this happens, then that will happen." Such a construction is a condition. However, is this statement actually a condition?

One person is promising to pay an amount of money for the purchase of the car. The word "if" in this sentence does not mean that the offer is conditional. A condition modifies the basic agreement between the parties; it inserts contingencies or stipulations. Does the sentence in this example do any of those things? Will the seller or the buyer be required to change any actions if an event does or does not occur? The answer is clearly no. Take a look at the sentence in Exhibit 8-2.

I promise to pay you $2,000, if a mechanic looks over your car and finds no major mechanical problems with it. You agree to sell me your car once the mechanic has said that everything is okay.

EXHIBIT 8-2: Examining conditions.

Is there a condition in the contract set out in Exhibit 8-2? Yes. How can we be sure? For one thing, this is no longer a straightforward transaction. The buyer has inserted a contingency, namely the inspection to be carried out by the mechanic. Will the mechanic's findings alter or modify the contract? Yes. In fact, if the mechanic reports a "major mechanical problem," the contract will be terminated. This certainly qualifies as a condition.

There is no requirement about where in the contract the condition is inserted. For instance, a condition is not required to be stated clearly at the beginning of the contract (although that would often make it easier for a judge to interpret it).

TYPES OF CONDITIONS

Conditions come in many different forms. In the next few sections, we will examine some of the most common types of conditions. It is not necessary to actually label a specific clause as a condition; it can be implied by the actions or the intentions of the parties.

Implied Condition

Conditions often are broken into two broad categories: implied conditions and express conditions. An implied condition is one that is not stated in the contract, whereas an express condition is one that is stated. An implied condition is one that is presumed to exist from the conduct of the parties. The most basic type of implied condition is that the parties will act lawfully. Stating such a condition in a contract is not required; it is assumed. Other types of implied conditions are set out in Exhibit 8-3.

- The contract will follow the applicable law
- The continued existence of the parties (death may void the contract)
- A manufacturing plant not be destroyed by fire or other catastrophe, and so on

---

EXHIBIT 8-3: Common implied conditions.

In the practical world of contract law, something as vague as an implied condition can create a wealth of potential problems. As such, courts are reluctant to read more than the most basic types of implied conditions into a contract. The court is under no obligation to create an implied condition. Consider Hypothetical 8-3.

HYPOTHETICAL 8-3   The Nondelivery Delivery

Maria has negotiated the purchase of new computer motherboards for her laptop manufacturing business. The company, Matrix Motherboards, Inc. (MMI) is a local company. As all of their other customers pick up the completed orders at its plant, the officers at MMI naturally assumed that Maria also would arrange to pick up her order at the plant. Maria has assumed just the opposite.

She has assumed that MMI would deliver the goods to her at her facility just outside of town. When MMI refuses to deliver the motherboards, Maria brings suit, claiming that delivery was implied under the contract. How does the court rule?

The court will probably rule that as nothing was stated in the contract about delivery, no delivery was promised. Courts generally will not impose implied conditions in contracts, absent negligence, bad faith, or fraud.[2] Maria must arrange to pick up the motherboards herself. (It was precisely this type of confusion among merchants that led to the creation of the UCC, which will be discussed in Chapter 9.)

To a certain extent, actions are presumed. For instance, in the example discussed in Hypothetical 8-3, the contract does not contain any provision specifying that the parties will act in accordance with state and federal law. Such activities are presumed and are therefore not spelled out in the contract. Why wouldn't contract law require that all conditions, whether presumed or not, appear in the contract language?

There are two problems with this approach. The first is that there is no way that the parties could anticipate all possible issues that might arise in a contract and requiring them to do so would be ridiculous. The second objection to this approach is more philosophical. Courts do not wish to restrict the parties' ability to contract with one another. Requiring every possible contingency to be agreed on in advance would have the practical effect of discouraging contractual relations in the first place. Who would want to enter into a contract when it must take into account every possible contingency? The negotiations alone would take weeks or even months.

Let's examine the sale of a home from a previous example. In this transaction, there are several, unstated assumptions in the contract. One assumption is that one party will produce the funds at a time and place agreeable to both parties. Other assumptions include that the seller will sign and deliver the title to the property to the buyers. The fact that the contract makes no mention of any of these details does not render it unenforceable. All these actions are implied conditions to the contract. When an action is necessary for the completion of the contract, and it is not stated in the contract itself, it will be implied. When we say that the courts are reluctant to create implied conditions contracts, what we are in fact saying is that courts are reluctant to create new conditions not contemplated by the parties in their negotiations. For instance, there is nothing in the contract that states that the house will be cleaned before the closing. Because this action is not necessary for the successful completion of the transaction, the court will be very reluctant to impose it. In the end, if courts take an overly active role in creating implied conditions, the end result will be a constraint on the parties' ability to negotiate whatever terms are agreeable to each other.

Our court system—and the U.S. Constitution—is founded on the belief that parties should be free to negotiate any type of contract, with any type of conditions, as long as the contract is not illegal. This is the reason that the courts take an essentially "hands off" approach to interpreting implied conditions in contracts.

Express Conditions

An express condition is one that is stated in the contract. It is set out by the parties and is part of the other expressed terms of the agreement. As such, both parties must agree to the condition before it will be imposed on the contract.

When an express condition exists, courts will usually attempt to follow the stated intentions of the parties, unless this is impossible. Later, we will discuss the rules that the court system uses to interpret express conditions when the wording is ambiguous or difficult to understand. However, one such rule should be noted here: when an express condition comes into conflict with an implied condition, the court is called on to interpret the contract in such a way as to give the express condition preference, unless it runs counter to the law.

Condition Precedent

So far, our discussion of conditions has been general. We have explored implied conditions and express conditions. Now, we must narrow our focus and explore two of the more complicated types of conditions: **conditions precedent** and conditions subsequent.

A condition precedent is a condition that must be met or performed before the agreement takes effect. If a condition precedent is not met, no binding contract results.

condition precedent: A condition, fact or occurrence that must occur before a contractual obligation is triggered.

We have already seen an example of a condition precedent in this chapter, although, at the time, we did not refer to it by that name. Under our first hypothetical involving Sandy and Ramon Cortez and their purchase of a home, we saw that they created an Offer of Purchase contract with a specified condition. This condition concerned obtaining financing. Sandy and Ramon made their offer conditional on their ability to obtain a mortgage for $95,000 at a specified interest rate. This is a condition precedent. In other words, the Cortezes must obtain the financing before the Offer of Purchase becomes a binding contract. (There are some jurisdictions where this contract provision would actually be considered to be a condition subsequent, i.e., a condition occurring after the initial agreement that would void the contract).

Other common examples of conditions precedent include the awarding of a government contract to A before his contract with B takes effect. Conditions precedent are common conditions and are designed to protect the parties. Suppose that A has negotiated a contract with B to rent B's trucks for a period of one year, conditional on the county awarding a hauling contract to A? If A did not have a condition precedent in his contract with B, and A did not receive the county's contract, he would be legally obligated to rent B's trucks, but he would have no use for them. By contrast,

A would like to arrange for the truck rentals before the government contract is awarded, so that he will know that he can meet the county's needs. Without a condition precedent, A would not approach B about renting trucks and therefore A might not bid on the county contract. A great deal of business enterprises would never get off the ground without such a condition.

When the contract contains a condition precedent that means that something must occur before the rights, duties, and benefits of the contract will be realized. This event can be any number of things, including an action by a third party, a natural event, or even an action by one of the parties themselves. The basic format of a condition precedent clause is "If this happens, then we agree to have a contract between each other."

Limitations on Conditions Precedent

There are certain limits to conditions precedent. For instance, one party cannot prevent the other party from meeting the condition. The defendant, in an attempt to avoid a contractual obligation, cannot actively interfere with the circumstances that would create the condition. In the example we outlined earlier, B is barred from contacting the county and insisting that the contract be awarded to someone else because he has realized that his rental charge to A is not as lucrative as it might be.

Another limitation concerns how the courts interpret these conditions. As a general rule, the condition must be stated clearly and precisely. If the courts are unable to decipher the parties' intentions, they will probably declare the condition to be void. As such, the parties must spell out their intention to create a condition precedent in unambiguous language. If they fail to do so, the court may rule that no condition precedent was created.

In most jurisdictions, courts do not favor conditions precedent. The reason that the courts do not look kindly on such a condition is that it imposes a contingency on the creation of a contract. In many situations, this condition may be difficult to interpret and can generate a great deal of litigation over the question of whether or not the condition precedent was met (see Exhibit 8-4).

Condition Subsequent

If a condition precedent refers to an action that must occur before a contract is created, a **condition subsequent** is just the opposite. Under a condition subsequent, the parties agree to be bound by the contract until a particular condition occurs. When that event occurs, the parties agree that they will dissolve the contract. In situations in which the there is confusion about whether or not a condition is a condition precedent or a condition subsequent, the courts usually opt for a condition subsequent.

Sidebar:
Conditions precedent also are known as "suspensive conditions," because they suspend the operation of the contract until a particular event occurs.

Sidebar:
Most courts require plain, concise, and unambiguous language to create a condition precedent. This is especially true when the condition involves an action that is outside the control of the parties.

condition subsequent: If a certain future event happens, a right or obligation ends.

✓ **PARALEGAL CHECKLIST**

When evaluating conditions in contracts consider the following questions:

☐ Is the condition stated clearly?

☐ Is the condition stated unambiguously?

☐ Are the parties' intentions clear from the wording of the condition?

☐ Is there an express condition that may conflict with an implied condition?

☐ Does the condition qualify as a condition precedent, which is not favored under the law, or a condition subsequent, which is favored under the law?

EXHIBIT 8-4

HYPOTHETICAL 8-4   The Mining Contract

Philip and Raul have entered into a contract to mine gold in land owned by Philip. The contract states, in a pertinent section, that Raul and Philip agree that they will share the profits and the expenses of the mining operation as long as the yield of gold is at least 10% per ton of material removed from the mine. Once the yield of gold slips below that amount for 30 consecutive days, Raul and Philip agree to dissolve the contract between them. Is this a valid condition subsequent?

Answer: Yes. Both Raul and Philip have entered into a legally binding contract to do something that they are entitled to do and they have also inserted a clause that will alter the contract when a certain event occurs, that is, when the yield of gold per ton drops below a specified amount. This is clearly a condition subsequent.

You may notice that in most of the contract clauses we have outlined in this chapter, we have consistently stayed away from sales of goods between merchants. The reason is that these types of transactions come within the jurisdiction of the UCC and, because that code has its own set of rules regarding contract clauses and conditions, we will address those issues when we discuss the UCC in Chapter 9.

Where conditions precedent refer to events that must occur before a binding contract is created, conditions subsequent always refer to future events. When the parties create a condition subsequent, courts will usually enforce it. The Restatement of Contracts takes a slightly different approach to conditions subsequent, referring to them as contract clauses that "terminate duty" under a contract.[3]

Sidebar:
A condition subsequent is one that, if it occurs, cancels the contract.

Sidebar:
Conditions subsequent are also known as resolutory conditions.

Sidebar:
An "aleatory" contract is one in which the parties condition their performance on a fortuitous event.

- Contract provision that required the defendant to deposit specified sum in account within 90 days of agreement or contract would be "null and void."[i]

- Contract provision stating that an employee's noncompete clause would be void if employment was terminated for any reason other than "substantial and material" reason.[ii]

- Contract clause stating that restaurant owners would have right to cancel contract for payment of maintenance fees if the other owners "discontinued maintenance on shared parking lot."

EXHIBIT 8-5: Examples of conditions subsequent.

[i] *Potrero Homes v. Western Orbis Co.,* 104 Cal. Rptr. 633 (1972).
[ii] *Chelsea Industries, Inc, v. Florence,* 260 N.E.2d 732 (Mass 1970).

Exclusions

Just as the parties may insert whatever conditions into the contract they wish (with certain exceptions), so, too, are they permitted to exclude certain matters from consideration. An **exclusion** is a particular item or subject that is not covered by the contract.

exclusion: Keeping (or leaving) someone out.

The general rule followed by most jurisdictions is that when the parties specifically state certain contract clauses they are implicitly excluding others. For instance, if the contract clearly states that the payment for services contemplated in the contract should be made by the 5th of each month that implicitly states that payment later in the month is contrary to the agreement. However, this is not a rule of law; it is a general, guiding principle. Courts will always look to the wording of the actual contract to determine what the parties did (and did not) intend to be covered.

Sidebar:
This principle was first laid down in the Latin phrase, "Expressio unius est exclusio alterius" (the expression of one is the exclusion of the other).

Proving Conditions at Trial

When a contract contains a condition, it is up to the judge to determine the legal effect of the wording. Often, conditions are pleaded as defenses to a failure to perform under a contract. That being the case, they are often raised in the defendant's answer.

Interpreting Contract Provisions

As we have already stated in previous paragraphs, the person usually called on to decide the legality of a particular contract clause is the judge. When a judge reviews a contested contract, he or she has certain rules to follow in evaluating contract clauses. We will summarize these rules in the follows paragraphs.

These rules of construction derive from previously decided cases and, in some instances, from rules set out by statutes. In almost all situations, the rules for interpreting contract language give a judge wide discretion. A judge's interpretation of contract provisions will only be overturned on appeal when it is clearly wrong. Although the rules presented in the next few paragraphs are numbered, the numbers are the creation of the author, not any statute, case law, or other authority.

RULE NUMBER 1: RECONCILE CONFLICTS

When the court is presented with contract clauses that apparently conflict, the first rule of construction is to find a way to reconcile them, unless that is clearly impossible.

RULE NUMBER 2: THE PARTIES' INTENTIONS ARE CONTROLLING

The court must interpret the contract in such a way as to effectuate the intention of the parties, at least as far as that can be determined. This means that the court is not supposed to imply contract clauses that the parties never intended, or that they never considered. Of course, the court is not bound by the parties' intentions when their intentions run counter to the law.

RULE NUMBER 3: WHEN THERE IS A CONFLICT BETWEEN AN EXPRESS CONDITION AND AN IMPLIED CONDITION, THE EXPRESS CONDITION WINS

When the court is presented with an express condition that conflicts with an implied condition, the court is required to give the express condition preference. Again, this rule, like so many others, is subject to the legality of the express condition. A close corollary to this rule is that if there are two possible interpretations of a contract clause and the first would make it meaningless whereas the second would give it meaning, always go with the second.

RULE NUMBER 4: WORDS ARE TO BE GIVEN THEIR NORMAL, ORDINARY MEANING

The words used by the parties will be given their ordinary, accepted meaning. Courts also will consider any qualifying terms associated with the particular words. Punctuation in the contract will often assist the court in construing meaning, but punctuation, by itself, is not the sole, controlling factor. **Strict construction** is the order of the day when reviewing contract language.

RULE NUMBER 5: WAS A CONDITION INTENDED?

Although specific legal terms are not required to create a condition, courts will review the choice of language used in the contract. Before a contract

strict construction: Strict construction of a law means taking it literally or "what is says, it means," so that the law should be applied to the narrowest possible set of situations.

will be considered to have a specific condition, the parties must manifest that intention by their choice of wording. The court will review the contract for words such as "if," "on the condition that," or "provided that," as guidance about the parties intention.

When a contract fails to include some language indicating the parties' intention to create a condition, the courts will usually not find one.

RULE NUMBER 6: ORAL TESTIMONY ABOUT WRITTEN PROMISES IS USUALLY NOT PERMITTED

When a contract is in writing, courts will usually refuse to hear testimony from the parties about what the contract actually "meant" to say. This oral testimony falls under the Parol Evidence Rules and will not be permitted.

The Parol Evidence Rule

Parol Evidence Rule: The principle that the meaning of a written agreement, in which the parties have expressly stated that it is their complete and final agreement, cannot be contradicted or changed by using prior oral or written statements or agreements as evidence.

The **Parol Evidence Rule** is an evidentiary rule that states that when a written contract purports to embody the entire agreement between the parties, no oral testimony will be permitted that seeks to modify or change the interpretation of the written contract provision.

Why should such a rule exist? The reason is both simple and complex. The simple answer is that the Parol Evidence Rule makes the written contract the final arbiter of what the parties actually intended. It must stand or fall on its own and no additional testimony should be permitted to affect is legal status.

Another reason for the Parol Evidence Rule is more complex. You will recall that we have said that the judge is the person who must decide the legality of certain contract clauses. A jury may be called on to decide specific facts in a case, but the judge always has the final say on questions of law. The Parol Evidence Rule furthers that role. If oral testimony were permitted to "interpret" the contract language, this would effectively remove the judge's authority from the case.

Exceptions to the Parol Evidence Rule

Although oral testimony about a written contract is usually not permitted, there are exceptions to this Rule. For instance, oral testimony is permissible when the actual circumstances surrounding the making of the contract are in dispute. If a party is alleging fraud, undue influence, or some other impropriety, oral testimony is not only permissible, it may be required.

Specific Contract Provisions

So far, we have discussed contract conditions in general terms. We have also discussed how the court system interprets contract clauses. Now we will address some specific types of contract provisions, explaining their function and how they are applied in a typical contract setting.

"Time Is of the Essence"

When a contract contains a "time is of the essence" provision, it means that the date set for the action contemplated in the contract is fixed. The action must occur on the date specified, or the contract is void. Why would such a provision ever be used? Consider Hypothetical 8-5.

HYPOTHETICAL 8-5   Time Is of the Essence

Sandy and Ramon Cortez eventually bought their first house and lived in it for five years. However, they are now considering selling it and moving into a bigger house. Their family has grown to include two children, a dog, and a cat, and the house is too small to accommodate everyone.

They place their home up for sale and get an offer within days. They accept the offer and then they begin looking for a new house.

When out looking at houses with a real estate agent, they find a house that they both like very much. They draft an Offer of Purchase contract and submit it to the current owner. Their offer is accepted immediately. The Cortezes have learned a lot of about real estate transactions since they purchased their first home and they realize that, before they can purchase their second house, they will need the funds from the sale of their first house. How can they insure that the closing on their house will take place before the closing on their new home? They insert the following language in their acceptance of the offer to purchase their current home: "Closing to occur on September 1st of this year; time is of the essence." What significance does this condition have?

Answer: If, for some reason, they do not close on their current home by September 1st, the contract for sale will be null and void. They also have inserted a condition in their offer on the new home that states that their offer is conditional on the closing of the sale of their current home. By making these arrangements, the Cortezes have insured that they will have the funds to purchase their new home with the proceeds of the sale of their current home.

This contract clause has the effect of galvanizing all parties involved in the transaction, because all parties realize that if the event contemplated in the contract does not occur on the date indicated, the contract will be void. Because the parties have a vested interest in making sure that the event occurs, there is a good chance that it will happen by the date indicated.

"Trade or Business Secrets"

Nearly all businesses have specific processes, methods, or special services that they offer their customers. When a person goes to work for a business, he or she must learn these processes in order to be effective at the job. Naturally, employers wish to safeguard their secrets from their competitors. Can they insert a condition into an employee contract that forbids the employee from ever revealing this secret? Consider Hypothetical 8-6.

HYPOTHETICAL 8-6   Cherry's Chunky Chicken Recipe

Walter "Cherry" Smith has developed a recipe for fried chicken that uses a special blend of herbs and spices. The public can't get enough of his chicken. At first, he sold his chicken from a roadside stand where he made all the chicken himself. However, with his success, he has opened a restaurant and expanded his operation. When he hires employees, he makes them sign an employment contract that has the following provision: "I hereby agree that I will not reveal the recipe for Cherry's Chunky Chicken for the rest of my life, I further agree that I will not work for any competing restaurant within a 500-mile radius for a ten-year period following my separation from Cherry's Chunky Fried Chicken, Inc."

One of Walter's employees quit two months ago and has gone to work for a competing restaurant that is 120 miles away from Cherry's Chunky Chicken Restaurant. Yesterday, the restaurant began offering fried chicken under the name, "Hunky Chicken." Walter wishes to enforce the clause in the employee's contract. Will he be successful?

Answer: Although Walter has the right to protect his trade secret, his protection must be reasonable. Courts have consistently held that any employment clause that has no time limit on how long the employee must keep a trade secret is unenforceable. The second question raised by this hypothetical concerns the geographic limitations. These, too, must be reasonable. When courts consider geographic limits in employment contracts they first consider the nature of the business. A geographic limit of 500 miles for a restaurant might also be considered excessive and unenforceable.

Businesses have the right to protect their trade secrets. However, this right is not absolute. A business's right to protect trade secrets must be reasonable. See "The Case of the Enron Employment Contract."

It is important to note that with many of these specific types of clauses the court is required to carry out a delicate balancing act. On the one hand, the court must attempt to effectuate the clear intent of the parties. On the other hand, the court must not permit any contract to restrain trade.

Unfair Restraint of Trade

The restraint of trade is an important consideration for the court system. Stemming from the U.S. Constitution, courts have consistently ruled that any contract that unfairly restrains trade is ultimately bad for the country and will not be enforced. Many litigants attempt, either rightly or wrongly, to shield their noncompliance with a contract with a claim that it is an "unfair restraint on trade." When this claim is raised, the court must attempt to find a balance between the individuals' right to contract as they please and society's freedom from contractual arrangements that unfairly restrict commerce.

"NONCOMPETE"

Noncompete, or noncompetition, clauses are very common in employment contracts. When a contract contains a noncompete clause, it usually contains some language barring a former employee from working for a direct competitor, within a specified geographic region, for a specified time. Noncompete clauses have been held to be invalid when they exceed these limitations. For instance, a noncompete clause that barred an employee from ever working for any competitor would be too restrictive for the employee and would doubtless be ruled as a restraint on trade. Noncompete clauses have come under increasing scrutiny in recent years and much of their impact has been curtailed. Courts have ruled that many noncompete clauses contained provisions encompassing too wide a geographic region, for example, or that the provision prevented the former employee from working with too many other possible employers.

"ARBITRATION"

When a contract contains an arbitration clause, this means that if the parties ever have a disagreement about the contract, they must first present their case to an arbitrator, rather than simply filing a lawsuit. Arbitration clauses have been held to be legal in a wide variety of contracts. However, an arbitration clause is not permitted to deny the parties any legal remedies whatsoever. An arbitration clause cannot, for instance, purport to waive any legal claim that either party may have at any time under the contract. Such a sweeping denial of access to the court system would never be sustained. Within these confines, however, an arbitration clause is perfectly valid.

ETHICS FILE: Lifting Contract Language

When it comes time to draft a contract, many legal professionals feel an understandable desire to avoid reinventing the wheel and lift language directly from previously written contracts. The problem with this approach is that each contract has unique features and there is no contract that can possibly anticipate all problems. In addition to that, the client is paying for a service and, when a legal professional simply copies other work and passes it off as new work, there is a good case for an ethical complaint that the professional has been paid for work that was never actually carried out. If their consideration weren't enough, there is also the added issue of copyright infringement. Published contracts—and contract forms—may be protected under federal copyright laws. Borrowing contract language verbatim without the author's permission is an actionable violation of U.S. copyright laws. Faced with all these potential dilemmas, the best course is to draft a new contract that meets the client's needs.

The Case of the Enron Employment Agreement[4]

JOHNSON, Judge.

Enron Capital & Trade Resource, Corporation is in the business of buying, selling, and supplying energy sources. Enron also trades energy commodities. Southern Electric International, Inc. is in the business of providing engineering and consulting services to power and other electric utility companies.

While employed by Enron in Texas, Joseph Pokalsky helped Enron develop procedures for trading energy commodities. Pokalsky eventually resigned his position at Enron and accepted employment with Southern in Georgia. On the day he resigned from Enron, he and Southern filed an action in Georgia seeking a declaratory judgment that the restrictive covenants contained in the employment agreements between Pokalsky and Enron were unenforceable. The agreements provided, in part, that the employee will not, at any time after employment, make any unauthorized disclosure of any confidential business information or trade secrets of Enron or its affiliates or make any use thereof; the employee will not, for one year after the termination of employment, engage in any business competitive with the business conducted by the employer, render any advice or services to, or otherwise assist any other person, association, or entity who is engaged in any business competitive with the business conducted by the employer, in any geographic area or market where Enron conducts any business, which may limit the employee's ability to engage in certain businesses "anywhere in the world." As part of the action, Pokalsky and Southern sought a temporary restraining order to enjoin Enron from seeking to enforce the restrictive covenants, from taking any other actions to preclude Pokalsky and Southern from engaging in an employment relationship, and from benefiting in any other fashion from the enforcement of the restrictive covenants. The court issued a temporary restraining order against Enron, prohibiting Enron from seeking to enforce the non-

competition obligations, acting to preclude Pokalsky and Southern from engaging in an employment relationship, and benefiting from the enforcement of those provisions. At about the same time, Enron filed a lawsuit in Texas against Pokalsky and Southern seeking to enforce certain obligations contained in the same agreements.

A few days later, Pokalsky and Southern amended their motion for interlocutory injunction seeking to enjoin Enron from seeking to enforce the non-disclosure or fiduciary obligations contained in the agreements, taking any action to preclude Pokalsky and Southern from engaging in employment relationships, benefiting from the enforcement of the non-disclosure provisions, and seeking to preclude Pokalsky from using information contained in his mind.

In a detailed order, the court granted the motion for interlocutory injunction as amended, denied the motion for contempt, and ordered Enron to dismiss and cease pursuing the Texas action. Enron appeals.

Enron argues that the trial court erred in enjoining it from proceeding with its Texas action or initiating any other action anywhere else against Pokalsky because the two cases involve different provisions of the agreements and the "anywhere else" restriction amounted to an abuse of discretion. We disagree.

Both actions involve the same parties, facts and agreements. Although the non-disclosure and fiduciary duty issues were not part of the motion for interlocutory injunction as originally filed, those issues were added when the motion was amended. The trial court properly ordered the Texas action to be dismissed. In addition, the Texas action was properly ordered dismissed as its filing violated the court's temporary restraining order.

The court's order prohibiting Enron from filing an action "anywhere else" did not preclude Enron from bringing its claims as counterclaims in the Georgia action. Indeed, such claims would be compulsory counterclaims.

The trial court did not err in finding that Georgia law, rather than Texas law, controls the enforceability of the covenants not to compete and not to disclose in the agreement. Contrary to Enron's argument, the choice of Texas law provision contained in the agreements is not controlling. Although the parties may have chosen the law of a foreign jurisdiction to govern, a Georgia court will not enforce the contract if it is "particularly distasteful." The non-competition provisions in this case were "particularly distasteful" because they prohibited a former employee from competing anywhere in the world in any capacity. Such covenants have been held to be unenforceable in Georgia. Moreover, the non-competition restriction is unenforceable as geographically overbroad, since it prohibits Pokalsky from working in an area where Enron has done business in the past 12 months or anywhere it currently conducts business; "area" is not defined. Moreover, the nondisclosure covenant is unenforceable in Georgia because it contains no time limitation.

"The law of the jurisdiction chosen by parties . . . will not be applied by Georgia courts where application of the chosen law would contravene the policy of, or would be prejudicial to the interests of, this state. Covenants against disclosure, like covenants against competition, affect the interests of this state, namely the flow of information needed for competition among businesses, and hence their validity is determined by the public policy of this state." We find no error.

Judgment affirmed.

Case Questions:

1. What were the provisions of the noncompete clause in this case?

2. What were Enron's contentions in this case?

3. Why did the court rule that the geographic limits in the contract were too broad?

4. Is the fact that the contract clause contains no time limit a significant point for the court? Why or why not?

5. What was the court's reasoning behind its decision?

The Case of the Terrible Tenants[5]

BOIS, Justice.

Action for recovery in quantum meruit involving a contract dispute wherein the plaintiffs agreed to construct a "breezeway" and garage addition to defendant's main house in return for the conveyance to them by the defendant of three acres of land and a so-called sap house situated thereon. The plaintiffs failed to render substantial performance of the contract. The defendant cancelled, evicted the plaintiffs and never conveyed the land. The Trial Court (Douglas, J.) denied relief in quantum meruit but awarded specific performance on condition that plaintiffs either fully perform their remaining contractual obligations or tender the cash value of those obligations. Defendants' exceptions have been reserved and transferred. We reverse.

On August 12, 1972, the parties entered into a written contract which provided in relevant part as follows:

"In consideration of Edmond Dandeneau building and completing a sun room and garage attached to the house owned by me in North Sandwich, N.H., the undersigned does hereby agree to deed a certain parcel of land containing a sap house. . . . Edmond Dandeneau does hereby agree to complete to satisfaction the above mentioned sun room and garage."

The parties further agreed that the construction value would approximately equal the $4,000 value of the land to be conveyed.

At the time the contract was formed, the defendant had been living in Florida and the Dandeneaus were renting her house in New Hampshire. This arrangement continued through most of 1973. Considerable work was done on the sunroom and garage in the latter part of 1972 and into early 1973, but thereafter the project was virtually abandoned. The court found the work incomplete in the following respects: one-half of the garage roof to be shingled, doors and windows to be installed, exterior siding to be applied on certain walls, the garage door to be strengthened, steps from the breezeway to the garage to be constructed, insulation and interior finish to be installed and completed in the breezeway. According to the value of labor and materials as found by the trial court, about 73% of the total job had been completed.

As the year 1973 progressed, the plaintiffs found themselves in increasing financial difficulties. Hoping to relieve themselves of rent payments, they directed their efforts to making the sap house livable. In December of 1973, they notified Mrs. Seymour that they had moved from the defendant's house to the renovated sap house and informed her that the purpose of the move was to save rent money which would later be used to finish their contract.

No substantial additional work was done and the plaintiffs continued to devote their attention to the sap house which, of course, by virtue of the original agreement, they hoped to eventually own. These improvements involved considerable cash outlays by the plaintiffs and plaintiffs admitted that, unbeknownst to the defendant, they had cleared and sold timber from the defendant's land and used the proceeds to improve the sap house.

Plaintiffs' finances continued to deteriorate and by their own account their indebtedness grew to the sum of $30,000 or $40,000. The defendant considered and rejected a plan proposed by the plaintiffs under which the agreed-upon land and building would be deeded to a relative of the plaintiffs who would then mortgage same to provide funds with which the plaintiffs could finish the breezeway and garage.

In February of 1975 one of plaintiffs' creditors initiated a suit and attempted to attach defendant's property. Mrs. Seymour traveled to New Hampshire from Florida and successfully contested the attachment in court. In connection with these proceedings, defendant learned that there were many claims outstanding against the plaintiffs. Concerned by the fact that plaintiffs' conduct had seemingly put her property in jeopardy, she decided to sell her New Hampshire house and cancel her contract with the plaintiffs. In June of 1975 she sent the following letter:

"This is to notify you that our home in N. Sandwich is for sale.

"Since no work has been done to the property in over one year and the project has been abandoned by you, our contract of August 12th '72 is hereby cancelled.

"We expect you to vacate the property within 30 days of the reciept (sic) of this notice."

The plaintiffs did not vacate without incident. In their displeasure over defendant's conduct, they vandalized the sap house. Undisputed testimony shows that the following damage was done:

"Trash and things throughout the house, busted lightbulbs in the sockets, and the well was full of garbage. The light wires had been cut from the 200 amp. entrance box. The circuit breakers were missing. The bathroom drains were all plugged. The kitchen drain in the sink was plugged. . . . The telephone wire was cut. . . . The water pipes were cut, and the water had run all over the floor. The stairtreads and the wall were taken up I presume to remove the hot water heater."

The court found that the partial construction of the breezeway and garage and the improvements to the sap house had conferred a net benefit to the defendant. However, relying on Roundy v. Thatcher, 49 N.H. 526 (1870), the court denied quantum meruit relief. In Roundy, at 529, this court reasoned: "So if it be expressly agreed that nothing shall be paid until the contract is fully performed, then the law will not, against such express stipulation imply a promise to pay for a part. . . . Upon the same principle, it would seem, that if the contract was to pay in a particular way, as in certain stocks, in land, or other specific articles, the law would not imply a promise, in case of a part performance, to pay in money."

"Quantum meruit is a restitutionary remedy intended for use by contracting parties who are in material breach and thus unable to sue 'on contract.'" The obligation thereby sued upon "is one that is created by the law for reasons of justice, without any expression of assent and sometimes even against a clear expression of dissent." The "reasons of justice" supporting quantum meruit recovery were enunciated in the early case of Britton v. Turner, 6 N.H. 481, 492 (1834):

"[W]here the party receives value takes and uses the materials, or has advantage from the labor, he is liable to pay the reasonable worth of what he has received."

While the principle of "unjust enrichment" has thus been invoked by this court from an early date, we are not inclined to depart from our holding in Roundy v. Thatcher. In the circumstances of the instant case, the law will not imply a promise by the defendant that she pay in money the value of plaintiffs' services under the contract.

The improvement of the sap house was not made pursuant to the August 12 written contract, and Roundy v. Thatcher thus presents no bar to quantum meruit recovery for the benefit conferred. However, the circumstances under which this building was improved will not permit the imposition of a quasi-contractual obligation on the defendant. Although the defendant had knowledge of the improvements, she could only assume that the plaintiffs would perform their contract and that the sap house would eventually be theirs. The improvements were made solely on the initiative of the plaintiffs in order that they might live in the sap house and avoid the obligation of paying rent for living in the defendant's house. Under these circumstances, it would be unfair to the defendant for the law to impose upon her an obligation to pay for the improvements.

"The rule that voluntary acceptance of benefits shows an implied promise to pay therefor, applies only where the party for whom the services are rendered is free to take their benefit or to reject it. If the services are of such nature that he has no choice but to accept them, he cannot be said to accept them voluntarily." In the instant case the defendant was not presented with such a free choice, since the benefits would not be hers unless and until the plaintiffs defaulted on their contract (an event within the plaintiffs' power). We conclude that the defendant is under no quasi-contractual obligation with respect to the improvements to the sap house.

We conclude that plaintiffs are entitled to neither legal nor equitable relief. This result may seem a harsh one. However, it is of the plaintiffs' own making and arises from their decision to devote their time and money to their own ends rather than their contractual obligations.

Case Questions:

1. Did the plaintiffs' own behavior in vandalizing the property contribute to the decision in this case?

2. According to the court, what is the definition of quantum meruit?

3. What is the rule of "voluntary acceptance of benefits?"

4. Was a "quasi" contract created in this case? Why or why not?

5. Was the defendant under an implied promise to pay for the plaintiffs' services?

Business Case File

Musical Group *Purpose*

Purpose is a gospel singing group that tours most of the southeastern United States. They have appeared in venues as diverse as churches and college campuses, but lately they've found themselves on stage at gospel music contests and on the Web with their first CD.

"We got our start singing in local churches and by singing an original arrangement of 'The Star Spangled Banner' for local leaders. The tragic events of September 11th had led to a huge increase in the demand for the national anthem. We named our group 'Purpose' because we have a mission to minister to community."

The group is composed of four members: Leslie McKesson, Vondra Evans, Mae Mills, and Valarie Connelly. Each has been singing individually and in other groups for years. They formed *Purpose* two years ago.

"Our name got out there because of all the singing we'd been doing," said Leslie. "We decided to enter a contest in Atlanta and we were awarded the Grand Prize. Part of the award package was six hours of studio time. After that, we entered a contest in Colorado and came in fourth place nationwide. That's not bad for a group who'd only been singing together for seven months."

"We started to think about our career as a business," said Vondra. "We had created verbal agreements with different promoters and they'd charge a varying amount as an honorarium. But we realized that we had costs: travel, hotel, meals and that in order for us to continue to afford performing, we'd have to consider those costs. We hired an accountant and Valarie took on the role of the 'money person.' She keeps track of billing and revenues. Leslie is the legal person," Vondra explained. The group members took on different roles.

"They noticed that I was organized," said Valarie. "This is an essential part of bookkeeping. The accounting classes that I took in high school and community college helped me be comfortable

Leslie McKesson and Vonda Evans

with the role."

Vondra agreed that having the different members take on different roles was helpful. "Valarie handles the money. Mae is the person who books our appearances and who really works well with people. Leslie is our law person. She makes sure that we are doing things right in regard to copyrights, permission, letters of request, things like that." Vondra is the administrator of the group; she keeps everything organized.

Their goal was to create a CD of their music and sell it to the public. "When we got into the studio, we had six free hours," said Leslie. "We wanted to put together a CD and we did thirteen songs in six hours. Our CD came out last year and it has been selling very well."

But creating a CD opened up a host of legal issues. "For one thing," said Leslie, "there were payments to writers and publishers. We had to keep track of royalty payments. Because we'd used pre-recorded music tracks, we also had to pay for those, too.

Royalty payments to various artists and composers are an important contract clause in any recording contract. Most of these contracts provide that the performers must pay these royalties themselves. This is another example of the importance of contract clauses: how and when others are

(continued)

paid can have a huge impact on the bottom line and affect the viability of the business.

"We never really put together a business plan," said Vondra. "Instead, we surveyed ourselves and asked, 'Where do we want to be in five years?' Nine months into our singing career, we'd already surpassed our five year goals."

What does it take to make it as a professional singing group? "It certainly takes more than talent," said Vondra. "What it really takes is sacrifice and attention to the details. You have to invest your own money, your own time, and even be willing to put your reputation on the line. You're away from your family a lot, singing in different states.

"There were so many things that we'd never considered before we decided to form a singing group," said Leslie. "There are issues about intellectual property law, agency, and contract law. It would be simple if all you had to worry about was the singing. That's the fun part. The rest of it is business. If you could leave out the legal mumbo jumbo it would be great, but that's as much a part of it as anything else."

"Before the group was formulated, I had no desire to run my own business," said Valarie. "But, as our music ministry began to increase, our needs did likewise. Signing a partnership agreement and opening the business account were the natural next step. So here we are. Four women who complement one another and have found our 'purpose' both in our ministry and in our business."

Chapter Summary:

Conditions are contract clauses that limit how a contract may be performed. Conditions come in two broad categories: implied conditions and express conditions. When a contract contains an implied condition, the condition is not stated but is interpreted to be present. An example of an implied condition would be that the parties would follow the applicable state or federal law. Express conditions are conditions that are specifically stated in the contract. They can be categorized as conditions precedent and conditions subsequent. A condition precedent is a condition that must exist before the rights and duties of a contract will be triggered. A condition subsequent is a condition that will terminate the contract.

When courts review contracts, they follow general guidelines about how to interpret contract language. Generally, courts try to give preference to the parties' intentions when they created a contract and they will attempt to interpret ambiguous or confusing contract clauses in such a way as to keep the contract in existence.

There are some specific contract clauses that are very common. "Time is of the essence," for example, is a contract condition that makes the date of performance of the contract mandatory. If the action is not carried out on the specific date, the contract is void. This provision is frequently seen in real estate contracts. Other typical contract provisions include noncompetition and trade secret provisions. These clauses are given great scrutiny by the courts because they often call into question a possible restraint on trade. Courts are vigilant in avoiding restraints on trade and will invalidate contract provisions that attempt to do so.

WEB SITES

WWW Virtual Library
http://www.interarb.com/
European database on legal issues.

U.S. Supreme Court
http://www.supremecourtus.gov
Web site for the United States Supreme Court, including recent decisions.

Florida Law Weekly
http://www.floridalawweekly.com
Information about recent Florida appellate decisions.

REVIEW QUESTIONS

1. What is an express condition?
2. How is an express condition different from that implied condition?
3. What is the relationship between an implied condition and statutory law?
4. What is a condition precedent?
5. What is a condition subsequent?
6. How is a condition precedent different from a condition subsequent?
7. When the contract contains an ambiguous term, how do the courts interpret the contract?
8. I agree to sell you 100 items, on the condition that I receive a bank loan in the amount of $10,000. What type of condition is this?
9. What is an example of an implied condition in a contract?
10. How do the courts interpret a contract when an express condition conflicts with an implied condition?
11. Draft a contract clause containing a condition precedent.
12. What is the importance of the party's intentions when a judge reviews the language of a contract?
13. Why is there no requirement that a contract specifically state that the parties will act in agreement with the law?
14. Analyze this contract clause: "If my grandmother leaves me more than $10,000 in her will, then you and I will go into a catering business with one another. I will use the $10,000 to finance the catering business, to purchase necessary equipment, and to assist you in the preparation of meals. You will market our new business, be responsible for planning and

preparing the meals, and we will both use our best efforts to further the business." Does this clause contain a condition? If so, what type of condition is it?

15. Why are the courts reluctant to insert implied conditions in a contract?

16. Explain the principle, "The inclusion of one thing is the exclusion of another."

17. Explain why Enron Corporation lost the appeal in the "Case of the Enron Employment Contract." What was there about the employment contract that the court found "distasteful?"

18. What are some techniques you can use to avoid having too much responsibility delegated to you when you work for an attorney?

19. Explain the rules used by the courts to interpret language in a contract.

20. Why is it necessary for the courts to interpret contract language in the first place?

HANDS-ON ASSIGNMENT

Locate a contract that contains some of the contract clauses and conditions that we have discussed in this chapter. Explain how these contract clauses modify the contractual language. Categorize each clause of the contract as one of the conditions presented in this text.

PRACTICAL APPLICATIONS

Deborah Dealer owns a craft store. On a recent buying trip to Atlanta, she located a vendor who manufactures birdhouses that have been carved from a single piece of wood. The man who makes these birdhouses is named Victor Vendor. Deborah believes that she could probably sell 10 or 20 of these birdhouses per week. She negotiates a purchase price of $9 for each birdhouse. Victor has one condition that he would like to insert into their written contract. He wants a provision that states that he has the right to terminate the contract should the lumber that he uses be declared illegal, or if the price of his lumber increases by more than 20%. Victor has recently heard that the South American wood that he uses for his birdhouses has recently been placed on the Endangered Species List.

Deborah would like to receive 200 birdhouses within 60 days of the contract date. She would then like to receive 100 birdhouses by the first day of each succeeding month, until a total of 1,000 birdhouses have been delivered. She will make payment by a certified check within 10 days of delivery. Deborah is concerned about the quality of the birdhouses and wishes to insert a contract provision that allows her to reject specific birdhouses if she feels that some of them do not meet her specifications. Victor and Deborah have worked out an overall list of specifications, which will be attached to the contract. You do not need to create this list of specifications, but you do need to refer to it in the contract itself. Draft a contract that clearly establishes the agreement between Victor and Deborah and includes their various contract conditions. You may wish to look at some of the sample contracts provided in the appendix for guidance on this assignment.

HELP THIS BUSINESS

Suppose that the group *Purpose* wishes to create a new contract binding on its members that provides the following:

- A condition that no member of the group will receive any type of remuneration until all of the expenses that the group incurred in producing its own CD have been paid
- A condition that states that each member agrees to actively participate in the creation of a second CD containing approximately the same number of songs
- A condition imposing a noncompetition clause on all members of the group should one or more leave and wish to create a competing musical group (keeping in mind the limitations on noncompete clauses imposed by the courts)

KEY TERMS

clause

condition

condition precedent

condition subsequent

exclusion

strict construction

Parol Evidence Rule

ENDNOTES

[1] *Modern Globe, Inc. v. 1425 Lake Drive Corp.*, 340 Mich. 663, 66 N.W.2d 92 (1954).

[2] *Town of Troy v. American Fidelity Co.*, 143 A.2d 469 (Vt. 1958).

[3] Restatement of Contracts, Second, §230.

[4] *Enron Capital & Trade Resources Corp. v. Pokalsky*, 490 S.E.2d 136 (Ga.1997).

[5] *Dandeneau v. Seymour*, 117 N.H. 455, 374 A.2d 934 (N.H. 1977).

 For additional resources, visit our Web site at www.westlegalstudies.com

CHAPTER 9

THE UNIFORM COMMERCIAL CODE

| *Focus of this chapter:* This chapter focuses on the development and the purpose of the Uniform Commercial Code. Special emphasis is placed on the articles of the Uniform Commercial Code, especially Article 1 dealing with the general definitions of the Uniform Commercial Code, and Article 2 dealing with sales. The history of the Uniform Commercial Code is examined and an explanation of how the Uniform Commercial Code has been adopted across the United States is provided.

Chapter Objectives:
At the completion of this chapter, you should be able to:

- Explain the basic function of the Uniform Commercial Code
- Explain how the Uniform Commercial Code was developed
- Explain the law of commercial transactions prior to the adoption of the Uniform Commercial Code
- Describe the organization of the Uniform Commercial Code
- Give a brief example of the types of transactions covered by each of the articles of the Uniform Commercial Code
- Explain the function of Article 1 of the Uniform Commercial Code
- Explain the importance of Article 2 of the Uniform Commercial Code
- Describe how the Uniform Commercial Code has an impact on day-to-day business activities
- Describe the function of Uniform Commercial Code financing statements
- Describe the significance of the Official Comments found in the Uniform Commercial Code

What Is the Uniform Commercial Code?

code: A collection of laws.

The Uniform Commercial Code is exactly what its name suggests. It is a nationwide **code** that seeks to standardize commercial transactions into a single, cohesive unit. However, the Uniform Commercial Code, like the Restatement of Contracts, is not a federal law. Instead, it is a suggested series of laws, a pattern that states are free to adopt or reject as they see fit.

The stated purpose of the Uniform Commercial Code is to simplify, modernize, and bring uniformity to the more than 50 independent commercial codes found throughout the United States. Before the adoption of the Uniform Commercial Code, each state had its own approach to commercial transactions and these approaches were widely divergent. Even the basic definition of "contract" was different from state to state.

In many ways, the Uniform Commercial Code is less like a series of statutes and more like a restatement of the law. Put together by legal scholars, the Uniform Commercial Code is a compilation of the entire nation's commercial statutes, boiled down to the most reasonable and efficient approaches to commercial transactions.

By itself, the Uniform Commercial Code is no more than a guideline. However, when it is adopted by a state, it becomes the state law on commercial transactions.

The Uniform Commercial Code also contains numerous protections and safeguards for buyers, sellers, and others involved in commercial transactions.

Sidebar:
Although the stated claim of the Uniform Commercial Code is to simplify and modernize commercial transactions, the greatest feature that it has contributed to American jurisprudence is uniformity.

A Brief History of the Creation of the Uniform Commercial Code

The Uniform Commercial Code (UCC) was created by a panel consisting of state lawmakers, law professors, and attorneys. It took this panel over a year to review the applicable laws in the 50 states and to condense and simplify all of these rules into what has become the Uniform Commercial Code.

The UCC was originally developed in the mid-1960s. The Code has been revised continuously since it was first developed. New articles have been added to the Code since it was created. The advent of electronic commerce and the Internet will undoubtedly cause additional revisions of the UCC in coming years. We discuss electronic commerce in Chapter 13 of this text.

Once the UCC was drafted, it was presented to the various states as a suggested series of statutes. States could adopt it in its entirety and therefore benefit from the UCC's organization and efficiency. However, the states were under no obligation to adopt the UCC. Some states, such as Louisiana, did not adopt the UCC for several years after its introduction in the late 1960s, whereas other states adopted it immediately.

When a state adopted the UCC, state lawmakers would, in most cases, specifically repeal previously existing statutory and case law governing commercial transactions in the state. The UCC itself provides that it is the framework for all future commercial transactions.

WHY THE NEED FOR A UNIFORM COMMERCIAL CODE?

The need for a Uniform Commercial Code was apparent to anyone who dealt with interstate commerce in the first half of the 20th century. With each state maintaining its own set of commercial laws, conducting business from state to state could be both confusing and costly. Because each state followed different rules regarding bills of lading, insurance, contract law, contract conditions, remedies, and a host of other issues, the overall effect was a restriction of business. Leaders in both the commercial and legal communities saw that in order to improve the overall efficiency and to increase business transactions, a uniform system was needed.

ADOPTION BY THE STATES

Most states that have adopted Uniform Commercial Code have adopted it virtually verbatim. This means that the UCC is virtually identical from Maine to California, Washington state to Florida. Because of the uniformity of the statutes contained in the UCC, businesspeople who understand it in their state already have a solid understanding of it in other states.

Although the states could not be compelled to adopt the Uniform Commercial Code, state legislatures saw the benefits of simplifying and modernizing their commercial codes to increase business traffic in their respective states. However, not all states adopted the Uniform Commercial Code word for word. Some states made modifications that bring it into line with earlier state law or case decisions. However, no state has radically altered the provisions of the Uniform Commercial Code.

Perhaps the greatest advantage conferred by the adoption of the Uniform Commercial Code is its uniformity. When an individual state legislature adopted the Uniform Commercial Code, it not only adopted the particular statutes dealing with commercial transactions but also adopted a well-thought-out analysis of commercial law, presented in a well-organized format, with practical examples and helpful comments. This package made the Uniform Commercial Code quite attractive.

The Organization of the Uniform Commercial Code

Entire books have been written about the Uniform Commercial Code, so our treatment of it in this chapter will not be exhaustive. Instead, we will focus on the organization and the application of the Uniform Commercial Code in everyday business practices.

Sidebar:
The process of creating a uniform system of laws and embodying them in the Uniform Commercial Code is similar to what has recently occurred in Europe. Members of the European Union also have adopted a uniform code, as well as a standard currency, to ease commercial transactions and to make it easier for member nations to conduct business with one another.

The best way to approach the Uniform Commercial Code is begin with the table of contents. As you can see in Exhibit 9-1, the organization set out in the table of contents reveals that Uniform Commercial Code covers a broad number of subjects. The UCC covers transactions ranging from sales to secured transactions. We will concentrate our attention on the first two articles, General Provisions (including definitions) and Sales.

Florida UCC §671-106: Remedies to be liberally administered

"(1)   The remedies provided by this code shall be liberally administered to the end that the aggrieved party may be put in as good a position as if the other party had fully performed but neither consequential or special nor penal damages may be had except as specifically provided in this code or by other rule of law.

(2)   Any right or obligation declared by this code is enforceable by action unless the provision declaring it specifies a different and limited effect."

Arizona UCC §47-1106: Remedies to be liberally administered

"A.   The remedies provided by this title shall be liberally administered to the end that the aggrieved party may be put in as good a position as if the other party had fully performed but neither consequential or special nor penal damages may be had except as specifically provided in this title or by other rule of Saw.

B.   Any right or obligation declared by this title is enforceable by action unless the provision declaring it specifies a different and limited effect."

New York UCC §1-106: Remedies to Be Liberally administered

"(1)   The remedies provided by this Act shall be liberally administered to the end that the aggrieved party may be put in as good a position as if the other party had fully performed but neither consequential, or special, nor penal damages may be had except as specifically provided in this Act or by other rule of law.

(2)   Any right or obligation declared by this Act is enforceable by action unless the provision declaring it specifies a different and limited effect."

EXHIBIT 9-1: Similarity in UCC provisions.

For purposes of our discussions on the Uniform Commercial Code, we will act as though the UCC is identical throughout all the states. However, you should keep in mind that your state may have a slightly different version of the Uniform Commercial Code. When in doubt, you should review your state's statutes to see how it approaches various commercial transactions.

ARTICLES

The UCC is organized into 11 articles (originally, it contained only nine, but two more articles were added). Presented in an elegantly simple plan, the articles describe different aspects of commercial transactions. For instance, if you wished to investigate the law concerning leases, you would go to Article 2A (see Exhibit 9-2).

Article 1. General Provisions

Article 2. Sales

Article 2A. Leases

Article 3. Negotiable Instruments

Article 4. Bank Deposit

Article 4A. Funds Transfers

Article 5. Letters of Credit

Article 6. Bulk Transfers and Bulk Sales

Article 7. Warehouse Receipts, Bills of Lading, and Other
          Documents of Title

Article 8. Investment Securities

Article 9. Secured Transactions

EXHIBIT 9-2: An overview of the articles of the Uniform Commercial Code.

Article 1 contains the general provisions governing the UCC as a whole and also has an extensive definitions section. Subsequent articles are devoted to specific topics and many also contain additional definitions sections relative to their specialty.

OFFICIAL COMMENTS

The Uniform Commercial Code comes with a series of official comments, designed to assist readers in the understanding and interpretation of various Uniform Commercial Code provisions. The official comments to the Uniform Commercial Code are usually not adopted as state law as are the other code provisions of the Uniform Commercial Code. However, some states have taken the extra step of enacting the official comments as well.

The Official Comments were created by the original drafters of the code. The purpose of these comments is to provide guidance about the objectives and interpretations of the code sections. The comments were designed to assist judges and others when faced with new or unanticipated problems in future cases.

TYPES OF TRANSACTIONS COVERED BY THE UCC

The Uniform Commercial Code lists all types of transactions that come within its jurisdiction. Each article lists the specific types of transactions that do, and do not, fall under its jurisdiction. For instance, Article 7 deals with warehouse receipts and bills of lading, whereas Article 9 deals with secured transactions. When in doubt about the coverage of a particular article, the reader should review the preliminary code sections under that article for a complete description of what the article covers.

TYPES OF TRANSACTIONS NOT COVERED BY THE UCC

The Uniform Commercial Code also limits the applicability of its articles. The UCC does not, for example, apply to any of the following:

- Probate matters
- Real estate transactions
- Divorce, family support, alimony, etc.
- Labor relations
- Prenuptial agreements

All of these issues are covered by other statutes outside the Uniform Commercial Code for a particular state.

Article 1 of the UCC

We will be examining Article 1 and Article 2 of the UCC in this chapter. Both of these articles are important but for different reasons. Article 1 is crucial to any matter that falls under the jurisdiction of the UCC because it contains the general provisions and definitions. Article 2, by contrast, is limited to sales. We consider that article in this chapter because "sales" encompasses a huge area and is also likely to be the one area that almost all legal professionals will come into contact with at some time in their careers.

DEFINITIONS AND BASICS

Article 1 of the Uniform Commercial Code contains definitions of terms and phrases that apply to the Code. These definitions are particular to the

Uniform Commercial Code and do not apply to other area of the law. The UCC's definition of "goods," for instance, would have no application to probate or criminal law (see Exhibit 9-3).

> "Agreement" means the bargain of the parties in fact as found in their language or by implication from other circumstances including course of dealing or usage of trade or course of performance as provided in this Act. Whether an agreement has legal consequences is determined by the provisions of this Act, if applicable; otherwise by the law of contracts.[i]

EXHIBIT 9-3: A simple definition from Article 1.

[i] U.C.C. §1-201. General Definitions.

STATE LAW PREVAILS

The Uniform Commercial Code is state law and must be applied as any other state law. Code provisions are subject to litigation and appeal. Appellate courts may interpret Code provisions and create decisions molding the UCC's application to future cases. The Uniform Commercial Code is, in all respects, a state statute and is treated as one.

Sources of Law for the Uniform Commercial Code

There are three different places to research UCC code provisions. The first such place is the Uniform Commercial Code itself. The Code is embodied in the state statutes and should be researched just as any other law would be.

The second source of law may be the Official Comments of the Uniform Commercial Code, if those Official Comments have been enacted by the state legislature. (They are a good source of background material even if they have not been enacted.)

The third source of law under the Uniform Commercial Code is the body of case decisions written by appellate judges interpreting Uniform Commercial Code provisions. These appellate cases are used by legal professionals to research particular areas of the UCC for future cases.

CONSTRUING UCC PROVISIONS

When the court is called upon to construe the language of a contract that is covered by the Uniform Commercial Code, it follows the same rules of construction outlined in Chapter 8. The general rules of construction remain constant whether or not the contract is a Uniform Commercial Code contract or a non-Uniform Commercial Code contract.

The Uniform Commercial Code was designed to be liberally construed. It contains language stating that its terms and definitions should be applied across a broad spectrum, instead of narrowly defined.

One of the advantages of the Uniform Commercial Code is that a judge can review decisions made in other states by judges who may have already considered the legal issue in their own version of the UCC. Because the Uniform Commercial Code is so similar from state to state, judges in one state can use court decisions from other states as a guide to resolving legal issues. In other areas of law, this is not true. Given the wildly divergent approaches among the states to other topics of law, decisions from other states are generally not helpful and can only be used as persuasive authority on a point of law.

Although the Uniform Commercial Code is nearly identical in each state, that does not mean that judges in those individual states are bound to interpret Code provisions in the exactly the same way. States are free to interpret the Code provisions as they choose. There is no oversight mechanism imbedded in the Uniform Commercial Code that forces states to reach similar conclusions on points of law. States have their own sovereignty and are permitted to make their own decisions about how Uniform Commercial Code provisions should be interpreted.

Article II of the UCC

Article 2 of the Uuniform Commercial Code discusses the sale of goods. The article was designed to assist merchants and nonmerchants alike in creating a safety net for commercial transactions. What Article 2 essentially does is create an infrastructure for the sale of goods that takes care of many of the details that are often not expressed by the parties themselves. For instance, the parties may only be interested in how much, how many, and when the items will be delivered. They may not discuss the details such as insurance or manner of payment and or who will pay shipping costs. The Uniform Commercial Code anticipates many of those issues and provides a framework for the parties to work out any disagreements about these, and many other, issues.

For instance, what happens when the goods are defective? Does the buyer have the obligation to ship them back at his or her own cost or should the seller absorb that cost? The Uniform Commercial Code answers these questions.

TYPES OF CONTRACTS COVERED BY ARTICLE 2

We will begin our exploration of Article 2 by examining its table of contents. When researching the UCC, the table of contents for a particular chapter is always a good place to start. As you can see in Exhibit 9-4, the article is broken down into seven parts, sometimes called chapters in some state statutory schemes.

- PART 1. SHORT TITLE, GENERAL CONSTRUCTION, AND SUBJECT MATTER
- PART 2. FORM, FORMATION, AND READJUSTMENT OF CONTRACT
- PART 3. GENERAL OBLIGATION AND CONSTRUCTION OF CONTRACT
- PART 4. TITLE, CREDITORS, AND GOOD-FAITH PURCHASERS
- PART 5. PERFORMANCE
- PART 6. BREACH, REPUDIATION, AND EXCUSE
- PART 7. REMEDIES[i]

EXHIBIT 9-4: Table of contents for Article 2.

[i] Illinois Compiled Statutes, Commercial Code, Uniform Commercial Code, §810 ILCS 5.

Each part contains provisions dealing with the listed area. We will skip Part 1, as it only explains the general rules of contract construction, and move directly to Part 2 (see Exhibit 9-5).

2-101. Short title

2-102. Scope; certain security and other transactions excluded from this Chapter

2-103. Definitions and index of definitions

2-104. Definitions: "Merchant"; "between merchants"; "financing agency"

2-105. Definitions: transferability; "goods"; "future" goods; "lot"; "commercial unit'

2-106. Definitions: "contract"; "agreement"; "contract for sale"; "sale"; "present sale"; "conforming to contract"; "termination"; "cancellation"

2-107. Goods to be severed from realty; recording SC UCC SECTION 36-2-101, etseq.

EXHIBIT 9-5: Index to Part 1 of Article 2.

Part 2 of Article 2

The index of Part 2, as shown in Exhibit 9-6, encompasses a broad range of topics relating to the formation of contracts for the sale of goods.

2-201. Formal requirements; statute of frauds

2-202. Final written expression; parol or extrinsic evidence

2-203. Seals inoperative

2-204. Formation in general

2-205. Firm offers

2-206. Offer and acceptance in formation of contract

2-207. Additional terms in acceptance or confirmation

2-208. Course of performance or practical construction

2-209. Modification, rescission and waiver

2-210. Delegation of performance; assignment of rights[i]

EXHIBIT 9-6: Index to Part 2 of Article 2 of the UCC.

[i] SC UCC §36-2-201, et seq.

As you can see from the list of topics in Exhibit 9-6, Part 2 of Article 2 covers topics that we have addressed in previous chapters. Here, however, the UCC codifies all of these various rules and brings them together in one subheading for ease of reference. This is one of the benefits of the UCC, the organizational scheme. Under traditional case law analysis, a legal professional would be forced to look in several different places to learn the law about seals, or the Statute of Frauds, or the law of offer and acceptance. The UCC puts it all in one place and, in many instances, simplifies, modernizes, and streamlines the rules about each of these topics. The UCC's coverage of the Statute of Frauds is particularly noteworthy.

The Statute of Frauds Under the UCC

We have dealt with the Statute of Frauds in Chapter 7. How does the UCC approach this topic? We will examine Section 2–201 (see Exhibit 9-7).

In Chapter 7, we learned that the Statute of Frauds, as that statute was originally created and later enacted by the various states, required certain types of contracts to be in writing. They included contracts for the sale/transfer of real estate, prenuptial agreements, and contracts for the sale of goods valued at $500 or more, among others. The UCC simplifies the Statute of Frauds, at least as it concerns commercial transactions. When we

> (1) Except as otherwise provided in this section a contract for the sale of goods for the price of $500 or more is not enforceable by way of action or defense unless there is some writing sufficient to indicate that a contract for sale has been made between the parties and signed by the party against whom enforcement is sought or by his authorized agent or broker. A writing is not insufficient because it omits or incorrectly states a term agreed upon but the contract is not enforceable under this paragraph beyond the quantity of goods shown in such writing.[i]

EXHIBIT 9-7:   UCC Section 2-201. Formal requirements; statute of frauds.

[i] SC UCC §36-2-201.

discussed the Statute of Frauds in Chapter 7, we explored memoranda of contract and other issues relating to whether a writing satisfied the statute. In Section 2-201, the framers of the Uniform Commercial Code have streamlined the statute. Under their approach, a writing is required "for the sale of goods for the price of $500." They have also simplified the rules regarding what qualifies as a "writing." Under the UCC, "some writing" is permissible, so long as it:

1.   Indicates that a contract for sale has been made between the parties
2.   Is signed by the party against whom enforcement is sought

This section also does away with a large body of cases devoted to the point of the sufficiency of a writing by making any writing sufficient that meets these requirements and further stating that a writing will be sufficient even if it misstates a term.

Defining "Contract" Under the UCC

Time and again, the framers of the Uniform Commercial Code work to simplify the rules and interpretations of commercial concepts. This is also evidence in the definitions section of Part 2, Article 2. The UCC defines a contract as "limited to those relating to the present or future sale of goods. 'Contract for sale' includes both a present sale of goods and a contract to sell goods at a future time. A 'sale' consists in the passing of title from the seller to the buyer for a price. A 'present sale' means a sale which is accomplished by the making of the contract."[1]

This definition takes into account a broad range of activities concerning goods and is fluid enough to be applied to a vast array of transactions. The definitions section also defines "goods" under the UCC and explain the limitations on this term (see Exhibit 9-8).

> "Unless the context otherwise requires, this Article applies to transactions in *goods*; it does not apply to any transaction which although in the form of an unconditional contract to sell or present sale is intended to operate only as a security transaction nor does this Article impair or repeal any statute regulating sales to consumers, farmers, or other specified classes of buyers.[i]

EXHIBIT 9-8: Defining "goods" under the UCC.

---

[i] New York UCC §2-102.

HYPOTHETICAL 9-1   Defining Time Under the UCC

§1-204 of the UCC defines reasonable time for transactions. It provides:

Whenever this Act requires any action to be taken within a reasonable time, any time which is not manifestly unreasonable may be fixed by agreement.

(2) What is a reasonable time for taking any action depends on the nature, purpose and circumstances of such action.

(3) An action is taken "seasonably" when it is taken at or within the time agreed or if no time is agreed at or within a reasonable time.

Boiled Beef Records has an agreement with nationwide retailer called Mutton Mart. The agreement provides that Mutton Mart must notify BBR about any problems with its CDs within a reasonable period of time, which for five years has been within 90 days of receipt. However, Mutton Mart claims that because of shipping and warehousing, it often doesn't learn about CD defects until after the time period. It brings action claiming that BBR's definition of reasonable time, 90 days, is too restrictive. How does the court rule?

Answer: The parties are free to define reasonable time between them and because they have previously agreed on a 90-day term, then 90 days is reasonable.

REMEDIES UNDER ARTICLE 2

Each Article of the UCC provides a list of its own remedies. Article 2, for instance, lists the remedies available for buyers and sellers.

Remedies of the Seller

Part 7 of Article 2 lists the types of remedies available to the parties. Although we will discuss contract remedies in Chapter 11, we will address UCC remedies here. The UCC is very specific about the types of remedies available to a seller when a buyer has acted wrongfully, that is, rejects acceptance of goods or fails to make payment on the goods.

The seller may employ any of the following remedies:

- Withhold delivery of the goods
- Stop delivery of the goods
- Resell and recover damages
- Recover damages for nonacceptance or the price of the goods
- Cancel the contract.[2]

Remedies of the Buyer

Article 2 also provides specific remedies for buyers. When a seller wrongfully refuses to deliver goods, supplies faulty goods, or breaches the contract, the buyer may:

- Cancel the contract
- Recover damages for nondelivery
- Recover the goods
- Obtain specific performance or use **replevin** to secure the goods[3]

UCC Financing Statements

replevin: A legal action to get back personal property wrongfully held by another person.

Although we have limited our discussion to Article 2 of the UCC, a brief statement about Article 9 is also important, at least to the extent of discussing financing statements.

A financing statement is a way for a debtor to record a security interest in personal property that is being used as collateral for a loan. In many ways, a financing statement acts in exactly the same way as a mortgage does on a home. When the homeowner fails to pay on the mortgage, the lending institution uses the mortgage (and more specifically the clauses relating to foreclosure) to take over the property in lieu of payments. Although repossessing personal property is a great deal easier than foreclosing a home, the idea is the same.

Financing statements provide a method for a creditor to create a public record of the security interest in the property and to use this public filing as a way to retake the property if the debtor fails to make payments on the loan.

UCC Financing statements are often filed in county land offices, or Register of Deeds offices—the same place where deeds and mortgages are filed.

They are important to legal professionals because they often form the basis of suits to recover personal property. A properly filed UCC financing statement may be required before such a suit will be allowed to continue. (For a sample UCC Financing Statement, see the Appendix.)

The Case of the Poorly Performing Pipes[4]
MEMORANDUM OPINION AND ORDER
TOM S. LEE, Chief Judge.

The facts alleged by IHP are as follows. IHP, a Missouri corporation qualified to do business in Mississippi, entered into a contract with PermAlert, an Illinois corporation, for the purchase of double-contained pipes. IHP needed the pipes in forty-foot sections to be used as part of an underground jet fuel distribution for the Mississippi Air National Guard at Key Field in Meridian, Mississippi, a fact of which PermAlert was aware. During the negotiation process, PermAlert represented to IHP that the pipes would be manufactured in a good and workman-like manner, free of defects and negligence, and that the factory joints, caused by the joining of two twenty-foot pipes, would be sealed and tested to withstand fifteen pounds of pressure per square inch. Based on these representations and relying on PermAlert's business judgment, IHP the contract. Following delivery of the first shipment of pipes, PermAlert informed IHP that a review of the quality assurance records indicated that PermAlert had failed to sign off on the test sheets. However, PermAlert did not reveal, in an effort to induce IHP's further reliance, that the pipes had never been tested. Relying on this material omission and further misrepresentations, IHP installed and tested the pipe at eight pounds of pressure per square inch in accordance with the instruction manual supplied by PermAlert, and with the assistance of PermAlert's field technician. IHP then backfilled the trenches in which the pipe was laid. Thereafter, IHP determined that water was infiltrating the outer containment pipes, necessitating that the pipes be re-tested at fifteen pounds of pressure per square inch. During the re-testing, many of the factory joints failed, requiring IHP to excavate the defective pipe, then field wrap all of the containment pipe joints. IHP, within eight days of discovering the failure, notified PermAlert that the factory joints were defective. As a result of PermAlert's actions, IHP was damaged in excess of $832,537.74 and alleges the following causes of action against PermAlert: 1) breach of express warranty; 2) breach of the implied warranties of fitness for a particular purpose and merchantability; 3) fraudulent misrepresentation; and 4) negligence. PermAlert seeks to have all of IHP's claims dismissed, save the claim for breach of express warranty. In support of its motion, PermAlert argues that, despite IHP's assertion to the contrary, the parties chose Illinois law to govern their contract and that pursuant to Illinois law, the disclaimer in PermAlert's order acknowledgment is effective to preclude IHP from recovery under an implied warranty theory. PermAlert further argues that application of §75-1-105, Mississippi's unique choice of law provision, would be unconstitutional because, utilizing the significant contacts requirement of the Second Restatement of Conflicts, this warranty action lacks a reasonable and appropriate relation to Mississippi. PermAlert also maintains that application of §75-1-105(1) to an out-of-state corporation with no significant contacts with Mississippi, not only defeats the purpose of §75-1-105(1)—to protect Mississippi residents—but also allows IHP to escape its contractual obligations.

As the case sub judice is a diversity action, under Klaxon this court must apply the law of the forum state, including the state's conflict of laws rules. Klaxon Co. v. Stentor Elec. Mfg. Co., 313 U.S. 487, 61 S.Ct. 1020, 85 L.Ed. 1477 (1941). As previously noted, §75-1-105, Mississippi's conflict of law rule for warranty claims, requires "the application of Mississippi substantive law on privity, warranty disclaimers and limitations of remedies in an action brought in Mississippi, notwithstanding any agreement by the parties that the laws of another jurisdiction would govern their respective rights and duties." Price v. International Tel. and Tel. Co., 651 F.Supp. 706, 709 (S.D.Miss.1986).

Under U.C.C. §1-105, the parties' contractual choice of law will be upheld "unless the transaction lacks a normal connection with the state whose law was selected." Superfos Inv., Ltd. v. FirstMiss Fertilizer, Inc., 809 F. Supp. 450, 452 (S.D.Miss.1992). Thus, "[o]nly when it is shown that the contact did not occur in the normal course of the transaction, but was contrived to validate the parties' choice of law [will] the relationship be held unreasonable." Id. While this court has indicated that this standard might apply to the transactional relation test for applicability of Mississippi law to implied warranty disclaimers and limitation of remedies, See Apache Prod. Co. v. Employers Ins. of Wausau, 154 F.R.D. 650, 656 (S.D.Miss.1994), in the instant case, it is apparent that the transaction is more than reasonably related to Mississippi.

Accepting as true IHP's allegations that PermAlert 1) entered into a contract to be performed in Mississippi; 2) shipped its product to Mississippi; and 3) sent a field technician to aid in the installation of the pipes in Mississippi, the court concludes that Mississippi is not only reasonably related to the transaction, but also has "a significant contact or significant aggregation of contacts, creating [a] state interest, such that choice of its law is neither arbitrary nor fundamentally unfair." Allstate Ins. Co. v. Hague, 449 U.S. 302, 313, 101 S.Ct. 633, 640, 66 L.Ed.2d 521 (1981). The court therefore concludes that, regardless of whether Mississippi has the most significant relationship to the transaction or whether the contract contained any choice of law provision to the contrary, Mississippi substantive law applies to IHP's implied warranty claims. Furthermore, the court finds that IHP's allegations are sufficient under Mississippi Code Sections 75-2-314 and 75-2-315 to state claims for breach of the implied warranties of merchantability and fitness for a particular purpose and thus PermAlert's motion to dismiss the implied warranty claim will be denied.

PermAlert next argues that, under the law of both Illinois and Mississippi, IHP's fraudulent misrepresentation claim cannot stand because the alleged misrepresentation refers only to future acts and thus constitutes only promissory fraud which is generally not actionable. Furthermore, PermAlert contends

that IHP's allegation does not fall within the narrow exception to promissory fraud recognized by both Mississippi and Delaware law which allows a claimant to go forward "where the false promise or representation of intention of future conduct is the scheme or device to accomplish the fraud." Bower v. Jones, 978 F.2d 1004, 1011 (7th Cir.1992); See Kidd v. Kidd, 210 Miss. 465, 49 So.2d 824, 827 (1951). Finally with regard to IHP's fraud claim, PermAlert, in its reply brief, asserts that IHP's claim "amounts to nothing more than a thinly veiled breach of contract claim," and thus, plaintiff's remedy, if any, is for breach of contract or express warranty.

No choice of law analysis is required for the purpose of determining whether Illinois or Mississippi law applies as IHP states a claim for fraudulent misrepresentation under both. The court rejects PermAlert's argument that IHP has merely alleged promissory fraud which is generally not actionable. In its amended complaint, IHP alleges that PermAlert did disclose that during a review of the quality assurance records related to the first of five shipments of pipe, it "discovered that the pneumatic tests on these pipes were not signed off on the test sheets," but it failed to tell IHP that no tests whatsoever were performed on the pipes. IHP submits PermAlert thereby omitted to apprise IHP of a material present fact. IHP also alleges that PermAlert's employee affirmatively misrepresented that he had inspected the pipes included in the first shipment and found them suitable for installation. These allegations are sufficient to state a claim for fraud.

Additionally, because IHP seeks punitive damages as a result of PermAlert's alleged fraudulent misrepresentations, its claim amounts to more than a "thinly disguised breach of contract claim," as asserted by PermAlert. The case sub judice is distinguishable from Furr Marketing, Inc. v. Orval Kent Food Co., 682 F.Supp. 884, 886 (S.D.1988), in which this court dismissed a plaintiff's negligence claim after finding that it was merely "a reiteration of the claim for breach of contract." Unlike the plaintiff in Furr, IHP has not alleged a willful breach of the contract, and thus a separate claim for fraudulent misrepresentation which includes a request for punitive damages is not duplicative of the breach of express warranty claim. Id. For these reasons, PermAlert's motion to dismiss IHP's fraudulent misrepresentation claim will be denied.

As to IHP's negligence claim, PermAlert asserts that Illinois law, which the parties agreed in their contract would apply to disputes arising under the contract, precludes recovery under a negligence theory since IHP alleges only economic loss which is "defined as 'damages for inadequate value, cost of repair and replacement of the defective product, or consequent loss of profit—without claim of personal injury or damage to other property.' " Moorman Mfg. Co. v. National Tank Co., 91 Ill.2d 69, 61 Ill.Dec. 746, 752, 435 N.E.2d 443, 449 (1982). PermAlert points out that under Moorman, tort law affords protection only if a "sudden and calamitous occurrence caused personal injury or property damage," and thus, where IHP discovered the defect in the pipes through pneumatic testing, it fails to state a negligence claim under Illinois law. IHP denies that Illinois law applies, and contends instead that Mississippi law applies. However, in the court's opinion, the law of both Mississippi and Illinois preclude IHP's recovery of economic losses under a negligence theory. This court held in East Mississippi Power Ass'n v. Porcelain Products Co., 729 F. Supp. 512, 514 (S.D.Miss.1990), that the Mississippi Supreme Court would deny recovery under either a strict liability or negligence theory "for a product defect where that defect results in damage to the product itself and thus causes only economic loss to its purchaser."

As in East Mississippi, IHP's claim that the factory joints in the pipes supplied by the PermAlert leaked

"is not a claim for the kind of accidental physical injury against which tort law was designed to protect consumers. In contrast, this is a commercial dispute in which commercial purchasers complain that a product has not functioned as was expected and intended." Id. at 517. Likewise, the court concludes that IHP has failed to plead a "sudden and calamitous occurrence causing personal injury or property damage," so as to bring its claim within the purview of Illinois law as established by Moorman. Accordingly, the court finds that PermAlert's motion to dismiss for failure to state a claim of negligence should be granted.

For the foregoing reasons, it is ordered that PermAlert's motion to dismiss is denied as to IHP's claims for breach of implied warranties and fraudulent misrepresentation and is granted as to IHP's negligence claim.

Case Questions:

1. Does the court mention any material omissions by the parties in this case? If so, what are they?

2. What does the UCC say about the parties' choice of law?

3. Why is Mississippi the court's choice for which law to apply to the contract in this case?

4. According to the court, what is promissory fraud?

5. Why does the court hold that tort (or negligence) law does not apply to this case?

The Case of the Calamitous Cable System[5]

TUTTLE, Circuit Judge:

This is an appeal from a verdict and judgment in favor of the Defendant-Appellee on its counterclaim when it was sued for the balance due on a construction contract wherein the plaintiff agreed to construct, and did construct, a cable television system for the defendant.

The jury found in favor of the defendant on Count One of the counterclaim, which was based on an implied warranty "that the said system would be well constructed of workmanlike quality and suitable for the purposes for which it was intended," and found damages on this counterclaim to amount to $56,000. The jury found in favor of the defendant on counterclaim number three, which was based upon alleged false representations as to the plaintiff's knowledge and intent that it could and would complete the contract within the sixty day period, upon which the defendant relied by entering into the contract, and which knowledge or intent did not in truth exist, all to the damage of the defendants. The jury found that such false representation did exist, and returned a verdict on this count in the sum of $21,591.

The issues before the court on appeal are: (1) Did the court properly submit to the jury the question of breach of implied warranty of fitness for use intended where the contract purported to waive all warranties except as expressly stated in the contract, and (2) was there sufficient evidence from which the jury could have found that the plaintiff made a fraudulent misrepresentation to the defendant.

We deal with the questions in reverse order.

Florida law of actionable misrepresentation was recently capsulated into the following elements: "(1) a misrepresentation of material fact. (2) (a) knowledge of the representor of the misrepresentation, or, (b) representations made by the representator without knowledge as to either truth or falsity, or, (c) representations made under circumstances in which the representor ought to have known, if he

did not know, of the falsity thereof, (3) an intention that the representation induce another to act on it, and (4) resulting injury to the party acting in justifiable reliance on the representation."

We now look at the facts in this case, which are substantially undisputed so far as they deal with the element of actionable misrepresentation. The contract, entered into after repeated statements by Bernard Karlen, Vice President of General Cablevision, that his company was strictly limited to the requirement that it have the job completed within sixty days, contained an express promise that Entron would construct and turn over a system on a "turnkey" basis within sixty days after beginning construction; the contract was not only not turned over within sixty days but was not offered for final acceptance until approximately three times that long, some 175 days after the contract was signed. Even this tender was not accepted by General Cablevision, because the system failed to operate properly, and it was not until nearly three months later that the system began operating completely satisfactorily; substantial damage accrued to General Cablevision as a result of this failure of Entron to live up to its promise of performance, since General Cablevision opened offices and started selling service to prospective customers on the assumption that the sixty day completion would be carried out; in response to questions asked by defendant of the president of Entron that he name several comparable jobs performed by Entron, several were named, including one in Laurinburg, North Carolina; the Laurinburg job required four or five calendar months for completion; the president of Entron testified that as far as he could recall this was the shortest time Entron had ever required to build and install a CATV System of comparable type.

It has been said that 'the state of a man's mind is as much a fact as the state of his digestion.' If this be true, if at the time a seller makes a statement as to what he proposes to do for the future when the true state of his mind would disclose that he knows he cannot do so, this is a misrepresentation of a material fact. The same would be true if the seller represents what he proposes to do at a time when he is either without knowledge as to his ability to perform or if he represents what he proposes to do under circumstances in which he should have known, but may not have known, of his inability to carry out his promise. These standards we derive from what has been quoted above as the Florida law. Here, also, there is no contention made by the appellant that whatever representations were made as to the sixty-day performance were not made for the purpose of inducing General Cablevision to act on them. Moreover, it is clear that General Cablevision did rely on the representation and this reliance resulted in injury.

Although not expressly argued on behalf of the appellee, we consider the very gross failure to perform the contract, even if standing alone, as strong evidence of the inability of the plaintiff-appellant to do what it promised to do—that is to complete the system within sixty days. Assuming, as we should, that when parties enter into a solemn written obligation to perform a contract involving a reasonably complicated mechanism and system as to which the promisor is presumed to be an expert, this should of itself be taken to be a holding out of a belief that the undertaking could be carried out, the failure of the promisor to carry out his agreement fully and adequately within anything like the terms of the formal contract is some evidence that the party did not intend to do it in the first place. To this there is to be added the testimony of the president of the appellant that the company had never performed a job of comparable size in a period of even twice as many days as the sixty-day period contemplated in this contract. We think this is sufficient to permit the jury to find all of the essential elements for actionable misrepresentation.

There remains the question as to the jury's verdict on count one charging that the CATV system constructed by Entron and sold to General Cablevision was not suitable and reasonably fit for the purposes for which it was intended, thus violating an implied warranty of fitness. The contract between the parties provides in paragraph 9(d) thereof, "Except for the express warranties set forth herein, Entron makes no warranty of any kind, express or implied and all warranties of merchantability, fitness for particular purpose, and other warranties of whatever kind are hereby disclaimed by Entron and excluded."

Appellant contends that this agreement in the contract precludes the possibility of a recovery on an implied warranty of fitness, because, although appellant concedes that otherwise the uniform commercial code, Section 672.2-102, Fla.Statutes, F.S.A., would apply, the provisions of the code do not apply here because what was called for by this contract was not a "sale." The uniform commercial code provides, 'Words or conduct relevant to the creation of an express warranty and words or conduct tending to negate or limit warranties shall be construed wherever reasonable as consistent with each other; but subject to the provisions of this chapter on parol or extrinsic evidence (672.2-202) negation or limitation is inoperative to the extent that such construction is unreasonable.

"(2) Subject to subsection 3, to exclude or modify the implied warranty of merchantability or any part of it, the language must mention merchantability and in case of a writing must be conspicuous, and to exclude or modify any implied warranty of fitness the exclusion must be by a writing and conspicuous. Language to exclude all warranties of fitness is sufficient if it states, for example, that "there are no warranties which extend beyond the description on the face hereof." Fla.Stat. 672.2-316, F.S.A. Although, of course, the language is not necessarily conclusive in the matter, it is significant to note that the first paragraph of the contract designated General Cablevision of Palatka as the "buyer."

Also, it is significant that the contract provided that "title and all incidence of title and ownership shall be and remain with Entron until completion of the work or any portion thereof required here-under. It is the intention of the parties that all equipment and material used hereunder shall be and remain personal property, at least until such time as acceptance of and final payment for the entire system is made." It seems clear that this contract for the sale of a system, many of the component parts of which were to be manufactured by Entron, was sufficiently a sale of goods as to bring it within the contemplation of the uniform commercial code.

Since the disclaimer of warranties must be judged by the provisions of the Uniform Commercial Code, it becomes obvious that the requirements of that code were not complied with in respect to the conspicuousness of the language purporting to disclaim an implied warranty.

In Boeing Airplane Co. v. O'Malley, 8 Cir. 1964, 329 F.2d 585, the court said:

"While the implied warranty could under the 1959 statute be disclaimed by the form of language used in Article VI of the contract, the 'writing must be conspicuous.' Here it is not so. It is merely in the same color and size of other type used for the other provisions and under the statutory definition of 'conspicuous' fails of its purpose."

The judgment of the trial court is affirmed.

Case Questions:

1. What were the material misrepresentations in this case?
2. Was the defendant's inability to perform the work in the time allotted the telling feature in this case, or was there another reason for the court's decision?
3. According to the court, does the Florida Uniform Commercial Code apply to this case?
4. Is this a case of fraudulent misrepresentation or simply underestimating the time it would take to complete a job? Explain your answer.
5. If this is a case of misrepresentation, what are the misrepresentations made?

Hypothetical 9-2   The Outboard Offer

§2-205 of the UCC provides:

"An offer by a merchant to buy or sell goods in a signed writing which by its terms gives assurance that it will be held open is not revocable, for lack of consideration, during the time stated or if no time is stated for a reasonable time, but in no event may such period of irrevocability exceed three months; but any such term of assurance on a form supplied by the offeree must be separately signed by the offeror."

Buzz Motors sends a fax to Mountain Marine, making the following offer: "Will sell 100 super-sized Melon brand outboard motors for $400 each. Offer remains open."

Four months later, Mountain Marine places an order for 75 supersized Melon brand outboard motors at $400 each. Buzz Motors returns the order, stating that the offer has been revoked. Mountain Marine brings suit, alleging that the offer was, by its own terms, irrevocable. What is the court's ruling?

Answer: The court rules that regardless of the wording of the offer, more than three months had passed since the original offer and the UCC authorizes revocation of offers after that time period.

ETHICS FILE: Current Legal Research of the UCC

Although legal research and ethical concerns do not, at first blush, appear to be related, actually they are very dependent on one another. When a legal professional researches a case or a provision of the Uniform Commercial Code, relying on outdated research can often produce faulty results. Requiring legal professionals to bring their research as up to date as possible is one way of ensuring that the client receives the best possible service. Appropriate and extensive legal research ensures that the client is getting the best possible service and also guards against recent cases that show that the client's cause of action is not authorized. In most states the individual provisions of the Uniform Commercial Code come with annotations that show how it has been applied. These annotations should be studied closely to make sure that there haven't been recent changes in the law that can have a devastating impact on a client's case.

Chapter Summary:

The UCC was developed as a means of bringing greater uniformity and predictability to commercial transactions. Developed by scholars and practitioners, the UCC is a model of efficiency and organization. The UCC is not federal law. Instead, it is a system of laws that the individual states were free to accept or reject. To date, all 50 states have adopted the UCC in whole or in part. The UCC is organized into 11 different articles, covering a broad range of topics. In addition to the articles, the UCC also provides Official Comments that explain or amplify the language in the Code provisions.

Articles 1 and 2 are the focus of this chapter. Article 1 is the General Provisions section that defines many of the major concepts and terms. Article 2 concerns sales. Each Article contains its own laws about interpretation, modification and enforcement of contracts. Article 2 provides its own body of laws about the Statute of Frauds and how transactions in goods are conducted.

Business Case File

Deb Bevans, Franchisee

Deb Bevans

Deb Bevans was a nurse for over 10 years before deciding to open up her own store. "I wanted the freedom that having my own business would give me." She researched several options and then decided to purchase a franchise in a scrapbook business. "I liked the idea of helping people preserve their memories and I've been a scrapbooker for years. It was a natural fit."

Once she had decided on her business and negotiated a franchise agreement, the next step was to consider the business structure. "I talked with a lot of business owners and knew that I wanted as much protection as I could get. She decided to incorporate her business under the name 'Scrapbook Company of Asheville.' "I was surprised by how straightforward the whole process was. I'd always had this idea that corporate law, like law in general, was all about complicated procedures and Latin terms. Actually, it was pretty simple."

Once her business opened up under the name of The Scrapbook Company, her next concern was ordering product to stock her shelves. "I didn't know very much about interstate shipments and some of the terms, such as F.O.B. (free on board) weren't familiar to me. I learned later about the UCC, and how it requires that manufacturers advertise how they will ship (and who will have to pay for it)."

She has been running her business since April 2004. "Things have gone a lot better than I would have imagined. Business has been great. We've even taken over the next unit and doubled the size of the store. That's not bad for just a few months in business!"

WEB SITES

North Carolina Department of the Secretary of State
http://www.secretary.state.nc.us/ucc/
Includes an in-depth discussion on the UCC.

Oregon Secretary of State's UCC listings
http://www.filinginoregon.com/ucc/
Provides a wide range of information about the UCC.

Vermont Secretary of State UCC Listings
http://www.sec.state.vt.us
Vermont's UCC information.

Uniform Commercial Code (Texas)
http://www.sos.state.tx.us
UCC information for the state of Texas.

REVIEW QUESTIONS

1. What is the purpose of the Uniform Commercial Code?
2. What types of transactions are covered by the Uniform Commercial Code?
3. What is the function of Article 1 of the Uniform Commercial Code?
4. Explain the coverage of Article 2 of Uniform Commercial Code.
5. The Uniform Commercial Code was developed by legal scholars but was not legal binding authority until what action was taken by the individual states?
6. What are the Official Comments to the Uniform Commercial Code?
7. Explain what the term "goods" means in Article 2 of the Uniform Commercial Code.
8. When the Uniform Commercial Code is enacted in a particular state, what happens to the preexisting statutory law on commercial transactions?
9. Why was a Uniform Commercial Code needed in the United States?
10. Can a state change the language of the Uniform Commercial Code?
11. What types of transactions are covered by the various articles of the Uniform Commercial Code?
12. What are examples of transactions that are not covered by the UCC?
13. Is the Uniform Commercial Code federal law or state law or both? Explain.
14. What are the rules that courts must follow in construing the language of the Uniform Commercial Code?
15. What types of remedies are available to a seller under the UCC?
16. What types of remedies are available to a buyer under the UCC?
17. Explain the court's ruling in the "Case of the Poorly Performing Pipes." What did the court mean by "choice of law provision?"

18. What are UCC financing statements? Why are they used?

19. Explain what sources of law relate to the UCC.

20. Explain why using accurate and updated legal research sources can be an ethical concern.

HANDS-ON ASSIGNMENT

Locate your state's own UCC provisions. How does your state define "contract" or "goods"? Does your state follow the same organizational scheme as the general Uniform Commercial Code? When did your state adopt the Uniform Commercial Code?

Do an Internet search for "UCC Financing Statements." Do any hits come up for your state? If so, what does your state site say about the Uniform Commercial Code in general and about UCC Financing Statements in particular?

PRACTICAL APPLICATION

Suppose that you wish to create your own independent paralegal firm. This firm will work as freelance paralegals for local attorneys, on a contractual basis, under the particular client–attorney's supervision. Is this arrangement covered by the Uniform Commercial Code? Why or why not?

HELP THIS BUSINESS

Your instructor has created a set of DVDs of class lectures and t-shirts bearing the logo "Business Law Rules." However, before your instructor actually starts selling the DVDs or the shirts, there is a UCC concern:

a. *Is the sale of DVDs and T-shirts covered by the Uniform Commercial Code in your state?*

b. *If yes, are there certain requirements that your instructor must meet when ordering supplies of DVDs and T shirts that would obviously exceed $500 in value?*

KEY TERMS

code
replevin

ENDNOTES

[1] SC UCC §36-2-106 (1).

[2] TX UCC §2.703.

[3] TX UCC §2.711.

[4] *IHP Indus., Inc. v. PermAlert, ESP.*, 947 F. Supp. 257 (S.D.Miss., 1996).

[5] *Entron, Inc. v. General Cablevision of Palatka*, 435 F.2d 995 (C.A.Fla., 1970).

 For additional resources, visit our Web site at www.westlegalstudies.com

CHAPTER 10

DISCHARGE, PERFORMANCE, AND CANCELLATION OF A CONTRACT

Focus of this chapter: In this chapter we will explore the issues relating to the successful completion of a contract and what happens when a contract is breached. We will begin with a discussion of discharge of a contract, then proceed to the legal issues associated with cancellation, rescission, and reformation of a contract, and how these legal issues affect contract analysis.

Chapter Objectives:
At the completion of this chapter, you should be able to:

- Explain the concept of discharge of contractual duty
- Explain abandonment as it relates to contracts
- Describe rescission and its effect on the contracting in parties
- Define legal impossibility
- Explain the concept of breach of contract
- Explain the ways that a contract may be terminated
- Explain the difference between rescission and cancellation of a contract
- Define the elements of rescission
- Explain the concept of impossibility due to an act of God
- Explain the effect that the death of a party has on the contract

When and How Does the Contract End?

In the preceding chapters we have devoted a great deal of attention to the formation of a contract and the interpretation of contract clauses. However, it may often be as important to the parties to a contract to establish when the contract actually terminates. Most contract suits are not brought over questions regarding the formation of a contract; they are brought because of what one party considers to be an improper termination of a contract. A contract can be terminated in a wide variety of ways, from successful performance of the terms to wrongful breach to the influence of some outside factor, such as an Act of God. We will begin our discussion of contract terminations with the relatively simple concept of performance and then progress to the more complex issues of rescission, impossibility, and supervening causes.

DISCHARGE OF A CONTRACT

discharge: To discharge a contract is to end the obligation by agreement or by carrying it out.

When we say that a contract has been **discharged**, it means that it has been performed and is no longer a pending, legal obligation. Relying on terminology from previous chapters, a discharged contract is an executed contract. A contract that has not been fully performed is an executory contract.

A contract remains in force as long as the parties continue to abide by it. In fact, continued performance of a contract is evidence of the continued obligation between the parties.

When a contract has been discharged, the rights, duties, and obligations of the parties have terminated at least as far as that particular contract is concerned. A discharged contract is a fully performed contract.

A contract may be discharged by completion of the act contemplated in the agreement. For instance, a unilateral contract will terminate on the performance of the action required in the contract. When a reward poster offers $1,000 for the arrest of a particular suspect, and the suspect is arrested, the contract is discharged. In this case, the contract contemplated a specific event and that event has occurred.

However, determining whether or not a contract has been discharged is not always such an easily answered question. When the parties have a continuing obligation, where one provides a service that the other pays for, when is the contract discharged? In a continuing relationship, is the contract ever really discharged? These are the types of issues we will address in the remainder of this chapter (see Exhibit 10-1).

• Agreement	• Operation of law
• Performance	• Breach

EXHIBIT 10-1: How a contract can be discharged.

Discharging a Contract Through Performance

A contract can be discharged through the performance of its terms. When it has been discharged, there is no longer any basis for a suit for breach of contract. A discharged contract is a nullity.

A contract that has been fully performed by one party cannot be terminated by the other prior to performance. The law presumes that all contracts are permanent and irrevocable by the parties, unless there is agreement to the contrary.

The performance must be those actions that were originally agreed on between the parties. There can be no substitution of one kind of performance with another, unless all parties agree to the substitution.

Duty to Perform

A party to a contract is under a legal obligation to perform. As long as the contract does not violate statutory provisions or public policy, a party must perform as originally agreed. Failure to do so gives rise to a cause of action for breach of contract.

This obligation to perform, however, is often strictly construed. The duty to perform is the duty to perform the specific actions assumed under the contract. As we will see later in this chapter, when performance is impossible, a different type of performance is not acceptable.

Sidebar:
Courts consistently have imposed a duty to perform on one party to a contract when the other has already performed.

Good Faith

Good faith is a requirement of all parties to a contract. This also is true of the party's duty to perform. The party to a contract is obligated to make reasonable efforts to perform duties outlined in the agreement.

What Duties Are Required?

The party is only required to perform the actions contemplated in the contract, and any assumed duties, as well. What are assumed duties? Suppose that Ramon has agreed to purchase 100 cases of alcohol to resell at his new bar. One of Ramon's assumed duties would be to arrange for a liquor license to sell the alcohol. Although this duty is not expressly stated in the contract, it is assumed by the parties and is reasonable under the circumstances. Put another way, can Ramon claim that he cannot live up to his obligations because he neglected to obtain a liquor license? The court would undoubtedly rule against him. A different issue is raised, however, if Ramon is refused a liquor license by the local government. We will address the issue of impossibility.

Of course, when a party wrongfully terminates a contract, such as through a unilateral cancellation, that party is subject to suit and may be forced to pay damages. We will discuss contract damages in a future chapter.

Sidebar:
One of the bedrock principles of law is to encourage performance of a contract and not to encourage breaches of contracts. To this end, courts will usually interpret a contract to impose a duty to perform on both parties.

Sidebar:
The rule about contractual performance is simple: when performance under the contract is lawful and possible, the party must perform.

Discharging by Termination

Many contract contain provisions allowing the parties to terminate the contract under certain conditions. Commonly referred to as "termination provisions," these clauses allow the parties to rescind the contract when specified events occur.

When no provision for termination exists in a contract, then the contract can be terminated either within a reasonable period of time or through the intentional act of the parties.

When a contract fails to state a particular event or date on which it terminates, and the termination of the contract is a point of controversy, the courts will look to the standard custom, if any, to determine a valid termination date. The courts also will consider all the surrounding circumstances relating to the formation of the contract and the contract clauses contained in the agreement. As we've seen on numerous occasions before, the courts will also attempt to interpret the intentions of the parties.

How does discharge of a contract differ from termination of a contract? A contract that has been terminated has been ended. Such a contract may or may not have been fully performed. A contract that has been discharged, by contrast, has been fully performed to the satisfaction of both parties.

Contracts without Termination Dates

Suppose that a contract has no agreed-on termination date? Does the contract continue in perpetuity? Perpetual contracts are frowned on, so some other construction must be given to the contract. The approach used by the courts is that the contract is revocable by either party after reasonable notice.

When a contract has no fixed termination date, it is capable of cancellation at either party's will.

Contracts that fail to give a specific date for termination or indicate how and under what circumstances the contract will be voided are enforceable, although they can present the court with a difficult problem. If the parties never indicated how they expected this contract to end, when did it actually end? The general approach is to rule that such a contract can be terminated by either party after reasonable notice.

Automatic Renewal   Contracts can contain provisions that automatically renew the contract for another term. Such a provision does not make a contract void for creating a perpetual contract. For example, some leases contain provisions that automatically renew the lease for another year if the parties indicate no desire to cancel it. These provisions are legal, as long as the parties are aware that such a provision exists.

Conditions Subsequent

When a contract contains a condition subsequent provision, the contract is no longer capable of being terminated at will by the parties. Instead, the contract language will be enforced, that is, the occurrence set out in the condition subsequent.

Termination for "Good Cause"

When a contract contains a clause stating that it may only be terminated for good cause it is usually construed to be terminable at will by the parties.

Termination for Any Reason

A contract is valid if it contains a provision stating that either party can revoke it at any time, for any reason.[1] The courts will enforce such a contract provision as long as it does not violate public policy or statutory law. Most jurisdictions impose a duty of good faith on the parties to a contract that contains such a clause.

An unconditional termination clause simply requires that one party notify the other of his/her intent to terminate the contract for any reason.

Notice of Termination   The method used to provide notice of termination can be set out in the contract. For instance, a contract may provide that the agreement may only be terminated on written notice from one party to another. Barring any such limitation, any communication that puts the other party on notice is sufficient.

Effect of Termination

Once the contract terminates, the legal obligations of the parties are extinguished. The contract's provisions and promises have no further legal impact. This does not terminate the parties' right to sue for beach of the contract, or any rights that they have acquired under the contract.

ENDING A CONTRACT THROUGH OTHER MEANS

Obviously, most contracts that end up in litigation do not involve satisfactory discharge or mutually agreed termination. Cases involving contract disputes often involve issues such as the nature of the agreement terminating the policy, whether one party abandoned the contract or actions to rescind the entire agreement.

Agreement

After creating a contract, the parties are free to mutually abandon, modify, or rescind the contract. The parties also may enter into an agreement to terminate the contract by a specific date. When the parties to the original contract enter into a new contract on the same terms, the original contract is deemed terminated and replaced with the new agreement. As always, the court will look to the intentions of the parties when creating a new contract. For instance, did the parties actually intend for the new agreement to be a replacement of the old agreement?

Sidebar:
In some situations, the parties create a second contract that contains a provision stating that this new contract succeeds the previous contract with no lapse in time. That way, there can be no claim of a "vacuum" in ownership or other rights.

Sidebar:
Many jurisdictions follow a rule that the parties' election to "abandon" a contract actually results in rescission.

Abandonment

When the parties abandon a contract, they are, in effect, agreeing to rescind the contract. We will discuss rescission in the next section. Abandonment and rescission are often used interchangeably, but there is an important difference between the two terms. Abandonment is often used in the context of deleting a particular contractual element, while keeping the rest of the contract in place. When the parties "abandon" a particular contract provision but keep the rest of the contract intact, this is actually a modification of the contract. The parties are free to renegotiate a contract as they sit fit. In this context, "abandonment" is too imprecise a term to pin down exactly what is happening between the parties. If the parties are "abandoning" a contract, it is more accurate to say that they are rescinding a contract (see Exhibit 10-2).

- By agreement
- By conduct
- By new or subsequent contract
- By inference from the party's actions

EXHIBIT 10-2: How abandonment can occur.

Rescission

When the parties agree to rescind the contract, they are terminating the contract in a very specific way. **Rescission** does not modify the contract terms; it eliminates them. When a contract is rescinded, the legal effect of the contract is canceled. The parties behave as though the contract never existed in the first place. Rescission is a joint undertaking, involving all of the parties to the contract. There is no unilateral rescission.

rescission: The annulment of a contract.

The right of rescission does not depend on a contractual term in the contract authorizing it. Parties have a right to rescind that exists independently of the contractual terms. Rescission is retroactive; it makes the contract unenforceable from the moment that it was first created.

All jurisdictions have a rule stating that there is no arbitrary right to rescind a contract. Rescission is a concept firmly grounded in equitable principles. Rescission must be based on some compelling reason or on a legally recognized ground (see Exhibit 10-3).

The Elements of Rescission

In order to demonstrate a valid rescission, there must be a demand or tender of full performance. (The failure to perform may help establish a clear breach.) There must also be an unambiguous, affirmative act by a party showing the intention to rescind the contract. An example would be a

Rescission is usually only available when the original contract was based on:

- Fraud
- Undue influence
- Lack of consideration
- Or when one of the parties causes a material breach

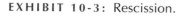
EXHIBIT 10-3: Rescission.

statement by the party refusing to carry out any additional actions under the contract.

Rescission has many of the same elements of proof as the original contract itself. There must be an offer to rescind, an acceptance of that offer and a mutual assent about the rescission. In addition to these elements, the same standards of mental competency needed to establish a valid contract are required to create a rescission. This means that the defenses of insanity, undue influence, coercion, fraud, and so on are all available to a party claiming that improper pressure was brought against him/her to rescind the contract.

In addition to these elements, the parties also must attempt to return themselves to their precontract positions. This means that any property or anything of value that has changed hands must be returned. The rule is that anything of value or any benefit derived from the contract must be returned to its original owner.

Agreement to Rescind the Contract   When the parties agree to abandon or rescind the contract, there are basic requirements that must be met. The agreement must be mutual and must be made prior to either party actually performing any actions. Some jurisdictions do allow contracts that have been substantially performed by one party to be rescinded, but these are the exceptions to the rule (see Exhibit 10-4).

> **Sidebar:**
> A contract may also be rescinded based on a finding that one of the parties is insane.

> **Sidebar:**
> Some states have statutes governing when, and under what circumstances, rescission may be obtained.

> **Sidebar:**
> A contract is deemed rescinded when both parties behave in a manner inconsistent with the contract and each acquiesces to the behavior of the other.[2]

☐   Lawful right to rescind

☐   Due notice of intent to rescind

☐   Return of benefits acquired under the contract

EXHIBIT 10-4: Elements of a successful rescission.

Who May Rescind

Only the parties to the contract may rescind it. A party's duly authorized agent or legal representative also may rescind a contract but, in this situation, the agent is acting for the party and is not an independent entity to the contract.

What Types of Contracts May be Rescinded

Sidebar:
A party's motive for rescission is irrelevant.

A fully discharged contract cannot be rescinded because such a contract no longer exists. In order to rescind a contract, there must first be a valid contract between the parties. Many jurisdictions also have a rule that prevents partially executed contracts from being rescinded. For instance, when one party has fully performed but the other has not, courts may not allow such a contract to be rescinded. Voidable contracts can be rescinded; void contracts cannot.

Cancellation versus Rescission

Although many jurisdictions indicate that these two terms are identical; in fact there is a subtle difference. Canceling a contract is a formal declaration that a contract is legally ineffective and cannot form the basis of a legal duty. By contrast, a rescission restores the parties to their positions prior to the creation of the contract (see Exhibit 10-5).

Termination + Reimbursement = Rescission

Cancellation = an end to the contractual obligation, without reimbursement

---

EXHIBIT 10-5: Rescission versus cancellations.

Waiving the Right to Rescind

As we have seen in other contexts, when a party has a right and fails to exercise it, that right may be lost. The same rule applies to rescission. When a party has this right, it must be exercised within a reasonable period of time or it will be waived.

The question in such cases often becomes what is a "reasonable period of time?" Courts have refused to come up with any definite time periods. Instead, they opt for a consideration of the contract and all of the surrounding circumstances. Courts will inquire if the party who had the right to rescind did so promptly, or if that party used reasonable diligence to rescind. Another factor the courts will consider is if the rescission was brought in sufficient time to restore the parties to their original positions. Many courts have ruled that once the parties' status has changed substantially, the right to rescind is lost.

Suits Seeking Rescission

Judges will usually not order rescission when the contract is illegal, or where the parties are equally at fault, or where someone other than the parties to the contract is seeking rescission (including a third party beneficiary) (see Exhibit 10-6). We will discuss the judicial remedy of rescission in the next chapter.

- Fraud
- Failure of consideration
- Material beach
- Insanity of one of the parties
- Unconscionability
- Non performance by a party[i]

EXHIBIT 10-6: Legal grounds for rescission.

---

[i] CJS Contracts §256.

Breach of Contract

Another way of terminating an agreement is by breach of contract. When a party breaches a contract, he or she violates some contractual duty. A party who is in breach of contract is generally barred from recovering benefits under the contract. The nonbreaching party has the right to sue for damages, specific performance and other remedies. (Remedies are discussed in Chapter 11.)

Negotiating Types of Breach

The parties are free to negotiate the possible remedies for a breach of a contract, and even to stipulate what types of actions will be considered a breach. Some contracts contain provisions specifying the consequences of a breach. For instance, a contract might provide, "contract becomes null and void when either party materially breaches this contract."

However, most contracts do not automatically terminate when a breach occurs. Instead, the contract may continue but with one party seeking damages against the other for breach.

> **Sidebar:**
> The party's motive for breach, whether good or bad, is usually irrelevant in the court's eyes.

One Party's Breach Does Not Relieve the Other of Legal Duty

When one party commits a breach the other party is not relieved of all contractual obligations. In a classic demonstration of the old maxim, "two wrongs do not make a right," nonbreaching parties are not relieved of their duties simply because the other parties failed to live up to their bargain. Laypersons are often confused on this point.

> ### HYPOTHETICAL 10-1   Tom's New Apartment
>
> Tom has moved into a new apartment. His rental agreement provides that the landlord will fix or repair damage to the property. During his second month living in the apartment, Tom reports that one of the steps leading up to his second floor apartment has broken. The landlord tells Tom that he will repair the step, but several weeks go by and nothing happens. Tom wants to withhold his rental payment as an incentive for the landlord to repair the step. Can he do so without also breaching the contract himself?
>
> Answer: No. Tom's obligation to pay rent is separate from the landlord's duty to maintain the premises. If Tom does not pay his rent, he will be in violation of his rental agreement. Tom can bring a civil action against the landlord, but he is obligated to pay rent until a judge enters an order in the case.

Allowing Party A to make the determination that Party B has breached the contract and therefore Party A is entitled to cancel the contract is a dangerous game. If Party A is wrong, he court might rule that Party A is in breach and award damages to Party B for breach of contract.

Anticipatory Breach

In some cases, a party may bring suit for a breach before the other party has actually committed one. Anticipatory breaches are recognized in most jurisdictions. Under this principle, a party may sue for breach when the other indicates a clear intention of violating the terms of the contract. This intention must be unambiguous. The party suing for such a breach may bring suit under the theory of anticipatory breach when waiting for the actual breach might cause additional hardship.

What Is a Material Breach?

Whenever a party does not perform as agreed on in the contract, this is a **breach**. A breach by one party gives the other party the right to receive damages. However, one category of breach, that is, material breach, gives the other party the right to rescind the contract. A material breach is the failure of one party to do some act that is so central to the agreement as to actually defeat the reason for having the contract in the first place. In order to qualify as a material breach, the action must be serious enough to place the entire contract in jeopardy. Therefore, not all breaches rise to the level of material breaches. When a party breaches an implied condition, or a minor duty, this is not considered to be a material breach and will not serve as the basis of rescinding the contract.[3] (See Exhibit 10-7 for examples of material breaches. See also Exhibit 10-8.)

breach: Failure, without legal excuse, to live up to a significant promise made in a contract.

> **Sidebar:**
> The Restatement of Contracts categorizes material breaches as "total" breaches and minor breaches as "partial" breaches.

> **Sidebar:**
> When one party's actions qualify as a total breach, the other party has a cause of action for breach of contract and is entitled to damages.[4]

HYPOTHETICAL 10-2   A versus B

Party A and Party B have a contract together. Party B has just contacted Party A and announced that not only does he not consider the contract to be legally binding, he also has no intention of honoring it and will do everything in his power to stop the contract from being carried out. Party A considers this to be a material breach and also stops his performance of the contract. He also files suit against Party B for breach of contract. Has Party A acted appropriately?

Answer: Yes. In this situation, Party B's actions would certainly seem to be an unambiguous (and wrongful) termination of the contract. Party B has repudiated the contract and that qualifies as a material breach. In this situation, when Party A abandons the contract she is not also committing a breach, because the contract has been dealt a mortal blow by Party B already. Party A's actions are simply an acknowledgment of the reality of the situation. Requiring Party A to continue to abide by a contract that Party B has totally repudiated would not make much sense.[5]

Material Breach (Total Breach)

- Failure to pay or compensate

- Failure to do the action contemplated in the contract

- Actively working to prevent the contract from being fulfilled

Minor Breach (Partial Breach)

- Compensating in a manner not contemplated in the contract, i.e., cash vs. certified funds

- Delay in carrying out the action contemplated in the contract

- Providing the service/thing in the contract but in a form different from that anticipated in the contract

EXHIBIT 10-7: Examples of breaches.

HYPOTHETICAL 10-3   The Stormy Stemware Provider

Anna owns a boutique that sells jewelry. She has a supplier named Renny who produces original and exotic wineglasses under the name "Renny's Stemware." Anna has an agreement with Renny to be the exclusive distributor for Renny's Stemware in the city limits where Anna's boutique is located. Yesterday, Renny stopped by Anna's store and told her that he has no intention of making any more stemware for Anna. He also told her that he is now going to be providing his stemware to one of Anna's main competitors. Anna has come to our firm and wants to know if she can rescind her contract with Renny and sue him for total breach of contract? Do Renny's actions qualify as a material breach?

Answer: Yes. Renny's actions are a material breach because of his refusal to provide the main object of the contract. This would not qualify as a minor or partial breach because this breach affects the whole reason for having the contract in the first place.

✓ PARALEGAL CHECKLIST

☐ How seriously will the nonbreaching party be affected by the breaching party's actions? (The more seriously the party is affected, the more likely the court will judge a particular action to be a breach; the opposite is also true.)

☐ Will the nonbreaching party be deprived of a benefit that he/she could have reasonably expected would flow from performance of the contract?

☐ Is the breach something that a reasonable third party would believe was material?

☐ Whether or not a particular action qualifies as a breach must be viewed from an objective, reasonable-person standard, not by the expectations of the parties themselves.

☐ Is the breach a fiduciary duty? (Those are definitely material breaches.)

EXHIBIT 10-8: Factors to consider when evaluating a potential breach of contract.

WHEN FAILURE TO PERFORM IS NOT ACTIONABLE: LEGAL EXCUSES

The general rule followed in most jurisdictions is that performance under a contract will only be excused in "extreme" circumstances or when the performance falls under a legally recognized excuse from performance. A legal excuse is one that provides insulation from liability for a party who fails to perform under the contract. Before we address specific examples of legal excuses, we will first address types of actions that do not qualify as legal excuses.

Examples of actions that do not qualify as legal excuses include a party's inconvenience, discomfort, or lower than expected income. Additional examples of actions that do not qualify as legal excuses are shown in Exhibit 10-9.

- Possible danger
- Change of circumstances
- Possible hardship
- Faulty equipment
- Unreliable workers
- That the contract was a "bad bargain"

EXHIBIT 10-9: Other actions that do not qualify as legal-excuses.

HYPOTHETICAL 10-4   Bert's Best Efforts

Bert has a contract with Ernie for the baking and delivery of cookies. The contract calls for 200 dozen cookies to be delivered every Monday. Bert made the first delivery, but the following weekend, he got involved in other activities and by Sunday night, he was too tired to bake any cookies. Bert had every intention of performing under the contract, but he found it simply too hard to do. Bert reports to Ernie that he used his "best efforts," but that he was not able to perform. Is this a legally valid excuse?

Answer: No. The contract contemplated that the party would carry out an act, not try to carry out an act. It is the act that was negotiated, not the effort.

However, the party's good faith and best efforts may have an impact on the ultimate damages awarded in the suit.

Categories of Legal Excuses

There are six general categories of legal excuses for breach of contract. They include:

- Impossibility
- Subsequent illegality
- Acts of God/nature
- Death of a party
- Destruction
- War

Impossibility

Impossibility of performance is a legally recognized excuse for failure to perform under a contract. However, what qualifies as "impossibility"? There are two types of impossibility: subjective impossibility and objective impossibility.

Under subjective impossibility, a party states that he or she cannot perform the duties outlined in the contract. In most jurisdictions, this claim is not a legal defense. A party who cannot perform must make alternate arrangements to have the contract performed or will be liable for breach of contract.

Objective impossibility, on the other hand, is a claim that the action itself cannot be done, whether by the party or anyone else. Examples of objective impossibility are provided in Exhibit 10-10. What all of the examples of objective impossibility have in common is that no one could perform the action. When the court finds that the action is impossible for anyone to perform, the court is more likely to excuse performance.[6]

- The party to perform has died
- The action to be performed has been found to be illegal
- War has broken out in the place where the contract is to be performed
- An unforeseen act of God/nature has occurred, i.e., flooding, hurricane, earthquake

---

EXHIBIT 10-10: Examples of objective impossibility.

HYPOTHETICAL 10-5   Signing the Singing Superstar

Salvador has an idea for a new promotional campaign for a new soft drink. He approaches a local bottler/distributor, Furry Fizz, and negotiates the following deal: if Salvador can get pop singing sensation Britannica Cheers to agree to wear a Furry Fizz t-shirt during her next performance, the company will pay Britannica $1 million and Salvador $10,000. The contract has a stipulation that states that Britannica must approve the arrangement.

Salvador, who has never met Britannica, tries to approach her at her home in Beverly Hills, California, but is turned away by her security guards. Later, he tries to stop her limousine by throwing himself in front of it. Britannica's attorneys take out a temporary restraining order against Salvador that requires him to stay at least 100 feet away from Britannica at all times.

Salvador returns to Furry Fizz and states that he is unable to perform under the contract due to impossibility. Is this a case of legal impossibility?

Answer: We must examine the various features of this contract before we can reach a decision. First, we must address the contract between Salvador and Furry Fizz. The company has promised to pay Salvador $10,000 if he can deliver Britannica's agreement to wear a t-shirt during her next performance. Salvador attempts to secure Britannica's agreement, but he is unsuccessful. The question raised here is whether the inability to secure a third party's agreement qualifies as a legal impossibility. Does it? In this case, the agreement sounds more like a condition. The agreement seems to contain a condition subsequent, making the contract operational only when Britannica agrees.

Otherwise, there is no contract. At this point, there doesn't appear to be any need to refer to the law of impossibility; this is a conditional agreement in which the condition was not met.

Consequences of Impossibility   When performance under a contract is impossible, a party cannot attempt to substitute a different type of performance. The parties obligated themselves to a specific type of performance and barring some new agreement, there is no provision to substitute another form of performance to satisfy the contract.

Sidebar:
Impossibility does not exist when one party has completed his or her performance and the only remaining act for the other party is to pay the agreed-upon compensation.

Subsequent Illegality

Suppose that at the time that the contract was negotiated, performance is possible and legal, but then the legislature passes a new statute making the action illegal. The party who is to perform is now in a difficult position: she can refuse to perform under the contract and face monetary damages, or she can perform under the contract and violate the law. The courts have intervened in this difficult situation with a ruling that makes the failure to perform in this situation excusable.[7]

Acts of God/Acts of Nature

When the performance under a contract is made impossible by an act of God, the performance is excused. However, there is a split among the jurisdictions about this issue. Some jurisdictions have ruled that if the act of God was reasonably foreseeable, then the parties should have anticipated it and made provision for it in their agreement and their failure to do so will not excuse performance. In these jurisdictions, unforeseen acts of God or nature follow the traditional rule and excuse performance and insulate the party from the payment of damages.

Examples of acts of God include earthquakes, hurricanes, tornadoes, and many of the natural phenomena that wreak havoc in people's lives.

Death of a Party

Death of the party who was to perform the duty under the contract usually results in a legal excuse. Although some jurisdictions have modified this rule to a certain extent, such as whether the party could have or actually did delegate performance to another or whether the act was personal to the party or could be applied to others, the general rule remains in effect in all jurisdictions: death of a party excuses performance.

Destruction

The same rule about death of a party applies to destruction. When the contract is based on the continued existence of a particular item and that item is destroyed, the obligation to perform under the contract is destroyed along with it.

Examples of destruction include:

- A mining contract when the mine collapses and is sealed off [8]
- The duty to maintain a dam when the dam is destroyed by flood [9]
- Fire that destroys the personal property sought to be purchased

If the categories listed under destruction sound similar to the types of events that will excuse performance for an "act of God," you would be correct. All of these events tend to intersect with one another and there is often no clear distinction between death, destruction, and an act of God. This is also true for our last general category of impossibility: war.

War

A contract may be canceled when war breaks out in the country in which the contract is to be performed. Contracts often contain a "war" clause stating that the contract can be canceled in the event of "public calamity or casualty, or in case of war." [10]

The Case of the Impossible Education [11]

COPELAND, Justice.

Plaintiff sets forth several arguments in support of his allegation that the Court of Appeals erred in reversing the trial court's order entering summary judgment in his favor. We have carefully reviewed each of plaintiff's contentions and find that summary judgment could not properly be granted in favor of either party. For the reasons stated below, we reverse that portion of the Court of Appeals' decision which remanded the case for entry of summary judgment in favor of defendant.

Plaintiff-appellant first contends that the doctrine of impossibility of performance and frustration of purpose should apply in this case to bring about a recission [sic] of the contract. Impossibility of performance is recognized in this jurisdiction as excusing a party from performing under an executory contract if the subject matter of the contract is destroyed without fault of the party seeking to be excused from performance.

Plaintiff's former wife's refusal to send the child to defendant school did not destroy the subject matter of

the contract; it was still possible for the child to attend the school. The doctrine of impossibility of performance clearly has no bearing on this case. In support of the applicability of the doctrine of frustration of purpose, plaintiff argues that his former wife's refusal to allow the child to attend defendant school was a fundamental change in conditions which destroyed the object of the contract and resulted in a failure of consideration. Judge Harry C. Martin agreed with plaintiff and dissented on this basis, discussing the doctrine of frustration of purpose at length. While we agree with Judge Martin's general discussion of the law concerning frustration of purpose, we hold that the doctrine does not apply to bring about a recission [sic] under the facts of this case.

The doctrine of frustration of purpose is discussed in 17 Am. Jur. 2d Contracts s 401 (1964) as follows:

"Changed conditions supervening during the term of a contract sometimes operate as a defense excusing further performance on the ground that there was an implied condition in the contract that such a subsequent development should excuse performance or be a defense, and this kind of defense has prevailed in some instances even though the subsequent condition that developed was not one rendering performance impossible. . . . In such instances, . . . the defense doctrine applied has been variously designated as that of 'frustration' of the purpose or object of the contract or 'commercial frustration.'

Although the doctrines of frustration and impossibility are akin, frustration is not a form of impossibility of performance. It more properly relates to the consideration for performance. Under it performance remains possible, but is excused whenever a fortuitous event supervenes to cause a failure of the consideration or a practically total destruction of the expected value of the performance. The doctrine of commercial frustration is based upon the fundamental premise of giving relief in a situation where the parties could not reasonably have protected themselves by the terms of the contract against contingencies which later arose."

If the frustrating event was reasonably foreseeable, the doctrine of frustration is not a defense. In addition, if the parties have contracted in reference to the allocation of the risk involved in the frustrating event, they may not invoke the doctrine of frustration to escape their obligations.

In the present case, plaintiff contracted to pay the tuition for the entire school year in advance of the first day of school. In consideration therefor, defendant promised to hold a place in the school for plaintiff's child, to make all preparations necessary to educate the child for the school year, and to actually teach the child during that period. Both parties received valuable consideration under the terms of the contract. After receiving plaintiff's tuition payment, defendant reserved a space for plaintiff's child, made preparations to teach the child, and at all times during the school year kept a place open for the child. This performance by defendant was sufficient consideration for plaintiff's tuition payment. A school such as defendant must make arrangements for the education of its pupils on a yearly basis, prior to the commencement of the school year. Many of these arrangements are based upon the number of pupils enrolled, for example, the teaching materials to be ordered, the number of teachers to be hired, and the desks and other equipment which will be used by the children. In addition, private schools are often limited in the number of pupils that can be accommodated, so that the reservation of a space for one child may prevent another's enrollment in the school. Had it been advised before the first day of school that plaintiff's child would not be in attendance, defendant might have been able to fill the vacant position. After the start of the school year, the probability of filling the position decreased substantially, thus to allow plaintiff to recover the tuition paid might deprive defendant of income it would have received had the contract not been entered into. Therefore, although plaintiff did not receive the full consideration contemplated by the contract, he received consideration sufficient to avoid the application of the doctrine of frustration of purpose. There was no substantial destruction of the value of the contract.

Furthermore, we find the doctrine of frustration of purpose inapplicable on an additional basis. Although the parties could not have been expected to foresee the exact actions of plaintiff's former wife in refusing to send the child to defendant school, the possibility that the child might not attend was foreseeable and appears expressly provided for in the contract. The contract states that tuition is "payable in advance of the first day of school, no portion refundable." This provision allocates to plaintiff the risk that the child will not attend, and prevents the application of the doctrine of frustration of purpose.

Because the doctrine of frustration of purpose does not apply and the terms of the contract are clear and unambiguous, the courts are bound to enforce it as written. This holding is consistent with prior cases in this jurisdiction which state that a contract providing for the nonrefundable payment of tuition is enforceable as written, regardless of the nonattendance of the pupil, where the failure to attend is not caused by some fault on the part of the school. Our decision is also in accord with the majority of jurisdictions in this country.

Defendant argues that even if the contract is not rescinded, this Court should find it unconscionable and refuse to enforce it. We disagree. A court will generally refuse to enforce a contract on the ground of unconscionability only when the inequality of the bargain is so manifest as to shock the judgment of a person of common sense, and where the terms are so oppressive that no reasonable person would make them on the one hand, and no honest and fair person would accept them on the other. In determining whether a contract is unconscionable, a court must consider all the facts and circumstances of a particular case. If the provisions are then viewed as so one-sided that the contracting party is denied any opportunity for a meaningful choice, the contract should be found unconscionable.

After considering all the facts before the trial court, we hold that the contract at issue cannot be declared unenforceable on the grounds of unconscionability. There was no inequality of bargaining power between the parties. Plaintiff was not forced to accept defendant's terms, for there were other private and public schools available to educate the child. The clause providing that tuition payments would be non refundable is reasonable when considered in light of the expense to defendant in preparing to educate the child and in reserving a space for him. The bargain was one that a reasonable person of sound judgment might accept. "Ordinarily, when parties are on equal footing, competent to contract, enter into an agreement on a lawful subject, and do so fairly and honorably, the law does not permit inquiry as to whether the contract was good or bad, whether it was wise or foolish." Roberson v. Williams, 240 N.C. 696, 700-01, 83 S.E.2d 811, 814 (1954). The contract is enforceable as written.

Plaintiff next contends that the clause prohibiting the refund of any portion of the tuition paid is in the nature of a penalty rather than a provision for liquidated damages, and therefore cannot be enforced. It is well established that a sum specified in the contract as the measure of recovery in the event of a breach will be enforced if the court determines it to be a provision for liquidated damages, but not enforced if it is determined to be a penalty. However, plaintiff's argument ignores the fact that there has been no breach of contract in this case. Both parties fully performed their obligations under the contract to the extent possible without the presence of the child in the school. Neither party promised that the child would attend. The nonrefundable tuition provision was simply one term of the contract, not a measure of recovery in the event of a breach, thus the law of damages has no bearing upon this case.

In paragraph five of his amended complaint, plaintiff alleged that after his former wife informed him that she did not intend to send the child to defendant school, plaintiff contacted Patsy Ballinger, headmistress of the school, who promised to refund to plaintiff the full tuition payment of $1,072.00. Before answering the other portions of plaintiff's complaint, defendant moved to strike the allegations of paragraph five. This motion was denied 19 September 1979 by an order which did not specify a time within which defendant was to reply to the allegations in that paragraph. On 25 September 1979 defendant filed an amended answer, for the first time denying the allegations of paragraph five. Plaintiff filed a motion to strike the amended answer on 27 September 1979, on the grounds that defendant failed to obtain permission of the court before filing the amended answer, in violation of G.S. 1A-1, Rule 15. Plaintiff's motion was allowed 16 October 1979. Plaintiff therefore contends that since the allegations of paragraph five were never denied, they are deemed admitted under G.S. 1A-1, Rule 8(d). We hold that the trial court erred in granting plaintiff's motion to strike defendant's amended answer, and therefore find plaintiff's argument without merit. Defendant's motion to strike paragraph five of the complaint was made under the authority of G.S. 1A-1, Rule 12(f). G.S. 1A-1, Rule 12(a)(1)a provides that when the court denies a motion permitted under Rule 12, a responsive pleading may be served within 20 days after notice of the court's action. Defendant's amended answer, which was the first responsive pleading to paragraph five of the complaint, was filed well within the 20 day limit. Thus, although Rule 15(a) mandates that defendant could only amend his answer after obtaining the court's permission or plaintiff's written consent, Rule 12(a)(1)a expressly authorized defendant to file without permission those portions of his amended answer which were a responsive pleading to the paragraphs of the complaint subject to defendant's motion to strike. Consequently, the court's 16 October 1979 order granting plaintiff's motion to strike the amended answer was in error to the extent that it struck those portions which were responsive pleadings to the paragraphs of the complaint subject to defendant's motion to strike. The allegations in paragraph five of the complaint were properly denied by defendant's amended answer, and plaintiff's arguments to the contrary are without merit.

However, we find that by his allegation that Ms. Ballinger agreed to refund the tuition paid, plaintiff raised an issue of fact sufficient to avoid the entry of summary judgment against him. If Ms. Ballinger did agree to refund plaintiff's payment, her agreement would constitute an enforceable modification of the provision of the contract prohibiting a refund. Where, as in this case, a contract has been partially performed, an agreement to alter its terms is treated as any other contract and must be supported by consideration. In return for defendant's promise to refund the tuition paid, plaintiff would relinquish his right to have his child educated in defendant school. Defendant received a benefit in being relieved of the responsibility to teach the child for the school year. It is well established that any benefit, right, or interest bestowed upon the promisor, or any forbearance, detriment, or loss undertaken by the promisee, is sufficient consideration to support a contract. We believe that there was consideration sufficient to support an agreement by Ms. Ballinger to refund plaintiff's payment, if such an agreement was made. Whether such an agreement was reached is a material fact to be determined by the jury. Summary judgment is properly granted only if all the evidence before the court indicates that there is no genuine issue as to any material fact and that one party is entitled to judgment as a matter of law. The burden of establishing the absence of any triable issue of fact is on the party moving for summary judgment. Plaintiff failed to meet his burden to prove, as a matter of law, that an enforceable agreement to refund his payments existed. Hence, the trial court erred in granting plaintiff's motion for summary judgment. Likewise, defendant did not prove, as a matter of law, that no agreement to refund plaintiff's payment was made, and that portion of the Court of Appeals' opinion which remanded to the trial court for entry of summary judgment in favor of defendant was also in error.

For the reasons stated, we reverse the decision of the Court of Appeals and remand to that court with instructions to remand to the District Court, Guilford County, for a NEW TRIAL.

Case Questions:

1. How does this court define impossibility of performance?

2. What is the doctrine of "frustration of purpose"?

3. According to the court, if the frustrating event was foreseeable, what effect does this have on a party's claim?

4. Does the court order that the tuition paid in advance should be returned? Why or why not?

5. The defendant in this case argued that the contract should not be enforced for several reasons. What are those reasons and did the court agree with them?

The Case of the Pushy Publisher[12]

CASTLE, Circuit Judge.

The contested issues are (1) whether the contract was rescinded by mutual agreement (2) whether plaintiff is estopped to charge defendant with breach of the contract (3) whether plaintiff repudiated the contract and (4) whether plaintiff failed to perform obligations under the contract which were prerequisite to defendant's duty to perform.

The contract alleged to have been breached was executed by plaintiff and defendant on January 18, 1951. In that contract plaintiff assigned to defendant all the volume publication rights in an unpublished literary composition to be written by plaintiff and entitled 'Mary Meade's Magic Cookery' and plaintiff agreed to deliver to defendant, on or before January 2, 1953, the manuscript of said literary composition, consisting of approximately 4,000 recipes, complete, legible and ready for the printer. The defendant agreed to publish the work in one volume in the style and manner it deemed best. The contract fixed no publication date or time requirement for the performance of any part of defendant's undertaking. Plaintiff's complaint charges that on or about November 13, 1957 the defendant wholly repudiated the contract.

The material facts as hereinafter set forth appear from the admissions, exhibits and affidavits submitted in support of and in opposition to the motion for summary judgment.

From the execution of the contract until 1956 plaintiff periodically supplied portions of the manuscript. During the period 1952 through 1955 plaintiff pursuant to separate contracts prepared two other manuscripts which were published by defendant. The first was a book entitled 'Mary Meade's Magic Recipes for the Electric Blender' published in 1952. The second book 'Mary Meade's Kitchen Companion' was published in 1955. It is conceded that the preparation and publication of the two intervening books retarded progress on the preparation and completion on the manuscript for 'Mary Meade's Magic Cookery, particularly since parts of the manuscript delivered earlier for 'Mary Meade's Magic Cookery' were taken from that work and incorporated in the 1955 book.

In September of 1952 the contract deadline for delivery of manuscript was formally extended by defendant to September 15, 1953. The letter of extension noted that the original contract was to remain in full force and effect except for the extension of the date for delivery of manuscript. There were no further formal extensions but it is admitted that the date for delivery of the manuscript was from time to time extended by mutual consent and that the contract was considered to be in effect at the time of the alleged breach.

Subsequent to 1955 no additional manuscript was submitted by the plaintiff. In February of 1957 plaintiff wrote the defendant that she had the last chapters ready except for a little final organization, but realized that there needed to be revision on earlier chapters due to taking out material used in the 1955 book. Plaintiff also inquired if there was any thought of publishing the manuscript in parts. The defendant replied under date of March 7, 1957 that it had no thought of publishing parts of the manuscript as small separate books and advised that to insure against possible failure of the project that:

'First, the manuscript must be right, every detail in the best and most attractive shape. This will take time, thought and effort. Second, we must choose the most favorable season in which to launch the book. (Before we have any real choice, the manuscript must be in final form, ready for manufacture.)'

Plaintiff made no further inquiry until August 21, 1957 and during the interval no additional or revised manuscript was supplied by plaintiff. Under date of August 21, 1957 the plaintiff wrote defendant stating that its Indianapolis office had 85% of the finished manuscript and advised 'I have the remaining chapters all but ready, but have not sent them as it seems now there is no definite plan for publication' and:

'Unless there is a firm, clear plan for the book I should like to have the manuscript back and present it to another publisher. Each chapter could be a book in itself'.

Under date of September 4, 1957 the defendant replied as follows:

'I take it from your letter that what you want us to do now is to set up a definite publication schedule for the book; and if we are not able to do that at this time, you would like to have the manuscript returned and the contract cancelled so that you could arrange for publication elsewhere. Nothing could be fairer than that. From time to time we have given you extensions of the delivery date for the final, complete, manuscript; and in every instance I believe that this has been a matter of mutual accord.'

The defendant further stated that plaintiff could expect a definite answer to her 'proposal' within four or five weeks. On October 17, 1957 the defendant advised plaintiff to the effect that she could expect a reply soon. Under date of November 13, 1957 defendant advised of its decision and that 'We will return promptly all the manuscript that we are now holding'.

Plaintiff admits receipt of the defendant's letters, return of the manuscript to her and its submission to other publishers.

Subsequent to its letter of September 4, 1957 defendant received no further communications from plaintiff except a letter under date of December 7, 1957 from a firm of attorneys consulted by plaintiff stating that defendant's conduct was a breach of its contract and that plaintiff would look to defendant for reimbursement for any and all damages suffered.

We find no genuine issue concerning any material fact in regard to the question of whether the actions of the parties effected a mutual rescission of the contract. The situation here presented did not require, as plaintiff contends, that a jury determine what plaintiff intended by her letter of August 21, 1959. It is admitted that this letter was addressed to the defendant at a time when plaintiff had furnished no more than 85% of the required manuscript, some of which had to be revised, and had furnished no manuscript for over a year and one-half. The letter informed the defendant that unless it had a firm, clear plan for the book, the plaintiff would like the manuscript back to present to another publisher. It suggested that each chapter of the manuscript could be published as a separate book. The contract called for publication as a single volume. A similar proposal by plaintiff to publish the manuscript material in parts as separate books had met with unfavorable response in March and plaintiff reminded that timing of the publication must await manuscript in final form, ready for manufacture. If there was ambiguity in plaintiff's letter of August 21, 1957 as to (1) whether it should be taken as a request for return of the manuscript unless contract requirements be altered as to the format of the publication—from a single volume, the material for which was not complete, to publication in parts as separate small books; or (2) be regarded as a demand that a definite date for future publication be then fixed; or (3) be deemed, as plaintiff urges, an attempt to accelerate an answer as to possible future publication plans, that ambiguity was resolved by defendant's reply. In its letter of September 4, 1957 the defendant in clear and unambiguous terms expressed its understanding of plaintiff's request of August 21, 1957. The material facts on the question of mutual rescission are plaintiff's request of August 21st, the defendant's expressed understanding of that proposal, which plaintiff admittedly knew, and the fact that plaintiff made no answer whatsoever during the period of over two months which intervened between defendant's letter of September 4th and its determination on November 13, 1957 that it elected to return the manuscript rather than to attempt at that time to set up a definite publication schedule for the book.

A contract may be rescinded by mutual agreement found in the acts of the parties and the attending circumstances. It is evidence that when a contract is rescinded by mutual consent or otherwise no action can be maintained for a breach thereof.

There is no dispute concerning any material fact relating to the acts or conduct of the parties and plaintiff was bound by defendant's interpretation of her request of August 21, 1957. Star-Chronicle Publishing Company v. New York Evening Post, 2 Cir., 256 F. 435. We therefore hold that as a matter of law defendant's acceptance of plaintiff's offer as understood by it, which understanding was known to plaintiff for over two months and not questioned before acted upon by defendant, effected a mutual rescission of the contract.

In addition plaintiff is estopped from asserting a breach of contract. Plaintiff's request for return of the manuscript was inconsistent with a performance of the contract by defendant. Defendant was under no duty to fix any definite schedule for publication until it had received the balance of the required manuscript. Plaintiff having originated the proposal had a clear duty to speak if defendant's interpretation was erroneous. She did not do so for a period of over eight weeks, even though she received an intervening reminder of defendant's reliance on its understanding of her proposal. Plaintiff by electing to remain silent while defendant proceeded to accept her proposal is estopped from charging defendant with repudiating the contract.

The return of the manuscript was induced by plaintiff's conduct.

The summary judgment for defendant was proper. We deem it unnecessary to consider the further issues discussed in the briefs.

The judgment of the District Court is affirmed. Affirmed.

Case Questions:

1. Was plaintiff's letter to the publisher proposing to turn each chapter into a separate book a rescission of the contract?

2. According to the court, is this a case of mutual rescission?

3. Is it significant that the plaintiff waited for over two months before taking issue with the defendant interpretation of the publishing contract?

4. Define the term "estoppel" as it is used by the court in this opinion.

5. Explain the court's rationale in reaching its decision.

ETHICS FILE: Documenting Discharge and Performance

It is always a good idea for legal professionals and parties to a contract to document specific acts of performance under a contract. This can take the form of a routine memo to a file that provides the date, time, and the manner of performance. That way, specific acts that show compliance with the contract's provisions can be documented and used if there is ever a dispute. Successful discharge of a contract should also be documented. In such a case, a brief letter or other communication to the other party that details successful discharge of the contract should be sent. Such language could be as simple as, "With this last shipment, our contract is now discharged." That way, if there is any controversy about when and if the contract was ever completed, one party can point to a clear and specific communication detailing what it believed to be the complete discharge of the contract.

Business Case File

Rezaz Restaurant

Rezaz is a Mediterranean-style restaurant in Asheville, North Carolina. It is always crowded with customers who come for the good food and the relaxed, elegant feel of the restaurant. The owner, Reza Setayesh, keeps a firm hand on the day-to-day business, monitoring business, meeting with customers, checking inventory, working out employee problems, and still finding time to cook many of the lunch and dinner meals himself.

"I'd always loved to cook," said Reza, during a rare, quiet moment at his restaurant. "I went to UCLA with the idea of getting a chemistry degree. Really, it was to please my parents. I became a chef to please myself. I worked in various restaurants around Los Angeles and then I heard about a culinary program in Asheville. I came here and enrolled in the program. I was hired by Marriott even before I graduated. I worked for them for six years. It was a valuable experience. They taught me a lot about management.

"When I decided to open my own business, my biggest concern was financing. There are only three ways to go: you can use your own money, you can use your family's money, or you can borrow. You can do some combination of both, but I had to go with the third option. I wrote up a business plan. It was much harder than I thought it would be. Once it was on paper, I could see areas where it was not complete. When I rewrote it, I showed it to my attorney, and he said, 'well this is all fine and dandy, but a banker wouldn't understand half of it.' He told that I had to rewrite it in from a banker's perspective.

"That business plan is a strong tool. I still refer to it, even after three years in business. I look at it to see how my day-to-day business compares with my original goals."

Running a restaurant, especially a large and successful one, presents some interesting legal issues.

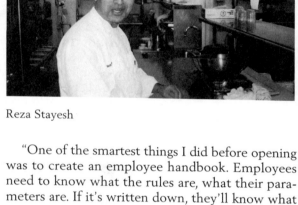

Reza Stayesh

"One of the smartest things I did before opening was to create an employee handbook. Employees need to know what the rules are, what their parameters are. If it's written down, they'll know what the rules and regulations are and what the results will be if you break them. With 40 employees, it's like a big family and that means forty different attitudes and 40 different types of problems. Having an employee handbook helps me and helps the employees."

Employee contracts, even oral ones, have conditions. For instance, when an employee fails to live up to the job's conditions, Reza is faced with firing the employee. That results in a complete discharge of the employment contract, severing any relationship between the restaurant and the employee.

"Restaurant work isn't for everyone. You have to love it, to have a passion for it. It's six days a week, 16 hours a day. If you didn't like it, you'd burn out quickly. My business is like a part of me. I love the food; I love the business." His passion for quality food is often reflected in the satisfied sighs of his customers.

Chapter Summary:

In this chapter, we explored the concepts of performance of a contract. When a contract has been discharged, it has been completed to the satisfaction of both parties. When a contract has not been successfully discharged, it can be the basis of a lawsuit between the former parties to the agreement. Failure of performance can come about through abandonment or rescission of a contract. Rescission is a term referring to the cancellation of the contract, either by the parties' agreement or through judicial action. Breach of contract is an important term because any breach will give the nonbreaching party the right to sue for damages. However, a material breach can give the nonbreaching party the right to cancel the contract entirely and sue the other party for damages associated with the cancellation. There are some breaches that may be legally excused. For instance, when a breach is brought about because of the impossibility of performance, the breach will be excused and the party will not be liable for damages. Other legal excuses include the death of one of the contracting parties, destruction of subject of the contract, and the declaration of war where the contract is supposed to be performed.

WEB SITES

Washburn University School of Law Legal Research on the Internet
http://www.washlaw.edu
Provides a wealth of legal links.

Versus Law
http://www.versuslaw.com
Online legal pay site.

Netlizard's Research Center
http://www.netlizard.com
Gives access and links to a wide range of other legal sites.

REVIEW QUESTIONS

1. What is rescission?
2. What are some grounds that would justify rescission of a contract?
3. Explain discharge of a contract.
4. What is meant by "abandonment" of a contract?
5. If a contract does not have a termination date, how does the court determine when the contractual obligation ends?
6. What is the "Doctrine of Mutuality"?
7. What effect does a declaration of war have on the performance of a contract?

8. What are some examples of "acts of God" that would cancel performance of a contract?

9. How is cancellation of a contract different from rescission of a contract?

10. Why is the question of when a contract ends considered to be important?

11. Explain the difference between abandonment of a contract and discharge of a contract.

12. When the contract does not contain a termination date how do the courts determine when the contract actually ends?

13. Explain the concept of good faith in regard to performance of a contract.

14. What effect does a declaration of war have on the performance of a contract?

15. In order to prove a successful rescission of a contract, what three elements must a party present?

16. Explain the doctrine of impossibility.

17. What effect does a party's death have on the contractual obligation?

18. Explain the doctrine of "frustration of purpose."

19. How does the subsequent illegality of a contract affect its performance?

20. Explain the difference between a technical breach and a material breach.

HANDS-ON ASSIGNMENT

Go through your local newspaper and find examples of situations that would provide legal excuses for a party's failure to perform.

PRACTICAL APPLICATION

In an earlier chapter, you drafted a contract based on your own course syllabus. What are some actions by a student or the instructor that would form a material breach of the contract?

HELP THIS BUSINESS

Suppose that Reza Setayesh, the owner of Rezaz restaurant, enters into a contract with Frank Felon, who supplies exotic fruits and vegetables that have been grown in molds to resemble a wide variety of items, such as the profiles of famous people, or everyday objects, such as cars and baseball bats. Reza is planning a new series of meals that will feature these fruit and vegetable creations as the centerpieces of the dinners. However, shortly after printing off new menus and paying for newspaper and magazine features advertising this unusual feature, Frank is arrested and sentenced to ten years' incarceration. What effect does this have on the contract?

KEY TERMS

discharge

rescission

breach

ENDNOTES

[1] C.J.S. Contracts §442.

[2] *In re Klugh's Estate*, 362 Pa. 166, 66 A2d 822 (1949).

[3] Andersen, "A New Look at Material Breach in the Law of Contracts," 21 U.C. Davis L. Rev. 1073 (1988).

[4] *Dalton v. Mullins*, 293 S.W.2d 470 (KY, 1956).

[5] *Cruse v. Clawson*, 137 Mont. 439, 352 P2d 989 (1960).

[6] 84 A.L.R.2d 12 (1962).

[7] C.J.S. Contracts §522.

[8] *Parrish v. Stratton Cripple Creek Min.* 116 F.2d 207 (C.A.10 1940).

[9] *Anderson v. Bradley*, 177 A.2d 227 (Conn. 1961).

[10] CJC Contracts §455.

[11] *Brenner v. Little Red School House, Ltd.*, 274 S.E.2d 206 (N.C. 1981).

[12] *Church v. Bobbs-Merrill Co.*, 272 F.2d 212 (C.A.7 1959).

 For additional resources, visit our Web site at www.westlegalstudies.com

CHAPTER 11

CONTRACT REMEDIES

▌ **Focus of this chapter:** This chapter examines the consequences of a
breach of contract. When one party sues another for breach, there are a
wide variety of options available to either enforce the contract or seek
monetary damages. The remedies available to the nonbreaching party can
be lumped into two broad categories: equitable remedies and monetary
damages. We will explore both categories in depth.

Chapter Objectives:
At the completion of this chapter, you should be able to:

- ■ Define "equitable remedy"
- ■ Explain quantum meruit and quantum valebant
- ■ Describe the difference between equitable remedies and monetary damages
- ■ Provide an example of specific performance
- ■ Explain situations where monetary damages would be preferable to equitable remedies
- ■ Explain how monetary damages are assessed
- ■ Define "mitigation of damages"
- ■ Explain the role of liquidated damages
- ■ Describe consequential damages
- ■ Explain the role of the court is assessing damages

Introduction to Remedies for Breach of Contract

In the past few chapters, we have discussed the various ways that a contract
is interpreted and how the courts determine when a party has breached a
duty under a contract. In this chapter, we will focus on what happens after

the breach. What damages will the breaching party be forced to pay? What actions may the court take in enforcing the contract? How does the court determine the exact amount of monetary damages?

The right to enter into a contract carries with it an inherent right to sue for breach of that contract. As we have already seen in the previous chapter, when a party breaches a contract, that party fails to perform as originally intended. In Chapter 10, we saw examples of legal excuses for nonperformance. Here we are assuming that the party does not have a legal excuse for the breach and the nonbreaching intends to bring suit to either enforce the contractual promise or to seek damages for the failure to perform.

THE CONSEQUENCES OF A BREACH

When one party to a contract breaches it, that breach relieves the other party of the duty to perform. However, as we saw in Chapter 10, the determination of breach is often a question for the courts. Often the safest route for the nonbreaching party to take is to file suit against the other party and show how that party failed to perform as promised.

When a breach of contract occurs, there are two immediate options: the nonbreaching party can consider the contract rescinded and sue for damages or ignore the breach and continue to deal with the breaching party. We will explore what occurs when the nonbreaching party seeks damages or equitable remedies.

THE CONTRACT PROVIDES A FRAMEWORK FOR REMEDIES

It is important, and a legal requirement of a contract, that the parties have some remedies available to them to enforce the contract. A contract that prevents one party from exercising any remedy for breach is void for public policy reasons and also may be voided because it violates statutory law.

Contracts may provide language specifically authorizing certain types of actions for breach, or they may have language that limits the parties' options. When evaluating a potential cause of action for breach, the obvious place to start is the contract itself. What does the contract say about breach and enforcement?

Unfortunately, most contracts are silent on the topic of nonperformance. This silence has required the court system (and sometimes the state legislature) to provide remedies.

Mutual Remedies

Is it necessary that both parties to the transaction have identical remedies? If the contract does not create mutual remedies, is it invalid?

There is no requirement that the parties enjoy identical remedies under a contract. In fact, in some contracts, that would be impossible. Consider a unilateral contract. In a unilateral contract we have one party giving a promise in exchange for an action by the other party. Obviously, the remedies available to the parties to this contract are different. These parties do not have, nor would they desire, identical remedies under the law.

There are two important terms that we should distinguish at this point: mutuality of obligation and mutuality of remedy.

Mutuality of obligation refers to the contractual duties and obligations created by the contract. In order to be binding, a contract must create mutuality of obligation. Without it, the contract is void and unenforceable. Mutuality of obligation is required in all jurisdictions for a valid contract.

Mutuality of remedy, by contrast, is a concept that originated in the distant past. There was a theory, now since abandoned, that a contract should create mutuality of remedy, as well. Under this construction, a contract should not be valid unless both parties had the same type of options to enforce it. However, as we have already seen in our example of a unilateral contract, this theory broke down under practical application. No jurisdiction now requires mutuality of remedy for a valid contract.

mutuality of obligation:
Describes the principle that, for a binding contract to exist, each side must have some obligation or duty to perform under the contract.

mutuality of remedy: Under equity law, a principle that requires that both parties have a similar recourse through the courts.

The Necessity of Damages

The law is clear that any breach of a contract, no matter how slight, is actionable. However, in the practical, hard-nosed world of business people, such a rule is almost meaningless.

What happens in situations in which there is a breach of the contract and the other party has incurred no appreciable loss or has failed to prove his losses? The general rule states that any breach is actionable, but does a minor breach justify the costs associated with bringing a legal action? After all, there are attorneys to pay, filing fees, and lost time from the business to attend court hearings, and so on. A minor breach, under such circumstances, would not justify such costs.

Courts take a similar view. Assessing the amount of damages is one of the major events that occur in contract litigation. If there are no damages, there is little likelihood of enough recovery to justify the time spent litigating the question.

In cases of minimal breaches, the Restatement of Contracts urges that the breaching party pay a small, fixed sum to the nonbreaching party. In many jurisdictions, the nonbreaching party would only be entitled to nominal damages. Determining the value of the damages is a question of fact for the jury. Both sides of the suit will present evidence to the jury suggesting that they award either a larger or smaller verdict depending on who is presenting the evidence.

Equitable Remedies: When Money Will Not Satisfy

Courts in the United States actually have two types of authority: legal and equitable. Most people are familiar with a court's legal power. When a court exercises its legal power, it makes rulings on the law, interprets cases and

equity: The name for a system of courts that originated in England to take care of legal problems when the existing laws did not cover some situations in which a person's rights were violated by another person.

statutes and generally follows precedents set out in prior appellate decisions. **Equity** law is a different matter entirely. A court can exercise its equity power to order an injunction, specific performance or other action that is normally not part of a court's authority under its legal power. Before we examine these two types of authority, we will first address how this disparity was created.

If a party wishes to bring a claim for equitable relief, he or she must show:

- There is no remedy at law that is adequate

- There is danger of an irreparable injury to the plaintiff if the court does not use its equity powers

- The contract is legally valid (consideration is sufficient, contract is not void for public policy reasons, etc.)

- The contract terms and clauses are clear and unambiguous

- The plaintiff has clean hands (has not been deceitful or breached the contract through his own actions)[i]

EXHIBIT 11-1: Bringing an equity claim.

[i] *Talley v. Talley*, 566 N.W.2d 846 (N.D. 1997).

A HISTORY OF EQUITY JURISDICTION

Under the English system, which forms the basis of the American judicial system, law courts and equity courts were separate. When persons sought an equitable remedy they went to the High Court of Chancery. That court was authorized to issue injunctions, order specific performance, and take other actions in particular cases to ensure that justice was done. When persons sought monetary damages, they sought redress in the regular court system. In the United States, the separate powers of law and equity were combined into a single court system. There may have been several reasons for this, but the most likely is that the early colonial court system could not support two separate court systems. Combining this power into a single court probably made a great deal of sense both in terms of finances and efficiency.[2]

jurisdiction: The persons about whom and the subject matters about which a court has the right and power to make decisions that are legally binding.

When a court has **jurisdiction**, it means that the judge is empowered to make rulings and enforce those rulings. A court's legal jurisdiction is based on the type of suit brought and the parties involved. For instance, if a person files for bankruptcy, this action must be brought in Federal Bankruptcy Court. This is the only court that has jurisdiction to consider the action. If a person filed for bankruptcy in a local small claims court, the court would be powerless to make any rulings. Courts in this country usually have limited jurisdiction: they are empowered to hear certain types of cases only.

On a local level, whether the court is referred to as superior court, state court, or district court, the court possesses both legal jurisdiction and equitable jurisdiction.

A court's equity jurisdiction does not derive from the type of the case; it derives from the court's willingness to enter the controversy and the necessity of reaching a decision.[3] If we were to come up with a shorthand reference for the two different types of jurisdiction, we might say that legal jurisdiction is the power of the court to enter a valid order, whereas equity jurisdiction is the power of the court to grant the relief sought by the parties.[4]

When a plaintiff seeks relief through the court's legal jurisdiction, the most that he can receive is monetary damages as a substitute for the performance that the defendant should have rendered. When a plaintiff seeks relief through the court's equity jurisdiction, the plaintiff is requesting that the court order the defendant to do some action, such as perform as promised (specific performance), or stop taking some action that harms the plaintiff (injunction). Equity jurisdiction does not give the court the power to order monetary damages; legal jurisdiction does not give the court the power to order the defendant to do or not do some action.

"Clean Hands"

One of the peculiarities of the equity jurisdiction is that the party seeking an equitable remedy must show "clean hands." This ancient doctrine of equity law requires that before a plaintiff can ask a court for an order sanctioning the other party, the plaintiff must show that he did not do anything wrong. The plaintiff must prove that at all times pertinent to the transaction, he did not engage in questionable or deceitful practices against the defendant. "Clean hands" is a defense that can be offered up to show that the plaintiff is not entitled to equitable relief.

The U.S. System: Legal and Equitable Jurisdiction Together

In the United States, a plaintiff is entitled to request that the court use both forms of jurisdiction in a single case. Put another way, a plaintiff can ask the court to function as an equity court for some of his claims and as a legal court for other claims. This sometimes creates confusion, not only for the litigants but also in the court system. A judge may issue a ruling that contains both legal and equitable remedies and fail to make a clear distinction between them.[5]

The situation is sometimes made even more complicated by a rule found in many states that a plaintiff must exhaust his legal remedies before seeking an equitable remedy.[6]

We will explore legal remedies later in this chapter. Those consist of monetary damages. Equitable remedies, by contrast, usually focus on actions. The most common types of equitable remedies are:

- Injunctions
- Specific Performance
- Reformation
- Rescission

INJUNCTION

injunction: A judge's order to a person to do or to refrain from doing a particular thing.

Injunctions are used in many different types of lawsuits. When a party seeks an injunction, the party files an action with the court stating that the defendant's actions will result in serious and irreparable damage to the plaintiff. The plaintiff asks the court to order an injunction, which uses the court's power to stop the defendant carrying out a specific action.

When the party moves for an injunction, the process usually involves several steps. The first step is the request for a temporary restraining order. When a court enters a temporary restraining order, the judge orders that a party cease a particular action for a specified amount time. The most common time period is ten days. The ten-day waiting time allows time for a more formal hearing so that the court can determine what permanent actions, if any, are required. In some states, a temporary restraining order is referred to as a preliminary injunction. During the formal hearing, the court will hear evidence and testimony and make a ruling as to whether a permanent injunction should be entered. If a court enters a permanent injunction, this means that the court orders a party to stop doing the particular action for the foreseeable future.

A request for an injunction is common in contract litigation. A party may seek an injunction against the other party for doing a wide variety of activities, all of which are alleged to be injuring the plaintiff's business interests or causing irreparable financial harm to the plaintiff.

SPECIFIC PERFORMANCE

specific performance: Being required to do exactly what was agreed to.

In most cases, there is one remedy that at least one side of the contract would always like to see ordered. **Specific performance** is a court order that requires a party to do that which he has already agreed to do in the contract. Other types of damages, such as monetary damages, might not be as satisfactory to a party as would be the actual performance of the contract itself. However, there are times when specific performance of a contract is either difficult or impossible. In those situations, other remedies must apply.

When a court orders a party to specifically perform, the court is using its contempt powers to force the party to carry out the action contemplated in the contract. If Bob Buyer enters into a contract to purchase Sal Seller's home and then, at the closing, Bob refused to go through with the sale, Sal might file suit seeking specific performance. In this situation, an eventual award of monetary damages will not help Sal very much. He is about to

Sidebar:
Specific performance may be impossible because the party has died or has gone bankrupt.

move out of his house, has, in fast, already arranged to purchase another house, and Bob's failure to perform under the contract causes serious difficulties for Sal. He wants Bob to buy his house and wants the court to order Bob to do so, as soon as possible.

If specific performance is a court order requiring a party to do as he or she originally agreed, why does it turn out that specific performance is not ordered in all cases? In fact, a party is far more likely to request an injunction, rescission or monetary damages, rather than specific performance. What is a possible explanation?

For one thing, the circumstances may have changed to such an extent that neither party wishes to have of the contract performed as it was originally intended. Commodity prices, business financing, or any of a number of other conditions may have altered significantly since the contract was originally created, and what was once a good bargain may now be a bad deal for both parties.

There is a more subtle reason why specific performance is not a remedy seen more often in cases. The plaintiffs often recognize that there is an important difference in the quality of performance between someone who is acting voluntarily and someone who is being compelled to act by court order.

REFORMATION

Reformation is another equitable remedy. When a party requests reformation, what the party is actually requesting is that the contract itself be changed to reflect the true intention of the parties. Reformation is often seen in contracts containing ambiguous phrases or terms.[9] A court action seeking reformation is usually brought when there has been:

- A bilateral mistake
- A written document that does not reflect the true intent of the parties

> In a reformation action, the plaintiff must prove:
>
> 1. That there was a mutual mistake of fact
>
> 2. That the resulting contract did not reflect the parties' intent[i]

EXHIBIT 11-2: Proof required in a reformation action.

---

[i] *Huss v. Huss*, 31 N.C. App. 463, 467, 230 S.E. 2d 159, 162 (1976).

When the plaintiff seeks reformation, it is usually the result of an oral agreement specifying certain promises and actions that is altered by one of the parties when it is put into writing. The writing creates a different contract, usually one that is far more advantageous to one party. The other party requests the court to use its equitable powers to recreate the terms of the original agreement before it was altered.[10]

Sidebar:
"If, when a man promised to labor to another, the law made him do it, his relation to the promisee might be called a servitude ad hoc with some truth. But that is what the law never does. It never interferes until a promise has been broken, and therefore cannot possibly be performed according to its tenor. It is true that in some instances equity does what is called compelling specific performance. But, in the first place, I'm speaking of the common law, and, in the next, this only means that equity compels the performance of certain elements of the total promise which are still capable of performance."[7]

Sidebar:
A party may breach a contract by announcing the intention not to assume any liabilities under it.[8]

reformation: A procedure in which a court will rewrite or correct a written agreement to conform with the original intent of the persons making the deal.

RESCISSION

As we saw in the previous chapter, a party may seek a court order rescinding the contract. Rescission is an action that cancels or voids the contract and places the parties back in the positions they were in prior to the creation of the contract.

When the court enters an order rescinding a contract, the contract is voided and all property and items of value exchanged are ordered returned to their original owners.[11]

Many jurisdictions impose limits on rescission actions such as only allowing the actions where some impropriety in the creation of the contract has occurred, such as fraud, undue influence, and so on.

For example of the complaint seeking equitable rescission of a contract, see the appendix.

When a party files a suit seeking rescission of a contract the party must show that:

- He/she is not in default under the contract

- The other party's breach is substantial

- The remedies available short of rescission are inadequate

- The parties can be returned to their original positions (status quo)

EXHIBIT 11-3: Making a case for rescission.

LEGAL DOCTRINES

We have seen many other instances in which courts use principles to guide them in their decisions in particular cases. Two such principles are important in equitable remedy cases. They are **quantum meruit** and **quantum valebant**.

Quantum meruit is a Latin term that translates "as much as merited." It is a legal doctrine that creates a presumption that a person who performs a service for another deserves to be paid. Quantum meruit becomes an issue when one party's services are not covered by the contract or arise under situations not originally anticipated by the parties. When the party is required to do additional work or services to complete the contract, the party is entitled to additional payments.[12]

Closely connected with quantum meruit is the concept of quantum valebant. This term means, "as much as it is worth." It arises in situations in which goods are sold and the parties have not specified the sale price of the goods. In this situation, when the receiving party refuses to pay for the goods, the supplier is entitled to bring an action requesting payment for

quantum meruit: "As much as he deserved." An old form of pleading used in a lawsuit for compensation for work done.

quantum valebant: "As much as they were worth." An old form of pleading used in a lawsuit for payment of goods sold and delivered.

the value of the goods. The supplier must then prove the actual value of the goods.

Monetary Damages

Damages refer to the monetary, property, or personal losses suffered by the plaintiff. The point of an award of damages is to restore the plaintiff to the condition he was in prior to the injury, if that is possible. A second consideration is to punish the defendant for his negligence and send a message to others that similar negligent actions will result in monetary losses. The damages seen most often in contract litigation are monetary damages.

Damages come in at least three broad categories, although some jurisdictions break them down in other ways. These broad categories include:

- Compensatory damages
- Punitive damages
- Nominal damages

COMPENSATORY

Compensatory damages are designed to restore the plaintiff to his or her original condition, or to reimburse the plaintiff for her expenses. Sometimes it is not possible to completely restore the plaintiff through monetary damages. In such a case, the court might award both monetary and equitable remedies.

When a court awards monetary damages, it orders the defendant to make a monetary payment to the plaintiff in a specific amount. If the defendant fails to make the payment, she can be held in contempt for failure to do so.

Assessing Monetary Damages

The principle that underlies the assessment of monetary damages in contract cases is relatively straightforward: the court creates an award for the nonbreaching party that is the financial equivalent of what the party would have received if the contract had been fulfilled as promised. Generally, these are the only types of monetary damages a party may receive. As we see in later sections, an award of punitive damages is rare. Limiting damage awards to the amount that would have been received under the contract may appear to drastically restrict the rights of the parties. After all, parties in other suits are permitted to seek punitive damages, loss of future income, even damages for psychological injuries. In most cases, parties to a contract dispute have no such options.

There is a side benefit to this limitation on contract damages. It creates a predictable system for assessing and awarding of financial damages in contract cases. Both the breaching party and the nonbreaching party will have roughly the same figure in mind when it comes time to assessing damages. A party considering breaching a contract might decide that the amount to pay out as damages is not worth whatever benefit would be received from breaching. However, the opposite is also true. There may be times when a party is willing to risk a potential verdict for damages because that amount is relatively small compared to the benefit he would receive from other quarters.

Just as we saw in the discussion about interpreting contract clauses, there are some general rules that the courts follow to assess monetary damages. Some of these rules create exceptions to the general rule that damages for a breach of contract are limited to what the party would have received if the contract had been fulfilled.

General Rules Used by Courts to Assess Damages

Here are the general rules used by the courts to assess damages. They are not offered in order of precedence. Judges are permitted to use some or all of these rules in any order that they see fit.

Rule Number One: Damages Must Be Foreseeable

When assessing an award, the damages must be both reasonable and foreseeable as a direct consequence of breach of contract. Damages that are not foreseeable at the time that the contract is created will not be assessed against the breaching party.

HYPOTHETICAL 11-1   "The Living Doll" Contract

Marty and Keisha have a service contract. Marty manufacturers tiny circuit boards for Keisha's newest product, the "Living Doll." Marty's circuit boards help control some of the doll's movements and make them appear more life-like. Keisha has been selling these dolls worldwide. Abdullah recently purchased such a doll for his daughter and because he is a computer programmer, he worked up an idea for a series of linked circuit board that would not only give the dolls lifelike movement but also would control sounds that they could make. He presents his idea to Keisha, who loves it. Unfortunately, she has a contract with Marty that runs for two more months before it expires. She wants to start using Abdullah's new circuit boards immediately and calculates that if she does, she can increase her profits by 200%. By contrast, if she breaches her contract with Marty, she will probably be assessed about $42,000. She contacts Marty and breaches the contract.

Marty sues for damages. He sues not only for the unfulfilled contract amount, which is $42,655.22, but also for mental distress. He claims in his contract that he had become emotionally involved in the production of the "Living Doll," and that the unlawful breach has caused him sleepless nights and anxiety attacks. Will he be awarded damages for mental pain and suffering in addition to his contract losses?

Answer: No. In contract cases, courts rarely, if ever, consider the psychological injury to the parties that arises from breach of contract. Courts reason that this is a business transaction and the parties should be thick-skinned enough to accept the vicissitudes of the business world.

Rule Number Two: The Parties Understand That Damages Follow a Breach

Under the second general rule of assessing damages, it is important that the parties understand that an award of damages is possible, should they breach the contract. In some cases, the parties may have attempted to negotiate away any right to monetary damages for a breach, or they may have some other understanding about the termination of the contract. In such cases, it is important for the non-breaching party to establish that monetary damages were a possibility under the contract.

Rule Number Three: Damages Are Specific

There must be some way of assessing the damages. Before a judge will order that a breaching party pay damages, there must be some way to determine what those damages were. Usually, a court will require a "reasonable degree of certainty" in the final award of damages. This rule of certainty will be explored in greater detail later in this chapter, but it stems from the practical concerns of legal remedies. If a judge is to order that one party pay a sum to the other, the judge must be able to determine what that amount is. If the judge cannot, there is a good chance that no award will be made at all.

Rule Number Four: Mitigation

Before a judge will order that the breaching party pay damages to the nonbreaching party, the nonbreaching party must show mitigation. **Mitigation of damages** is an ancient, and very sensible, principle of law.

A plaintiff is obligated to mitigate or lessen his damages whenever possible. In a contract case, this principle demands that when a contract is breached, the plaintiff must seek some alternative method of disposing of the property. If the plaintiff sells the item for less than the contract price, the plaintiff can sue for the difference. If the plaintiff makes a reasonable attempt to dispose of the property in some other way and is unable to do so, once that is proved in court, the defendant may then be forced to pay for the total loss.

mitigation of damages: The principle that a person suing for damages must have taken reasonable steps to minimize the harm done, or the amount of money awarded will be lowered.

HYPOTHETICAL 11-2　The Ice Cream Contract

Teresa makes large batches of ice cream for a local amusement park. The amusement park contacted Teresa shortly after she made her latest batch and announced its intention to breach the contract. Teresa is left with 100 gallons of various flavors of ice cream. She leaves the gallon containers on her shipping room floor where they eventually melt. She then sues for the total loss of the shipment and the costs for cleaning up the mess. Will she get what she requests?

Answer: No. Under the principle of mitigation, Teresa must take some action to attempt to mitigate her damages. This means that she must contact other possible purchasers and offer to sell the ice cream to them. Even if she sells the ice cream for a lower amount, she can sue for the difference, but she cannot simply allow the ice cream to melt and sue for the total loss.

Rule Number Five: Damages Should Not Exceed the Total Contemplated in the Contract

The final rule in assessing damages is that the ultimate award should not exceed the amount that the nonbreaching party would have received if the contract had been fully performed. To allow any other rule would be to encourage parties to sue for any type of infraction in the hopes that they might receive a windfall without actually having to perform under the contract.

Although these five rules seem simple and straightforward to apply, in the real world of contract litigation, things do not always work out quite so neatly. For one thing, determining the overall value of performance may not be that easy. Consider the next two hypotheticals.

HYPOTHETICAL 11-3   Dan's Damages

Dan and Barbara have entered into an agreement to purchase a tractor. Although the tractor is used, Dan assures Barbara that the tractor is in very good shape and well worth the offering price of $5,000. Barbara agrees to pay the $5,000. Dan then refuses to deliver the tractor. How does the court assess damages?

Answer: The value of Barbara's damages are equal to the total value of what she would have gained if the contract had been fully performed. In this case, the negotiated price of the tractor was $5,000 and so Barbara's damages equal that sum.

Sidebar:
Damages are assessed as of the day that the breach occurred.

HYPOTHETICAL 11-4   Calvin's Coins

Calvin and Ramon entered into negotiations to purchase Calvin's 1932 mint condition Liberty quarter. The sale price of this very rare coin is $100. Ramon, who is in the business of buying and reselling coins, has already lined up a buyer to purchase the coin for $150. Before the transaction is complete, Calvin learns from another source that the coin is actually worth $1,000. He no longer wishes to sell the coin to Ramon for $100. Ramon has also learned the value of the coin and has renegotiated with his new buyer for the sum of $1,500. When Calvin refuses to deliver the coin pursuant to the original agreement, what is the measure of damages?

Answer: We must look at the transaction point by point. Is the value of the contract $100, which is the amount originally agreed to buy Calvin and Ramon, or is the value of the contract and $1,000, which is the value of the item that was being discussed? In most jurisdictions, the answer would be that Ramon is entitled to damages in the amount of $100, because that was the price negotiated between Calvin and Ramon.

The two previous hypothetical situations have pointed out how quickly the issues can become complicated when assessing monetary damages.

Suppose, in Hypothetical 11-2, we change one small fact in the negotiations. Suppose that instead of negotiating a price of $100 for the coin, the parties agreed that they would pay an amount assessed by a third party? Calvin submits the coin to an independent coin dealer who assesses the value at $1,000. When Calvin learns of the coin's value, he decides to hang on to it. Ramon could have produced the $1,000 and was willing to do so. What is the measure of damages? Should the court award Ramon what essentially amounts to a windfall of $1,000 or should the court to step back from the transaction and simply award Ramon an amount for his time and aggravation involved in the transaction that didn't come off?

PUNITIVE DAMAGES

Punitive damages are rare in contract cases. An award of punitive damages is the jury's way of punishing the defendant for some action. These damages are awarded in addition to any compensatory damages that may have already been awarded. Because of the general rules for assessing damages in contract cases, the defendant's actions must be particular reprehensible to justify an award of punitive damages.

NOMINAL DAMAGES

We have seen that any breach of a contract justifies an award of damages, but that doesn't necessarily mean a large award. Nominal damages refer to an award of a small or token amount to a plaintiff. When a jury awards nominal damages, it is essentially agreeing with the plaintiff that there was a breach of contract, but the breach was minor.

When a breach is minor and the possibility is that only nominal damages will be awarded, most attorneys and clients would likely decide that it is not worth going through expensive litigation to be awarded a token sum, such as $1.

CONSEQUENTIAL DAMAGES

We have discussed compensatory damages as those damages that flow logically and foreseeably from the contract itself. However, there is another category of damages that are often seen in contract cases: consequential damages.

Consequential damages are different from compensatory damages in that the final award amount contains not only the amount that would have been obtained under the contract but also losses tied to a particular contract breach. Seen this way, compensatory damages are the losses associated with any contract breach; consequential damages are the losses associated with a particular contract breach. When a party seeks consequential damages, she must show how these damages were inextricably tied to the defendant's actions. These damages are, in effect, unique to this case and should be

Sidebar:
Many jurisdictions place limits on consequential damages. For instance, consequential damages will only be awarded if they were within the "contemplation" of the parties at the time that the contract was made.[13]

added to the amount that the defendant must pay. Lost profits, for example, do not always flow from a breach of contract. In a particular case, if a plaintiff wishes to sue for lost profits, she must present them as consequential damages and show that these damages were a proximate cause of the defendant's actions. In many jurisdictions, consequential damages will only be awarded if they were foreseeable at the time that the parties entered into their contract.

✓ PARALEGAL CHECKLIST

In order to prove consequential damages, the plaintiff must present evidence showing:

☐   The damages were caused by the breach of the contract[i]

☐   Consequential damages were foreseeable at the time that the contract was created

☐   The amount of damages can be determined with reasonable certainty

FIGURE 11-4: Recovering consequential damages.

---

[i] *Mahmood v. Ross*, 990 P.2d 933 (Utah 1999).

- *Expectancy*

  The value of the profit that the nonbreaching party would have received on the contract; sometimes called the "benefit of the bargain."

- *Reliance*

  The amount spent by a party in reliance that a contract would be carried out. These damages are usually sought in cases where the contract is breached early and other damages may be difficult, if not impossible, to determine.

- *Restitution*

  The amount required to put the breaching party back into the financial position he was in before the breach.

EXHIBIT 11-5: Other types of consequential damages.

LIQUIDATED DAMAGES

As we have seen on numerous occasions, courts give the contracting parties wide latitude in creating contractual duties with one another. This is also true in the area of damages. With certain limitations, the parties are free to negotiate the terms and payments due on a breach of contract by either party. The most common way to achieve this is through **liquidated damages**.

A liquidated damages clause is one in which the parties set out in advance what constitutes a breach and how the damages for this breach will be assessed. Liquidated damages clauses are often a good idea when the contract involves a transaction for which assessing damages might be difficult. The liquidated damages clause can set out a method for determining the value of damages when a breach occurs. This has the effect of eliminating some future litigation and streamlining any litigation that actually does occur.

Common types of liquidated damage clauses might include:

- Limitation or exclusion of consequential damages
- Exclusion of restitution damages
- Limitations on expectancy damages

> **liquidated damages:** A specific amount of money agreed to in a contract as compensation for a breach of that contract.

Limiting Damages Through Agreement

There are other methods of limiting damages as well. Another method is to limit the types of remedies that the parties have on a breach. These arrangements are not looked on as favorably by the courts as are liquidated damages clauses. Courts are reluctant to impose a contract clause that eliminates a party's right to seek redress through the court system. Contract clauses that purport to bar a party from bringing suit for a breach are routinely voided by the courts.

Another option for the parties is to create an alternative method for working out differences. A clause might contain a provision for Alternative Dispute Resolution. ADR clauses require that the parties submit their differences to a pre selected arbitrator or mediator before any party is authorized to bring suit. As long as the clause does not attempt to bar a party's right to the court system, ADR clauses are routinely upheld in contract disputes.

Liquidated Damages Under the UCC

The UCC uses a slightly different approach to liquidated damages. Under the UCC, any agreement between the parties that acts as a liquidated damages provision will be enforced if:

1. The stipulated amount is reasonable in relation to the actual damages incurred
2. Proving damages without the clause is difficult
3. The plaintiff would have no other remedy without such a provision[14]

Rights Under Bankruptcy

Although not typically thought of as a contract remedy, what rights does a party have when the other party to a contract declares bankruptcy? Does the contract still apply? What about payments due under a contract?

What Is Bankruptcy?

Bankruptcy is a process that allows a person who is overwhelmed with debt to enter into a court-administered plan to either repay a portion of that debt or to cancel the entire amount. There are different types of bankruptcies that follow the pattern set out in title 11 of United States Code. For instance, a Chapter 7 bankruptcy is a complete liquidation of the debtor's assets that repays creditors a portion of the money that is owed to them and cancels the balance of the debt. Chapter 11, by contrast, creates a reorganization of the debt and allows the person or business entity to remain in business and continue to make regular payments on the debt load. It is possible for a business to later emerge from bankruptcy with its credit intact. Other provisions of title 11 focus on debts owed by other business entities and also control how and when the debtor's assets will be divided amongst the creditors.

One of the most important aspects of a bankruptcy is the petition filed by the debtor that requests bankruptcy relief. Many law firms specialize in bankruptcies and spend their time preparing bankruptcy petitions and working with United States Bankruptcy Court to protect their clients' interests.

ETHICS FILE: Using the Court System to Harass or Intimidate

The court system is a party's recourse to enforce contract provisions and use legally authorized remedies to obtain redress, but it is not designed as a means for one party to harass or intimidate another. All state and federal jurisdictions have rules that specifically prohibit a party from using frivolous lawsuits as a means to harass or intimidate others. No legal professional should take part in a bogus lawsuit that is designed primarily to inflict revenge or intimidation on a party. The court system should be used to enforce legitimate contract provisions and to seek remedies for valid wrongs, not as a forum for personal vendettas.

The Case of the Uncharitable Charter Rights[15]

ABRAMS, Justice.

We consider whether an employee, serving under a contract of employment terminable at will, may recover for lost wages and fringe benefits in addition to commissions related to past services, when the employee is discharged in bad faith. See Fortune v. National Cash Register Co., 373 Mass. 96, 364 N.E.2d 1251 (1977). After a trial in the Superior Court, the jury returned a verdict for the plaintiff on his claim that he was discharged in "bad faith." By interrogatories accompanying the general verdict, see note 6, infra, the jury determined that the plaintiff would have earned $61,000 in commissions for past services. The judge also submitted the issue of damages to the jury on a quantum meruit theory. The jury determined that on a quantum meruit basis, the plaintiff was entitled to damages in the amount of $28,000. The judge entered a judgment on the quantum meruit theory. Both parties appealed. The Appeals Court concluded that the plaintiff was entitled to $61,000 in lost commissions, and that the issue of damages for lost wages and fringe benefits should have been submitted to the jury. For the reasons set forth in this opinion, we agree with the Appeals Court that the plaintiff was entitled to $61,000 in damages for lost commissions. A majority conclude that the judge correctly declined to allow the jury to consider the issue of the plaintiff's damages for lost wages and fringe benefits.

We summarize the evidence most favorable to the plaintiff and resolve in his favor all reasonable inferences that could be drawn from that evidence. The plaintiff was hired by the defendant, Western Mass. Bus Lines, Inc. (WMBL), as general manager in April, 1964. At that time, the president of WMBL, John F. Fortier, was interested in obtaining a grant of interstate charter rights from the Interstate Commerce Commission (ICC). The plaintiff had considerable experience appearing before the Massachusetts Department of Public Utilities (DPU) and

the ICC, in order to secure new operating authorities. Besides dealing with the ICC, the plaintiff's duties as general manager of WMBL included arranging the operating schedule, soliciting, advertising for, and quoting prices on charter trips, preparing the billing, checking employee time-cards, and generally overseeing the entire operation.

About six weeks after the plaintiff was hired, the plaintiff drafted, and the parties executed, a contract setting forth the terms of his employment. No definite term of employment was set out in the contract, and thus the contract was terminable at will. The contract provided that the plaintiff would receive a salary of $120 a week plus Blue Cross and Blue Shield insurance benefits. Additional weekly compensation was to be provided at the discretion of the defendant. The contract also provided that after the ICC granted the defendant interstate charter rights, the plaintiff would receive a five per cent commission on the special and charter revenues of the defendant as reported to the DPU and the ICC. The commission was to be paid to the plaintiff on the fifteenth of each month.

The defendant obtained interstate charter rights in June, 1966, and the plaintiff received the commissions called for in the contract for five and one-half months. In November, 1966, the grant was revoked after the United States District Court for the District of Massachusetts held that the ICC had erred in granting the interstate charter rights to the defendant. The plaintiff's commissions under the contract ceased thereafter.

In September, 1970, Mario Cantalini bought WMBL and became its president. The plaintiff remained as general manager. In October or November, 1970, the plaintiff met with Cantalini and his attorney to discuss the need for obtaining interstate charter rights. Cantalini then took out the plaintiff's employment contract and handed it to his attorney to read. The attorney read it and returned it to

Cantalini, stating that "this would be all right with the company." Sometime later the plaintiff and Cantalini sought to obtain from the ICC a grant of interstate charter rights. On October 1, 1973, the ICC again granted interstate charter rights to the defendant. About a week later, the plaintiff told Cantalini, "[N]ow that we [have] received the operating authority from the I.C.C., . . . that portion of my agreement on the commission [is] now in effect." Cantalini replied that "he didn't understand it to be that way, but that . . . he would check the agreement." On November 14, 1973, a day before the plaintiff's commissions for October became payable under the contract, Cantalini telephoned the plaintiff and asked him if he had to pay the five percent commission for the month of October. The plaintiff responded, "[Y]es, that was in accordance with the agreement he [Cantalini] had accepted." Cantalini replied "that it was a lot of money, that it was cream off the top." Cantalini sought to postpone the discussion, but the plaintiff stated, "We are not going to talk about it later because tomorrow is the day that I am supposed to be paid. . . ." The last thing Cantalini said before he hung up was "all right."

In addition to the payment for October, the plaintiff received commissions for November and December. On January 19, 1974, Cantalini discharged the plaintiff from his employment. Cantalini stated that he was discharging the plaintiff because the plaintiff was responsible for the poor profit statement which Cantalini claimed was inhibiting his attempt to sell the company. "[B]esides," stated Cantalini, "you wanted to get paid the commission under the agreement you made with Jack [Fortier]." Thereafter, the plaintiff filed a complaint in the Superior Court alleging that the defendant's termination of the contract was based on a bad faith attempt to avoid paying the plaintiff his commissions.

1. Liability of defendant for breach of contract. The defendant claims that there was insufficient evidence to support the jury's verdict, and that the judge should have granted its motion for a directed verdict or judgment notwithstanding the verdict. The Appeals Court concluded that "[f]rom the evidence as set out above, the jury could have found facts which bring this case within Fortune." We agree.

In Fortune, we held "that an employer may not in every instance terminate without liability an employment contract terminable at will. . . . [W]e upheld the plaintiff's claim for future commissions based on past service when the employer terminated the plaintiff's employment without good cause and for the purpose of retaining the sales commissions for itself." In that case we declined to "speculate as to whether [a] good faith requirement is implicit in every contract for employment at will." Fortune v. National Cash Register Co., supra at 104, 364 N.E.2d 1251. We believe that the plaintiff in this case, like the plaintiff in Fortune, could reasonably expect that his employment would not be terminated by the defendant in order to deny him commissions.

The defendant argues that there was insufficient evidence of bad faith in this case, and that the judge should have granted its motion for a judgment notwithstanding the verdict. We do not agree. The evidence and the reasonable inferences to be drawn therefrom support the jury's verdict. At the time of his discharge the plaintiff had been in the transportation business for approximately thirty-eight years. He had been the defendant's general manager for six years before Cantalini acquired WMBL, and for approximately four years since Cantalini acquired the company. After Cantalini acquired another bus company, he made the plaintiff its general manager, and the two companies were run out of the same office. By January, 1974, the plaintiff's salary was $250 a week. It is not clear from the record how much of the increase in salary was authorized by Cantalini. (The record indicates that he authorized at least $50 a week.) In 1972, the plaintiff was provided with pension benefits, apparently authorized by Cantalini. In addition, for the four years that Cantalini owned WMBL, the plaintiff was provided each year with a new, fully equipped automobile with all expenses paid. Finally, although there was evidence of poor profits prior to the time that the plaintiff's commissions became payable under the contract, Cantalini did not discharge the plaintiff until after the commissions became payable. From this evidence, the jurors could conclude that Cantalini discharged the plaintiff to avoid paying the plaintiff's commissions. The jurors were not required to believe

Cantalini's testimony that the plaintiff was discharged for legitimate business reasons.

When evidence on a contested matter is conflicting, the issue is for the trier of fact.

Damages. The jury were instructed that, in determining damages, they should answer two questions, Mass.R.Civ.P. 49(b), 365 Mass. 812 (1974), concerning the amount of commissions due under the contract. The judge refused to allow the jury to consider lost wages and fringe benefits. Although the jury determined that the plaintiff could reasonably have expected to be paid $61,000 in commissions during the course of his employment, the judge awarded the plaintiff $28,000 (the amount the jury determined was "attributable" to the plaintiff's work and effort). See note 6, supra. The Appeals Court concluded that the plaintiff was entitled to $61,000 in commissions rather than $28,000. We agree.

By limiting commissions to the amount "attributable to [the plaintiff's] work and efforts," the judge permitted recovery on what appears to be a quantum meruit theory. However, as in Fortune, "in this case there is remedy on the express contract." Thus, we need not reach any issues raised by a theory of quantum meruit recovery. The plaintiff was entitled to $61,000, the amount which the jury determined would be payable in commissions for his services in accordance with the contract. There is no merit to the defendant's claim that the plaintiff's interest in the commissions is distinguishable from the interest of the plaintiff in the Fortune case. The defendant claims that the plaintiff's right to commissions only vested each month that the plaintiff was employed, and, therefore, there were no commissions due the plaintiff. Contrary to the defendant's argument that the commissions payable in Fortune are distinguishable because they had already vested, in that case we stated, it is "clear that under the express terms of the contract Fortune . . . received all the bonus commissions to which he [was] entitled."

In this case the plaintiff used his skills, knowledge, and experience to assist the defendant in obtaining interstate charter rights from the ICC. The contract provided for compensation in the form of commis-

sions if the charter rights were secured. The plaintiff is entitled to receive the commissions, and a discharge to avoid payment of commissions is a discharge in bad faith. An employer may not discharge an employee in order to avoid the payment of commissions or to reap for itself financial benefits due its employee.

In his appeal, the plaintiff claims that the jury should have been allowed to consider the issue of damages for lost wages and fringe benefits. In Fortune v. National Cash Register Co., we left open the question whether such damages "might be justified in cases of bad faith termination." A majority of the court believe that the judge properly refused to instruct the jury on the issue of lost wages and fringe benefits unrelated to past services. In Fortune v. National Cash Register Co., supra, and Gram v. Liberty Mut. Ins. Co., supra, we imposed an obligation of good faith and fair dealing to prevent an employer from being unjustly enriched by depriving the employee of money that he had fairly earned and legitimately expected. However, a majority do not believe that an employee should be entitled to benefits which he neither contemplated nor included in his contract.

We therefore vacate the judgment and remand the case to the Superior Court for entry of judgment for the plaintiff in accordance with this opinion.

So ordered.

Case Questions:

1. According to the factual background provided by the court, why did the defendant hire the plaintiff?

2. Explain the commission arrangement created in this case?

3. What were the defendant's reasons for firing the plaintiff?

4. Did this court find that the defendant had acted in bad faith? If so, in what way?

5. According to the court, is the theory of quantum meruit the primary focus in this case? Why or why not?

The Case of the Callous Co-signor[16]

HANDWORK, P.J.

This appeal is from the June 3, 2003 judgment of the Wood County Court of Common Pleas which granted partial summary judgment to appellees, Suzanne and Stanley Harris. Upon consideration of the assignments of error, we affirm the decision of the lower court. Appellants, Nikki Isbell, Garry Isbell, and Debra Isbell, assert the following single assignment of error on appeal:

"The trial court committed prejudicial error by granting summary judgment against appellants on the equitable concept of specific performance."

Appellees filed their complaint against Brian J. Reiff (Suzanne Harris's son), and Nikki, Garry, and Debra Isbell to either quiet title, compel a sale in partition, or recover damages for breach of contract. This case arose out of an oral contract between appellee Suzanne Harris, Reiff, Nikki Isbell, and Garry Isbell.

Suzanne Harris, along with her husband, Stanley Harris, sought to be declared the sole owners of the property and quite title to certain property. Suzanne Harris also sought to recover $20,000 plus interest in damages resulting from the breach of the above-mentioned contract. Alternatively, appellants sought to compel a sale in partition since Reiff and Nikki Isbell own an undivided one-half interest in the property.

Thereafter, the Harrises filed a motion for partial summary judgment. Attached to the motion was the affidavit of Suzanne Harris. In that affidavit, she attested to the following facts.

Around July 24, 2001, Harris agreed to loan Reiff and Nikki Isbell $20,000 for the purchase of a home. Garry Isbell, Nikki Isbell's father, also made the same oral agreement. While the Isbells contend in their motion in opposition to the Harrises' motion for summary judgment that the initial loan was for $16,300, the Isbells admitted in their answer that the loan was for $20,000.

Both Suzanne Harris and Garry Isbell agreed to execute quit claim deeds in favor of Reiff and Nikki Isbell upon repayment of the loans. The parties intended that Reiff and Nikki Isbell would immediately refinance the loan and repay the loans to Garry Isbell and Suzanne Harris. All four parties purchased a home together on July 24, 2001.

Reiff and Nikki Isbell obtained a mortgage from American General Mortgage Company. The Isbells admit in their answer that they repaid Garry Isbell's loan and that on September 25, 2001, he signed a quitclaim deed transferring his rights in the home to Reiff, Nikki Isbell, and Suzanne Harris.

Suzanne Harris further attested that in the fall of 2001, Reiff and Nikki Isbell expressed a desire to refinance the home in order to make certain improvements. In consideration for Suzanne Harris' consent to the refinancing loan, Reiff, Nikki Isbell, and Garry Isbell orally agreed to refinance the property by December 31, 2001. If they failed to do so, they agreed that all of their names would be removed from the property and Suzanne Harris would become the sole owner of the property. The Isbells admitted in their answer to the complaint that they entered into a written agreement on November 30, 2001 affirming the oral agreement.

Suzanne Harris also attested that Reiff and Nikki Isbell failed to refinance the property by the deadline. Reiff executed a quitclaim deed in Suzanne Harris' favor on July 22, 2002, but the Isbells refused to execute a quitclaim deed, refused to repay the loan, and refused to permit Suzanne Harris to take possession of the home.

Garry, Debra, and Nikki Isbell opposed the motion for summary judgment and presented the following affidavits. Debra Isbell attested that Suzanne Harris and Garry and Debra Isbell agreed to loan Reiff and Nikki Isbell $16,300 to help Reiff and Nikki Isbell purchase a home for $32,500. Because the loaned funds were insufficient to enable Reiff and Nikki Isbell to make the home habitable, the parties agreed that they would obtain a $37,000 loan against the house in order to make repairs. From the proceeds of the loan, Garry Isbell was reimbursed $20,000. Garry Isbell used the entire $20,000 he received to make improvements to the home. Because there was still insufficient funds to repair the house, the loan was refinanced in November 2001 to increase the face amount to $48,060, giving them an additional $11,000 to repair the home after paying off the first loan. Suzanne Harris refused to sign this note, but she did sign the mortgage. Debra Isbell further attested that Suzanne Harris only signed the mortgage after the parties signed the November 30, 2001 agreement.

Reiff, Nikki Isbell, and Garry Isbell attempted to obtain a second $20,000 mortgage on the property in order to repay Suzanne Harris' loan, but they were unable to do so because Reiff was delinquent on a loan for a vehicle in the amount of $9,000, which resulted in a judgment lien on the home. Suzanne Harris had led Debra Isbell to believe that Harris was making payments of the vehicle loan, but she was not. Debra Isbell believed that Suzanne Harris refused to cooperate with any of the financing transactions that would enable her to be repaid. Debra Isbell also attested that she and Garry Isbell have paid the real estate taxes, mortgage payments, and utilities on the property.

In their motion in opposition, the Isbells did not contend that there were genuine issues of material fact in this case. Rather, they contended that the court should not grant summary judgment in favor of the Harrises because the Isbells are not in breach of the contract; that it would be unconscionable to quiet title in favor of the Harrises when Suzanne Harris' failure to pay the vehicle loan prevented the Isbells from obtaining refinancing so that they could repay the loan owed to her; that the Harrises would be unjustly enriched by such a judgment due to the fact that significant improvements have been made to the house; and that the quiet title remedy is not available for one who claims an entire estate but is not in possession of the property.

On April 11, 2003, the trial court granted partial summary judgment to the Harrises. The court found that they were entitled to specific performance of the contract and that there was no right to restitution or a claim of unjust enrichment by the Isbells.

On appeal, the Isbells assert in their sole assignment of error that the trial court erred in granting partial summary judgment to the Harrises.

Because specific performance is an equitable remedy, the Isbells argue that it cannot be awarded unless the contract was fair and equitable. The Isbells contend that the contract was not fair or equitable because they would lose the $20,000 investment they made in improving the property and would not fulfill the purpose of the contract which was to provide Nikki Isbell with a home. The Harrises argue that the Isbells did not raise this issue in the trial court and, therefore, have waived the issue for purposes of appeal.

However, the Isbells did argue that the Harrises would be unjustly enriched by an award of specific performance due to the fact that the Isbells have made significant repairs to the home. Therefore, this issue has been preserved for consideration on appeal. The Isbells' second argument, that equity requires that they be credited with the contributions they made to improve and maintain the property, will be considered in conjunction with the first argument.

Generally, unjust enrichment is an equitable doctrine to justify a quasi-contractual remedy that operates in the absence of an express contract or a contract implied in fact to prevent a party from retaining money or benefits that in justice and equity belong to another. Because there was a valid, enforceable contract in this case, this doctrine is not applicable.

Rather, the substance of the Isbells' argument is that the court should not have awarded specific performance in this case. The Isbells argue that this was inequitable because that award would transfer title of the house to the Harrises after the Isbells have made significant improvements to the property and maintained the property.

We agree with the trial court that the Isbells, had they filed such a claim, were not entitled to restitution for the benefits they conferred upon the Harrises since the Harrises did not request that the Isbells improve or maintain the home.

Generally, specific performance can be awarded if there was a valid enforceable contract that was breached. The court's goal is to carry out what the parties had intended to do under the contract. If the terms of the contract are unambiguous, the court must enforce the intent of the parties as expressed by the contract.

The following factors are the general prerequisites to the award of specific performance: "The contract must be concluded, certain, unambiguous, mutual, and upon a valuable consideration; it must be perfectly fair in all its parts; free from any misrepresentation or misapprehension, fraud or mistake, imposition or surprise; not an unconscionable or hard bargain; and its performance not oppressive upon the defendant; and finally, it must be capable of specific execution through a decree of the court."

However, in an arms length transaction, the parties are free to make whatever contract they desire so long as there is no fraud, duress, overreaching, or undue influence involved. A contract does not have to be fair or equitable to be enforceable. Nonetheless, specific performance will not be granted where it will cause unreasonable hardship, loss or injustice to the party in breach. The court has the discretion, if the circumstances require, to modify the award of specific performance of a contract in order to make it equitable.

Thus, the trial court, after considering the circumstances of the particular case, has the discretion to determine whether specific performance is the appropriate remedy. On appeal, the trial court's decision will not be disturbed unless the trial court abused its discretion. The term "abuse of discretion" has been defined as a decision which is arbitrary, unreasonable, or unconscionable.

The contract in this case was unambiguous. It clearly reveals that Suzanne Harris' sole intent was to recoup her initial $20,000 investment. The parties made an agreement which protected Suzanne Harris' investment while enabling Reiff and Nikki Isbell to obtain another loan. The fact that the Isbells made a poor bargain cannot be rectified by the courts. We find that the trial court did not abuse its discretion by awarding the Harrises specific performance in this case.

The Isbells also argue that the Harrises were not entitled to relief since they did not come into equity with clean hands. They contend that Suzanne Harris allowed a loan she agreed to pay to become delinquent and a lien upon the house, thus preventing Reiff and Nikki Isbell from being able to obtain a refinancing loan without Suzanne Harris' participation.

We find no merit to this argument either. Even if the evidence that Suzanne Harris had stated that she was going to pay off Brian Reiff's vehicle loan is accepted as true, there was no legal obligation for her to do so. Furthermore, there is no basis for imposing such a burden on her in order to protect her investment.

Having found that the trial court did not commit error prejudicial to the Isbells, the judgment of the Wood Court of Common Pleas is affirmed. Pursuant to App.R. 24, the Isbells are hereby ordered to pay the court costs incurred on appeal.

JUDGMENT AFFIRMED.

Case Questions:

1. What was the original agreement in this case?

2. Why did the parties enter into this agreement?

3. According to the Isbells, why are the Harrises not entitled to receive the property?

4. Why did the court reject the Isbells argument concerning the actions of Suzanne Harris in failing to pay a vehicle loan?

5. Explain the court's decision in this case?

Business Case File

Robert Harbour, Harbour Communication, Incorporated

Robert Harbour isn't a typical business entrepreneur. He worked for over 20 years as a high school and college instructor before launching Harbour Communication, Inc. "I was doing a lot of applied physics courses and a I realized that there was a need for local Internet service. There were no local dial up services for the Internet and I knew that I could pull all of the systems together to make it happen."

In 1995, he began Harbour Communication, Inc. as a side venture out of his home while still working full time as a high school applied physics teacher. One of his first contacts with the law came when he retained an attorney to incorporate the business. "I thought incorporation was essential." Once formed, his business grew by leaps and bounds. "By summer, 1995, we had 16 modems up and running. In just a few months, it was up to 100. By the following year, it was over 300. Business mushroomed so fast that I had to make a decision: do I continue to exist on two hour's of sleep each night, keep teaching and also try to run this business? I decided to quit teaching and give one hundred percent to the business. Business just kept taking off. My wife was working with me and, during the summers, so were my sons. Eventually, I had to hire additional employees. By spring 1999, we decided to relocate to a new office building." That decision to relocate—and to provide additional services at his new location—brought up a whole host of new issues. "We had to look into the Americans with Disabilities Act," he said. "If you're running a business that's open to the public, then you have to be in compliance." Eventually, he installed an elevator at a substantial cost to make sure that he fully complied.

A rapidly growing and successful business has also brought other headaches. Besides the enormous amount of time that Harbour continues to

Robert Harbour

give his business, there are also legal questions to consider. For instance, he sometimes has to threaten collection action against customers who won't pay. For another, he is currently involved in a long-running dispute with a service provider who is going through bankruptcy. "When this bankruptcy issue came up, I contacted a lawyer who is a friend of mine and asked him to help educate me about all of this. I didn't know anything about bankruptcy and I wasn't sure how I could safeguard my business with this provider going under."

Harbour must often consider the various contract and other remedies available to him to enforce contracts, or to try to recoup money through bankruptcy.

The rapidly changing pace of technology in general and the telecommunications industry in particular continues to provide challenges. Although business has been good, Harbour keeps his eyes on the fundamentals. "Word of mouth advertising is what got us off the ground. I want people to be happy with our service. We're in the problem solving business." With that attitude, Harbour Communication, Inc. will probably be in business for a long time.

Chapter Summary:

When a breach of contract occurs, the nonbreaching party has several possible options. The party can sue for an equitable remedy. An equitable remedy is a court order compelling a party to take some action. When a court has equity jurisdiction, it means that it has the power to order injunctions, specific performance or several other actions. Courts in the United States possess both equity jurisdiction and legal jurisdiction. Legal jurisdiction gives the court the power to assess damages against a breaching party. Damages can come in the form of compensatory, punitive, or nominal damages, although compensatory damages are the most common in contract litigation. Compensatory damages are designed to place the nonbreaching party as close to his or her original financial position as possible. A plaintiff may request that a court use either or both of its jurisdictional powers: equity and legal jurisdiction.

The parties are as free to negotiate the terms of a breach as they are any other point in the contract. Parties can, and often do, insert liquidated damages clauses in contracts. These clauses provide a method for determining the actual amount of damages. Parties also may attempt to limit the types of remedies available, but courts take a dim view of such limitations. The parties also may negotiated alternative dispute resolution clauses, which require that the parties submit their grievances to an arbitrator or mediator before they can file suit.

WEB SITES

Georgetown University–E.B. Williams Law Library
www.law.georgetown.edu
Georgetown University School of law.

Duke Law
www.law.duke.edu
Duke Law School.

Law.com
www.law.com
Offers legal news and information.

Courts.net
www.courts.net
Offers links to court sites around the United States.

REVIEW QUESTIONS

1. Under what circumstances would a party not want the other party to specifically perform under the contract?
2. How did the English court system's Equity Court affect the organization of the American court system?
3. What is the difference between equity jurisdiction and legal jurisdiction?
4. What are some of the rules that courts use to assess damages in contract cases?
5. One of the basic doctrines of equity is that the plaintiff must have "clean hands." What does this phrase mean?
6. What elements must a plaintiff present in order to prove a case for rescission?
7. What are the basic steps involved in obtaining an injunction?
8. Explain mitigation of damages.
9. Under what circumstances can a plaintiff seek both an equitable remedy and a legal remedy?
10. What is an injunction?
11. Explain specific performance.
12. How is reformation different from rescission?
13. Are punitive damages common in contract litigation? Why or why not?
14. What is mitigation of damages?
15. What are the five rules that the courts use to determine monetary damages?
16. Why are damages for psychological injury usually not found in contract cases?
17. Explain liquidated damages under the UCC.
18. How can the parties limit damages through the contract?
19. What are typical examples of liquidated damages provisions?
20. What are some examples of consequential damages?

HANDS-ON ASSIGNMENT

Draft a contract based on the facts in the "Case of the Uncharitable Charter."

PRACTICAL APPLICATION

Which court in your state can exercise both equity jurisdiction and legal jurisdiction?

What is the standard the plaintiff must meet in your state in order to make out a case for rescission of contract?

HELP THIS BUSINESS

Danny and Hilda wish to go into business together. Danny has an idea to create a new type of insurance company. Hilda will use her expertise as an internationally renowned art expert to examine paintings owned by clients that Danny will produce. Danny will then issue a policy for the paintings and insure their increase in value. The way that Danny sees it, paintings constantly increase in value. If a particular painting does not increase in value as much as Hilda believes, then Danny will pay a claim made on the policy.

Hilda has some concerns about this scheme and wishes to create a liquidated damages clause in their partnership contract that will limit the total amount of damages she might have to pay to Danny if she wishes to terminate the partnership. Draft an agreement that helps Hilda with her concerns.

KEY TERMS

mutuality of obligation

mutuality of remedy

equity

jurisdiction

injunctions

specific performance

reformation

quantum meruit

quantum valebant

mitigation of damages

liquidated damages

ENDNOTES

[1] *Davenport Osteopathic Hospital Asso. v. Hospital Service*, Inc., 261 Iowa 247, 154 NW2d 153 (1967).

[2] *Carrick v. First Criminal Court of Jersey City*, 20 A.2d 509 (N.J.1941).

[3] *Moore v. McAllister*, 141 A.2d 176, 216 Md. 497 (1958).

[4] *Williams v. Cedartown Textiles*, 208 Ga. 659, 68 S.E.2d 705 (1952).

[5] *Clark v. Board of Ed.*, Hamilton Local School Dist., 51 Ohio Misc. 71, 367 N.E.2d 69 (1977).

[6] *Spector v. Loreck*, 342 Mass. 685, 175 N.E.2d 262 (1961).

[7] *The Common Law*, Oliver Wendell Holmes, Harvard University Press, 1963, p. 236.

[8] *Matheney v. McClain*, 248 Miss. 842, 161 So. 2d 516 (1964).

[9] *Tuel v. Gladden*, 234 Or. 1, 379 P.2d 553 (1963).

[10] *Mutual of Omaha Ins. Co. v. Russell*, C.A.Kan., 402 F.2d 339 (C.A. Kan., 1968).

[11] *Abdallah, Inc. v. Martin*, 242 Minn. 416, 65 N.W.2d 641 (1954).

[12] *Bignold v. King City*, 65 Wn. 2d 817, 826, 399 P.2d 611 (1965).

[13] *Long v. Abbruzzetti*, 254 Va. 122, 487 S.E.2d 217 (1997).

[14] UCC §2-718.

[15] *Maddaloni v. Western Mass. Bus Lines, Inc.*, 438 N.E.2d 351 (Mass., 1982).

[16] *Harris v. Reiff*, unpublished decision Ohio App. 2003.

For additional resources, visit our Web site at
www.westlegalstudies.com

CHAPTER 12

DRAFTING CONTRACTS

> **Focus of this chapter:** This chapter focuses on the various resources that a paralegal can use in researching contract law and to assist in drafting contracts. Actual contract clauses are examined in detail.

Chapter Objectives:
At the completion of this chapter, you should be able to:

- Explain the resources available to a paralegal who wishes to research and write contract clauses
- Explain the role of form books in drafting contracts
- Be able to draft specific types of contract clauses
- Explain the resources that are available in print media for legal professionals drafting a contract
- Detail the Internet resources for legal professionals drafting a contract
- Be able to draft a contract dealing with specific factual situations
- Explain how the use of checklists and other aides can assist a legal professional in drafting a contract
- Explain the types of contracts that law firms are usually carry called on to draft
- Define a contract of adhesion
- Examine a contract for legal sufficiency through the use of contract checklists

Legal Professionals and Contracts

Law firms are often called on to either assist in the creation of a contract or to actually draft a contract as a whole. It is important to keep in mind that a contract is more than a legally binding instrument. A contract is the expression of the intent of the parties. As such, a contract should not only contain all of the legal language that we have encountered in previous chapters, but it also should be drafted in such a way that businesspeople can understand it. A contract that contains overly technical legal phrases may actually create more problems than it solves.

WHY BUSINESS PEOPLE WANT TO AVOID LITIGATION

As a general rule, business people do not like to litigate. Litigation is a long, drawn-out, and costly procedure. Cases may take years to successfully litigate. Even if a party wins, the legal expenses could eat up any possible profit. One of the best ways to avoid the litigation is to draft a contract that anticipates and solves many of the problems businesspeople face.

> "Of all the ways in which business people interact with their own attorneys, probably the most usual, but also one of the most crucial, has to do with the drawing up of contracts. Unfortunately, the terrible truth is that contracts are too often drawn up without any creativity at all.
> "Some lawyers, overly proud of their own areas of expertise, take it upon themselves to make substantive changes in aspects of deals that they're not really in a position to understand. This type of lawyer likes to knock off the rough edges, so that the finished contract is a marvel of symmetry and elegance-regardless of the fact that sometimes it's the rough edges in which the deal's real benefits consist." [1]

AVOIDING "LEGALESE" IN CONTRACTS

One of the biggest temptations for a legal professional when preparing a contract is to use legal-sounding jargon and other impressive words to emphasize the seriousness of the document. In many circles, this is referred to as "legalese." Common examples of legalese are provided in Exhibit 12-1. Although these phrases certainly sound as though they have a particular legal meaning, more often than not they cause more confusion than they solve. Legal professionals should always strive for clarity in their writing. This is as true of a contract clause as it is of an appellate brief. What this means, on a practical level, is that impressive-sounding phrases often don't communicate as well as simpler phrases. When in doubt, strive for clarity instead of jargon.

Contract Law Resources

In this section, we will explore the types of resources available to legal professionals who must either research or assist in drafting the contract for a client. We will begin our discussion with one the most frequently used: formbooks.

- Heretofore
- Party of the first part
- Party of the second part
- Hereunder
- Hereafter
- Infra
- Supra
- Whomsoever

EXHIBIT 12-1. Common examples of legalese.

FORMBOOKS

Formbooks have existed in one form or another for centuries. Formbooks are used in a wide variety of legal areas. There are formbooks dealing with real estate, bankruptcy, and even criminal law. All formbooks contain forms that are used in a specific area of law. A contract formbook contains a wide variety of contracts, clauses, and other materials that act as a guideline for a person creating a new contract. Laypersons often make the mistake of assuming that a form from such a book is the only thing that they need to address all of their legal concerns. This is far from the truth. A formbook is a guideline; it is not a substitute for clear thinking or research. Formbooks were never designed to anticipate all possible legal problems. Instead, a formbook simply provides a template for how a particular legal document should look. There are many fine contract formbooks available. Forms also are available on Westlaw and other Internet pay services, as well as through standard print publications.

Suppose, for instance, that you are looking for a form for a person to sign to waive copyright issues? A formbook might provide you with a good, basic form that sets out a copyright waiver. However, a formbook cannot—and was never designed to—substitute for a legal professional's experience and research.

Sidebar:
Formbooks are a good place to begin your research; they should never be relied upon exclusively.

TREATISES

Treatises are specialized works on specific topics of law. Written by eminent legal scholars, a treatise focuses on a narrow area of the law and explores it in detail. There are treatises for topics as diverse as real estate law to admiralty law. There also are several excellent treatises on contract law. Treatises are a great resource when you are faced with a particularly difficult question of law. The authors of legal treatises have explored their topic in minute detail and can often provide excellent guidance. Some treatises, like *Corbin on Contracts*, have been around for decades.

These treatises may run to 10 or more volumes. Treatises sometimes contain general forms as well.

CASEBOOKS

Another resource for the legal professional is a casebook. Casebooks contain interesting and seminal cases on particular topics of law. Compiled by some of the most learned and eminent scholars in the field, casebooks provide an overview of the critical cases in a particular area of law.

STATUTES

Although state statutes are not a good resource to help you draft a contract, they are absolutely essential in assuring that your contract is legally valid. Some contracts have specific requirements set out in statutes. If you fail to meet these legal prerequisites, the contract may be void.

APPELLATE DECISIONS

Closely associated with statutory law, state appellate decisions are another invaluable resource for a legal professional intent on drafting a contract that is legally valid. Appellate cases interpret and expand on statutory laws. In an area such as contract law, in which there are relatively few statutes, cases take on an even more important role in helping to explain and amplify certain legal concepts.

INTERNET SITES

No discussion of the types of resources available to legal professionals could be complete without a discussion of the Internet. Ten years ago, when the Internet was in its infancy, Web-based legal resources were almost nonexistent. However, in the last few years, legal research sites have expanded considerably. Pay sites, such as Westlaw or Lexis-Nexis, provide a wealth of the information that would be almost impossible to duplicate in print form. There is also a plethora of free legal research sites on the Internet. If you were to type in "contract clauses" in your search engine, you would undoubtedly receive hundreds of hits. However, when it comes to legal research, quantity is not synonymous with quality. Many of the free legal research sites do not have the extensive coverage found on the pay sites. Cases and statutes may not be up to date and may not cover more than just a few years of appellate decisions. Although Internet sites are improving constantly, your best bet with online research is still a pay site.

GENERAL BOOKS ON CONTRACTS

A quick perusal of the public library or any bookstore will reveal dozens of books about business and contracts. Some of these books claim to be the best source for drafting "absolutely legal" contracts in all states. For a legal professional, these books are essentially useless.

Drafting Contract Clauses

Now that we have discussed the various resources available, we will begin to focus on specific contract clauses. We will develop these clauses as we have discussed these topics throughout this text. We will begin with an offer, then proceed through acceptance, the establishment of consideration, mutual assent, and all of the additional contractual elements we have explored in previous chapters. We also will set out some general contract clauses that may, in most situations, be considered legally sufficient. However, the same caveat applies to this material as it does to formbooks or any other general topic of law: you should always research the particular facts and circumstances of your client's case, and you should never rely exclusively on a general summary or general contract form.

In the following paragraphs, we will detail specific contact clauses and contract elements. Each section is followed by a short checklist to assist you in double-checking an existing contract, or to help you draft the components of a new contract.

CHECKING FOR THE CONTRACT BASICS

In the first few chapters of this book, we explored the basic contract elements that must be present in all contracts to make them binding, legal, and ultimately enforceable. The final contract is the written expression of those basic elements.

✓ PARALEGAL CHECKLIST

- ☐ Are the essential elements of a valid, legal contract present in the written document?
- ☐ Is there a valid offer and acceptance?
- ☐ Is mutual assent established in the contract?
- ☐ Is there consideration for the contract?
- ☐ Is the contract legally valid?
- ☐ Is the contract for a legal subject?
- ☐ Is the contract voided for public policy reasons?
- ☐ Do the parties have capacity?

Offer and Acceptance

It is often difficult to review an existing contract for valid offer and acceptance. Contracts usually do not detail the history of the negotiations between the parties. Instead, the contract presents the final form of those negotiations. However, this does not mean that offer and acceptance can be ignored. It is always a good idea to gather evidence about those negotiations, especially the offer-acceptance period because it may become an issue later.

✓ **PARALEGAL CHECKLIST**

☐ What evidence is there about the client's interactions with the other contracting parties?

☐ Are there any writings, memoranda, or other documents supporting the fact that a valid offer was made and that it was validly accepted?

Mutual Assent

Unlike offer and acceptance, mutual assent is a contract detail that not only can be gathered from the contract but also should be presented clearly and unambiguously. We have already seen examples of contracts that have been voided for mutual mistake. A close reading of the contract language concerning the understandings of the parties will help avert any later claims of lack of mutual assent.

✓ **PARALEGAL CHECKLIST**

☐ Is there a common design or purpose in the contract?

☐ What is the subject of the contract?

☐ Who will be bound?

☐ Is there an agreement about what will be exchanged, who will exchange, what its value is and who will pay?

Capacity

Capacity is another legal requirement of a contract that is often not actually presented in the document. It is rare to find a contract clause that reads, "Party A is over the age of 21 and has not been declared to be legally incompetent." Because of this, other sources must be used to determine capacity. This may require some research into the parties' backgrounds as well as additional information about the negotiations themselves.

✓ **PARALEGAL CHECKLIST**

☐ Are all the parties legal adults?

☐ Have any of the parties ever had their mental competency challenged?

☐ Were there any unusual behaviors exhibited by any of the parties during the negotiations or the signing of the contract that might indicate capacity issues?

Legal Subject of Contract

Although this sounds obvious, the contract should be checked to make sure that it contemplates actions that are legal in the jurisdiction where it will be performed. States have widely different laws and what may be legal in one state may not be legal in another. It is always a smart move to double-check the legality of your contract.

We also have discussed occasions where a contract, although technically legal, has been voided by the courts for public policy reasons. In addition to confirming the legality of the contract subject, a legal professional should also research the contract clauses and provisions to see if any have been voided on prior occasions for public policy reasons.

DRAFTING AN OFFER

There are times when the legal team will be called on to draft an offer. We have explored the legal requirements of an offer in Chapter 2. An offer must contain specific language and show an evidence to enter into a contract. Consider Hypothetical 12-1.

HYPOTHETICAL 12-1   Offer Posted on a Sign or in a Newspaper

"Daffy Shoes has just received 200 pairs of assorted sizes of Hound-dog brand children's shoes, just in time for "Back to School!" Each pair of Hound-dog brand shoes will be sold for $3.00 each, on a first come, first served basis. Limit of three pairs per customer. They won't last long at this price! Sale starts Monday at 8:00 A.M."

Is this a valid offer?

Answer: Yes. Although advertisements are generally not considered to be offers, this ad does satisfy all of the requirements of a valid offer. It is specific as to subject matter, price and the manner in which the contract can be formed. Whoever arrives at the store after Monday at 8:00 A.M. and presents $3 can purchase a pair of the listed shoes.

C. DRAFTING AN ACCEPTANCE

In addition to drafting an offer, the law firm also may be called on to draft an acceptance. We know that an acceptance must meet some basic requirements. An acceptance is valid if it unequivocally accepts the offer as stated, without changing any of the essential terms.

D. RECITALS OF CONSIDERATION

Moving beyond the basics of offer and acceptance, we will now address some of the specific, foundational requirements of a valid contract. One such requirement is consideration. We have seen that consideration is the legal detriment assumed by both parties to the transaction. One party gives up something of value in exchange for the other party giving up something of value. The "something of value" could be money, a promise or an action, but whatever the consideration is, it should be listed in the contract. A simple phrase such as "in consideration of . . ." is often sufficient.

HYPOTHETICAL 12-2 Considerate Consideration

Uma and Troy enter into a contract that states the following:

"I, Uma, agree to allow Troy to work as hard as he can to further my acting career, including, but not limited to, trying to find me work in television and film. The consideration for this contract is the warm feelings that we have for one another."

Is this consideration?

Answer: This extremely vague contract doesn't appear to bind Uma to do anything. Nothing of value is exchanged (and Uma's obligation under this contract is unclear). Without more, there is no consideration and no contract.

SPECIFIC CONTRACT CLAUSES

In the next six sections, we will focus on specific contract clauses and ways to ensure that the final contract contains the appropriate language creating such a clause.

Goods and Services

Contracts involving the sale of goods are a common form of contract. There are many issues involved in such contracts, not the least of which involves delivery and payment. The transaction also may fall under the UCC.

✓ **PARALEGAL CHECKLIST**

☐ Does the contract clearly point out the specific time at which ownership of goods changes hands?

☐ Which party is responsible for insuring the goods?

☐ Is the transaction covered by the Uniform Commercial Code? If so, the code should be referred to because it has its own provisions about insurance and transfer of ownership.

Statute of Frauds

This entire chapter is devoted to the discussion of written contract provisions, so discussing the Statute of Frauds is almost superfluous.

However, when a contract falls under the jurisdiction of the state Statute of Frauds, the statute must be followed closely.

✔ PARALEGAL CHECKLIST

Does this contract cover:

- ☐ Contracts involving testamentary transactions (wills, etc.)
- ☐ Contract to answer for the debt of another
- ☐ Contracts in anticipation of marriage (pre-nuptial/ante-nuptial agreements)
- ☐ Contracts for the sale of land
- ☐ Contracts that cannot be performed within one year of the date of their creation

---

"Time Is of the Essence"

In Chapter 8, we saw that a provision providing that time is of the essence in a contract means that performance must occur by a specific date or the contract will be voided. When reviewing a contract, or inserting language creating such a provision, you should look for a clause similar to that found in Exhibit 12-2.

The parties hereby agree that time is of the essence in this contract. If either party fails to perform as anticipated in this contract by the time fixed in this contract, the other party may elect to terminate the contract.[i]

EXHIBIT 12-2: Time is of the essence contract clause.

[i] Am. Jur Legal Forms, Contracts §68:239. 2003.

"Trade or Business Secrets"

If the client wishes to insert a provision preventing an employee from releasing sensitive information about trade or business secrets, the contract must contain some provision that specifically states what types of information should not be released. Courts are reluctant to enforce vague contract clauses dealing with trade or business secrets.

"Noncompete"

Noncompetition clauses in contracts are usually reserved for employment contracts. Courts will generally not enforce such provisions when they are overly broad.

✔ **PARALEGAL CHECKLIST**

☐ Does the contract contain reasonable geographic limitations on an employee's future employment?

☐ Does the contract contain reasonable limitations about the other types of businesses that the employee may enter following termination with the current company?

Contract of "Adhesion"

The small print found on the reverse of airline tickets or other types of forms is just as binding as the large print on the obverse. These are often referred to as **contracts of adhesion.** Such contracts have often been found to be invalid because they impose contractual obligations on persons when there is no negotiation and no power to alter any of the terms of the contract.

contract of adhesion: A contract in which all the bargaining power favor one side.

✔ **PARALEGAL CHECKLIST**

A contract may be ruled an adhesion contract if:

☐ One party has no bargaining power

☐ One party has no ability to change contract terms

☐ The contract is unconscionable

☐ The contract involves a matter of practical necessity

☐ Person signing contract had no real alternative

Sidebar:
Contracts of adhesion are strictly interpreted and any ambiguity is construed against the drafter.

THE FINE PRINT

Laypeople often refer to contract clauses and provisions as "fine print." This term makes it appear that the language in provisions contained in these paragraphs are simple technicalities that may only be applied at some future date. However, for a legal professional, the fine print *is* the contract. As a general rule, a party is presumed to have read the entire contents of any contract that he or she has signed. When a contract contains some provision that is not favorable to party, and the party's signature appears on the contract, the law presumes that the party not only read it that provision but also agreed to it.

Conditions

When reviewing a contract for language that could potentially qualify as a condition, some important considerations come to mind. First of all, is the language used in the clause open to interpretation as a condition? If so, what type of condition is it? We have discussed at least three different types of conditions in Chapter 8. They included conditions precedent, implied conditions, and conditions subsequent.

✔ **PARALEGAL CHECKLIST**

When a clause is a *condition precedent* it:

☐   Imposes a condition that must be satisfied before the contractual duty is assumed

☐   Specifically states that the failure of the condition to materialize will void the contract

---

✔ **PARALEGAL CHECKLIST**

When a clause is an *implied condition* it:

☐   Is not actually stated in the contract

☐   Is a duty or fact that is assumed by the parties to be true

---

✔ **PARALEGAL CHECKLIST**

When a clause is a *condition subsequent* it:

☐   Is an event that occurs after the contract has been completed

☐   Is an event that will affect the existence of the contract

---

Payment

Payment is one of the most important contract clauses for the parties, even though it may have no greater significance to the contract drafter than any other contract provision. The parties always want to know how much they will be paid and when.

Damages

Damages are the focus of Chapter 11. In that chapter, we saw that damages can come in many forms, from consequential to punitive. Although most contracts are silent about the topic of damages, it would be prudent to include some provision about damages in a contract.

✓ **PARALEGAL CHECKLIST**

- ☐ What type of payment is required under the contract?
- ☐ May payment be made in cash, personal check, certified funds, or through other means?
- ☐ When and where is payment to be made?
- ☐ Who is authorized to receive payment?
- ☐ Are partial payments permissible?
- ☐ Is the payment to be made at the same time every month, or when the goods are delivered?
- ☐ Is the payment to be made on the date that the goods are delivered or within a certain time period afterward?

✓ **PARALEGAL CHECKLIST**

- ☐ Is there any provision for damages?
- ☐ Should the contract contain a provision about liquidated damages?
- ☐ Are there any limitations on consequential damages?
- ☐ Are there any limitations on the remedies available to the parties when the breach occurs?
- ☐ Is there any provision, or should there be any provision, about equitable remedies? For instance, should specific performance be excluded?
- ☐ Is there a reasonable method to calculate damages?

Time

There are several important considerations about time that should be considered in a contract. The most obvious concern is the effective date of the contract. Exactly when will the contractual obligations negotiated in the contract become effective? There should be no ambiguity on this point. Other considerations about time include the manner and method of performance of the contract. When is performance to be carried out? Time is also an important consideration when discussing termination of the contract.

✓ **PARALEGAL CHECKLIST**

☐   What is the effective date of the contract?

☐   When do the contractual obligations of the parties commence?

☐   Is the date specific and unambiguous?

☐   Are there conflicting dates in the contract, such as a signature date and effective date?

☐   Did the party have authority to enter into the contract on the date in question? (For instance, if one of the parties is a corporation, was the corporation a valid, legal entity when the contract was created?)

Choice of Law

In situations in which both of the contracting parties are located within the same state, a choice of law provision is usually unnecessary. However, you should pay close attention to the business dealings in negotiations between the parties. If one of the parties is a business entity, the matter can become complicated. Are any of the corporation's branch offices, warehouses or sales facilities located outside the state? If they are, then a choice of law provision may be required. A choice of law provision is simply a contract clause that states which jurisdiction will have the power to hear and decide any litigated issues under the contract. In situations where the parties to a contract are residents of different states and there is no choice of law provision, there may be extensive litigation about where the case should be heard, before the actual issues in the case are reached.

✓ **PARALEGAL CHECKLIST**

☐   What law governs the contract?

☐   If the parties reside in different states, which state law will be used to interpret the contract provisions?

☐   Are any of the parties a business entity, such as corporation, with offices outside the jurisdiction?

Parol Evidence Rule

We have discussed the parole evidence rule in different contexts before. The parol evidence rule is an evidentiary rule that states that when a contract is written it is the sole and exclusive evidence of the contractual obligations between the parties and a court will refuse to hear any oral testimony that attempts to modify those contract provisions. Because that is the rule, is there any need to address the parol evidence rule in the contract? The answer is yes. Despite the existence of the parol evidence rule, there are certain situations in which the court will allow testimony about contract. One of those exceptions occurs when the parties do not include a provision in the contract that states that the contract is the sole and exclusive evidence of the contractual obligation. Other exceptions, such as fraud and undue influence, cannot be foreclosed with a contractual clause, but including language to the effect that the written contract is the only evidence of the contractual duties between the parties will help satisfy part of the parol evidence rule.

✔ PARALEGAL CHECKLIST

- ☐ Does the contract contain a clause specifically stating that the written contract is the sole and exclusive evidence of the binding agreement between the parties?

- ☐ Are there any oral "understandings" about the contract that are not embodied in the contract?

- ☐ Are there any other documents relevant to the contract that are not referred to in the actual contract?

Death of the Parties

In most situations, when an individual dies his contractual obligations die with him. However, we have already seen exceptions to this rule. Including a clause in the contract that specifically deals with this topic is simple common sense. When one of the parties is a business entity, such as a corporation, the contract provision must read differently. After all, corporations do not die, but they can be dissolved. Anticipating problems here can be a huge time-saver later on.

✔ PARALEGAL CHECKLIST

- ☐ Does the contract contain a provision dealing with the death or dissolution of a party?

- ☐ Are any of the parties married? If so, is there a contract provision concerning possible divorce?

Many contract drafters also include a provision dealing with divorce under this heading. If the parties to a contract are a married couple, then their divorce may have a profound impact on the discharge of the contract. Anticipating this possibility is always a wise move.

Bankruptcy

Bankruptcy is an action filed in federal court to discharge an individual or a business liability. These liabilities can include contractual obligations. A clause dealing with bankruptcy might be as simple as stating that the contract is terminated when any of the parties to the contract files for bankruptcy. However, there may be additional, and more complex, issues raised by a bankruptcy filing. In the contract that contemplates years or months to complete, additional research about the effect of bankruptcy on this contract is essential.

✓ **PARALEGAL CHECKLIST**

☐   Is there provision in the contract that takes into account the bankruptcy of any of the parties?

Attorneys' Fees

The "attorneys' fees" provision in the contract is a simple statement that provides for the payment of an attorney for any expenses related to litigating issues under the contract. Although many contracts are silent about attorneys' fees, some include language detailing that any claim found to be brought in bad faith makes the party bringing it liable for all attorneys' fees.

✓ **PARALEGAL CHECKLIST**

☐   If there is a breach of contract, is there provision detailing which side must pay attorneys' fees for the litigation?

Alternative Dispute Resolution

When we discussed arbitration in a previous chapter, we said that arbitration is often an alternative to costly and time-consuming litigation. An arbitrator is a person who is appointed either by the courts or selected by the parties who will attempt to resolve the differences between the parties. Mediation, by contrast, is often compulsory. Parties agree that they will be bound by the decisions of the mediator, whatever that decision might be. Both mediation and arbitration are attractive alternatives to long and drawn-out court proceedings. When the contract contains an alternative dispute resolution clause, special attention should be paid to how this clause interacts with the "Choice of Law" provision. For example, if this clause is triggered, which state's arbitration system will be used?

✓ PARALEGAL CHECKLIST

- ☐ Should the contract contain a provision that forces the parties to go through arbitration before commencing lawsuit?
- ☐ How will the arbitrator be selected?

Notice

Notice is one of the vitally important contract clause provisions. Although the term "notice" is often used in relation to notice of termination or voiding the contract, there are many other types of notice provisions. The party should be given sufficient time to receive notice and to take action based on it. However, the notice period cannot be so long as to make it impractical to give it in the first place.

✓ PARALEGAL CHECKLIST

How much notice is required to:
- ☐ Modify the contract
- ☐ Cancel the contract
- ☐ Terminate the contract
- ☐ What form must the notice take?
- ☐ Is notice by fax sufficient?
- ☐ Is notice by e-mail sufficient?
- ☐ Is notice by telephone sufficient?
- ☐ Is notice required by mail? If so, must be sent by certified mail?

Termination

We have examined termination in depth in a previous chapter. We have seen that a contract can terminate for any of a number of reasons. Contracts can terminate by the agreement of the parties or by some other factor. When the parties wish to terminate by agreement, is there a contract clause that provides a mechanism for doing so? Termination also has important legal consequences. For example, a party's right to sue may or may not terminate with the contract. This issue of the survivability of certain legal claims can often be worked out when drafting a termination clause.

✓ **PARALEGAL CHECKLIST**

☐ Is there a set termination date for the contract?

☐ Does the contract terminate by its own terms?

☐ Is there provision that allows the parties to cancel a contract after giving specific notice?

Modification

The parties are always free to modify their agreements in an executory contract. However, the manner of modification should be expressed in the contract so that all the parties know how it can be done. More importantly, the parties also must know when the modification is ineffective. For instance, many contracts contain a provision that states that an oral modification is ineffective for a written contract. Such a contract clause might also include language specifying exactly how the modification must be made. For instance, the clause might provide that a modification must be in writing, signed by all parties and dated.

✓ **PARALEGAL CHECKLIST**

☐ Does the contract provide any mechanism for modification of the contract?

☐ Are modifications to be made in writing?

☐ Can the parties modify the contract orally?

☐ Is the current contract a modification of a prior contract? If so, where is the prior contract?

Signature Provisions

The parties officially identify themselves in the signature section of a contract. When they sign the contract they are expressing their intent to be bound by the entire terms. The signature provision should be clearly set out so that each party knows exactly where to sign. Whenever practical, the person's title also should be used. When a corporation or other business entity is a party to the contract, the person signing on behalf of the business should have the capacity to do so. State statutes will provide which corporate officer is entitled to sign for the contract. If there are to be witnesses, their signature lines also should be clearly set out.

✔ **PARALEGAL CHECKLIST**

- ☐ Are the parties human beings or some type of business entity?
- ☐ If they are individuals, do they possess the authority to sign the contract?
- ☐ If the party is a corporation or some other type of business entity, is the person signing for the business authorized to do so?
- ☐ Are witnesses required?
- ☐ Must the signatures be notarized?

Exhibits and Attachments

Contracts often contain exhibits and attachments to which the contract refers. A contract might contain a "deal memo" or a memorandum of contract. When this document is critical to the interpretation of the contract, it should be attached and referred to in the contract itself.

✔ **PARALEGAL CHECKLIST**

- ☐ Does the contract refer to any document, exhibit or other attachment?
- ☐ If so, is it attached to the contract?
- ☐ If not, where is it?
- ☐ If the contract makes any reference to any other document, is this document in the possession of the legal team?
- ☐ Does the contract refer to any other writings or memorandum?
- ☐ If so, are they physically attached to the contract itself?

Contracts Under Seal

In most jurisdictions, the old common law form of "contract under seal" has been abolished. As we learned in Chapter 4, when a contract is under seal, the seal creates the presumption that consideration is adequate. These days, seals are rarely used and, even when they are, they have no greater significance than any other contract provision.

DOUBLE-CHECKING THE CONTRACT

Although it sounds so obvious that it should go without saying, most errors in contracts are typographical. The final contract should be reviewed very closely. Each contract clause and provision should be examined to make sure not only that it is the actual agreement between the parties but also that it does not contain any grammatical or spelling errors. One method, used for centuries to double-check the language of a contract, is to read the contract out loud to someone else. Reading the contract aloud will help you catch problems in wording and syntax. Better to catch the problem when the contract is being drafted rather than have a judge point out the problem during a lawsuit. The final contract should be compared with notes about the preliminary negotiations and any other writings that have been used as a basis to create the contract. This is where attention to detail pays huge dividends. If you should locate a contract clause that seems out of place or incorrect, you should bring it to the attention of the attorney immediately. Poorly drafted contracts can be the basis of a legal malpractice action.

✓ PARALEGAL CHECKLIST

- ☐ Is there any unusual feature of the contract that should receive additional attention or research?

- ☐ Has the contract been checked for grammatical or spelling errors?

- ☐ Does the contract contain overly technical legal phrases and terms? (Here is where you will want to avoid "party of the first part," etc.)

- ☐ Are there any missing pages?

- ☐ If the paragraphs are numbered, are there any missing paragraphs?

- ☐ If the contract makes a reference to some other paragraph in the contract is that cross-referenced paragraph actually present in the document?

The Case of the Messy Mobile Home Contract[2]
OPINION
PER CURIAM

In this original proceeding, Oakwood Mobile Homes, Inc. seeks relief from the denial of its motion to compel arbitration. Because the trial court abused its discretion in denying arbitration, and because Relator has no adequate remedy by appeal, we conditionally grant the writ. Shirley and David Brandon purchased a mobile home from Oakwood. Three days before completing the sales transaction, and again on the closing date, the Brandons signed Oakwood's Arbitration Agreement. This Agreement required the parties to submit all disputes arising out of the sale to binding arbitration under American Arbitration Association rules. When they began experiencing problems with the mobile home, the Brandons twice wrote to Alan Warren and Charles Boyner of Oak Creek Homes, the manufacturer of the home, and requested that they arrange an arbitration hearing. Receiving no response, the Brandons sued Oakwood for rescission of the contract.

Oakwood moved to compel arbitration under the Agreement. In support of its motion, Oakwood submitted a copy of the Agreement, together with an affidavit attesting that it was voluntarily executed and negotiated at arm's length. The Brandons responded, claiming that the Agreement was unconscionable and void for fraud, duress, and misrepresentation. In support of their contentions, the Brandons submitted affidavits stating that they were told, "we had to sign [the Agreement] or we couldn't finance the house," and "we had to sign the arbitration provision or we could not take possession of the house." The Brandons also claimed Oakwood waived the right to compel arbitration by failing to respond to their letters requesting an arbitration hearing. The trial court denied Oakwood's motion to compel arbitration. The court of appeals concluded that the Brandons' uncontroverted affidavits provided sufficient evidence for the trial court's summary disposition of the motion to compel arbitration, and denied Oakwood's petition

for mandamus. [not reported in SW Reporter] 1998 WL 210813. Oakwood now petitions this Court for relief.

A party seeking to compel arbitration must establish the existence of an arbitration agreement, and show that the claims raised fall within the scope of that agreement. See Cantella & Co. v. Goodwin, 924 S.W.2d 943, 944 (Tex.1996). Once the party establishes a claim within the arbitration agreement, the trial court must compel arbitration and stay its own proceedings.

Here, Oakwood met its burden of presenting evidence of an arbitration agreement that governs the dispute between the parties. The burden then shifted to the Brandons to present evidence that the Agreement was procured in an unconscionable manner, induced or procured by fraud or duress, or that Oakwood had waived arbitration under the Agreement. Id. Oakwood contends the Brandons presented no evidence to support their claims; therefore, they did not satisfy their burden and the trial court erred in denying arbitration. We agree.

To establish fraud in the formation of an arbitration agreement, a party must prove, inter alia, that (1) a material misrepresentation was made, and (2) it was false. See Green Int'l, Inc. v. Solis, 951 S.W.2d 384, 390 (Tex.1997); see also Perry v. Thomas, 482 U.S. 483, 492 n. 9, 107 S.Ct. 2520, 96 L.Ed.2d 426 (1987) (noting that under the FAA, state law should be applied to assess the validity of arbitration agreements "if that law arose to govern issues concerning the validity, revocability, and enforceability of contracts generally"). The Brandons' fraud and misrepresentation claims rest solely on their contention that Oakwood represented the sale would not go through if they did not sign the Agreement. Because neither party asserts that these representations were false, they cannot support the Brandons' fraud or misrepresentation claims.

In support of their claims of unconscionability and duress, the Brandons contend the Agreement "is a classic example of a contract of adhesion where one party . . . had absolutely no bargaining power or ability to change the contract terms." Even if this contention is true, however, adhesion contracts are not automatically unconscionable or void. Moreover, "there is nothing per se unconscionable about arbitration agreements." EZ Pawn, 934 S.W.2d at 90; see Emerald Tex., Inc. v. Peel, 920 S.W.2d 398, 402–403 (Tex.App.—Hous. [1 Dist.] 1996, no writ) (holding that to find the arbitration provision unconscionable under the evidence presented would negate the public policy in favor of arbitration). The Brandons did not present the trial court with evidence of unconscionability or duress in their affidavits. See Tenneco Oil Co. v. Gulsby Eng'g, Inc., 846 S.W.2d 599, 604 (Tex.App.—Hous. [14 Dist.] 1993, writ denied) (defining "duress" as "a threat to do some act which the threatening party has no legal right to do"). Accordingly, the Brandons failed to meet their burden.

The Brandons next contend Oakwood waived its right to arbitrate when it failed to respond to their requests for arbitration. Because public policy favors resolving disputes through arbitration, there is a strong presumption against the waiver of contractual arbitration rights. See In re Bruce Terminix Co., 988 S.W.2d 702, 704 (Tex.1998); Prudential Sec., Inc. v. Marshall, 909 S.W.2d 896, 898 (Tex.1995). Whether a party's conduct waives its arbitration rights is a question of law. See In re Bruce Terminix Co., 988 S.W.2d at 703–704. We should resolve any doubts about waiver in favor of arbitration.

Waiver may be found when it is shown that a party acted inconsistently with its right to arbitrate and such actions prejudiced the other party. See In re Bruce Terminix Co., 988 S.W.2d at 704. The Brandons contend Oakwood's failure to respond to their letters requesting arbitration was inconsistent with Oakwood's right to arbitrate. However, in In re Bruce Terminix Co., we held that, absent an agreement to the contrary, "a party against whom a claim is asserted does not waive its right to arbitrate by failing to initiate arbitration of that claim." In re Bruce Terminix Co., 988 S.W.2d at 706. It was never Oakwood's burden under the Agreement to initiate the arbitration process against itself or assist the Brandons in doing so. The Agreement specifically provides that the parties shall arbitrate in accordance with "the applicable rules of the American Arbitration Association." By agreeing to these rules, the parties placed the burden of initiating arbitration on the claimant, in this instance the Brandons. Accordingly, Oakwood's failure to initiate arbitration in response to the Brandons' letters is not a waiver as a matter of law.

We conclude that the trial court abused its discretion by denying Oakwood's motion to compel arbitration. A party erroneously denied the right to arbitrate under the FAA has no adequate remedy on appeal, and mandamus relief is appropriate. See Jack B. Anglin Co. v. Tipps, 842 S.W.2d 266, 272–73 (Tex.1992). Accordingly, without hearing oral argument, Tex.R.App. P. 2.8(c), we conditionally grant the writ of mandamus. We are confident the trial court will grant Oakwood's motion to compel arbitration in accordance with this opinion. We instruct the clerk to issue the writ only if the trial court fails to do so.

Case Questions:

1. What were the terms of the arbitration agreement in this case?

2. What claims did the Brandons make about the contract?

3. According to this court, why did the trial court commit error by denying arbitration?

4. What evidence must a party present in order to prove fraud in procuring an arbitration agreement?

5. Is this a "classic case" of adhesion? Why or why not?

The Case of the Condition Precedent[3]

The defendant, Robert Hare, was the owner of a three-quarters section of land in Ottawa County, Kansas. The land was used solely for grazing cattle and Carl Nelson claimed a lease on the land for the 1962 grazing season. The pleader did not know the terms, duration or form of the purported lease and could not plead whether or not the claim was valid.

Hare retained James H. Seng, a real estate broker of Salina, Kansas, as his agent to obtain a purchaser for the land. The plaintiff, George H. Wallerius, became a willing purchaser and on February 20, 1962, gave the agent a check for earnest money in the sum of $5,000 and executed an instrument designated 'agreement for warranty deed.' The agreement contained the usual provisions, described the land and provided:

'And the said party of the second part hereby covenants and agrees to pay the Party of the first part the sum of Twenty-eight Thousand eight hundred ($28,800.00) DOLLARS, in the manner following: Five Thousand ($5,000.00) DOLLARS, cash in hand, paid as earnest-money, the receipt of which is hereby acknowledged, and balance to be paid upon approval of title. *Full possession to be given 2nd party on or before April 1, 1962.* This contract must be accepted on or before the 1st day of March, 1962, or it automatically becomes cancelled at the option of the party of the 2nd part.' (Emphasis supplied.)

On February 20, 1962, the agent forwarded the agreement and the check to Hare accompanied by a letter which read in part: "There are only two provisions that are not absolute. One is the possession clause, and the other is the acceptance of the sale by you on or before March 1, 1963. "I do not feel that the tenant is being fair to you, but I do think that he will let you cancel his lease for a nominal sum.

"It is barely possible that, should you not be able to deliver possession, that my client might accept the property subject to tenants rights. We will cross that bridge if and when we get to it.'

On February 28, 1962, having received the agreement and the Five Thousand Dollar check, Hare transmitted a telegram to his agent, Seng, containing the following message:

'Accept offer Wallerius providing obtain cancellation pasture lease from Nelson any litigation lawyers fee or damages paid by purchaser.'

Also on February 28, 1962, Hare transmitted a telegram to Carl Nelson, the tenant, containing the following message:

'Sold pasture: must cancel lease for 1962.' Seng informed the plaintiff, Wallerius, of the receipt of the telegram whereupon he, on March 1, 1962, transmitted a telegram to Hare containing the following message:

'Accept counter-proposal via telegram in connection with contract to purchase land in Ottawa County, Kansas. Letter follows.' Which was delivered to the defendant on March 1, 1962, 2:00 P.M., Pacific Standard Time.

After receipt of the above telegram Hare transmitted to his agent, Seng, a telegram on March 2, 1962, 7:45 A.M., Pacific Standard Time, containing the following message:

'Recd offer today $32,000.00 net to me. Therefore withdrawing land from sale. Thanks for help. Will contact you when ready to sell.'

The letter referred to in the telegram dated March 1, 1962, from Wallerius to Hare, was signed by the agent and read in part:

'Mr. Wallerius sent you a telegram of acceptance of your counter proposal this afternoon, which you will have received long before receipt of this letter.

'In checking with the telegraph office, I found that they had been unable to obtain an answer at the Nelson residence, so I suggested they contact Mrs. Nelson at her place of work here in Salina. I also requested that they notify me of delivery of the message to the Nelsons, but because of rules governing giving out information in connection with telegrams, they did not wish to supply me with any information in connection with it. They finally agreed to call me if it were or were not delivered, but instead, they asked

Mrs. Nelson to call me, which she did. She seemed to accept the message completely and give no indication whatever of any unwillingness to abide. She did want to know who had bought it and what they had paid. I didn't figure it was any of her business, but rather than antagonize her, I give her the information. The purchaser was sitting in my office listening.

'It appears that we should have no further difficulty, and I will anticipate receipt of the original and copy of the signed contract, along with the check, which I will convert into a Cashier's Check. You may instruct me to deduct the commission therefrom, and I will mail you a Cashier's Check for the balance. Please also send the abstract of title, so that we may proceed with extension and examination.'

We are not informed as to the date on which the letter was received. The appellees argued in the court below and contend here that their telegram was not an acceptance of appellant's offer but indicated a willingness to accept appellant's offer upon cancellation of the pasture lease and that appellees by their telegram made cancellation of the pasture lease a condition precedent to the formation of a contract. Appellees state:

'Treating defendant's telegram of February 28, 1962, as a counter-offer, plaintiff, on March 1, 1962, sent a telegram to defendant as follows:

"Accept counter-proposal via telegram in connection with contract to purchase land in Ottawa County, Kansas. Letter follows.'

'While this message may have bound plaintiff to pay any expenses incurred, or damages assessed against defendant in attempting to obtain cancellation of the pasture lease, it certainly does not constitute a contract between plaintiff and defendant for the purchase and sale of the land. Cancellation of the pasture lease was still a condition precedent to the formation of that contract.

'In order to establish a completed contract for the purchase and sale of this land, it would be essential that plaintiff be able to plead and prove fulfillment of this condition.

'We suggest that it would be rather a harsh rule which would make appellant liable under its telegram, 'accepting counter-proposal,' for the payment of 'any expenses incurred, or any damages assessed against defendant in attempting to obtain

cancellation of the pasture lease' and place no responsibility whatsoever upon appellees in connection with the cancellation of such lease. However, we do not care to base our decision upon this limited issue.

We agree with appellee that the telegrams created a condition precedent.

The word 'provided' when used in a contract is usually used in the conjunctive sense. As so used the word means 'on condition' and a condition precedent is created. Webster's New Twentieth Century Dictionary, Unabridged, Second Edition, defines 'provided' as follows: 'on condition; on these terms; this being understood, conceded or established; if: frequently followed by *that*.'

The word 'provided' is defined in 73 C.J.S. Provided, p. 266, as follows:

'It has been said that there has been much nice discussion on the word, and it is regarded as an apt word to create, express, or introduce a condition or exception, or for creating a condition precedent; and it is an apt and appropriate word to indicate an intention to give contingently. It frequently indicates a condition, and it has been said that ordinarily it indicates that a condition follows; and is recognized as implying a condition without the addition of any other words.'

Since we admittedly have involved a condition precedent, the condition being the cancellation of the pasture lease to make possible the delivery of possession by April 1, 1962, the question is, what application is to be made of the condition?

The appellees contend that the cancellation of the lease was a condition precedent to the formation of a contract and that it was essential that appellant plead definite fulfillment of the condition, i.e., that the lease was actually cancelled.

The appellant contends that the condition contained in appellees' telegram and accepted by appellant was incorporated in the original offer and a complete contract was consummated but that the cancellation of the lease was a condition precedent to requiring performance of the contract which was complete in all of its terms. Appellant further contends that having bound himself to pay any expenses incurred, or damages assessed against appellees in their attempt to obtain cancellation of the pasture lease, they were bound to exercise a reasonable effort to cancel the lease.

We are inclined to agree with appellant's contention.

A condition precedent is something that it is agreed must happen or be performed before a right can accrue to enforce the main contract. It is one without the performance of which the contract, although in form executed and delivered by the parties, cannot be enforced. A condition precedent requires the performance of some act or the happening of some event after the terms of the contract, including the condition precedent, have been agreed on before the contract shall take effect. (See Words and Phrases, Conditions Precedent, Vol. 8, pp. 713–785.)

While the condition precedent must have happened before the contract can be enforced or relief sought in the way of specific performance, the party who has demanded the condition precedent cannot hinder, delay or prevent its happening for the purpose of avoiding performance of the contract. We believe the rule announced in Talbott v. Nibert, 167 Kan. 138, 206 P.2d 131, is applicable here. On page 146 of 167 Kan., on page 138 of 206 P.2d, of the opinion it is stated:

'The rule is clear and well settled, and founded in absolute justice, that a party to a contract cannot prevent performance by another and derive any benefit, or escape any liability, from his own failure to perform a necessary condition. And this is the universal rule.

Considering the facts as alleged in the petition, in the light most favorable to the pleader, as we are bound to do our responsibility is to determine whether they raise a reasonable inference that the pasture lease was cancelled in fact, if not in deed, or could have been cancelled by appellees had they not desired to avoid performance of the contract of sale because they had received an offer of a higher price.

A brief review of the facts most favorable to appellant discloses that the appellees had at least until April 1, 1962, in which to seek cancellation of the lease, yet they attempted to cancel the agreement by telegram March 2, 1962, the next day after their condition was accepted by appellant, because they had received an offer of $32,000.00 net to them. They did so after being informed that Mrs. Nelson, the wife of the lessee, on whose decision reliance appears to be placed, seemed to accept the message completely and give no indication whatever of any unwillingness to abide.' The agent also informed the appellees prior to the attempted cancellation that 'It appears we should have no further difficulty'

It appears that the facts as alleged leave much for the appellees to explain by way of answer if they are to avoid performance. We must conclude that the petition states facts sufficient to constitute a cause of action for specific performance of the contract for a warranty deed.

Approved by the Court.

Case Questions:

1. According to the court, was the telegram an acceptance of the offer, or simply an indication of a willingness to enter into a contract?

2. Was cancellation of the previous lease condition precedent to the formation of a contract?

3. If cancellation of the lease was a condition precedent, was this condition incorporated into the original offer?

ETHICS FILE: Is It Unauthorized Practice of Law to Draft Contracts?

It is common for a paralegal to be asked to research and even help to compose a contract for a client. When the paralegal performs this function it is under the direct supervision of the attorney who remains responsible for the final end product. In this case, there is no unauthorized practice of law. However, the situation changes dramatically when the paralegal is asked to draft a contract for a friend or a colleague. In this scenario, the paralegal is usually approached by a person who has a "simple" contract and just needs a little help to complete it. Although some states allow paralegals to assist members of the public in completing forms, this protection does not extend to actually creating the contract. When the paralegal drafts a contract, almost every jurisdiction would rule that this is unauthorized practice of law. The best practice is to avoid creating contracts for others unless under the direct supervision of an attorney.

Business Case File

Diane Bartle, Small Business Center

Diane Bartle

Diane Bartle has been the Small Business Center coordinator for seven years. "A lot of people don't realize the kind of resources that are available at Small Business Centers." In Diane's state, each community college has a separate Small Business Center, which exists solely to help people with business questions and offer other resources. "We offer counseling services, educational classes, assistance with creating business plans, tips on obtaining loans, marketing, taxes and accounting. We even have a list of local attorneys and accountants who work with small business people.

Businesspeople are always seeking legal assistance. "When someone comes to me and asks any questions about incorporation, or any other legal issue, I always tell them that they need to talk to a lawyer. The couple of hundred dollars that you may spend conferring with a lawyer is one of the best investments you will ever make. It's your business, you don't want second-hand information, or to follow advice that your neighbor gives you."

What is the most common misconception about starting a new business? "It would have to be that there is a lot of free money out there that will help you get started. There isn't. You have to get your own funding. And you need a business plan.

"A lot of people who are thinking about starting a business carry the details around in their heads. They've done a lot of homework, but they haven't put it on paper. That's what a business plan is all about. Once you get it on paper, you begin to see the strengths and the weaknesses of your plan. You can then start to focus on the weak points. We have volunteers who work through our Small Business Centers who help people with business plans. We even have a program called SCORE (Service Corps of Retired Executives). These are retired executives and businesspeople who will give free advice and counseling to people thinking about going into business."

One of the most important concerns for any new business owner is not only to get the details down on paper but also to make sure that those details appear in the contract. Paying close attention to contract clauses, and making sure that they reflect the true nature of the agreement, can mean the difference between a successful business and a failure.

The Small Business Centers offer a wide range of resources to assist new business owners in pinning down the details, whether they be in business plans, partnership agreements, or contract clauses.

Chapter Summary:

In this chapter we explored the issues surrounding drafting contracts. The paralegal has several excellent resources available to assist in both researching and preparing basic contract provisions. These resources include formbooks, treatises, and statutes. In addition to these resources, a paralegal also must use common sense and experience in interpreting the language of an existing contract or preparing a new one. To this end, checklists are helpful to double-check work on a contract (but they are no substitute for researching and thinking through a contract problem). Specific types of contract clauses, such as arbitration clauses or "time is of the essence" provisions, have their own sets of problems and should be reviewed closely.

WEB SITES

U.S. Department of Justice/Antitrust Division
www.usdoj.gov
See its Antitrust Division for information about commercial issues.

The Sixth Judicial District of Florida
http://www.jud6.org
An excellent Web site providing tremendous information on a well-designed Web site.

Superior Court of Arizona, Maricopa County
http://www.superiorcourt.maricopa.gov/
Offers a wide variety of information about legal issues.

Thomas Legislative Information on the Internet
http://thomas.loc.gov
Library of Congress site devoted to legislative issues.

REVIEW QUESTIONS

1. Why are business people eager to avoid litigation?
2. It is often been said that business people and lawyers approach contracts from completely different perspectives. Explain.
3. What are some considerations when drafting an offer?
4. What are some of the considerations when drafting an acceptance to an offer?
5. What is the most common type of error when drafting the contract? How could this error be avoided?
6. When drafting a contract provision what are some of the considerations to keep in mind about time?
7. Why is a choice of law provision important?
8. How does the parole evidence rule affect the drafting of a contract?
9. What is meant by the "entire agreement" clause in the contract?
10. What are some important considerations to keep in mind about the death of one of the parties?
11. How would you draft a contract clause to take into account the dissolution of the corporate party to the contract?
12. What is significant amount bankruptcy, and why should it be considered when drafting a contract?
13. What are some of the considerations when drafting a contract clause concerning alternative dispute resolution?

14. Why are notice provisions so important to a contract? Why is it important to buy a method for terminating the contract?

15. What are some important considerations when drafting a clause concerning future modifications of the contract and?

16. What are formbooks?

17. What are treatises and how are they helpful to someone drafting a contract?

18. Explain the types of Internet resources available to a contract drafter.

19. How do Internet pay sites compare with free Internet legal research sites?

20. What are some of the considerations in the final double-check of a contract?

HANDS-ON ASSIGNMENT

You have decided to open up a freelance paralegal firm, providing legal services to local attorneys. Draft a contract that you will use to form the basis of your working relationships with these attorneys. Make sure that your contract is thorough and addresses as many of the possible problems as you can anticipate. Some of the concerns should include how you will be paid for your services, how you will void ethical dilemmas when serving different attorneys, whether you will charge for filing court documents at the courthouse.

PRACTICAL APPLICATION

Provide examples of contract clauses that have been held to be in violation of public policy in your state.

HELP THIS BUSINESS

Locate at least ten Web sites, in addition to the ones listed in this chapter, that could help a new business owner gather information about starting a business.

KEY TERM

contract of adhesion

ENDNOTES

1. *The Terrible Truth About Lawyers*, Mark H. McCormick, Beech Tree Books. Copyright © 1987 by Mark H. McCormack Enterprises, Inc., p. 132.

2. *In re Oakwood Mobile Homes, Inc.*, 987 S.W.2d 571(Tex., 1999).

3. *Wallerius v. Hare*, 94 Kan. 408, 399 P.2d 543 (1965).

 For additional resources, visit our Web site at www.westlegalstudies.com

CHAPTER 13

BUSINESS LAW IN THE INTERNET ERA

Focus of this chapter: This chapter focuses on the emerging industry of e-commerce and the unique challenges, and opportunities, it presents to business people. Special attention is paid to the legal issues of binding contractual agreements, security, confidentiality, regulation, and the common legal problems for business people who carry out some or all of their business on the Internet.

Chapter Objectives:
At the completion of this chapter, you should be able to:

- Explain some of the problems unique to online commerce
- Define privacy concerns inherent in e-commerce
- Explain the function of digital signatures
- Describe how the basic elements of contracts are satisfied by Internet transactions
- Explain some of the confidentially concerns inherent in online commerce
- Explain why copyright infringement is such an important issue for Internet commerce
- Define the types of Internet-based crimes that can occur
- Explain how an Internet-based company can be liable for revealing sensitive customer information
- Explain why e-mail is not protected in the same way under the law as other forms of communication
- Describe why creating legislation governing the Internet is often difficult

An Introduction to E-Commerce

Twenty years ago, the idea of running an entire business in "cyberspace" would have seemed the purest form of science fiction. The successes of businesses such as e-Bay and Amazon.com have shown that Internet businesses are here to stay. Like all new industries, however, e-commerce has suffered its share of successes and disasters. Doing business on the Internet raises some unique and interesting questions about business law. We will explore some of those questions in this chapter and also examine the role of the legal professional in the maze of cyberspace.

Unlike the Industrial Revolution, which concentrated power and resources into the hands of a relatively few individuals, the Technological Revolution has empowered individuals all over the world. If you have a product, a Web site, and a computer, you could become an Internet entrepreneur. This pervasiveness of the Internet is both its greatest strength and its greatest flaw.

The Rise of a New Industry

brick and mortar: A business or other entity that maintains a physical structure with buildings, parking lots, and on-site employees

Internet Service Provider (ISP): A business that provides Internet access through dial-up modems.

Although the Internet seems ubiquitous now, even a few years ago the idea of actually running a business on it seemed preposterous. Business was something that you ran out of a **brick and mortar**, not through an **Internet Service Provider (ISP)**.

Like the Industrial Revolution before it, the rise of the Technological Revolution has caused some rapid changes in society, displaced workers, and raised new legal issues. Unlike the Industrial Revolution, however, which concentrated power and resources into the hands of a few rich and powerful individuals, the Technological Revolution is a dispersed change. Seemingly, anyone with a dream, a computer, a Web address and modem can become the next J. P. Morgan or Bill Gates. Although creating and running an Internet-based business is not that simple, the basic premise is. However, any businessperson who is considering opening an Internet-based business, or expanding a brick-and-mortar operation into cyberspace, must consider some of the unique challenges presented by the Internet.

GROWING PAINS

All new industries have growing pains. There are supply and service problems to work out. There are legal challenges. Web-based businesses are no exception. Over the past ten years, we have seen the dot-com wave crest and fall flat. Seemingly overnight, young computer whizzes went from rags to riches to rags again. The stock price for Internet businesses went through the roof with every investment advisor clamoring for investors to get on the ship before it sailed. Unfortunately, the ship turned out to be the *Titanic* and, when it hit the inevitable iceberg, in this case the failure to produce profits, a lot of people were caught onboard without lifeboats.

Discussing the world of e-commerce and all of its ramifications is too large a topic for this book. Instead, we will focus on the basic business issues raised by Internet commerce, especially the basics of contract formation and the specific legal issues that often arise in this new industry.

Problems Presented by E-Commerce

In this section, we will explore some of the more basic issues presented by e-commerce. We will begin with contract formation.

CONTRACT FORMATION ON THE INTERNET

As soon as we begin addressing the issue of contract formation, we run into a wealth of potential problems, such as proving the basic requirements of a valid, legal contract. Consider these questions:

- How do we prove that there was a valid offer?
- How do we know that there was a valid acceptance of that offer?
- How can the parties prove mutual assent?
- How do we prove that both parties had legal capacity?
- How do we establish consideration?
- How do we determine what law applies if we have a dispute?

All of these questions revolve around the unusual nature of the Internet. Most forms of communication on the Internet are asynchronous communications. An **asynchronous communication** is one in which both parties to the message are not present at the same time. A message scrawled on a wall is an example of an asynchronous message. Suppose that the message reads, "Watch out for the hole in sidewalk!" You are walking on the sidewalk and you see the sign. You immediately stop and look around. You spot the large hole and step around it. The message was communicated, but the person who sent it was not actually present when it was received. If you then write "Thanks!" on the wall, just below the warning message, you have engaged in two-way asynchronous message transfer.

E-mail is the modern equivalent of messages scrawled on walls. Someone sends you an e-mail message providing you with specific information. You might respond within a minute, an hour, or a day. You might not respond at all. This is the perceived problem with Internet commerce: most of it involves asynchronous transactions. When you visit a Web site offering products for sale and you locate something that you would like to buy, there is usually no salesperson on the other end monitoring what you are viewing and who is ready to ring up your sale on the spot. It is all done automatically, and that often makes people uneasy. Can you form a valid contract under these circumstances? After all, at the time that you make an offer, there is no one on the other side to respond immediately with an acceptance. How can you even know when your offer was received, or even if it was received?

Looking to History for Answers to New Problems

If you approach the Internet as simply a new method of communication instead of a brand new "cyberworld," then many of these seemingly intractable issues become easier to analyze. For instance, is there really a

asynchronous communication: The transmission of information as it is completed, rather than when the party to whom it is addressed is ready to receive it. Example: E-mail.

synchronous communication:
The transmission of information when the party to whom it is addressed is ready to receive it. Example: telephone conversation.

problem with asynchronous business communications? When an offer is sent by traditional mail delivery, commonly referred to as "snail mail" by online aficionados, isn't this another form of asynchronous communication? Although merchants may be accustomed to the **synchronous communication** of a telephone call or a face-to-face meeting, asynchronous communication is not a new development. People communicated asynchronously for centuries. Letters, rewards posters, and advertisements are all forms of asynchronous communication, and millions of perfectly legal contracts have resulted from these communications.

The basic requirements of a contract do not change simply because it happens to involve a transaction in cyberspace. A contract must meet all of the foundational requirements: offer, acceptance, mutual assent, capacity, consideration, and legality, among others.

More important, the way that we prove these elements does not change. An offer must have all of the same legal requirements regardless of whether it is posted on a wall or on a Web page. The same is true for acceptance. The rules for interpreting contracts do not change because the transaction occurs in cyberspace.

Because we now know that the basics of contract interpretation do not change between real-world and cyberspace transactions, we will concentrate on some of the issues that are unique to the Internet. The two most prominent are digital signatures and the lack of regulation.

Digital Signatures

It is essential to online commerce that a consumer can do online what she can do in a store: select merchandise, present a credit card, sign the receipt, and receive the merchandise. The easier it is for a Web site to duplicate this process, the more likely that it will survive in the highly competitive world of e-commerce. As you can see from the process just outlined, there is a potential stumbling block: how does a consumer "sign" a receipt when the entire transaction is virtual and the process of putting pen to paper and signing a name never occurs?

Digital signatures were created to deal with that problem. Although, at first blush, the signature requirement would seem to create an insurmountable problem for e-commerce, a quick review of contract law history reveals that this problem was actually solved a hundred years ago. In the early 1900s, courts ruled that a signature didn't necessarily mean an actual handwritten name. A telegram containing a purported signature could satisfy this requirement.[1]

Federal legislation authorizing digital signatures includes the Electronic Signatures in Global and National Commerce Act.[2] This act specifically addresses some of the lingering questions about digital signatures. For instance, the act provides that a contract will not be invalidated simply because the signature was not made by a person signing his or her name to a piece of paper.

LACK OF REGULATION

Almost all new industries begin with virtually no rules or regulations. The Industrial Revolution is a prime example of this maxim. Early railroad companies and manufacturing firms ran their businesses without regard for health or environmental restrictions. There were no trade unions, no workers' rights, no rules about child labor, and no accountability to anyone but themselves. They were free to set prices as they saw fit and even to engage in "cutthroat" competition that artificially lowered their price to drive out competitors and then raise those prices as high as they wished once their competitors had been destroyed. Only after years (and sometimes decades) of such practices were lawmakers and others motivated to place restrictions on their practices.

Many argue that the Internet has enjoyed a similar freedom. In the early days of the World Wide Web, there were no restrictions on business practices, no sales taxes to pay, and no one to answer to but the investors. In many ways, it was a new frontier.

The "Wild West" of Business Transactions

Many traditional businesses were reluctant to create an Internet presence for their companies because of the perception (often valid) that the Internet was an unregulated frontier populated by anarchists and computer hackers. Stability, the essence of business, was completely lacking on the Internet. There were other, more basic problems with the early Internet. It was designed as a research tool, not as a forum for commerce. The early Internet was almost exclusively based on text, not images. It depended on a working knowledge of programming and other skills to negotiate it successfully.

Graphic user interfaces and the World Wide Web helped tame the wild image of the Internet and make it more accessible to the average consumer. However, in many ways, the Internet is still in its infancy and legislation has lagged behind the technology.

Attempts at Federal and State Regulation

In recent years, several new federal and state laws have been enacted that focus directly on the Internet. The Federal Trade Commission (FTC) has become actively involved with Internet business transactions. The FTC, for example, has been empowered to act against companies that violate their privacy policies and sell customer information to other companies.[3] Other examples of federal legislation are found in Exhibit 13-1.

In addition to these federal initiatives, some states have made attempts at regulating certain aspects of the Internet. Nearly every state has statutes governing child pornography Web sites and similar illegal activities. Some have even taken a step towards regulating other practices, such as unwanted e-mail.

> - The Gramm Leach Bliley Act provides sanctions for companies that release financial information about an individual.[i]
> - There are numerous federal and state statutes designed to protect children in their online activities.[ii]
> - The Fair Credit Reporting Act has been applied to online companies as well as traditional brick and mortar companies.[iii]
> - The Electronic Communications Privacy Act protects e-mail and other types of online communication from interception or disclosure by the federal government.[iv]

EXHIBIT 13-1: Federal regulation.

---

[i] 15 USCA §6801.
[ii] 15 USCA §6501.
[iii] 15 USCA §1681.
[iv] 18 USCA §§2510-2522.

SPECIFIC INTERNET-BASED BUSINESS PROBLEMS

So far, we have discussed general problems faced by Internet-based businesses. In the following sections, we will explore specific problems.

Cyberpiracy

Piracy, in one form or another, has existed for thousands of years. In a classic example, a group of pirates would disguise their vessel to look like a ship belonging to a particular fleet. The ship would fall in line with a convoy of other ships and then attack one. Modern pirates use similar tactics. Cyberpiracy refers to the practice of copying existing software and reselling it to a customer, often at a lower price.

In the early days of desktop computers, the practice was commonplace. Many people didn't see making copies of some corporation's software as illegal, or even immoral. However, society's attitude to this practice has changed. Many people recognize that this practice has consequences, including:

- Lost revenue
- More layoffs at businesses
- Bootleg copies can contain viruses
- Businesses that carry out such practices, or allow their employees to do so, run the risk of civil suits and fines

Software Licensing

Licensing is the flip side of piracy. When a company obtains a license to use the software, it means that it has permission to use the software and has lawfully obtained the copy. A businessperson should always make sure to have sufficient licenses to cover all employees actually using the software. Otherwise, the business owner may be liable to the software company.

Tax Issues

Taxes present another unique problem for Internet-based businesses. So far, federal and some state governments have stayed out of the picture by not imposing taxes on Internet transactions in the same way that they do for other types of transactions. For an example of how difficult assessing taxes can be, consider Hypothetical 13-1.

HYPOTHETICAL 13-1   Taxes on the Internet

Lamar is sitting in his home in California and pulls up a Web site for fly fishing equipment. The actual store is located in New York. However, the fly rod that Lamar would like to order is actually located in Florida. Lamar clicks on his preference and gives his credit card number as payment for the purchase. Which state's taxes apply: New York, Florida, or California?

Answer: Unknown. States have yet to work out a credible scheme for assessing sales taxes in this scenario. Some states simply require a sales tax for any sale made and eventually delivered in their state. Under this scheme, Lamar would owe sales tax in his home state. However, this question is very much up in the air.

Spam

We have all received "junk mail" in our mailboxes. Junk mail is any unwanted, unsolicited mail that either seeks to introduce us to a new product or find some other way for us to spend our money.

Spam is the modern equivalent of junk mail. In recent years, spam has become a huge problem, with unsolicited e-mails filling servers with offers of everything from weight loss products to pornography. Some states have passed legislation aimed at reducing the quantity of spam directed at consumers. California's antispam statute is provided in Exhibit 13-2.

Meta Tags

A meta tag is a method used by some companies to increase the number of hits that their site would receive under a search engine. A Web designer will bury certain phrases in the Web page's HTML code to take advantage of the way that some (but not all) online search engines categorize and store information about Web pages. Some search engines, for examples, review only the first 50 words on a posted Web page and use this material to categorize the site for future retrieval. Consider the language used in two different sites. Site 1 reads, "This site is devoted to the maintenance and presentation of fine quality gifts and cards created with recycled materials." The other site reads, "recycled-gifts-recycled products-gifts-environmentally

> §17538.4. Prohibition against e-mailing documents containing unsolicited advertising material; notification to stop e-mailing
>
> (a) No person or entity conducting business in this state shall electronically mail (e-mail) or cause to be e-mailed documents containing unsolicited advertising material for the lease, sale, rental, gift offer, or other disposition of any realty, goods, services, or extension of credit unless that person or entity establishes a toll-free telephone number or valid sender operated return e-mail address that the recipient of the unsolicited documents may call or e-mail to notify the sender not to e-mail any further unsolicited documents.

EXHIBIT 13-2: California's anti-spam legislation.

friendly-bargains." When an indexing program evaluates the site, it reviews the words listed and indexes them all. The first site will have the words "devoted," "maintenance" and "presentation" indexed along with "quality," "gifts" and "recycled." When the indexing program reviews the second site, however, only the essential key words that relate to the business will be indexed. Because of this, the second site will be ranked higher on a list of hits for anyone searching for gifts made from recycled products.

Although some would see this as simple good business practice, others view meta tags as questionable, if not illegal. Pornographic sites, for instance, might index seemingly innocuous words just to list higher on a search engine and bring in people who would not ordinarily view such sites.

The same technology that created the possibility of meta tags may be making them obsolete. Many search engines no longer strictly rely on the first 50 words of a site to index it.

LEGAL NOTICES ON WEB SITES

Sidebar:
Web notices should always be displayed prominently so that any visitor to the site will be aware of them.

Given the unregulated nature of the Internet, many business owners opt for a cautious approach to issues such as spam, piracy, and copyright issues. One way of attempting to insulate themselves from legal action is to post notices on the Web site. These notices attempt to limit the company's civil or criminal exposure by specifically stating what visitors to the site can do.

Notices might include limitations on how the material posted on the Web site can be used. The site might include a notice stating that the material posted is copyrighted or that company logos and trademarks are protected.

Other notices might include limitations on liability for the actions of visitors to the web. Several such notices are provided in Exhibit 13-3.

> - "The material provided on this site is copyrighted. Although you may read this material, you do not have permission to copy it and disseminate it to others for any reason."
>
> - "The Web master is not responsible for statements, representations, or promises made by members of this chat room. Users are warned that inappropriate, threatening, or illegal statements will not be tolerated. Any user who engages in such practices will be barred from the site."
>
> - "The owners of this site make no claims of warranty or guarantee for any product referred to on this site."
>
> - "The links provided on this site are not endorsements by this company of any product, statement or political agenda offered on the linked site."
>
> - "This site complies with all federal and state laws."

EXHIBIT 13-3: Typical Web site notices.

Privacy and Confidentiality Issues

Privacy is a huge concern on the Internet. One disgruntled employee can sell thousands of customers' credit card numbers to criminals who will use this information to purchase millions of dollars of goods, ruining the credit ratings of the customers in the process. Consumers continue to be wary about Internet-based transactions. Encryption of customer data has helped calm some of these fears but so has rigid enforcement of company privacy policies and prosecution of information theft.

However, some Internet practices continue to come under question. Consumers worry that "cookies," "data mining," and other practices may invade their privacy.

COOKIES

Cookies are small bits of programming that are stored on an individual's computer that make it easier to access a particular site in the future. Cookies store information about the user. When the user logs back onto the same site, the Web server at the other end will pull up the cookie and use it to generate a personalized Web page. Some of this information is also stored on the Web server. When the individual returns, this information is used to streamline the two-way communication between the individual's computer and the Web server.

Unfortunately, cookies are open to abuse. Because a cookie stores personalized information about a particular user, a cookie can provide a business with valuable intelligence about its consumers. A cookie is also created without the user's consent (and often without the user's knowledge). The Web server can then begin to create a picture of the user's preferences in a way that many find highly intrusive.

Chat Rooms

Chat rooms are designed to allow many different people to log into a virtual space and type real-time messages to one another. There are chat rooms devoted to a dizzying array of topics from apples to aardvarks, zoning to zoos. Chat rooms become a legal problem when the participants use them to further a criminal enterprise or to threaten one another. Companies that have chat room capabilities on their Web pages should monitor them closely and kick off any member who breaks the chat room rules.

Surveillance

It is possible to install a tiny device on a person's computer that tracks every single keystroke. Some companies track their Web site visitors' movements through the Web page. For consumers already worried about surrendering too much of their privacy, this could be the final straw. Companies with a Web presence must often balance two conflicting desires: the desire to know which of their products get more attention from Web surfers and the desire to keep the customer comfortable with the level of attention and scrutiny they get when visiting the site.

Data Mining

Using specially designed software, data miners bore through computer data, seeking previously unknown information and relationships and then present it in such a way that it will be understandable to people. One of the most common uses for data mining is customer profiling and detecting fraud. However, data mining can have some disquieting undertones. For instance, when a database contains a great deal of information about people, it can come up with information and relationships that most consumers would find intrusive. For instance, a data mining operation might come up with a list of names of men who frequently use credit cards, who live in a specific geographic region, have an annual salary between $50,000 and $100,000, travel frequently, and might be open to a liaison with a prostitute. These men would then be targeted the next time they travel away from home. When data mining is used by the government as part of an investigative tool, it begins to have overtones of Big Brother.

E-Mail

As new technologies emerge, there is always a period of abuse, followed by legislative action. When the telephone first became widely used, the U.S. Supreme Court ruled that individuals had no privacy rights in a telephone call. This ruling was later changed, but it exemplifies a tension between technology and law. Technology moves quickly; the law does not. The legal field sometimes takes years to catch up with the reality of every day technology. Early audio tape recordings were not admissible in court. When fax machines were first introduced, it took years before a fax transmittal copy could be used as evidence.

The Supreme Court's approach to e-mail has a familiar ring. E-mail is not protected as a private communication, although most e-mail users consider it to be a private exchange similar to a letter sent through the mail. E-mail is not considered to be a protected form of communication for several reasons, including:

- E-mail is composed of data packets that follow varying routes to get to their final destination
- E-mail is often provided for employees to further their company's business (not for their personal use)
- E-mail can be viewed and intercepted by the Internet Service Provider

However, whether e-mail continues to be classified as a nonprotected communication is a question that may be answered differently in the future.

Business Issues on the Internet

Along with concerns about practices such as data mining, spam, and tracking customer information, there are some business issues that face special challenges on the Internet.

Domain Names

When the Internet first became popular with computer users, some individuals began engaging in a process known as "cybersquatting." A cybersquatter would obtain a URL (Uniform Resource Locator) address from the Internet Corporation for Assigned Names and Numbers (ICANN) and then attempt to sell the rights this URL to a company, often at an overinflated price. Consider Hypothetical 13-2.

HYPOTHETICAL 13-2   Marvin's Foolproof Plan to Make a Million

Several years ago, before ICANN began limiting the practice, Marvin petitioned and was awarded the Web address www.HarrysHotDogs.com. There is a business in town called "Harry's Hot Dogs," that has several sites in town and is spreading across the state. It has recently announced plans to create a Web site. Marvin sends a letter to the owner of Harry's Hot Dogs, offering to sell the Web address to the company for $1 million dollars. Instead, the owner brings action against Marvin for cybersquatting. In the action, Harry's alleges that the only reason that Marvin acquired the Web address was to hold the restaurant hostage for a URL that any Web surfer would naturally assume belonged to it.

The court rules against Marvin.

Sidebar:
The World Intellectual Property Organization (WIPO) has recently enacted provisions similar to ICANN's to limit the ability of individuals to seek URLs that would obviously be associated with businesses, charities, or celebrities.

ICANN, which is responsible for assigning all Web addresses or URLs, has been cracking down on this practice for several years.

COPYRIGHT ISSUES

Copyright is literally the right of a creator to copy and distribute a work. The form that the work takes is usually not important; it can be written, oral, and even posted in cyberspace. The rules about copyright can be complex, but the essential basis is that copyright in any work automatically attaches when the work is completed and fixed in some tangible form. That tangible form can be printed words on a page, electromagnetic pulses on a tape, or HTML coding on a Web page. There is no requirement that a person register a particular work before copyright exists. The law creates a presumption of copyright. Although registration with the U.S. Copyright Office is helpful in proving an infringement claim, a work is copyrighted when it is completed. The law does not even require that the work bear the copyright symbol: "©."

Although a person may quote portions of a copyrighted work under the "fair use" exception, any lengthy presentation of a copyrighted work requires the permission of the copyright holder.

Public Domain

Sidebar:
"A work that is created (fixed in tangible form for the first time) on or after January 1, 1978, is automatically protected from the moment of its creation and is ordinarily given a term enduring for the author's life plus an additional 70 years after the author's death."[4]

Copyright is no longer an issue when a work enters the "public domain." A work could enter the public domain because the author has specifically waived all copyright protections and submitted it to the public. Some forms of clip art are an example of public domain works. When a work is part of the public domain, it can be used in any manner without first obtaining permission from the author. Works also may enter the public domain when their original copyright protection expires. In 1978, federal legislation created a copyright period of 70 years after the author's death for any work created after that year. Works created before that period have a different protection.

When a person opens a Web page, a copy of that page is automatically stored inside the user's computer. This is not a violation of copyright, because Web page creators impliedly grant this right. However, copying the material and using it in another program or work may be a violation of copyright.

Infringement Actions

Copyright can be an important issue to a company because customers or users might use the company's forum to violate copyright law. For instance, suppose that the company provides a forum for visitors to exchange copyrighted music online? Is that a violation of copyright? Read "The Case Against Napster."

Sidebar:
The Digital Millennium Copyright Act was signed into law in 1998. It protects Web site owners for infringement actions based on providing Web links and other common Internet practices but not for enabling violation of copyright law.

Crime on the Internet

The creativity that criminals exhibit in creating scams is apparently limitless. The Internet has opened up a whole new venue for people intent on deceiving others and taking their money. Internet crime and fraud has become a major concern in recent years with the widespread availability of the Internet. Crime on the Internet ranges from fraud to theft of information to solicitation of prostitution and child molestation. This topic is far too large to be covered in a book on business law. Instead, we will focus on specific types of Internet crimes that are directly related to business.

FRAUD

Internet fraud can run the gamut from bilking innocent consumers out of their money to incredibly complicated schemes. Two of the most common forms of Internet fraud are identity theft and skimming.

Identity Theft

Identity theft is a growing problem in the United States. Armed with your personal information, a criminal can establish a series of accounts in your name, max out the credit limits on all these accounts, and then disappear, leaving you with thousands of dollars of debt and a credit rating that has been destroyed.

identity theft: The process of obtaining a person's credit card and other identifying information, such as birth date and Social Security Number, to create bogus accounts that are then used to purchase items or obtain loans

Skimming

The process of **skimming** involves obtaining a credit card number from a victim and passing this card through a hand-held device that stores the card's information. Hundreds of cards can be passed through this machine, which can then be downloaded into a computer. Because a consumer's critical information is stored on the magnetic strip the back of his card, this information can be deciphered and used to create new accounts in the customer's name.

skimming: Obtaining a person's credit card information by running the card through a hand-held device that stores the card information in downloadable form

INTERNET SCAMS

Some of the more common Internet scams include bogus auction sites and offers of amazing returns on investments. Some scams involve obtaining individual credit card numbers from legitimate businesses and then using these credit card numbers and other information to create a new credit card account that is then used to purchase items. The purchased material is then resold to other suppliers or returned to the original company for a re-fund. Other scams include Internet service providers that require three- to five-year contracts with hefty cancellation fees or "work at home schemes" that promise amazing amounts of monthly income, for relatively small work. Of course, there is a fee to receive the information about the work at home program. See Exhibit 13-4 for an example of another common Internet scheme.

> **Sidebar:**
> Although statistics on the defect are hard to come by, some estimates the state that there are 700,000 cases per year.

VIRUSES

By now, anyone who has spent time on the Internet is aware of computer viruses. A **virus** is a computer program that was developed specifically to damage or destroy computer systems. A virus can be embedded in software

virus: A computer program designed to destroy computer data and disable computer systems.

or e-mail. Viruses can spread from one computer to another, often through sharing files or forwarding e-mails.

Dear _____

Strictly confidential

We are the members of National Committee for Budget and Planning for the country of X. This committee is principally concerned with contract awards. We have amassed a total of $25 million that we plan on dispersing in the United States for the purchase of food, medicine, and other commodities for our people. Based on informaion that we have obtained about you, we believe that you would be in an excellent position to assist us in transferring this money from our country to yours. In order to carry out this transaction, we must be able to transfer the money into an account to which you have sole and complete authority. By providing us with this service, you will be reimbursed a total of 15% of the total funds transferred into your account. We will pay all necessary transfer fees and taxes associated witth this transaction. Please contact us immediately with your full legal name and account numbers so that we may begin this transfer of much needed material to our country.

EXHIBIT 13-4: A common e-mail scam.

HACKING

Computer hacking refers to an individual's unauthorized access of a computer system. A hacker might access a computer system to destroy data or simply to prove that she can do it. Prosecutions of computer hackers have become more common in recent years. Hackers access computer databases and other systems and sabotage them. They can cost a company millions of dollars in damaged or destroyed data and lost time.

Denial of Service Attacks

Another way that a computer hacker attacks a computer system is through a denial of service attack. A computer hacker launches a denial of service attack by creating software that causes hundreds, even thousands, of computers to send nonsense messages and data to a company's Web site. This effectively crashes the company's Web server and makes it impossible for others to access the site for normal purposes.

The Case Against Napster

A&M Records, Inc. v. Napster, Inc., 284 F.3d 1091 (C.A.9,2002).

Before SCHROEDER, Chief Judge, BEEZER and PAEZ, Circuit Judges.
BEEZER, Circuit Judge.

This appeal involves challenges to a modified preliminary injunction entered by the district court on remand from a prior appeal, A&M Records, Inc. v. Napster, Inc., 239 F.3d 1004 (9th Cir. 2001). At issue is the district court's order forcing Napster to disable its file transferring service until certain conditions are met to achieve full compliance with the modified preliminary injunction. We entered a temporary stay of the shut down order pending resolution of this appeal. We have jurisdiction pursuant to 28 U.S.C. §1292(a)(1). We affirm both the district court's modified preliminary injunction and shut down order.

I

Plaintiffs' action against Napster claims contributory and vicarious copyright infringement stemming from Napster's peer-to-peer music file sharing service. In the prior interlocutory appeal, we affirmed the district court's decision to issue a preliminary injunction and reversed and remanded with instructions to modify the injunction's scope to reflect the limits of Napster's potential liability for vicarious and contributory infringement. Napster, 239 F.3d at 1027.

We now consider the district court's modified preliminary injunction, which obligates Napster to remove any user file from the system's music index if Napster has reasonable knowledge that the file contains plaintiffs' copyrighted works. Plaintiffs, in turn, must give Napster notice of specific infringing files. For each work sought to be protected, plaintiffs must provide the name of the performing artist, the title of the work, a certification of ownership, and the name(s) of one or more files that have been

available on the Napster file index containing the protected copyrighted work. Napster then must continually search the index and block all files which contain that particular noticed work. Both parties are required to adopt reasonable measures to identify variations of the file name, or of the spelling of the titles or artists' names, of plaintiffs' identified protected works. The district court carefully monitored Napster's compliance with the modified preliminary injunction. It required periodic reports from the parties and held several compliance hearings. The district court also appointed a technical advisor to assist in evaluating Napster's compliance. Napster was able to prevent sharing of much of plaintiffs' noticed copyrighted works. Plaintiffs nonetheless were able to present evidence that infringement of noticed works still occurred in violation of the modified preliminary injunction. After three months of monitoring, the district court determined that Napster was not in satisfactory compliance with the modified preliminary injunction. The district court ordered Napster to disable its file transferring service until certain conditions were met and steps were taken to ensure maximum compliance.

The record company plaintiffs and the music producer plaintiffs appeal the modified preliminary injunction, and Napster cross-appeals. Napster also appeals the district court's shut down order.

II

"As long as the district court got the law right, it will not be reversed simply because [we] would have arrived at a different result if [we] had applied the law to the facts of the case." Gregorio T. v. Wilson, 59 F.3d 1002, 1004 (9th Cir. 1995).

III

Plaintiffs challenge the requirement that they provide file names found on the Napster index that correspond to their copyrighted works before those works are entitled to protection. Plaintiffs argue that Napster should be required to search for and to block all files containing any protected copyrighted works, not just those works with which plaintiffs have been able to provide a corresponding file name. Napster, on the other hand, argues that the modified preliminary injunction's articulation of its duty to police is vague and fails to conform to the fair notice requirement of Federal Rule of Civil Procedure 65(d).

We are unpersuaded that the district court committed any error of law or abused its discretion. The notice requirement abides by our holding that plaintiffs bear the burden "to provide notice to Napster of copyrighted works and files containing such works available on the Napster system before Napster has the duty to disable access to the offending content." Napster, 239 F.3d at 1027. Napster's duty to search under the modified preliminary injunction is consistent with our holding that Napster must "affirmatively use its ability to patrol its system and preclude access to potentially infringing files listed on its search index." Id. The modified preliminary injunction correctly reflects the legal principles of contributory and vicarious copyright infringement that we previously articulated.

Napster's challenge on grounds of vagueness is without merit. A preliminary injunction must "be specific in terms" and "describe in reasonable detail . . . the act or acts sought to be restrained." Fed.R.Civ.P. 65(d). We do not set aside injunctions under this rule "unless they are so vague that they have no reasonably specific meaning." E. & J. Gallo Winery v. Gallo Cattle Co., 967 F.2d 1280, 1297 (9th Cir. 1992). Napster has a duty to police its system in order to avoid vicarious infringement. Napster can police the system by searching its index for files containing a noticed copyrighted work. The modified preliminary injunction directs Napster, in no vague terms, to do exactly that.

IV

Napster challenges the district court's use of a technical advisor. Napster does not contest the appointment of the advisor but rather challenges the manner in which the district court relied on the advisor. Napster argues that the district court improperly delegated its judicial authority. We disagree. At no time did the technical advisor displace the district court's judicial role. The technical advisor never unilaterally issued findings of fact or conclusions of law regarding Napster's compliance. See Kimberly v. Arms, 129 U.S. 512, 524, 9 S.Ct. 355, 32 L.Ed. 764 (1889) (holding a court may not, through appointment of a master or otherwise, "abdicate its duty to determine by its own judgment the controversy presented"); Reilly v. United States, 863 F.2d 149, 157–58 (1st Cir.1988) (stating a trial court may not rely on technical advisor to contribute evidence, determine legal issues or undertake independent factual findings). The district court's use of the technical advisor was proper.

V

Napster challenges the district court's shut down order. The district court was dissatisfied with Napster's compliance despite installation of a new filtering mechanism. The new filter analyzed the contents of a file using audio fingerprinting technology and was not vulnerable to textual variations in file names. Napster had voluntarily disabled its file transferring service to facilitate installation and debugging of the new filtering mechanism. Users were still able to upload files and search the Napster index during this period. The district court ordered Napster to keep the file transferring service disabled until Napster Satisfied the court "that when the[new] system goes back up it will be able to block out or screen out copyrighted works that have been noticed. . . . and do it with [a] sufficient degree of reliability and sufficient percentage [of success]. . . . It's not good enough until every effort has been made to, in fact, get zero tolerance. . . . [T]he standard is, to get it down to zero." The shut down order was issued after the parties had filed notices to appeal the modified preliminary injunction.

Napster contends that the shut down order improperly amends the modified preliminary injunction by requiring a nontext-based filtering mechanism and ordering a shut down of the system pursuant to a new "zero tolerance" standard for compliance. Napster additionally argues that the district court lacked authority to further modify the modified preliminary injunction while the injunction was pending on appeal.

A.

Napster argues that the new filtering mechanism is unwarranted as it lies beyond the scope of Napster's duty to police the system. By requiring implementation of the new filtering mechanism, the argument goes, the shut down order fails to recognize that Napster's duty to police is "cabined by the system's current architecture." Napster, 239 F.3d at 1024. We are not persuaded by this argument. "Napster has the ability to locate infringing material listed on its search indices, and the right to terminate users' access to the system." Id. at 1024. To avoid liability for vicarious infringement, Napster must exercise this reserved right to police the system to its fullest extent. Id. at 1023. The new filtering mechanism does not involve a departure from Napster's reserved ability to police its system. It still requires Napster to search files located on the index to locate infringing material.

A district court has inherent authority to modify a preliminary injunction in consideration of new facts. See System Federation No. 91 v. Wright, 364 U.S. 642, 647–48, 81 S.Ct. 368, 5 L.Ed.2d 349 (1961) (holding that a district court has "wide discretion" to modify an injunction based on changed circumstances or new facts); Tanner Motor Livery, Ltd. v. Avis, Inc., 316 F.2d 804, 810 (9th Cir.1963) (same). Napster's original filtering mechanism was unsuccessful in blocking all of plaintiffs' noticed copyrighted works. The text-based filter proved to be vulnerable to user-defined variations in file names. The new filtering mechanism, on the other hand, does not depend on file names and thus is not similarly susceptible to bypass. It was a proper exercise of the district court's supervisory authority to require use of the new filtering mechanism, which may counter Napster's inability to fully comply with the modified preliminary injunction.

B.

Napster argues that the shut down order improperly imposes a new "zero tolerance" standard of compliance. The district court did not, as Napster argues, premise the shut down order on a requirement that Napster must prevent infringement of all of plaintiffs' copyrighted works, without regard to plaintiffs' duty to provide notice. The tolerance standard announced applies only to copyrighted works which plaintiffs have properly noticed as required by the modified preliminary injunction. That is, Napster must do everything feasible to block files from its system which contain noticed copyrighted works. The district court did not abuse its discretion in ordering a continued shut down of the file transferring service after it determined that the new filtering mechanism failed to prevent infringement of all of plaintiffs' noticed copyrighted works. Even with the new filtering mechanism, Napster was still not in full compliance with the modified preliminary injunction. The district court determined that more could be done to maximize the effectiveness of the new filtering mechanism. Ordering Napster to keep its file transferring service disabled in these circumstances was not an abuse of discretion.

C.

Napster argues that the district court lacked authority to modify the injunction pending appeal. The civil procedure rules permit modifications. While a preliminary injunction is pending on appeal, a district court lacks jurisdiction to modify the injunction in such manner as to "finally adjudicate substantial rights directly involved in the appeal." Newton v. Consolidated Gas Co., 258 U.S. 165, 177, 42 S.Ct. 264, 66 L.Ed. 538 (1922); Stein v. Wood, 127 F.3d 1187, 1189 (9th Cir.1997). Federal Rule of Civil

Procedure 62(c), however, authorizes a district court to continue supervising compliance with the injunction. See Fed.R.Civ.P. 62(c) ("When an appeal is taken from an interlocutory or final judgment granting, dissolving, or denying an injunction, the [district] court in its discretion may suspend, modify, restore, or grant an injunction during the pendency of the appeal . . . as it considers proper for the security of the rights of the adverse party.").

The district court properly exercised its power under Rule 62(c) to continue supervision of Napster's compliance with the injunction. See Meinhold v. United States Dep't of Def., 34 F.3d 1469, 1480 n. 14 (9th Cir.1994) (holding modification of preliminary injunction during pendency of appeal was proper to clarify injunction and supervise compliance in light of new facts).

VI

We affirm both the modified preliminary injunction and the shut down order. The terms of the modified preliminary injunction are not vague and properly reflect the relevant law on vicarious and copyright infringement. The shut down order was a proper exercise of the district court's power to enforce compliance with the modified preliminary injunction.

AFFIRMED.

Case Questions:

1. What did the District Court order Napster to do in its preliminary injunction?

2. According to the court, what information was the plaintiff originally ordered to provide to Napster concerning copyright infringement?

3. Napster argued that the original order was "vague." Did the court agree? Why or why not?

4. What grounds does Napster use to challenge the shut-down order?

5. What does the court say about Napster's obligation to find people who are sharing copyrighted material on its site?

ETHICS FILE: Internet Ethics

The Internet presents an interesting and, in many ways, unique challenge to ethical standards. Given the fact that interactions on the World Wide Web provide a level of anonymity rarely found in any other aspect of life, individuals might find themselves tempted to abandon many of their long-standing ethical business practices. The Internet presents concerns for legal professionals, as well. We are all aware that a telephone call, and even a fax, from a client can be a confidential communication that is fully protected under the law, but that same ruling has not been applied to e-mail. Clients who communicate through e-mail every day may find it surprising, or even awkward, to learn that they cannot ask for legal advice using the same medium. E-mail does not receive the same level of protection as other forms of communication. You should guard against breaching a client's confidentiality by sending any sensitive information through e-mail.

The Case of the Dicey Domain Name[5]

ELLERIN, J.

This appeal raises issues of good faith and fair dealing in contractual relations and deceptive consumer-oriented business acts and practices in the context of the Internet.

Defendant Register.Com, Inc. (with which defendant Forman merged in 1999) provides Internet services, among them the registration of domain names, i.e., unique names for the addresses of Internet Web sites. Pursuant to an online contract, plaintiff paid defendant $35 to register the domain name "Laborzionist.org" in his name for one year and defendant did so. Not stated in the contract is the fact that a domain name newly registered with Register.com forwards users to a "Coming Soon" page that contains banner advertisements for Register.com and other organizations. A person who types the newly registered domain name into the Internet is brought to a page that reads, "Coming Soon! We recently registered our domain name at … Register.com the *first* step on the web." There follows directly a list of so-called "Additional Services" and, further down on the page, various advertisements. Looking at the page, it appears that these services are provided by the entity—the "we"—whose domain name forwarded the user to this page, although in fact they are provided by Register.com. Similarly, it appears that the advertisements for Register.com and for other companies are in some way endorsed by or, at the least, associated with the entity whose domain name forwarded the user to this page. After plaintiff discovered that his newly registered domain name was pointing users to this "Coming Soon" page, he followed defendant's procedures for removing his registered domain name from the page, a process he asserts took several months.

Plaintiff alleges that he bargained for the right to exclusive use and control of the domain name "Laborzionist.org" and that defendant, by the deception of concealing in its Web site and not disclosing in the agreement that it intended to use the name, deprived him of this benefit by usurping the name and using it to direct those who typed in the domain name to defendant's own site, which contained advertising for defendant and others. Thus, plaintiff claims that defendant breached the covenant of good faith and fair dealing implied in every contract by "act[ing] in a manner that, although not expressly forbidden by any contractual provision, would deprive the other party of the right to receive the benefits under their agreement."

Defendant moved to dismiss the complaint. Defendant argued that it performed the contract, i.e., it registered the domain name "Laborzionist.org" in plaintiff's name; that the contract did not promise plaintiff exclusive use and control of the domain name; and that its policy of placing newly registered domain names on the "Coming Soon" page was fully disclosed in materials found in its Web site, namely, in the text of the "Frequently Asked Questions" (FAQ) and "Help" sections of the website, which were prominently posted on or around the date on which plaintiff registered the domain name.

The motion court found, as a matter of law, that plaintiff received "everything he bargained for" under the contract, pursuant to which he paid defendant to register the domain name "Laborzionist.org" in his name. The court ascribed to the word "register" its ordinary meaning, i.e., make a record of, because the word is not defined in the contract. The court found that, moreover, the word "control" never appears in the contract. The court also cited, although without explaining its significance, a provision permitting defendant to "suspend, cancel, transfer or modify [plaintiff's] use of the Services at any time, for any reason, in [defendant's] sole discretion." On appeal, defendant contends that this provision shows that the express terms of the contract give plaintiff no exclusive right to control the domain name.

There is no question that the instant contract does not in express terms grant plaintiff control over the domain name or the exclusive right to use the name. However, the benefit to plaintiff of his contract with defendant would be rendered illusory if the effect of registering the domain name in his name were merely to have the domain name placed next to his name in some official record, as the motion court found, and not to grant him exclusive use and control of it. The courts will not adopt an interpretation that renders a contract illusory when it is clear that the parties intended to be bound thereby. Moreover, even if the paragraph cited by the motion court accorded defendant the discretionary right to use plaintiff's domain name, it did not insulate defendant from the duty of good faith and fair dealing.

With respect to whether the contract conferred upon plaintiff the exclusive right to control his newly registered domain name, the custom and usage of "registration" of a domain name in the Internet context is certainly more relevant than the literal definition of "registration" found in the dictionary. Defendant itself incorporated custom and usage into the contract in a provision that permits it to "suspend, cancel, transfer, or modify [plaintiff's] domain name registration" in certain circumstances, such as plaintiff's use of his domain name "in contradiction to either applicable laws or customary acceptable usage policies of the Internet."

Indeed, the exclusiveness of the use of a registered domain name is already a familiar concept in the law. Once a domain name is registered to one user, it may not be used by another. Thus, whether "registration" in the context of Internet domain names confers exclusive use and control presents a fact question that should not have been decided upon a motion to dismiss.

In alleging that he was deprived of the essence of his bargain, i.e., the right to exclusive use of the domain name, plaintiff showed a "causal connection between some injury to [himself] and some misrepresentation [or omission] made by defendants" (*Small v. Lorillard Tobacco*, 252 A.D.2d 1, 15, 679 N.Y.S.2d 593, *affd.* 94 N.Y.2d 43, 698 N.Y.S.2d 615,

720 N.E.2d 892). That he paid for the registration of the domain name is sufficient to demonstrate damages (*see Batas v. Prudential Ins. Co. of America*, 281 A.D.2d 260, 261, 724 N.Y.S.2d 3 ["Although plaintiffs sustained no out-of-pocket costs, actual injury is sufficiently alleged in the nonreceipt of promised health care (under the agreement), for which restitution of premiums paid may be an appropriate remedy"]).

The motion court properly dismissed plaintiff's claim for unjust enrichment since there is no dispute that a written contract exists or that it covers the subject matter of plaintiff's action (*see Clark-Fitzpatrick v. LIRR Co.*, 70 N.Y.2d 382, 388, 521 N.Y.S.2d 653, 516 N.E.2d 190).

Accordingly, the order of the Supreme Court, New York County (Karla Moskowitz, J.), entered July 27, 2001, which granted defendants' motion to dismiss the complaint, should be modified, on the law, so as to reinstate plaintiff's claims for breach of implied covenant of good faith and fair dealing and for deceptive practices pursuant to General Business Law §349, and otherwise affirmed, without costs.

Order, Supreme Court, New York County (Karla Moskowitz, J.), entered July 27, 2001, modified, on the law, so as to reinstate plaintiff's claims for breach of implied covenant of good faith and fair dealing *183 and for deceptive practices, and otherwise affirmed, without costs.

All concur.

Case Questions:

1. What services does defendant provide?

2. What is plaintiff's contention in this case?

3. According to the court, did the plaintiff receive exclusive control over the domain name registered by defendant?

4. How does the court define the term "register" in relationship to an Internet domain name?

5. According to the court, was the plaintiff denied the essence of his bargain? Explain.

Business Case File

Fiction Addiction

Fiction Addiction is a used bookstore that also sells books online. Owned and operated by Jill McFarlane, the store has bookshelves from floor to ceiling containing books on a dizzying variety of topics. Besides officering Internet sales, the store also boasts a feature not seen in most bookstores: a spunky kitten named Miles. Jill, like many business owners, had thought about opening up her own business for years.

"I used to live in New York and I owned the apartment that I lived in. When the business that I was working for went bankrupt, I sold my apartment and used the profits to start this business. Even though I knew the book market and felt confident, it was still a little scary opening up my own business."

For Jill, extensive research and planning were the keys to success. "I put together a detailed business plan. None of the numbers on my plan turned out to be accurate, but the whole picture turned out to be right. Part of my success came from knowing the area. I knew that there wasn't a bookstore in this area. Also, the little shopping center that I'm in is nice. You get a lot of people waiting for prescriptions or for pizza; they stop in while they're waiting. Part of it is just looking at your assumptions. When you're doing a business plan and doing the numbers, you must double-check your assumptions. As long as they are working out, then you know that you're doing all right. There are some industry standard figures like the number of times that you should turn over your inventory. Your business plan sets up that you need to make this amount of money per year, the store is this size, so it will hold x amount of books. You take your industry figure and then you see if that will give you the income you're looking for. If you're going into a business to support yourself, you have to learn the numbers. You can't be afraid of the basics."

Like most business owners, Jill found that starting up the business required attention to detail.

Jill McFarlane

"I registered our store logo as a trademark. The instructions were incredibly hard to understand. Then I registered as an LLC [Limited Liability Company], which is comparable to a subchapter S corporation.

"You have to get inspected a few times. The fire inspector comes out. He told me that I needed aisles that were at least 42 inches wide from the front to the back door. ADA [Americans with Disabilities Act] only requires 36-inch-wide aisles. Fortunately, my aisles were already wide enough."

There were other details to attend to as well. "It's important for a small business owner to have a will. When we were discussing the form of the business, the topic of a will came up. This was the first time that I ever had a will. The main thing you have to decide is whether your heirs would want to take over your business or sell it. You have to figure out what your heirs would want to do. It really involves two considerations: who the heirs are and the type of business that you're in. Your heirs might not want to run the business and you have to be prepared for that. You might also want one of your heirs to already be named on a joint account, so that they can write checks and take care of bills while your estate is being probated. It might take too long if they have to

(continued)

wait to go through probate before they can do all of that."

But with the headaches, come certain rewards. "The best thing about owning your own business is being your own boss. Nobody tells you what to do or when to do it. Any ideas that you have, you can follow up on them."

Chapter Summary:

E-commerce presents some new and interesting challenges. Although the basic requirements of a contract do not change simply because the contract was negotiated on the Internet, there are some issues that arise in cyber-based commerce that do not occur in brick and mortar operations. The issue of the party's signature on a contract has been addressed by the creation of a digital signature. E-commerce continues to be relatively unregulated. Internet businesses are unhindered by many of the tax concerns faced by more traditional businesses. However, e-commerce does face cyberpiracy, spam, and other issues not seen in brick-and-mortar businesses. In addition to concerns about regulation, Internet consumers are also concerned about the privacy of their information. E-commerce also faces problems from criminal enterprises. Identify theft and Internet scams are a common dilemma faced by both traditional businesses and Internet-based businesses.

WEB SITES

Federal Trade Commission
http://www.ftc.gov
The U.S. Federal Trade Commission's home page, featuring information on many Internet-based commerce issues.

E-Commerce Times
http://www.ecommercetimes.com/
Provides a wealth of information about Internet-based businesses.

U.S. Copyright Office
http://www.loc.gov/copyright/
Provides information about registering artistic and other works, as well as information about infringement actions.

Lawyer Tool
http://www.lawyertool.com
Gives basic information about legal research and an extensive list of links to other legal sites.

Computer Law Research
http://www.complaw.com
Provides a wealth of information about computer law issues.

REVIEW QUESTIONS

1. The chapter mentions the Industrial Revolution and compares it with the Technological Revolution. How are they alike? How are they different?

2. In what ways is running a business on the Internet different from running a business in a traditional "brick-and-mortar" framework?

3. What is computer hacking?

4. Explain the court's ruling in the "Case against Napster."

5. What are some of the confidentiality concerns for law firms dealing with clients over the Internet?

6. Is e-mail as confidential as a telephone conversation? Why or why not?

7. What are "cookies?"

8. What are some of the privacy concerns for e-commerce?

9. What is skimming?

10. What is a digital signature?

11. What is "spam?"

12. Copyright is often a concern on the Internet. Explain why.

13. What are some ways that a business owner can protect a client's Internet information?

14. What is a "denial of service attack?"

15. What is a computer virus?

16. The text draws a similarity between online commerce and historical business transactions. How are these transactions similar? How are they different?

17. What is the difference between synchronous communication and asynchronous communication?

18. What are some examples of federal legislation that are designed to protect online consumers?

19. What are some common Internet scams?

20. What concerns do businesspersons have about computer hacking?

HANDS-ON ASSIGNMENT

Visit any online retailer and order a product. How does this transaction satisfy the elements of a binding contract? Are there procedures in place on the site that were obviously developed as a way of ensuring that a valid contract is created?

PRACTICAL APPLICATION

You have a product that you like to sell over the Internet. Does your state require you to register your product, your Web site, or to pay taxes on sales of that product?

HELP THIS BUSINESS

We have a client who has created a Web site on which he sells exotic jewelry. What are some of the disclaimers that he should place on his site to protect himself from legal problems? If a purchaser wishes to buy with a credit card, what should his policy be about privacy and releasing credit card information to other retailers?

KEY TERMS

asynchronous communication

brick and mortar

identity theft

Internet Service Provider (ISP)

skimming

synchronous communication

virus

ENDNOTES

1. *Selma Sav. Bank v. Webster County Bank,* 206 S.W. 870 (Ky. App. 1918).
2. 15 U.S.C.A. §7001.
3. 15 U.S.C.A. §45.
4. "Copyright Basics," U.S. Copyright Office, 2003.
5. *Zurakov v. Register.Com, Inc.,* 760 N.Y.S.2d 13, 304 a.d.2d 176 (2003).

 For additional resources, visit our Web site at www.westlegalstudies.com

CHAPTER 14

NEGOTIABLE INSTRUMENTS, SECURITIES, AND SECURED TRANSACTIONS

Focus of this chapter: In this chapter we will explore negotiable instruments such as drafts, checks, and other transactions, as well as secured transactions such as the transfer of stocks and bonds and the requirements placed on these transactions by federal law and the Uniform Commercial Code.

Chapter Objectives:

At the completion of this chapter, you should be able to:

- Define negotiable instruments
- Explain how negotiable instruments are used in commerce
- Compare and contrast cash dispersals with transactions governed by negotiable instruments
- List and describe various types of negotiable instruments
- Describe the organization of the Uniform Commercial Code for negotiable instruments
- Explain how title to negotiable instruments and securities are transferred
- Define securities
- Explain which provision of the Uniform Commercial Code governs investment securities
- Explain the difference in various types of securities
- Explain what secured transactions are

What Are Negotiable Instruments?

negotiable instrument: An unconditional promise or order to pay a fixed amount of money, with or without interest

What we today call **negotiable instruments** were once known under the more general category of "commercial paper." Although neither description encompasses the broad range of this topic, each term gives a clue to the topic's importance. Negotiable instruments are the tools of commerce. Negotiable instruments are the way that manufacturers and merchants pay for their transactions.

draft: A bill of exchange or any other negotiable instrument for the payment of money drawn by one person on another.

Examples of negotiable instruments include drafts and notes. **Drafts** are negotiable instruments that order payment to be made. The most common example of a draft is a check. **Notes,** by contrast, are instruments that promise payment in the future. An example of a note is a Certificate of Deposit or a promissory note. Both will be converted into cash at some later point.

note: A written promise to pay a debt.

"Negotiable Instrument" is a term that encompasses a broad range of business transactions. Merchants have used some form of negotiable instrument for hundreds of years. The use of drafts, checks, and notes was a practical alternative to the risk of carrying large amounts of cash. A negotiable instrument can be issued for the benefit of a specific person or business, making it much harder to convert into cash for someone who intercepted it.

CASH VERSUS NEGOTIABLE INSTRUMENTS

We all know that cash has no pedigree and no method for checking its history. Currency is designed to be anonymous and to pass freely from person to person. Although this ease of use has great benefit to society, there are times when it is better—and safer—to limit the exchange of value between specific parties.

Cash and negotiable instruments are not the same thing. Cash is actual currency and is value in itself. Negotiable instruments, by contrast, can be converted into cash at some point. They represent value and the possibility of future cash dispersal. Negotiable instruments have existed, in one or another, for hundreds of years. A draft that is payable to a specific merchant is a safer form of payment for a traveling salesperson than cash would be. Cash can be used by anyone and does not indicate where or from whom it was collected. Negotiable instruments, such as bank drafts, notes, and checks all have features that help identify the source of the funds, what the funds are to be used for, and who should benefit from them. In this way, they are superior to cash.

Negotiable instruments are both more secure and more easily regulated than the use of cash. We will explore the various uses of negotiable instruments in this chapter.

NEGOTIABLE INSTRUMENTS ARE GOVERNED BY THE UCC

Just as we have seen in other commercial contexts, the Uniform Commercial Code also governs negotiable instruments. The adoption of Article 3 by all states has created the same degree of standardization in this area that the UCC has brought to other commercial transactions, such as sales and secured transactions (see Exhibit 14-1).

---

§ 3-101. Short Title

This Article may be cited as Uniform Commercial Code — Negotiable Instruments.

§ 3-102. Subject Matter

(a) This Article applies to negotiable instruments. It does not apply to money, to payment orders governed by Article 4A, or to securities governed by Article 8.

(b) If there is conflict between this Article and Article 4 or 9, Articles 4 and 9 govern.

(c) Regulations of the Board of Governors of the Federal Reserve System and operating circulars of the Federal Reserve Banks supersede any inconsistent provision of this Article to the extent of the inconsistency.

EXHIBIT 14-1: Article 3, Uniform Commercial Code.

What Makes a Document Negotiable?

UCC §3-104 explains that a document becomes negotiable when it contains an unconditional promise to pay money and is payable to a bearer or payable on demand. This section also explains that, for most purposes, checks are considered to be negotiable instruments, with certain exceptions.

Checks fall into an unusual category under Article 3. They are also covered by Article 4, Bank Deposits and Collections. We will address checks throughout this chapter in their capacity as negotiable instruments, but you should always keep in mind the dual nature of the common check. It straddles two different sections of the Uniform Commercial Code (see Exhibit 14-2).

- Checks
- Drafts
- Bearer bonds

EXHIBIT 14-2: Examples of negotiable instruments.

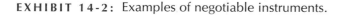

Organization of Article 3

Just as we have seen with other UCC articles, Article 3 has a very specific format. Its subparts are set out in Exhibit 14-3.

Part 1.   General provisions and definitions

Part 2.   Negotiation, transfer, and indorsement

Part 3.   Enforcement of instruments

Part 4.   Liability of parties

Part 5.   Dishonor

Part 6.   Discharge and payment

EXHIBIT 14-3: Parts of Article 3.

Part 1, Article 3

By its own terms, Article 3 does not apply to money or securities. Instead, it only applies to instruments that are payable to the bearer or to order at the time that they are issued. The article also applies to instruments that are payable on demand or at a definite time.

The term "payable on demand" refers to any financing instrument that can be presented for payment at a financial institution. The term is synonymous with "payable on sight," or "payable at the will of the holder."[1]

Other terms defined in Part 1 of Article 3 include, "payable at a definite time." This refers to an instrument that is payable when a specific period of time has elapsed or at some time that is obvious from the wording of the instrument itself. For an example of this language, see Exhibit 14-4.

This document is payable on demand . . .

This document is payable ninety (90) days from the date affixed above . . .

This document does, by its presents, authorize payment to the bearer . . .

EXHIBIT 14-4: Payable on demand language.

Identifying Parties to Be Paid

Article 3 provides that the means for identifying the party to be paid must come from the language of the document and the intent of the signor. A person is free to designate payment to a person when he doesn't know the person's full name. This is true even when the signor knows the person by some name other than his actual, legal name. Consider Hypothetical 14-1.

Hypothetical 14-1   Jack Cherry

Enrique Juarez has been known as "Jack Cherry" since he was a child. He even has a name badge on his work uniform that reads "Jack Cherry." Although this isn't his legal name, he opens a certificate of deposit at a local bank that matures in six months under this name. Can Enrique collect the funds when the note matures?

Answer: Absolutely. The funds were designated for Enrique, even if no one actually knows him by that name. Here, the intent of the note is clear and unambiguous. We might reach a different decision if there actually was a Jack Cherry in the area. Fortunately for Enrique, that is not a problem.

Article 3 not only allows a person to be designated by some name other than his own, it also allows a person to be identified solely by an account number or other identifying number.

When an instrument is made payable to two or more people and they are listed as alternates, any one of them may cash it. By contrast, when an instrument is made out to Party A and Party B, they must both be present to cash it. When two or more people are endorsers, drawers, or makers of an instrument, they are jointly and severally liable.[2]

The term "joint and several liability" means that the parties can be liable both individually and as a group. Each member of the group can be made to pay a portion of the damages assessed in a suit.

Holder in Due Course Rule

When a negotiable instrument, such as a draft or note, is transferred from one person to another, the subsequent purchaser acquires the same rights that the previous owner had in the instrument. But Article 3 provides an additional protection. The **Holder in Due Course Rule** grants complete and legal title to an instrument even when there are outstanding claims against it. The Holder in Due Course Rule protects buyers who act in good faith. If the subsequent purchaser had no way of knowing that there was some impropriety in the transaction, such as forgery or alteration, the subsequent purchaser acquires complete title to the instrument, even if the previous seller didn't actually have those rights.[3]

The Holder in Due Course Rule is an exception to the general rule, commonly referred to as the Derivative Title Rule. Under this rule, a subsequent purchaser can never acquire any greater rights to any property than the previous owner possessed. The Holder in Due Course Rules was created out of a need to protect good faith financial transactions. Unlike real property or items of personal property, negotiable instruments usually have no public

Holder in Due Course Rule: Under this rule, when a person acquires the instrument in good faith, he or she takes title free and clear of any defects or outstanding claims on it.

records to substantiate title. Instead, purchasers must rely on the draft as it is presented. The Uniform Commercial Code helps to ease the concerns of subsequent purchasers not only through the Holder in Due Course Rule but also by creating warranties that accompany each transaction.

Warranties

In addition to protection under the Holder in Due Course Rule, the person who receives a negotiable instrument is also protected by warranties. These warranties are set out in Article 3 and include:

- That the signatures on the instrument are authentic and authorized
- That the instrument has not been altered
- That the person who transferred the instrument has no knowledge of an insolvency proceeding concerning the transaction

These warranties help protect people who handle negotiable instruments. The warranties are assumed for each draft or check and subsequent purchasers are entitled to rely on these warranties, even when they are not actually stated on the document.

Accord and Satisfaction

Article 3 has an accord and satisfaction provision that is similar to the old common law provision that we have discussed in other contexts. Article 3-311 provides that when an instrument contains a conspicuous statement that the instrument was tendered as payment in full, the debt is discharged and no further actions are warranted.[4] Under this ruling, when a person pays a disputed amount with a check or other instrument and writes out "accord and satisfaction" of the debt, the person who cashes the check is tacitly agreeing that the dispute is over. Cashing the check in this situation amounts to waiving any further litigation on the disputed amount. In order to avoid this drastic result, the person receiving payment that contains such language must refuse to cash it and return it to the person who tendered payment.

Negotiable Instruments and Securities

Securities and negotiable instruments are sometimes confused with one another. A security, as we will see in the next section, is a share or ownership interest in a company. Securities can be bought and sold, but they do not qualify as negotiable instruments. A negotiable instrument promises payment; a security is evidence of company ownership.

Securities

security: A share of stock, a bond, a note, or one of many different kinds of documents showing a share in a company or a debt owned by a company or a government.

A **security** is defined as a share in a corporation or an obligation by an issuing company. Although we will discuss corporations in Chapter 15, securities law deserves its own discussion in this chapter. Corporations are organized in such a way that ownership is spread across a wide number of people. These people are referred to as shareholders and their interest in the company is referred to under the broad category of securities. Shareholders own stock in a company and stock falls under the larger category of securities.

Securities can be bought, sold, and transferred in ways that are similar to negotiable instruments. However, there is an important difference between negotiable instruments and securities. A security is an ownership interest in a company. When a security is sold, the seller is actually selling her interest in the company to another person. The purchaser will then acquire an ownership interest in the company.

Securities also are sold through securities' markets that exist all over the world. People frequently buy shares in companies out of a belief that the company's overall wealth will increase and the price of the share will have a corresponding increase in value.

WHAT QUALIFIES AS A SECURITY?

Securities law is controlled not only by state law, through the Uniform Commercial Code, but also through various federal statutes. Before we discuss the applicability of federal and state law, we must first address the broader question of what types of instruments qualify as a security.

Securities consist not only of company stock but also apply to a broad range of other financial instruments, including:

- Corporate notes
- Treasury stock
- Bonds
- Debentures
- Collateral Trust Agreement
- Voting Trust Certificate
- Oil, gas, or mineral interests

The laws about securities are construed liberally, so that a wide range of arrangements fall under the jurisdiction of both state and federal definitions of securities (see Exhibit 14-5).

- Interests in general partnerships
- Shares in limited liability companies are not securities (unless they are traded on the stock market)
- Credit card receipts

EXHIBIT 14-5: Items that do not qualify as securities.

The Case of Contested Condominium[5]

JACOBS, Circuit Judge.

New York investors who purchased condominium apartments in a Chattanooga, Tennessee housing development brought this putative class action against the real estate promoter, SEC Real Estate Corp., and its legal counsel in the transaction, alleging that nondisclosure of a gas well on the property and discrepancies in the closing documents constitute federal securities fraud, common law fraud (or, in the alternative, negligent misrepresentation) and racketeering.

Claims asserted under §10(b) of the Securities Act of 1934, 15 U.S.C. §78j(b), as to which the statute of limitations defense was not pleaded, were dismissed on substantive grounds: the §10(b) claim relating to non-disclosure of the gas well was dismissed (along with the common law and racketeering claims premised on the same non-disclosure) on the ground that title was marketable; the §10(b) claim relating to discrepancies in the closing documents was dismissed (along with the related common law and racketeering claims) because the discrepancies had not caused the purchasers any loss.

We affirm the judgment of the district court. However, we do so on different grounds as to some claims, chiefly because we hold that the condominium purchase contracts are not investment contracts, and therefore are not "securities" under the federal securities laws.

BACKGROUND

This controversy arises from the conversion of a 484-unit apartment complex in Chattanooga, Tennessee into a condominium project called Lake Park Condominiums ("Lake Park"). The Lake Park units were marketed primarily to New York investors. Defendant-appellee SEC Real Estate Corp. ("SEC Realty") was the owner of the complex and the promoter of the condominium project.

In 1985, SEC Realty retained the Nashville law firm of Dearborn & Ewing ("D & E") to prepare the Lake Park Offering Plan. The D & E partner in charge of the representation was Stephen Baker, a member of the board of directors of SEC Realty. D & E and Baker, who are defendants-appellees on this appeal, prepared the Offering Plan and, as required by New York's Martin Act, N.Y.Gen.Bus. Law art. 23-A, filed it with the New York State Department of Law.

Marketing of the Lake Park units began in July 1986. SEC Realty encouraged prospective investors to consider the tax shelter advantages of the units, the income to be derived from rentals, and the prospect of capital appreciation upon resale. To minimize the initial cash requirement, SEC Realty offered to furnish up to 99% financing. All buyers were also offered the opportunity to enter into an on-site management contract with the Nashville management firm of Harvey Freeman & Sons, Inc., for such services as advertising, leasing, lease renewal, interior maintenance, and rent drop.

In the condominium transactions, the buyers gave SEC Realty adjustable-rate promissory notes and deeds of trust, which were subsequently assigned to defendants-appellees Boatmen's Bank and Sovran Bank (the "Banks"). It is undisputed that the Banks are holders in due course of these deeds and notes.

By December 1989, it became clear that the tax advantages and capital gains forecast by SEC Realty would not soon materialize. Thereafter, plaintiffs discovered allegedly false representations in the Lake Park Offering Plan. These consisted of (i) the failure to disclose the existence of a gas well on the Lake Park property, and (ii) discrepancies between the sample debt instruments contained in the Offering Plan and the actual debt instruments presented to plaintiffs (and signed by them) at their respective closings.

A. The Gas Well

Some or all of the Lake Park site became subject to an oil and gas lease executed in January, 1954. The lease, known as the Bunch/Perkins lease, had an initial term of ten years and continued indefinitely "as long thereafter as oil, gas, or other mineral is produced from" the land. A gas well was drilled on the Lake Park property in 1972. Although the well was later designated as "dry and abandoned," it was not plugged until 1989.

The Offering Plan provided a detailed description of the Lake Park units and explicitly stated that any conveyance of title would be subject to:

Lease of oil and gas and other minerals as set forth in instrument of record in Book 1129, page 256, Register's Office for Hamilton County, Tennessee.

The Offering Plan made no mention of the gas well drilled in 1972. However, the location of this well was on file in the Hamilton County Register's Office.

SEC Realty contracted to "convey or cause to be conveyed to Buyer good, marketable, fee simple title to the Unit." Since the title insurance policy provided to purchasers listed a number of exceptions, including the oil and gas lease, and since the Offering Plan pointed purchasers to the registry book (and the page) recording the lease terms, plaintiffs do not allege non-disclosure of the lease itself. Rather, plaintiffs complain of the failure to disclose the existence of the gas well. The well allegedly placed a cloud on title because (i) it was theoretically capable of further production, thus causing confusion as to the viability of the Bunch/Perkins lease, and (ii) an unexpired mineral lease raises vexed questions under Tennessee law concerning the separation of titles to surface and mineral rights. In sum, there was arguably a cloud on title when the units were sold, and it continued to affect marketability, at least until the well was plugged in 1989.

B. Alterations to the Debt Instruments

When SEC Realty began marketing the Lake Park units, it gave each potential investor a copy of the Offering Plan. It included a "Certification of the Sponsor and the Sponsor's Principals," signed by Baker, which represented that the Offering Plan did not "omit any material fact" or "contain any untrue statement of a material fact". The Offering Plan also contained sample forms of the adjustable rate promissory note and the deed of trust that SEC Realty would require the purchasers to execute at the title closing. It is undisputed that the actual promissory note and the deed of trust presented to plaintiffs at closing differed from the forms in the Offering Plan in the following respects.

The specimen deed of trust in the Offering Plan provided in Paragraph 19 (headed "Acceleration; Remedies") that the buyer would be given notice of default and allowed at least ten days from the date of that notice to cure the default before the lender could accelerate and foreclose on the property. Paragraph 20 of the specimen deed of trust in the Offering Plan provided:

20. Lender in Possession. Upon acceleration under Paragraph 19 or abandonment of the property, Lender . . . shall be entitled to enter upon, take possession of and manage the property and to collect the rents of the property including those past due.

The deed of trust presented to plaintiffs at closing, and signed by them, allowed the lender to take over the unit without affording the investors notice of default and an opportunity to cure:

20. Lender in Possession. Following borrower's default in the payment of any sum secured by the Security Instrument for a period in excess of ten (10) days, Lender . . . shall be entitled to enter upon, take possession of and manage the property and to collect the rents of the property including those past due.

Neither SEC Realty nor its lawyers informed the purchasers that the Lender in Possession clause had been changed in this way. Although all of the closings occurred between June, 1986 and November, 1987, plaintiffs state that they did not become aware of the change in the Lender in Possession clause until they looked at their closing papers in May, 1991.

The adjustable-rate note signed at the closings also differed from the specimen document filed with the Offering Plan. The specimen stated:

C. Notice of Default

If I am in default, the Note Holder may send me a written notice telling me that if I do not pay the overdue amount by a certain date, the note holder may require me to pay immediately the full amount of principal which has not been paid and all the interest that I owe on that amount. That date must be at least 30 days after the date on which the notice is mailed to me or if it is not mailed, 30 days after the date on which it is delivered to me.

In the closing documents, however, the 30 day notice of default had been curtailed to a 10 day notice period. Plaintiffs allegedly did not discover this change until December, 1991.

Plaintiffs' failure to detect the changes in the debt instruments is no doubt due in part to the plaintiffs' decision not to retain counsel for the closings. No counsel was needed, plaintiffs believed, because the Offering Plan recited that it did not "omit any material fact" or "contain any untrue statement of a material fact," and was approved by the New York State Department of Law. Nevertheless, the Offering Plan clearly warned prospective buyers that

THE PURCHASE OF A CONDOMINIUM UNIT HAS MANY SIGNIFICANT LEGAL AND FINANCIAL CONSEQUENCES. THE ATTORNEY GENERAL STRONGLY URGES YOU TO READ THIS OFFERING PLAN CAREFULLY AND TO CONSULT WITH AN ATTORNEY BEFORE SIGNING A PURCHASE AGREEMENT

In addition, the purchase agreement contained in the Offering Plan revealed the following:

16. Seller's Attorney. Buyer acknowledges that Seller's attorneys are representing only Seller in this transaction.

DISCUSSION

I. THE SEC REALTY DEFENDANTS

We hold that the condominium transactions are not investment contracts, and therefore are not securities for purposes of the federal securities laws. Affirming the dismissal of the securities claims on that ground, we have no reason to consider the district court's rulings concerning expiration of the statute of limitations on the §12(2) claims and the lack of loss causation under §10(b). Since the Lake Park units are not securities, we affirm the dismissal of plaintiffs' RICO claims on the ground that there was no "racketeering activity". We also affirm the dismissal of all common law claims, because plaintiffs have suffered no injury caused by the alterations to the debt instruments, and the SEC Realty defendants had no duty to disclose the existence of the gas well.

A. The Securities Claims

Section 2(1) of the Securities Act of 1933, 15 U.S.C. §77b(1), defines a "security" as any note, stock, treasury stock, bond, debenture, evidence of indebtedness, certificate *87 of interest or participation in any profit-sharing agreement, collateral-trust certificate, preorganization certificate or subscription, transferable share, investment contract, voting-trust certificate, certificate of deposit for a security, fractional undivided interest in oil, gas, or other mineral rights, or, in general, any interest or instrument commonly known as a "security," or any certificate of interest or participation in, temporary or interim certificate for, receipt for, guarantee of, or warrant or right to subscribe to or purchase, any of the foregoing. If the Lake Park offering is to constitute the sale of a "security," it must fall within the definition of an investment contract. The district court found that it does; we disagree.

The Supreme Court long ago defined the term "investment contract" to include any "contract, transaction or scheme whereby a person invests his money in a common enterprise and is led to expect profits solely from the efforts of the promoter or a third party." SEC v. W.J. Howey, Co., 328 U.S. 293, 298–99, 66 S.Ct. 1100, 1103, 90 L.Ed. 1244 (1946). The investors in Howey bought parcels of land in a citrus grove. The land was offered together with a service contract under which the seller would jointly cultivate the groves and market the produce, and would remit the profits to investors based on the acreage they owned. The Court held that the transaction was an investment contract, emphasizing that the seller was offering "something more than fee simple interests in land, something different from a farm or orchard coupled with management services."

Id. at 299, 66 S.Ct. at 1103. The "something more" was the opportunity to join in a "common enterprise"; investors would "contribute money and . . . share in the profits of a large citrus fruit enterprise managed and partly owned" by the seller. Id.

The three elements of the Howey test must all be present for a land sale contract to constitute a security: (i) an investment of money (ii) in a common enterprise (iii) with profits to be derived solely from the efforts of others. We hold that the Lake Park venture does not constitute a common enterprise.

A common enterprise within the meaning of Howey can be established by a showing of "horizontal commonality": the tying of each individual investor's fortunes to the fortunes of the other investors by the pooling of assets, usually combined with the pro-rata distribution of profits. In a common enterprise marked by horizontal commonality, the fortunes of each investor depend upon the profitability of the enterprise as a whole:

Horizontal commonality ties the fortunes of each investor in a pool of investors to the success of the overall venture. In fact, a finding of horizontal commonality requires a sharing or pooling of funds.

Some circuits hold that a common enterprise can also exist by virtue of "vertical commonality," which focuses on the relationship between the promoter and the body of investors. In an enterprise marked by vertical commonality, the investors' fortunes need not rise and fall together; a pro-rata sharing of profits and losses is not required. Two distinct kinds of vertical commonality have been identified: "broad vertical commonality" and "strict vertical commonality." To establish "broad vertical commonality," the fortunes of the investors need be linked only to the efforts of the promoter.

This Court has not previously considered whether vertical commonality (strict or otherwise) satisfies the common enterprise requirement of the Howey test. There is nothing in the record to indicate that the fortunes of the Lake Park purchasers were interwoven with the promoter's fortunes so as to support a finding of strict vertical commonality. Accordingly, we need not address the question of whether strict vertical commonality gives rise to a common enter-

prise. We do consider whether broad vertical commonality satisfies Howey's second requirement, and we hold that it does not.

In concluding that the sale of Lake Park units constituted the sale of securities, the district court evidently adopted the broad vertical commonality approach. A critical factor in the district court's analysis is that many of the plaintiffs enlisted the management services of Harvey Freeman & Sons, Inc. to oversee all rental arrangements. Such a service contract may tend to demonstrate that (at least some) investors expected profits to be derived from the efforts of others. The district court relied on the same arrangement to establish a common enterprise, as the broad vertical commonality analysis invites the finder of fact to do. We do not interpret the Howey test to be so easily satisfied. If a common enterprise can be established by the mere showing that the fortunes of investors are tied to the efforts of the promoter, two separate questions posed by Howey—whether a common enterprise exists and whether the investors' profits are to be derived solely from the efforts of others—are effectively merged into a single inquiry: "whether the fortuity of the investments collectively is essentially dependent upon promoter expertise."

We next consider whether horizontal commonality exists among the Lake Park investors so as to satisfy Howey's common enterprise requirement. Plaintiffs do not allege, and the SEC Realty defendants vehemently deny, that any rent-pooling arrangement existed among the Lake Park investors. The rents and expenses attributable to each unit were not shared or pooled in any manner, but were instead the sole responsibility of the unit owner. Plaintiffs owned individual units, and could make profits or sustain losses independent of the fortunes of other purchasers. There are simply no indicia of horizontal commonality. The fact that many purchasers employed the services of Harvey Freeman & Sons, Inc. in renting their units establishes, at most, a common agency, not a common enterprise. Accordingly, the Lake Park venture does not constitute a common enterprise within the meaning of Howey and the sale of the Lake Park condominium units cannot be considered the sale of securities for purposes of the federal securities laws.

Our analysis is consistent with the approach adopted by the Securities and Exchange Commission (the "SEC") in applying the principles of Howey to condominium offers. The SEC recognizes that the sale of a condominium, without more, does not constitute a security transaction.

CONCLUSION

Since the sale of Lake Park units did not constitute the sale of "securities" for purposes of the federal securities laws, we affirm the district court's dismissal of the § 12(2) and § 10(b) claims as well as the dismissal of the attendant RICO claims.

Case Questions:

1. What are three elements that this court says are required in order to prove that an arrangement is a security as that term is defined under federal law?

2. Why did this court determine that the arrangement in this case was not a "common enterprise?"

3. What is "horizontal commonality?"

4. How does horizontal commonality compare to "vertical commonality?"

5. Why is it significant that the rents for the condominiums were not pooled by the various investors and owners?

SECURITIES AND FEDERAL LAW

Although securities fall under the jurisdiction of Article 8 of the Uniform Commercial Code, they also fall under federal law as well. This was not always the case. Before the stock market crash in 1929, securities law was almost exclusively a state law issue. However, with the tremendous financial losses that occurred after that financial disaster, the federal government passed a series of statutes governing the securities field, with the result that this topic falls under both state and federal jurisdiction (see Exhibit 14-6).

Often referred to as the "truth in securities" law, the Securities Act of 1933 has two basic objectives

- It requires that investors receive financial and other significant information concerning securities being offered for public sale

- It prohibits deceit, misrepresentations, and other fraud in the sale of securities

---

EXHIBIT 14-6: Securities Act of 1933.

Federal Laws That Apply to Securities

The first of a series of federal legislative initiatives aimed at the securities field was the Securities Act of 1933. This act provided, among other things, that investors must receive complete and accurate financial information about companies that offered their securities for public sale and authorized penalties for fraudulent and deceitful practices on the part of stockbrokers, financial institutions, and companies. The Securities Act was quickly followed by the Securities Exchange Act of 1934, which authorized the creation of the Securities and Exchange Commission.

The Securities and Exchange Commission

The Securities and Exchange Commission (SEC) has been a potent force in the securities field since its inception. Today, it polices stock exchanges, brokers, investment advisors, financial institutions, and publicly traded companies. On average, the SEC brings about 500 actions per year for actions as diverse as insider trading, fraud, and giving false information to investors or government agencies (see Exhibit 14-7).

There are numerous other types of stock, including:

- Assessable
- Blue-chip
- Control
- Common
- Cumulative
- Growth
- Guaranteed
- Penny
- Preferred
- Registered

EXHIBIT 14-7: Other types of stock.

Registration with the SEC

One way of ensuring that investors receive accurate information is the SEC's requirement that all securities sold in the United States must be registered. Registration information includes descriptions of the following:

- The company, its business, and basic features
- The security being offered for sale
- The company's management
- Financial statements filed by accountants supporting the information about the security

Viewing Registration Information   One of the most helpful features of the SEC is its database of information about companies, securities, and financial information. The SEC maintains all of this information in a public-access database called EDGAR. This database can be accessed directly from the SEC's Web page at http://www.sec.gov.

SECURITIES AND STATE LAW (THE UCC)

Article 8 of the Uniform Commercial Code governs securities. Like negotiable instruments, securities law is based on state law applications of the Uniform Commercial Code. However, unlike negotiable instruments, there also are several important federal law limitations on securities transactions.

Article 8 limits its scope to investment securities, not the complex world of share transfers and shareholder rights. The article was originally created out of a need to protect investors from fraudulent schemes and other potential abuses that were once common in the securities market. However, securities also are controlled on the federal level.

Provisions of Article 8 of the UCC

Article 8 of the Uniform Commercial Code governs a wide variety of activities associated with securities. Among these features is a definitions section, §8–102, which sets out definitions specific to this article. Other features in Article 8 include a provision making the Statute of Frauds inapplicable to securities agreements. The article is comprehensive in its coverage of securities and should always be referred to whenever a securities question arises.

STOCK

Stock represents ownership interest in companies. Article 8 provides specific rules about the transfer of stock between individuals. As we will see in the next chapter, there are different types of corporations and there are different types of stock. Not all shares issued by all types of corporations qualify as securities under Article 8. For instance, some closely held family corporate stock is not considered to be securities. The same ruling holds true for professional corporations, often formed by lawyers or doctors to facilitate their practice—and take advantage of favorable tax rules. Although stock comes in many different forms, there are two types that are seen more often than any other: common stock and preferred stock.

Common Stock

common stock: Shares in a corporation that depend on their value on the value of the company.

Common stock is the stock that a company issues in order to raise capital. This stock is sold on stock exchanges around the world. The stock price is based partly on the base value of the stock (called the par value) and the perceived wealth of the company. Holders of common stock are entitled to dividend payments (if the corporation declares a dividend for a particular year). Common stock qualifies under Article 8 as a security.

Preferred Stock

The other type of stock frequently seen is preferred stock. **Preferred stock** is a class of stock that entitles the person who possesses it with priority when it comes to paying dividends. Preferred stockholders must be paid before common stockholders. However, with this advantage comes a disadvantage: preferred stockholders do not have voting rights in the corporation. Without voting rights, they cannot vote to remove directors or seek to affect corporate policy.

preferred stock: A class of stock that entitled the holder to a stated dividend that must be paid before any dividend payment is made to holders of common stock. Holders of preferred stock generally do not have any voting rights in the corporation.

Article 9

Article 9 of the UCC concerns secured transactions. A **secured transaction** is any promise to pay on a loan that is guaranteed by some form of **collateral**. If the borrower fails to make payments on the loan, the lender may seize the collateral and sell it to satisfy the obligation.

secured transaction: A secured transaction is a secured deal involving goods or fixtures that is governed by Article 9 of the Uniform Commercial Code.

collateral: Money or property put up to back a person's word when out a loan.

Hypothetical 14-2   Collateral

Dion wants to expand his business and decides to apply for a loan at a local bank. He wishes to borrow $10,000 and the bank asks if he has any collateral. He offers the title on his car, which he says is worth about $11,000. The bank agrees to loan Dion the money. When he stops making payments one year later, the bank hires a repossession expert (otherwise known as a "repo man") to find the car and seize it for the bank. Later, the bank auctions the car off for $10,500 and applies the proceeds to Dion's outstanding debt.

As you can imagine, there is a great deal of potential abuse and fraud that could be carried out in a secured transaction. Article 9 was enacted to provide solid ground rules for all transactions in which property is offered as security for the loan. For one thing, Article 9 provides an extensive definition section that spells out meanings for a wide variety of terms, from "account debtor" to "secured party." Under Article 9, an "account debtor" means a person obligated on an account, chattel paper, or general intangible. The term does not include persons obligated to pay a negotiable instrument, even if the instrument constitutes part of chattel paper. A "secured party," by contrast, means (A) a person in whose favor a security interest is created or provided for under a security agreement, whether or not any obligation to be secured is outstanding; or (B) a person that holds an agricultural lien; or (C) a consignor; or (D) a person to which accounts, chattel paper, payment intangibles, or promissory notes have been sold.[6]

Sidebar:
An "unsecured" loan has no collateral to support the loan.

CARE AND MAINTENANCE OF THE COLLATERAL

Other rules enforced under Article 9 include the requirement to care for the collateral. Article 9-207 requires the party in possession of collateral to use reasonable care in its custody and preservation. This means that if the debtor retains possession of the collateral, such as continuing to drive the car that was pledged as security for a loan, he must take care of the car and not allow it to fall into disrepair. The possessor must pay reasonable costs to maintain the collateral, including paying insurance premiums, taxes, and storage fees, if required.

PRIORITY IN PAYING CLAIMS

Article 9 also creates rules for priority of claims. Priority refers to the order in which claims will be paid. For instance, in many situations, the party who has the oldest claim is paid first. Once that party is fully paid, the remaining money is paid to the creditor who is next in line. As you can imagine, there is usually not enough value to pay everyone with a claim. This is why any rule that places one party ahead of another is important. In most situations, priority is determined chronologically. The first party to file is first in line when it comes to distributing value. However, there are some exceptions to this rule. For instance, the government usually takes highest priority for claims of unpaid taxes, no matter when the claim was filed.

UCC FINANCING STATEMENTS

Article 9 also provides that proof of a secured transaction in property must be filed in order to substantiate the claim. These documents are often referred to as "UCC Financing Statements" and can often be located in the local courthouse. They provide information about the collateral, the terms of the loan, and the ability of the creditor to seize the collateral in the event of nonpayment.

ETHICS FILE: Insider Trading

The term "Insider trading" has received great deal of publicity in recent years. With the media attention surrounding the Martha Stewart case and the Enron Case, to name only two, brokers, company presidents, and others have come face-to-face with an ethical concern that is also a criminal law violation. Legal professionals also must consider the implications of insider trading. Under the broad definition of insider trading, anyone who uses secret or otherwise not disclosed information to reap financial gain may have committed insider trading with regard to stocks and bonds. Legal professionals are in an excellent position to discover this type of information. They must be on guard not only to the implications of using this information but also to the ethical concerns that this use has for the firm. Ethical rules for legal professionals almost always follow the line that when there is an appearance of impropriety there is an ethical violation. Under this standard, when a legal professional who works for a corporation, a stock exchange, or any other financial institution uses confidential information to gain a reward, this is certainly an ethical violation, even if it does not rise to the level of a criminal violation.

The Case of the Missing Note[7]

STONE, J.

The issue on appeal is whether a mortgagee by assignment, State Street Bank, may pursue a mortgage foreclosure in the absence of proof that either the mortgagee, or its assignor, ever had possession of the missing promissory note. A summary judgment was entered in favor of the mortgagor, Hartley Lord. We affirm.

State Street sought to establish the promissory note and mortgage under section 71.011, Florida Statutes. State Street alleged that Hartley executed the note and mortgage and that, after multiple assignments, the documents were assigned to State Street by EMC Mortgage Corporation. Although State Street alleged in its pleading that the original documents were received by it, the record established that State Street never had possession of the original note and, further, that its assignor, EMC, never had possession of the note and, thus, was not able to transfer the original note to State Street.

The trial court correctly concluded that as State Street never had actual or constructive possession of the promissory note, State Street could not, as a matter of law, maintain a cause of action to enforce the note or foreclose the mortgage. The right to enforce the lost instrument was not properly assigned where neither State Street nor its predecessor in interest possessed the note and did not otherwise satisfy the requirements of section 673.3091, Florida Statutes, at the time of the assignment.

To maintain a mortgage foreclosure, the plaintiff must either present the original promissory note or give a satisfactory explanation for its failure to do so. §90.953(1), Fla. Stat. (2002). A limited exception applies for lost, destroyed, or stolen instruments, where it is shown that "the person was in possession of the instrument and entitled to enforce it when loss of possession occurred." §673.3091, Fla. Stat. (2002).

Section 673.3091 provides, in part:

(1) A person not in possession of an instrument is entitled to enforce the instrument if:

(a) The person was in possession of the instrument and entitled to enforce it when loss of possession occurred;

(b) The loss of possession was not the result of a transfer by the person or a lawful seizure; and

(c) The person cannot reasonably obtain possession of the instrument because the instrument was destroyed, its whereabouts cannot be determined, or it is the wrongful possession of an unknown person or a person that cannot be found or is not amenable to service of process.

Here, it is unrefuted that State Street was unable to meet the requirement of section 673.3091. The undisputed facts show that the note was lost before the assignment to State Street was made. This court has previously refused to allow a mortgage foreclosure under similar circumstances. In *Mason v. Rubin*, 727 So.2d 283 (Fla. 4th DCA 1999), the appellant brought a foreclosure action on a second mortgage, the trial court denied the foreclosure, and this court affirmed on the basis that the appellant had failed to establish the lost note under section 673.3091. Likewise, here, where State Street failed to comply with section 673.3091, the trial court correctly entered summary judgment denying its foreclosure claim.

Although it appears that O'Donovan permits foreclosure even where the promissory note is not re-established, the Third District applied section 71.011 governing enforcement of lost papers, records, or files, and not section 673.3091. This court, however, has concluded that lost promissory notes are negotiable instruments and are actually governed by section 673.3091.

State Street cannot succeed under an assignment theory. We recognize that this court, and the Third District, have held that the right of enforcement of a lost note can be assigned. Here, however, in contrast to National Loan, Slizyk, and Deakter, there is no evidence as to who possessed the note when it was lost.

In Slizyk, we held that the assignee of a note and mortgage was entitled to foreclose despite his inability to produce the original documents. This court concluded that because the assignor was in possession of the notes, he had the right to enforce them. When the notes were assigned to the appellee, the right to enforce the instruments was assigned to him as well. In contrast, here, the undisputed evidence was that EMC, the assignor, never had possession of the notes and, thus, could not enforce the note under section 673.3091 governing lost notes. Because EMC could not enforce the lost note under section 673.3091, it had no power of enforcement which it could assign to State Street. Were we to allow State Street to enforce the note because some unidentified person further back in the chain may possess the note, it would render the 673.3091 rule meaningless. We do not, and need not, reach any question as to whether Slizyk and National Loan may be applied where there is proof of an earlier assignor's possession further removed than the most immediate assignor.

We recognize that applying the statute as we do will result in a windfall to the mortgagor and a likely injustice to the mortgagee, unless it is able to obtain new evidence. In *Dennis Joslin Company v. Robinson Broadcasting Corp.*, 977 F.Supp. 491 (D.D.C.1997), the district court rejected the right to assign the enforcement of a lost note. Apparently, in response to that opinion, the Uniform Commercial Code was amended to delete the requirement that the transferee be in possession at the time the instrument was lost and now provides that the person seeking to enforce the instrument either was entitled to enforce the instrument when loss of possession occurred, or acquired ownership of the instrument from a person who was entitled to enforce the instrument when loss of possession occurred. See U.C.C. §3-309(a)(1) (2002). Florida, however, has not similarly amended its code and still requires possession either by the assignor at the time of loss or by the person seeking to enforce the note. Any remedy must, therefore, be left to the legislature.

Case Questions:

1. Was it significant in this case that State Street Bank never had actual possession of the promissory note?

2. Does Florida law ever allow a creditor to foreclose a mortgage when the promissory note is missing?

3. Is there any provision for foreclosing on collateral when the original note is destroyed or goes missing?

4. If a lost note can be assigned, why didn't this give State Street Bank the right to foreclose on it?

5. Doesn't the result in this case mean that the person who owns the house now owns it forever and has no future responsibility to pay a mortgage? Is this fair?

Business Case File

Seaside Pharmaceutical, Inc.

Seaside Pharmaceutical is run by pharmacist Robert Tretheway and Lisa Burnett, Registered Nurse. They have been in business for about two years. Lisa Burnett says, "If I had to give a basic description of our business, I'd say that we are a pharmacy with a difference. We do in home services, like IV therapy for patients. We provide medical equipment and we are a compound pharmacy. Compounding means that we actually make medications from raw chemicals. The advantage of compounding is that when a large pharmaceutical company discontinues making a drug, we can take that formula and recreate it for the person. We can also adjust the balance of the medicine to create a prescription that best suits the person. It's not just a "one size fits all." We can adjust the balance of the different compounds and customize the medication for the person. We actually make the pill right here in our office. Sometimes it takes a couple of hours; sometimes it takes a couple of days, if we have to order rare materials.

"When we started our business, we knew that we wanted to incorporate. We formed an S Corporation with the two of us as officers.

Seaside Pharmaceutical works with negotiable instruments on a day to day basis. "We pay for our

Lisa Burnett and Robert S. Tretheway

supplies through bank drafts and sometimes directly on line from our commercial account. Our customers pay us with personal checks, cash and credit cards. We also get routine direct deposits from Medicaid. We had to learn a lot about billing, deposits and drafts to make sure that we got paid.

"The best part about our business is that we help people feel better. Some of them have been on prescriptions for years and they've never found the right dosage. We tailor the prescription to the person's needs and you'd be surprised what a difference that can make in a person's overall health."

-Lisa Burnett

Chapter Summary:

A negotiable instrument is any commercial paper that promises to pay money to another. Negotiable instruments come in a wide variety of forms, from drafts to promissory notes. What they all have in common is a promise to pay a specific amount at a specific time. They may be payable on demand or payable on a specific date. Negotiable instruments have rules that are specific to their category. One such rule is the Holder in Due Course Rule. This rule provides that a good faith purchaser of a negotiable instrument may take complete and unchallenged title to the instrument, even when the person selling it did not have that same degree of title. The Holder in Due Course Rule protects subsequent, good faith purchasers by giving them better title than the previous possessor had.

Securities are shares in a corporation or any obligation to pay issued by a company. All securities are governed by both federal law and state law. On the federal level, there are statutes, such as the Securities Act of 1933, that penalize fraudulent or deceptive practices in securities. Securities also are governed by Article 8 of the Uniform Commercial Code. Stocks are one type of security; they come in many different forms, including common stock and preferred stock. Common stock consists of shares in a company; preferred stock gives the owner priority in the payment of dividends but no voting rights for the shareholder.

Secured transactions involve loans that are guaranteed by collateral. Governed by Article 9 of the UCC, secured transactions are a very common arrangement. Article 9 not only establishes the rules for how and when property can be used as collateral for a loan but also how the collateral can be used during the loan period.

When legal professionals deal with company clients, it is always a good idea to keep in mind the rules about the use of confidential information. The Securities and Exchange Commission is a federal agency that is authorized to investigate claims of insider trading. Legal professionals should always be cautious when attempting to gain personal advantage from client information.

WEB SITES

Federal Reserve
http://www.federalreserve.gov
The central bank of the United States. This site provides a wealth of information about many aspects of the financial transactions.

Legal Information Institute
http://www.law.cornell.edu
Provides a wealth of information about negotiable instruments, secured transactions and securities.

Securities and Exchange Commission
http://www.sec.gov
Arguably one of the best sites on the Web for a wide range of information about investment securities, insider trading, and many other topics relating to securities.

REVIEW QUESTIONS

1. What is a negotiable instrument?

2. What types of transactions are governed by Article 8 of the Uniform Commercial Code?

3. Explain why federal and state law plays such a significant role in Article 9 transactions.

4. What types of transactions are governed by Article 9 of the Uniform Commercial Code?

5. Why are negotiable instruments important to commerce?

6. What are some examples of negotiable instruments?

7. What is the difference between cash and negotiable instruments?

8. Which article of the Uniform Commercial Code governs negotiable instruments?

9. According to the Uniform Commercial Code provisions concerning negotiable instruments, what other rules must be followed in identifying parties to be paid with negotiable instruments?

10. Explain the joint and several liability clauses found in Article 3.

11. What is the "Holder in Due Course" rule?

12. How does accord and satisfaction operate under Article 3?

13. What are securities under Article 8?

14. When there is a conflict between Article 3 and Article 8, which one takes priority? Why?

15. Explain the differences between common stock and preferred stock.

16. What are secured transactions?

17. What is the purpose of the Securities and Exchange Commission?

18. What is the purpose of Article 9?

19. Explain the priority rules under Article 9.

20. Explain the restrictions placed on the party in possession of collateral to protect and preserve the secured property.

HANDS-ON ASSIGNMENT

1. Locate newspaper or online news sites concerning insider trading. What are the allegations raised? Was the SEC involved and, if so, what charges did the SEC bring?

2. Are there publicly traded corporations headquartered in your area? What kind of information can you discover about the company through the SEC Web site?

PRACTICAL APPLICATION

Visit the your state's Secretary of State's Web site and locate the following:

Corporate names and information

Company filings

Information about fraudulent business practices

Use the EDGAR service under the Securities and Exchange Commission Web site to locate filings on regional companies or companies in your area.

Contact a local bank and inquire about the terms for certificates of deposit. Does the certificate of deposit qualify as a negotiable instrument?

Why or why not?

HELP THIS BUSINESS

Seaside Pharmaceuticals has decided to seek more financing to expand its business. They wish to apply for a secured loan. What kind of collateral can they offer?

KEY TERMS

collateral	note
common stock	preferred stock
draft	secured transaction
Holder in Due Course Rule	security
negotiable instrument	

ENDNOTES

[1] UCC §3-108.

[2] UCC §3-116.

[3] UCC §3-302.

[4] UCC §3-311.

[5] *Revak v. SEC Realty Corp.*, 18 F.3d 81 (C.A.2 N.Y., 1994).

[6] UCC §9-102(3).

[7] *State Street Bank and Trust Co. v. Lord*, 851 So.2d 790 (Fla.App. 4 Dist., 2003).

For additional resources, visit our Web site at
www.westlegalstudies.com

CHAPTER 15

BUSINESS ENTITIES

> **Focus of this chapter:** In this chapter we will explore the various types of business organizations, from sole proprietorships to multinational corporations. Along the way, we will examine how the legal structure of business affects aspects as varied as initial startup, day-to-day management, and transfer of ownership interests.

Chapter Objectives:
At the completion of this chapter, you should be able to:

- Explain why the choice of business organizational structure is important for a new business
- Explain the liability concerns for sole proprietors
- Compare and contrast the liability for various types of business structures
- Discuss the role of the legal professional in helping to create and maintain specific types of businesses
- Describe how different types of business entities are created
- Define limited liability and the role it plays in certain types of business structures
- Explain the differences between general partnerships and limited partnerships.
- Describe the significance of various types of corporate structures
- Explain the ethical concerns peculiar to corporate business entities
- Define the concerns of business owners in obtaining financing and running their businesses

Introduction to Business Organizations

Throughout this book, we have seen the importance that business plays in every society. We have examined areas as diverse as the creation of contracts, the Uniform Commercial Code, and negotiable instruments. In this final chapter, we will address the topic of creating business structures.

The way that a business is set up is often as important as how it is run, and the choice of business entity often has a huge influence on the eventual success—or failure—of that business.

The topic of business organizations is rich and diverse. Authors have written entire texts on the topic. In this chapter, we will examine various business structures, from sole proprietorships to corporations, and explore not only how these business structures are created but also the legal significance of the business structure and the role that it plays in the day-to-day operation of a commercial enterprise.

A business can be as simple as a sole proprietorship and as complex as a vast, multinational corporation. The organization of these businesses has profound implications for the owners, whether they are local merchants or the shareholders of a huge corporation.

We will examine the various types of business organizations by starting with the simplest form and then moving through progressively more complex arrangements. The simplest form of business is the sole proprietorship.

Sole Proprietorships

Sole proprietorships are the oldest, and simplest, form of business structure. In a sole proprietorship, there is a single individual who conducts all aspects of the business. One person acts as the boss, employee, marketing department, billing department, customer service representative, and any other role required by the business. Consider Hypothetical 15-1.

HYPOTHETICAL 15-1 The Lawn Business

Ned is 13 years old and wants to earn some extra money. He decides to go door-to-door in the neighborhood and ask the neighbors if they would like to have their lawns mowed. He hasn't decided what price he will charge. He gets his first customer later that day. The neighbor offers to pay Ned $8 if he will mow his lawn. If the neighbor likes Ned's work, he'll have Ned come by every week and mow the lawn for the same amount.

Ned has just embarked on his business career.

A sole proprietorship is a very simple form of business. Sole proprietors have great flexibility in how the business will be run and in making changes in the direction that the business will go. However, this degree of freedom does come at a price. One of the biggest concerns for any sole proprietor is legal liability.

LEGAL LIABILITY OF SOLE PROPRIETORS

When a business owner speaks of legal liability, she is usually referring to the possibility of having a lawsuit brought against her and the further possibility of having to pay a judgment in the event that she loses the suit. If a

unlimited liability: A concept that places all of a person's personal assets within reach of a civil judgment.

sole proprietor is sued because of some business disagreement, her personal assets are in danger. This is true because there is no legal boundary between a sole proprietor's business assets and personal assets. If the plaintiff obtains a judgment against the sole proprietor, then this judgment can be enforced against the sole proprietor's bank accounts, personal holdings, and, in some cases, her personal residence. This puts the sole proprietor in a tenuous position. The sole proprietor has the freedom that comes from being her own boss, but she also faces the specter of **unlimited liability**.

Unlimited liability is the biggest disadvantage to sole proprietorship. In fact, this one factor may be such a disadvantage that a sole proprietor often searches out other business structures as a way of protecting her personal assets. Later in this chapter, we will examine business entities that were created specifically to address this issue.

HYPOTHETICAL 15-2   The Broken Window

Ned's business has grown over the past few weeks. He now has four regular customers. He has been smart about his money: he's been putting 90 percent of everything he makes into the bank. (He allows himself to spend 10 percent on video games and candy.) One day, when he is mowing the yard of one of his regular clients, he runs over a rock and it flies out from under the motor and breaks the front window of the customer's house. The customer rushes out, angry and yelling. The final bill to repair the window is $20. Who pays?

Answer: Ned does, even though the bill is $20.00, more than twice what he would have made on the lawn job. Ned has no choice in paying the bill; he is a sole proprietor and responsible for any damage his business causes.

THE ADVANTAGES OF A SOLE PROPRIETORSHIP

One of the most obvious advantages to a sole proprietorship is the freedom given to the owner to make business decisions. The owner is not obligated to confer with anyone else before making a decision. If the owner wishes to change the way that business is done, she can simply do it. There are no committees, no partners, and no shareholders to consider. This gives a sole proprietorship a degree of freedom that is not seen in any other type of business. Another important advantage of sole proprietorship concerns income taxes.

Tax Consequences of Sole Proprietorship

One of the major advantages of a sole proprietorship concerns income taxes. When a sole proprietor sustains a major income loss during the year, she can pass this loss through on her personal income tax return. This often results in paying fewer taxes and perhaps qualifying for a tax refund. Of course, the opposite situation is also true. If the sole proprietor earns a substantial income, she must pay taxes on it. Consider the following hypothetical.

HYPOTHETICAL 15-3   Ronnie's New Consulting Business

After years of working in corporate America, Ronnie has decided to open her own consulting business. She will advise local businesses on the best way to obtain government contracts in specific areas. She creates an office in her home, has business cards printed up, and, because of her reputation, builds a strong customer base almost immediately.

Now that Ronnie is working on her own and is no longer employed by a large corporation, she can enjoy some tax benefits that she didn't have as an employee. For one thing, if she has any business losses over the year, she can assess them against her personal income taxes and lower her overall tax liability. She can "write off" business expenses and can deduct a certain amount from her income for a home office deduction.

THE DISADVANTAGES OF A SOLE PROPRIETORSHIP

Oddly enough, the features that make a sole proprietorship so advantageous are also what cause the most problems for business owners. Because the business is so closely associated with a single person, the death or incapacity of that person causes the business to fail. There is usually no way for the business to continue without the owner.

Sole proprietors also frequently suffer from **undercapitalization**. With only their personal credit and financial resources to rely on, many sole proprietors find it difficult to expand their businesses or to pay unexpected bills. In fact, the financial limitations are one of the biggest reasons why many sole proprietors move to the next level of business organization: the general partnership (see Exhibit 15-1).

undercapitalization: Lacking enough cash or short-term profit to stay in business.

☐ Who will own the business?

☐ What degree of formality is required to create the business structure?

☐ What is the owner's income tax situation?

☐ How difficult will it be to acquire additional investments?

EXHIBIT 15-1: Factors in choosing a business organizational structure.

General Partnerships

A partnership consists of two or more people working together in a joint business venture. Partnerships have several obvious advantages over sole proprietorships. First of all, there are more people to share the load. Partners can bring additional financial and other resources to bear for the good of the business. However, with these greater resources come more limitations. The partners must consult with one another before making business decisions and all partners face the possibility of losing their personal assets in a judgment against the partnership. We refer to this arrangement as a **general partnership** in order to distinguish it from a limited partnership, discussed later in this chapter.

general partnership: An unincorporated business organization co-owned by two more persons.

HYPOTHETICAL 15-4   N&L Lawn Association

Ned's lawn business has done so well in recent months that he needs help. Although Ned would like to have one of his friends work with him, Ned's mother suggests that Ned should talk to his sister, Lisa. She is 12 and, as much as Ned would hate to admit it, she is a good worker. Ned also suspects that some of his friends would slack off and not get the work done. Swallowing his objections, he works out the following agreement with his sister:

"I, Ned, agree to work with you, Lisa, to run N&L Lawn Association. We will split the profits 60–40. I'll get 60% of whatever we make; you'll get 40%. I'll run the mower and you'll do the trim work, like running the weed wacker and trimming bushes and stuff."

(Signed) Ned

(Signed) Lisa

Ned and Lisa have just created a general partnership.

FORMING A GENERAL PARTNERSHIP

In most situations, forming a general partnership is a simple matter. The partners simply agree to be bound to one another in a business and to pledge their financial assets for the business. Although many partners write out a General Partnership Agreement, in most situations it is not required. For an example of a General Partnership Agreement, see the appendix.

ADVANTAGES OF GENERAL PARTNERSHIPS

The advantages of a partnership are obvious: with two or more people, the business can expand and serve more customers. Partners also can contribute more financial resources than a single individual. A second person in the business sometimes helps to balance the personalities and abilities of all partners.

DISADVANTAGES OF GENERAL PARTNERSHIPS

Like sole proprietorships, general partners also suffer from one major disadvantage: unlimited liability. A general partner's personal assets could be seized to pay a judgment, sometimes putting the general partnership in a precarious situation. The partners need their personal resources to run the business but risk losing them because of a business problem. This shortcoming, found in both sole proprietorships and general partnerships was one of the motivating factors behind the creation of a new type of business entity: the limited partnership.

In addition to financial and liability issues, the death of a general partner often dissolves the partnership. Although a partnership agreement may anticipate the death of a partner and make provisions to allow the business to continue after this event, in practical terms that may be impossible.

Limited Partnerships

In a **limited partnership**, there are two classifications of partners. There are general partners and limited partners. General partners are responsible for the day-to-day management of the business in the same way that general partners are in a regular partnership arrangement. Limited partners, by contrast, have no right to control day-to-day operations, but they also enjoy a protection that the general partners do not. Limited partners are protected by **limited liability**. This means that the extent of their financial loss in the business is limited to the extent of their financial contribution. If a limited partner puts up $1,000 in a limited partnership and the business fails or a large judgment is assessed against the business, the most that the limited partner can lose is her $1,000 investment. Limited partners will receive a percentage of the profits if the business does well but enjoy limited liability protection for losses. The general partners who run the Limited Partnership are not protected by limited liability but usually enjoy a larger percentage of the profits.

limited partnership: A partnership formed by general partners (who run the business and have liability for all partnership debts) and limited partners (who partly or fully finance the business, take no part in running it, and have no liability for partnership debts beyond the money they put in or promise to put in).

limited liability: A legal concept that, when used in the context of business, refers to the protection of an investor's personal assets. Potential loss is limited to the total amount invested in the venture, not the investor's total personal assets.

ETHICS FILE: Keeping Clients on Track with Business Filings

When legal professionals work with business clients, it is always important to keep in mind the legal requirements imposed on those various business entities. As we've already seen in this chapter, corporate officers who ignore the divisions between corporate and personal property face drastic sanctions. Sometimes, the legal professional is placed in the position of having to gently remind clients about these important differences. This means that a legal professional must always stay abreast of important changes in statutes and other laws governing business entities and be prepared to advise clients about these changes as they develop. In addition to annual filings with various government offices, there also may be Internal Revenue Service documents and other agency filings to consider. This is where attorneys or paralegals really earn their fees. Keeping clients apprised of legal and ethical obligations is not only god legal practice; it also helps keep the client on the right side of the law.

The Case of the Peeved Partner[1]
BEACH, Associate Justice.

Ben D. Kellis, assignee of a limited partnership interest in an apartment house project, sued defendant Ellis Ring, a general partner in the limited partnership and an officer or director in companies that allegedly provided management services for the apartment complex. Kellis sought declaratory relief and an injunction; he asked the court to make a "judicial determination and declaration as to plaintiff's and defendants' respective rights and duties with respect to said Limited Partnership and specifically whether by being an officer and director of, and having an interest in Ring Brothers Corporation and Ring Brothers Management Corporation and their affiliates and by doing acts in furtherance of such interest, defendant Ellis Ring is in violation of his fiduciary and trust relationships to plaintiff." The second cause of action was to enjoin Ring "from holding any employment or managerial position with or have any interest in Ring Brothers Corporation. Ring Brothers Management Corporation or affiliated companies." An order of dismissal was entered. The order sustaining the demurrer stated, "(t)he complaint pleads a cause of action for breach of fiduciary duty, but plaintiff has no standing to bring the action."

Kellis appeals from the order dismissing the action and from the order denying the motion for reconsideration or in the alternative for a new trial.

CONTENTIONS ON APPEAL:

Appellant contends:

1. The Uniform Limited Partnership Act does not bar an assignee of a limited partnership interest from suing the general partner for breach of fiduciary duty. A construction prohibiting such an action is contrary to the act, contrary to general principles of law and equity, and contrary to analogous cases.

2. If section 15519 is construed to deprive an assignee of a limited partnership interest of his right to bring an action to protect his property interest in the limited partnership, the statute is unconstitutional as an unlawful "taking" of property.

Respondent contends:

1. The trial court properly ruled that an assignee of a limited partnership interest has no authority or right to maintain an action against a general partner for breach of fiduciary duty. The assignee's rights are limited by section 15519.

2. The court should not hold section 15519 unconstitutional as the issue was not properly raised below, nor is any constitutional principle offended by a construction of the Limited Partnership Act which precludes an assignee from seeking to interfere in the management of the partnership and from obtaining information concerning partnership finances and business operations when the assignee has not alleged any damage to his sole right to income and profits.

DISCUSSION

1. Section 15519 delineates the rights of assignees of limited partners who are not substituted limited partners.

The Uniform Limited Partnership Act (§ 15501 et seq.) describes four classes of persons with interest in a limited partnership: general partners, limited partners, substituted limited partners, and assignees of a limited partners interest who do not become a substituted limited partner. (§§ 15501, 15519.)

Subsection 3, section 15519 describes the rights of an assignee who is not a substituted limited partner as follows: "An assignee, who does not become a substituted limited partner, has no right to require any information or account of the partnership transactions, to inspect the partnership books, or to vote on any of the matters as to which a limited partner would be entitled to vote pursuant to the provisions of section 15507 and the certificate of limited partnership; he is only entitled to receive the share of the profits or other compensation by way of income, or the return of his contributions, to which his assignor would otherwise be entitled."

Appellant contends that this section is not exclusive and must be read in conjunction with section 15529 which provides: "In any case not provided for in this act the rules of law and equity . . . shall govern."

Respondent, while conceding that appellant would have the right to sue for damages if his profits or other compensation were impaired, contends that subsection 3 defines all the rights of the assignee who is not a substituted limited partner and that under that section appellant does not have standing to sue.

We agree with respondent that section 15519 limits the rights of assignees of limited partners who are not substituted limited partners. While appellant has a right to receive "the share of the profits or other compensation by way of income, or the return of his contributions to which his assignor would otherwise be entitled," he has no right to interfere in the management of the limited partnership.

Viewed forthrightly, substantively and apart from the niceties of pleading and form it is clear that appellant seeks to interfere in the management of the limited partnership totally contrary to the statutory provisions.

Any other construction of section 15519 would thwart the legitimate purposes of the statutory scheme. Those purposes are based on the fact that limited partners themselves have only circumscribed opportunities to inquire into or challenge the management of the partnership, for reasons associated with the very nature of the limited partnership relation. Even greater restrictions are understandable for one who is involved only as an assignee of that interest and who for whatever reasons has not been accorded the status of a substituted limited partner. Thus it may be that the very assignee at bench may have sought entry into the partnership in question as a limited partner and had been refused such status by the general partner. Possibly the presence of the assignee would have chilled or prevented the association of the current limited partners if he had been accepted as such; or it may be that the assignee having sought a limited partnership interest and been refused found a person acceptable to the general partner who purchased a limited interest for the sole purpose of transferring that interest to the assignee at bench and did not make such purpose known to the general partner. Personality is the very essence of a general partnership and although not as inherently pervasive in a limited partner, it is clear that the section 15519 and the nature of this legal entity does place a premium on personality. The law has provided for the limited preservation of that relationship. It is reasonable to assume that a general partner, about to form a limited partnership for the conduct of a business would not bring into the business association limited partners with whom he had unfavorable contacts or who he considered meticulously curious or one who he thought was litigation minded anymore than he would have a general partner subject to the same shortcomings. One conclusion clearly stands out. A person definitely rejected as a limited partner could nevertheless by becoming an assignee of an acceptable limited partnership defeat the decision of those who originally formed the limited partnership.

It is apparent that because appellant may have acquired his assignment under one of the several circumstances described above, his right to raise the kind of issue he seeks to present may justifiably be less than one who was a participant as a limited or substitute partner. When the statute provides that one who has come into his interest by assignment without more "Has no right to require any information or account of the partnership transactions," has "No right to inspect the partnership books," no right "To vote on any of the matters" etc. and that he is "Only entitled to receive a share of the profits" etc. the restrictive character of the language is intentional even if not categorically exclusive. On the facts pleaded at bench we cannot come to any other conclusion.

In summary, we hold that beyond the limits described in the statute a mere assignee has no voice in the internal management of a partnership. The statute does not thus deprive an assignee of property, but merely recognizes the different business associations and conditions that persons may lawfully make and the legitimate reasons therefor.

The judgment (order of dismissal) is affirmed.

Case Questions:

1. Why did the court rule that the plaintiff was not a person who has an "interest" in the limited partnership?

2. Under what circumstances would the appellant be entitled to bring suit about the management of the limited partnership?

3. What rights does the court say the appellant is entitled to from the limited partnership agreement?

4. According to the court, what rights do limited partners have in the management of a limited partnership?

5. What role does "personality" play in general partnerships and limited partnerships?

Limited Liability Companies

limited liability company:
A limited liability company is a cross between partnership and a corporation owned by members who may manage the company directly or delegate to officers or managers who are similar to a corporation's directors.

Limited liability companies (LLC) are a relatively recent invention. They resemble limited partnerships but have legal protections that are similar to those of a corporation. Like limited partnerships, investors in an LLC enjoy limited liability. However, the day-to-day business of an LLC is run more like a corporation.

FORMING A LIMITED LIABILITY COMPANY

In order to form a limited liability company, a company must file several documents with the state. One of the most important is the Articles of Organization. This document contains the basic information about the company, including the company name, registered agent, and the names of the persons forming the company. The LLC also may file an operating agreement that sets out the duties of the members and details how the business will be run.

NAMING A LIMITED LIABILITY COMPANY

Sidebar:
Many states passed legislation authorizing the creation of limited liability companies in the 1970s and 1980s.

The name of a limited liability company must contain the phrase "Limited Liability Company" or some other easily recognizable abbreviation, such as "LLC." This name requirement places individuals on notice that they are dealing with a business that is protected by limited liability. Therefore, the individual may not be able to obtain judgments from individual owners, only from business assets.

Like corporations, limited liability companies designate agents who must be served with lawsuits. LLCs are also required to file annual reports with the state secretary of state's office.

ADVANTAGES OF LIMITED LIABILITY COMPANIES

Limited liability companies have several advantages. For instance, they can take advantage of the protection of limited liability. They also can enjoy some of the flexibility of a partnership, the financial advantages of spreading investment over a larger pool of individuals, and the ability of individual owners to pass through losses on their personal income tax returns.

ORGANIZATION OF A LIMITED LIABILITY COMPANY

Individuals who own shares in limited liability companies are referred to as "members," not partners or shareholders. The day-to-day management of a limited liability company is handled by "managers." Unlike limited partnerships, in which only the general partners have the right to manage the company, all members enjoy this right. However, the members usually delegate this responsibility to specific individuals.

Although limited liability companies do enjoy the protection of limited liability, there are other concerns. For one thing, setting up an LLC (or a corporation) can be expensive. These charges come at a time when the new business is usually strapped for cash.

Corporations

A **corporation** is a business entity that is, in many ways, unique. A corporation isn't just another form of business. Investors in a corporation enjoy the full range of limited liability, but the real strength of a corporation goes beyond that concept. A corporation enjoys both substantial protection and substantial freedom.

corporation: An organization that is formed under state corporate law exists, for legal purposes, as a separate being or an "artificial person." The stockholders have no liability for corporate debts beyond the value of their stock.

CREATING A CORPORATION

Although corporations enjoy limited liability similar to limited partnerships and limited liability companies, a corporation is an entirely different animal as far as the law is concerned. What makes a corporation so unique is that unlike a limited liability company, a corporation is considered be an artificial person. Like a person, a corporation can own property, hire employees, pay taxes, and even survive the death of the people who created it. Once created, a corporation continues to exist separate and distinct from the people that compose it.

> **Sidebar:**
> Corporations even enjoy some of the constitutional protections that natural persons do. For instance, corporations have limited rights of freedom of speech of under the First Amendment.

TYPES OF CORPORATIONS

There is a wide range of corporation types, ranging from small privately held corporations to huge multinational corporations with offices scattered across the globe. Whether the corporation is a small family affair, or a huge corporate entity, there are some features that all have in common.

CORPORATE SHAREHOLDERS

The persons who own the corporation are called **shareholders**. A person can buy a share in a corporation and this share represents a percentage of ownership. The more shares that a person owns, the more of an ownership

shareholder: A person who owns shares in a corporation.

dividend: A share of profits or property; usually a payment per share of the corporation's stock.

interest she has in the corporation. Shareholders are also entitled to an annual payment, referred to as a **dividend**, based on corporate profits.

CORPORATE OFFICERS AND DIRECTORS

Shareholders do not engage in the day-to-day management of the business. Corporations have officers who manage corporate affairs. These officers are responsible for negotiating with vendors, hiring and firing employees, and all of the other tasks that we would associate with any business manager. Corporations also have boards of directors. Directors decide on long-term goals and strategies for the corporation, which they then put into effect through the corporate officers.

Although shareholders do not have any direct control over corporate affairs, they do have indirect control. For instance, shareholders vote on the appointment of the members of the corporate board of directors. If the shareholders are dissatisfied with the performance of a particular director, they may vote to remove that director.

Like limited liability companies and limited partnerships, corporate shareholders also are protected by limited liability. In this context, a shareholder's liability is limited to the number of shares he or she has purchased in the corporation. The shareholder's maximum possible liability is the extent of investment in corporate shares. Corporate officers and directors, by contrast, have substantially more liability than shareholders.

DISADVANTAGES OF CORPORATIONS

Although the corporate business form enjoys great benefits, both in terms of business flexibility and legal protection for its investors, corporations do have some disadvantages. For one thing, shareholders do not enjoy the "pass through" provisions for income tax purposes that are seen in sole proprietorships, general partnerships, and other business structures that we discussed in this chapter. A corporation pays its own income taxes. This means that a corporation's net losses for the year cannot be reflected on individual shareholders' income tax returns. However, this disadvantage is more than offset by the tremendous advantages conferred on the corporate structure.

ADVANTAGES OF CORPORATIONS

As an artificial person, a corporation may own property, negotiate contracts, and, in many ways, enjoy a degree of flexibility that resembles sole proprietors or partnerships.

Corporate Existence

Among the advantages of the corporate structure, one of the most obvious is that a corporation does not die. As we've seen in our discussions about sole proprietorships and general partnerships, the death of the business owner usually terminates the business structure. This is not true with corporations. Although a corporation may cease to exist because of bankruptcy or by merger with another corporation, it does not cease to exist when individual shareholders, directors, or officers die. This gives a corporation a sense of continuity and reliability that attracts many investors.

Transfer of Ownership

Another advantage of a corporation structure is that ownership in the corporation is easily transferable from one individual to another. Shares in corporations are bought and sold by the millions every day on the various stock exchanges around the world. Share ownership, in the form of stock certificates, is a source of wealth for millions of people. Revenue from stocks comes not only from declared dividends, but also from the innate value of the company. Many people purchase stocks out of the belief that a specific corporation will generate future income and make the stock more valuable over time (see Exhibit 15-2).

Sidebar:
Even the disadvantage of not being able to pass through profits and losses on an individual income tax return disappears with a specific type of corporation. An S Corporation, which usually consists of a small closely held business, permits a certain amount of losses to be passed through on the income tax returns of the individual owners.

☐   Who will record corporate minutes?

☐   How should the corporate seal be aquired?

☐   Should the company issue stock certificates?

☐   What should the corporate bylaws state?

☐   How does the company acquire a business checking account?

☐   Are there any issues regarding patents?

☐   Are there any issues regarding copyrights?

☐   How easy will it be to borrow money?

☐   Should the company arrange for unemployment insurance?

EXHIBIT 15-2: Questions that often arise in forming a corporation.

STEPS IN FORMING A CORPORATION

All states have rules about how a corporation is formed. In most situations, parties form a corporation by filing Articles of Incorporation with the state. In many states, the Secretary of State's office is responsible for maintaining records on corporations.

Articles of Incorporation

The articles of incorporation set out the basic details of the corporate entity. The articles will contain information on:

- The name of the corporation
- The number of shares the corporation is authorized to issue
- The classes of stock issued
- The name and address of the Registered Agent
- The names and addresses of the principal incorporators

States charge a fee for filing articles of incorporation that varies considerably from state to state. Once the articles are filed, the next step in creating a corporation is the organizational meeting.

Corporate Organizational Meeting

Once appropriate documentation has been filed with the state, the next step in creating a corporation is the organizational meeting. This meeting, held among the people who create the corporation, has several purposes. First of all, the parties elect officers for the corporation and then enact bylaws for the day-to-day management of the corporation. The corporate officers will decide how much stock to issue. Other matters that may come up at the organizational meeting include creating a corporate seal for all documents to be signed by the corporate officers and what other licenses and permits must be obtained in the corporate name in order to run the business (see Exhibit 15-3).

> The U.S. Securities and Exchange Commission maintains a database of publicly held corporations across the United States. The Database is called EDGAR and can be accessed at <http://www.sec.gov>.

EXHIBIT 15-3: U.S. Securities and Exchange Commission.

Piercing the Corporate Veil

Once a corporation is created, it operates as an entity that is separate and distinct from its creators. This separation is not only a feature of the corporate character; it is actually a necessity. Business owners sometimes run into trouble when they ignore the distinction between corporate property and private property.

One concern for any corporate officer or director is the legal principle of "piercing the corporate veil." This doctrine holds that when a person uses corporate property interchangeably with his private property, the court may disregard the existence of the corporation and seize the person's personal assets. These actions often come up in the context of small, closely held corporations in which there are few shareholders and officers. Occasionally, an officer may feel the temptation to ignore the concept of separate corporate property and treat all assets as his own. In such a case, the officer may take possession of, borrow against, or even sell corporate property without permission. In such cases, the courts may rule that the corporate structure is simply a sham and permit creditors and others to ignore the corporate structure in pursuing a judgment against the individual.

The Case of the Overpaid President[2]

HALLER, Associate Justice.

laintiff Donald F. Sammis and defendant Robert Stafford formed a corporation in 1984. Approximately five years later, Sammis brought two actions against Stafford. First, he brought a shareholder's derivative suit, alleging Stafford committed misconduct while he was president and majority shareholder. Second, he brought his own individual action, alleging Stafford committed fraud in inducing Sammis to transfer his majority shareholder position to Stafford. The actions were consolidated for trial; the parties waived jury.

After trial, the court entered judgment in Stafford's favor on the fraud action. Sammis does not appeal from this ruling. The court entered judgment against Stafford on the shareholder's derivative action, awarding Sammis $64,801. Sammis appeals from this ruling, contending the court erred in failing to award additional damages, principally the amount of Stafford's annual salary and pension benefits from 1990 through 1992.

We conclude Stafford's conduct was properly ratified under Corporations Code section 310, subdivision (a)(3). We conclude substantial evidence supported the court's finding that Stafford proved his salary was fair and reasonable within the meaning of the code section. Accordingly, we affirm the judgment.

FACTUAL AND PROCEDURAL BACKGROUND

In 1984, Sammis and Stafford formed Fabric and Structure Technology, Inc. (FAST), to design, manufacture, and market fabric structures. Sammis initially contributed $2,500 and Stafford contributed $2,450. Sammis thus owned 51 percent interest and Stafford owned 49 percent interest. Sammis held the majority interest because he was responsible for arranging financing and guarantying loans.

FAST's board of directors consisted of Sammis and Stafford. Stafford was the corporate president responsible for all aspects of the business. Although Sammis was also an officer, his role was primarily limited to providing financing. Stafford received a salary. Sammis did not.

From 1984 through 1986, FAST developed patents related to fabric building structures. FAST then began manufacturing the product. By 1988, FAST owed Sammis approximately $272,500. In addition, Sammis had arranged and personally guaranteed a $300,000 line of credit for FAST.

In 1988, FAST discontinued its manufacturing operation and focused on developing patents and licensing the patents. Stafford thereafter began negotiating licensing agreements with two entities. During the negotiations with one of the entities (Canvas Specialties), Canvas's manager, Irwin Sack, told Stafford that Canvas would not enter into a license agreement unless Stafford was either the sole owner or the majority shareholder of FAST.

In response to Sack's concerns, on June 22, 1989, Sammis and Stafford executed a written agreement (entitled "Shareholders' Agreement"), in which Sammis sold 2 percent of his FAST stock to Stafford. After that time, Stafford owned 51 percent of the corporation. As part of this Shareholders' Agreement, the parties agreed that if any employee was paid more than $30,000, FAST would enter into an employment contract with the employee and board approval would be required for the contract.

FAST thereafter entered into licensing agreements with Canvas and another entity. As a result of these agreements, FAST received approximately $725,000. FAST used these funds to retire corporate debt and to repay obligations owing to Sammis.

In approximately May 1990, Sammis failed to return Stafford's telephone calls and refused to countersign checks. Concerned by Sammis's refusal to cooperate, Stafford consulted FAST's attorney, Michael Shea. Shea suggested that Stafford call a shareholder's meeting. Shea said that if Sammis failed to attend the meeting, Stafford could reduce the Board of Directors to one, elect himself to that position, and then eliminate the requirement that Sammis approve FAST's expenditures.

Relying on this advice, Stafford noticed a shareholder's meeting for June 27, 1990. Sammis received the notice, but did not attend. At the June 27 meeting, Stafford created a board of one and elected himself as the sole board member. Stafford then took action on several matters, including signing an employment agreement authorizing a salary of up to $150,000 for himself, establishing a pension for himself, and hiring his wife and paying her both salary and a pension. Before 1989, Stafford was paid less than $50,000 annually. In 1989, he was paid approximately $86,000. After Stafford elected himself sole director, he paid himself approximately $118,000 in 1990, $146,000 in 1991, and $127,000 in 1992.

In June 1991, Sammis learned of Stafford's actions. After protracted negotiations, the parties agreed to reconstitute the board to five directors. Stafford elected himself, his wife, and his sister. Sammis elected himself and his son.

Six months later, on January 27, 1992, a board meeting was held, at which a majority of the board (Stafford, his wife, and his sister) voted to ratify all of Stafford's actions while he was the sole director.

In December 1992, Sammis bought all of Stafford's shares in FAST for $156,000. Sammis filed two actions arising from the foregoing events. First, Sammis, on behalf of the corporation, brought a shareholder's derivative suit alleging Stafford committed misconduct while he was majority shareholder in that he (a) paid himself excessive salary and benefits and (b) diverted corporate funds for personal uses. Second, Sammis filed an action against Stafford, alleging that in 1989 Stafford fraudulently induced Sammis to transfer 2 percent of FAST stock to Stafford and falsely promised he would limit his salary to $30,000. The two cases were consolidated.

After a 10-day trial, the court issued a written statement of decision. The court explained it was ruling in Sammis's favor on the shareholder's derivative suit because Stafford improperly diverted

$64,801 of corporate funds for his personal use. The court determined, however, that Stafford's salary and pension benefits were "neither excessive nor inappropriate" and thus did not award Sammis any damages in connection with Stafford's salary. The court additionally ruled in Stafford's favor on Sammis's fraud action, finding Sammis failed to prove he was fraudulently induced to transfer his majority interest to Stafford or that Stafford had agreed to limit his salary to $30,000. The court thus entered a $64,801 judgment against Stafford on the shareholder's derivative suit and entered judgment in Stafford's favor on the fraud suit.

DISCUSSION

Sammis challenges the court's ruling that Stafford's salary and pension benefits were not a misappropriation of corporate funds. Sammis contends Stafford's conduct after 1989 was not properly authorized and therefore the court erred in failing to determine Stafford must return his salary and benefits received from the corporation during that time.

Section 310 governs situations where a matter before a board of directors is one in which a director has an interest. Section 310(a) provides that a vote on the matter is not void or voidable because the interested director is present at the board meeting if one of three alternatives are satisfied:

"(1) The material facts as to the transaction and as to such director's interest are fully disclosed or known to the shareholders and such contract or transaction is approved by the shareholders (Section 153) in good faith, with the shares owned by the interested director or directors not being entitled to vote thereon, or

"(2) The material facts as to the transaction and as to such director's interest are fully disclosed or known to the board or committee, and the board or committee authorizes, approves or ratifies the contract or transaction in good faith by a vote sufficient without counting the vote of the interested director or directors and the contract or transaction is just and reasonable as to the corporation at the time it is authorized, approved, or ratified, or

"(3) As to contracts or transactions not approved as provided in paragraph (1) or (2) of this subdivision, the person asserting the validity of the contract or transaction sustains the burden of proving that the contract or transaction was just and reasonable as to the corporation at the time it was authorized, approved or ratified." (§310, subd. (a)(1)(2)(3), italics added.)

At trial, Stafford acknowledged that a one-person board is not proper under California law (see §212) and therefore his actions from June 1990 through January 1992 were not initially authorized. Stafford, however, relied on the January 27, 1992 ratification vote (see ante at p. 592) to argue that his 1990–1992 conduct as director was nonetheless valid because the conduct was later ratified by a majority of a five-person board. Stafford recognized such board approval did not fall within the first two statutory alternatives (§310(a)(1) or §310(a)(2)) because his vote was necessary to obtain a majority to approve the resolution. Stafford maintained, however, that the approval was proper as to section 310(a)(3), italicized above.

In its statement of decision, the trial court stated it did "not find that [Stafford] misapplied any funds of the corporation with regard to the salary paid to himself." Although the court did not specifically identify section 310(a), Sammis did not raise any objections to the statement of decision. We therefore are required to presume the trial court made all findings necessary to support the judgment. Accordingly, we interpret the court's statement to mean the court found Stafford proved his salary was "just and reasonable" within the meaning of section 310(a)(3).

Sammis contends section 310(a) is inapplicable because Stafford's salary was not an "interested director" transaction, but rather it was an "ultra vires" act. " '[U]ltra vires' refers to an act which is beyond the powers conferred upon a corporation by its charter or by the laws of the state of incorporation. . . ." A corporation may recover damages when a director engages in ultra vires activities, and the director may not defend such action by alleging ratification. If, however, the director's act was within the corporate powers, but was performed without authority or in an unauthorized manner, the act is not ultra vires.

There is no evidence in the record that Stafford acted beyond the purpose or power of the corporation. Rather, Stafford's acts were within the scope of FAST's corporate powers, but were not validly authorized by a properly constituted board of directors. Thus, Stafford's acts were not ultra vires and therefore were subject to later ratification.

Sammis alternatively argues Stafford's conduct was not properly ratified because as a matter of law section 310(a)(3) applies only where the board "authorized, approved or ratified" the action, without the vote of the interested director.

We are required to interpret a statute according to its plain meaning. In so doing, we must consider the language in context of the entire statutory scheme.

Applying these principles, we conclude the January 27, 1992 ratification vote could qualify as a ratification within the meaning of section 310(a)(3). Section 310(a)(3) applies "to contracts or transactions not approved as provided in paragraph (1) or (2) of this subdivision. . . ." In other words, section 310(a)(3) addresses the situation where the approval was based on a vote by the interested director.

Considering section 310(a) as a whole, this interpretation makes sense. If section 310(a)(3)'s phrase "authorized, approved or ratified" was construed to mean only those approvals made without the interested director's vote, then section 310(a)(3) would be unnecessary. Section 310(a)(2) and section 310(a)(3) both permit interested director transactions where the board of directors approves the transaction. The sections differ, however, depending on whether the approval was obtained with or without the interested director's vote and whether there was full disclosure. Where a disinterested majority approves the transactions and there was full disclosure, section 310(a)(2) applies, and the burden of proof is on the person challenging the transaction. Where, however, the approval was not obtained from a disinterested board vote, section 310(a)(3) applies and requires the person seeking to uphold the transaction to prove it was "just and reasonable" to the corporation.

Section 310's legislative committee comment, which discusses each of the three "independent procedures for the validation of 'interested' transactions," supports our view. In referring to sections 310(a)(1) and 310(a)(2), the comment makes clear that the specified "approval" refers to the requirement that the vote be without the vote of the interested director. By contrast, with respect to section 310(a)(3), the comment does not mention the disinterested vote requirement and instead states, "a transaction may be validated if the person asserting its validity sustains the burden of proving that the transaction was just and reasonable as to the corporation at the time it was approved."

Finally, we reject Sammis's reliance on his expert's opinion that the January 27, 1992 ratification was ineffective because "it was done in a blanket fashion, not a separate consideration of each item of conduct. . . ." Sammis fails to direct us to any statutory or decisional law prohibiting a general ratification as occurred here.

DISPOSITION
Judgment affirmed.

Case Questions:

1. What was the basis of the plaintiff's shareholder's derivative suit in this case?

2. What role did ratification play in this case?

3. Was the salary and other benefits that Stafford voted himself a misappropriation of corporate funds?

4. Were Stafford's actions ultra vires? Why or why not?

5. What are the allegations in this case about a "blanket ratification?"

The Role of the Legal Team in Creating a Business

So far, our discussion has centered on the complexities of creating new business structures. Businesspeople often seek out legal advice in both creating and running their businesses. They may seek legal advice on a wide variety of issues, from creating the business to tax consequences of liquidating it. As a paralegal in a business firm, you will be called on to engage in many different activities to help create a business. Legal professionals often are involved in every step of business activities and assist with the drafting and filing of Articles of Incorporation to bankruptcy actions if the business isn't able to stay afloat.

LICENSES AND PERMITS

Sidebar:
Paralegals are often called upon to research the applicable zoning certification.

New business owners are often ignorant of the many different types of licenses and permits that are required to run a business. For instance, local ordinances may require business licenses or other permits to run specific types of business. If the business will be run out of the client's home, there is also the issue of zoning permits. If the zoning certification does not permit the type of business that the client wishes to run, then a request for zoning variance may be required. In addition to business licenses, there are a wide variety of other types of permits and certifications that may be required.

Business Case File

Olive Hill Economic Development Corporation

Beverly Carlton started Olive Hill Economic Development Corporation (EDC) four years ago as a way of helping serve low- to moderate-income people in rural North Carolina. For Carlton, the choice of business entity was critical. Creating a nonprofit corporation requires great attention to detail, but the payoff comes in the protection that the corporate form offers. It frees Olive Hill to concentrate on its mission.

"The most important thing that we do is direct traffic. We put them on the right path to finding the information that they are looking for for business, development, or for their personal home or business, or anything in general," said Carlton.

Beverly Carlton works with Jasper Hemphill to educate people about finances and to help them reach some of their personal goals. "We're in the business of helping people achieve the American dream," said Hemphill.

Getting an economic development corporation started was not easy. "It took a lot of research," said Carlton, "both to find out what the process is to get a nonprofit organization going and then attending a lot of conferences. I talked to a lot of people across the state that were in the practice already."

Jasper Hemphill

Olive Hill EDC has three main goals in its service to the community.

"Our three main components are affordable housing, business development and economic empowerment," said Hemphill.

"The best part of my job is helping people realize their dreams and fulfilling their needs," said Carlton. "Over the four years, we've helped about 400 people."

By offering programs on home buyer education, personal finance, micro enterprise loans, among many others, Olive Hill EDC is making a valuable contribution to its community and helping others to create new business opportunities and achieve their lifelong dreams.

Chapter Summary:

There are many different types of business organization models. The sole proprietorship is the most basic and, in many ways, the most flexible. When a business is a sole proprietorship, the business is owned and run by a single individual. This individual has the right to control all aspects of the business and to take all the profits from the business. However, a sole proprietorship has certain disadvantages. Perhaps the most important disadvantage is the fact that a sole proprietor's personal assets are not protected when a judgment is entered against the business. Other types of business organizations, including limited partnerships, limited liability companies, and corporations, all enjoy some additional measure of protection. With limited liability companies and corporations, members enjoy limited liability. Limited liability refers to the concept of a member's financial liability limited to the extent of his investment. Paralegals working with business clients often are called on to do much of the legwork in tracking down business licenses, permits, inspections, and other statutory requirements for a new business.

WEB SITES

New York Department of State
http://www.dos.state.ny.us/
Contains numerous links and forms for the creation of corporations, limited liability companies, and limited partnerships.

Texas Secretary of State
http://www.sos.state.tx.us
This site has a large database of business forms and publications to help people negotiate the world of business entities.

SBA Online Women's Business Center
http://www.onlinewbc.gov/womens_business.html
Provides a wide range of links and other information for women considering opening a small business.

REVIEW QUESTIONS

1. What is a sole proprietorship?
2. Are there any tax advantages to a sole proprietorship? Explain.
3. What is the difference between a sole proprietorship and other forms of business?
4. What are some of the legal or liability concerns for a sole proprietor?
5. Explain the concept of unlimited liability.
6. Why is the choice of business organization so important?
7. What are some examples of licenses or permits that a new business owner might be required to obtain?
8. What is a general partnership? How do general partnerships compare to sole proprietorships?
9. What is a limited partnership?
10. Explain the role of general partners and limited partners in a limited partnership.
11. Explain the concept of limited liability.
12. What is a limited liability company?

13. How is a corporation different from other forms of business organizations?
14. What duties and benefits are conferred on corporate shareholders?
15. What is the function of a corporate board of directors?
16. Who is responsible for the day-to-day management of a corporation?
17. What is undercapitalization?
18. This chapter states that corporations are considered to be "artificial persons." Explain.
19. What advantages does a corporation structure bring to a business?
20. What are the consequences to business owners when they ignore the distinction between personal property and corporate property?

HANDS-ON ASSIGNMENT

Suppose that you have a client who is interested in creating a corporation in your state. What online, state-level resources can you locate to help provide not only information but also forms and other documentation to begin the process?

PRACTICAL APPLICATION

1. Contact your local government agencies and ask about the requirements for business licenses and permits to run the following types of businesses:

   An attorney's office

   A certified public accountant

   A paralegal firm

   A pharmacy

2. Prepare a checklist of questions that should be asked of a client who is seeking to create a new business as a sole proprietor.

3. Locate your state secretary of state's office or other governmental agency that is responsible for maintaining filings on business entities like corporations. What type of information can you locate on around the Web site? For instance, can you do a search of corporate names? What types of forms are available on this Web site?

HELP THIS BUSINESS

Olive Hill Development Corporation has decided to open an operation in your town. What types of business permits, licenses, and other documentation would it need to open a non-profit corporation? Contact your local government and find out.

KEY TERMS

corporation

dividend

general partnership

limited liability

limited liability company

limited partnership

shareholder

undercapitalization

unlimited liability

ENDNOTES

1. *Kellis v. Ring*, 92 Cal.App.3d 854, 155 Cal.Rptr. 297 (1979).
2. *Sammis v. Stafford*, 48 Cal.App.4th 1935, 56 Cal.Rptr.2d 589 (Cal.App. 4 Dist., 1996).

 For additional resources, visit our Web site at www.westlegalstudies.com

APPENDIX: BASIC CONTRACT FORMS

This section contains some contract clauses and complete contract forms. These forms are for reference purposes only and should not be used in business transactions.

Contract Employing a Law Firm

STATE OF PLACID

COUNTY OF BARNES

EMPLOYMENT CONTRACT

THIS AGREEMENT, made and entered into this the _____ day of _____,20___, by and between _____, hereinafter referred to as "Client"; and CLARENCE D. ARROW, P.A., hereinafter referred to as "Attorneys";

WITNESSETH:

WHEREAS, Client has a claim against _____ _____ arising out of an accident which occurred on or about the day of _____, 20___, and desires to employ the Attorneys on a contingent fee basis;

NOW, THEREFORE, the Attorneys agree to represent, through trial court, as attorney for the Client and the Client agrees to pay the Attorneys Thirty-Three and One-Third (33 1/3%) percent of the amount recovered or which may be recovered in this matter, whether by compromise or settlement at any time before suit is instituted or by compromise, settlement or judgment after suit is instituted, plus expenses incurred in the preparation of the case. Both parties agree that neither party will compromise or settle this action without consent of the other party.

This the _____ day of _____, 20___.

_____
Attorney
CLARENCE D. ARROW, P.A.

Agreement between a real estate agent and a seller to list property for sale

Brokerage Agreement

This agreement, dated the 20th day of July, 2003 between Pruitt Real Estate Professionals, Inc. and Sal Seller provides the following:

Sal Seller grants to Pruitt Real Estate Professionals, Inc. the right to show the property located at 21 Maple Street, Placid City, Placid for a period of 180 days from the date of this agreement.

Sal Seller appoints * to act as his agent for purposes of listing this property for sale.

The property shall be sold for a purchase price of not less than $150,000.

Upon the presenting of a qualified buyer for said real estate, Pruitt Real Estate Professionals, Inc. shall be entitled to a commission of 6% of the purchase price.

Sal Seller represents that he is sole owner, in fee simple of the property located at 21 Maple Street and agrees to convey said property by general warranty deed if and when Pruitt Real Estate Professionals, Inc., presents a qualified buyer, ready, willing and able to purchase the property.

In witness of this agreement, the parties have affixed their signatures to this agreement.

This the 20th day of July, 2003.

_____

Sal Seller, Owner

_____

Prudence Pruitt
President and CEO of Pruitt
Real Estate Professionals, Inc.

Breach of contract clause provision

The parties hereby agree that is payment is not made within fifteen days of payment date, then the agreement shall be null and void. All rights, obligations, covenants, guarantees and warranties of whatever kind shall terminate as if this agreement had never been entered into between the parties listed below.[1]

Parol Evidence clause

This contract contains all of the promises and obligations between the parties. All previous communications between the parties, whether by oral, electronic or written form that are not contained in this contract are expressly withdrawn and shall not form the basis of any right, obligation, promise or guarantee under this contract.[2]

The following forms are taken from *Advising Small Businesses: Forms,* available through International Thomson Company.

§ 48:2. AUTHORITY OF PERSONAL REPRESENTATIVE TO OPERATE BUSINESS

"The following provision is designed to be included in the will of an individual who holds an interest in one or more closely held businesses. The provision makes it clear that the personal representative of the individual's estate has the authority to hold and deal with the business interests."

SECTION 1. BUSINESS INTERESTS

I authorize the Personal Representative of my estate to hold, manage, and operate any interest in any sole proprietorship or closely held partnership, limited partnership, joint venture, limited liability company, corporation, or other business entity (Business Interest) owned by my estate for such period of time as is deemed by the Personal Representative to be in the best interests of my estate. Any Business Interest shall be operated at the risk of my estate, and not at the risk of iothe Personal Representative. Unless otherwise provided in my will or by law, the profits and losses from the operation of the Business Interest shall inure to the benefit of, or be chargeable to, my estate as a whole. The Personal Representative may perform any other act or exercise any other power that may be exercised by a person owning a similar Business Interest in the person's individual capacity that the Personal Representative deems necessary or advisable in connection with the operation, retention, or disposition of a Business Interest, including without limitation, the power to:

1.1 *Create Entities.* Form corporations, limited liability companies, limited partnerships, or other entities for the purpose of holding and operating Business Interests; transfer to those new entities part of my estate in exchange for stock, other ownership interests, securities, or obligations of the new entities; and continue to hold the same.

1.2 *Changes in Form.* Cause or permit the reorganization, consolidation, merger, liquidation, or other similar change in a Business Interest.

1.3 *Exercise Options.* Exercise conversion, subscription, purchase, or other options.

1.4 *Securities.* Deposit, surrender, or exchange securities.

1.5 *Voting Arrangements.* Enter into and perform the terms of voting trusts, proxies, and other voting arrangements, and make agreements or subscriptions in connection therewith.[3]

§ 2:2. CHECKLIST OF ADVANTAGES AND DISADVANTAGES OF BUSINESS ENTITIES[4]

CHECKLIST OF BUSINESS ENTITY ADVANTAGES AND DISADVANTAGES

1. Sole Proprietorship
    a. Advantages:
        (1) ☐ No organizational formalities.
        (2) ☐ Decision making is informal and centered in the owner.
        (3) ☐ No qualification requirements for doing business in other states.
        (4) ☐ Minimal reporting to governmental entities.
        (5) ☐ Business profits are subject to only one tax, at the individual level, and are not subject to double tax as would be the case if the profits were realized by a C corporation.
        (6) ☐ Losses are available on the owner's personal income tax return and can offset other income (subject to the passive loss rules).
    b. Disadvantages:
        (1) ☐ Owner has unlimited liability for obligations and liabilities of the business.
        (2) ☐ Death or disability of owner terminates business.
        (3) ☐ Sale or other transfer of business requires transfer of individual assets.
        (4) ☐ No opportunity to utilize equity capital contributed by persons other than the owner.
        (5) ☐ Business profits are taxed as income to the owner and, as a result, will be subject to self-employment tax as well as income tax.
2. General Partnership
    a. Advantages:
        (1) ☐ Multiple owners can provide a combination of individual resources and talents.
        (2) ☐ Minimal formalities are required for organization.
        (3) ☐ Decision making may be informal.
        (4) ☐ No qualification requirements for doing business in other states.
        (5) ☐ Minimal reporting to governmental entities.
        (6) ☐ Business profits are subject to only one tax, at the individual partner level, and are not subject to double tax as would be the case if the profits were earned by a C corporation.
        (7) ☐ Losses are available on the partners' personal income tax returns and can offset other income (subject to the passive loss rules).

(8) ☐ Special allocations may be made for income tax purposes.

(9) ☐ Disproportionate distributions may be made to partners.

b. Disadvantages:

(1) ☐ Partners have unlimited liability for obligations and liabilities of the business.

(2) ☐ Death, disability, or withdrawal of a partner may terminate partnership.

(3) ☐ All partners have the right to participate in management.

(4) ☐ All partners have broad authority to act on behalf of, and incur debts and liabilities for, the partnership.

(5) ☐ Business profits are taxed as income to the individual partners and, as a result, may be subject to self-employment tax as well as income tax.

3. Limited Partnership

a. Advantages:

(1) ☐ Limited partners enjoy limited liability.

(2) ☐ Only general partners participate in management so that limited partners can be equity owners without the general partners giving up control.

(3) ☐ There are no limitations on the number or types of partners.

(4) ☐ Existence is unaffected by the death or transfer of interest by a limited partner.

(5) ☐ Business profits are subject to only one tax, at the individual partner level, and are not subject to double tax as would be the case if the profits were earned by a C corporation.

(6) ☐ Losses are available on the partners' personal income tax returns and can offset other income (subject to the at risk rules and passive loss rules).

(7) ☐ Special allocations may be made for income tax purposes.

(8) ☐ Disproportionate distributions may be made to partners.

b. Disadvantages:

(1) ☐ Formalities are required for organization.

(2) ☐ Qualification is required for doing business in other states.

(3) ☐ Regular reporting to governmental entities is required.

(4) ☐ General partners have unlimited liability for obligations and liabilities of the business.

(5) ☐ Death, disability, or withdrawal of a general partner may terminate partnership.

(6) ☐ Limited partners have no ability to participate in management or decision making.

(7) ☐ Business profits are taxed as income to the individual partners and, as a result, may be subject to self-employment tax as well as income tax to the extent they are allocated to general partners.

(8) ☐ Transfer of interests may be subject to securities law regulation.

4. Limited Liability Company
   a. Advantages:
      (1) ☐ All members enjoy limited liability.
      (2) ☐ No limitation on the number or types of members.
      (3) ☐ Centralized management is available if an LLC is manager managed.
      (4) ☐ Business profits are subject to only one tax, at the individual member level, and are not subject to double tax as would be the case if the profits were earned by a C corporation.
      (5) ☐ Losses are available on the members' personal income tax returns and can offset other income (subject to the at risk rules and passive loss rules).
      (6) ☐ Special allocations may be made for income tax purposes.
      (7) ☐ Disproportionate distributions may be made to members.
   b. Disadvantages:
      (1) ☐ Formalities are required for organization and operation.
      (2) ☐ Qualification is required for doing business in other states.
      (3) ☐ Regular reporting to governmental entities is required.
      (4) ☐ Termination results from the death, disability, or withdrawal of a member under the laws of some states.
      (5) ☐ Interests are not freely transferable.
      (6) ☐ Business profits are taxed as income to the individual members and, as a result, may be subject to self-employment tax as well as income tax.
      (7) ☐ Transfer of interests may be subject to securities law regulation.

5. Corporation
   a. Advantages:
      (1) ☐ All shareholders enjoy limited liability.
      (2) ☐ Ownership interests are freely transferable.
      (3) ☐ Perpetual existence unaffected by the death of shareholders or transfer of shares.
      (4) ☐ Centralized management.
      (5) ☐ No limitation on the number or types of shareholders.
      (6) ☐ Flexibility of financing is available through the sale of various types of securities to many investors.
      (7) ☐ Tax-favored fringe benefits are available to employee-shareholders.

(8) ☐ Income is taxable at corporate rates, which are for the most part for the most part lower than individual rates.

(9) ☐ Noncorporate shareholders may qualify for an exclusion from federal income tax of one-half of the capital gains realized on stock of a small business corporation organized as a C corporation.

b.   Disadvantages:

(1) ☐ Formalities are required for organization and operation.

(2) ☐ Qualification is required for doing business in other states.

(3) ☐ Regular reporting to governmental entities is required.

(4) ☐ Stock transfers are subject to securities law regulation.

(5) ☐ Income is subject to double taxation.

(6) ☐ Losses of business may not be deducted by individual shareholders.

(7) ☐ The distribution of property by a C corporation to its shareholders is generally a taxable event for income tax purposes as to both the corporation and the shareholders. Thus, withdrawing property from a corporation can be extremely expensive from a tax standpoint.

6.   S Corporation

a.   Advantages:

(1) ☐ All shareholders enjoy limited liability.

(2) ☐ Ownership interests are freely transferable (subject to restrictions imposed by contract to preserve S corporation status).

(3) ☐ Perpetual existence unaffected by the death of shareholders or transfer of shares.

(4) ☐ Centralized management.

(5) ☐ Business profits are subject to only one tax, at the individual shareholder level, and are not subject to double tax as would be the case if the profits were realized by a C corporation.

(6) ☐ Losses are available on the shareholders' personal income tax returns and can offset other income (subject to the at risk rules and passive loss rules).

b.   Disadvantages:

(1) ☐ Formalities are required for organization and operation.

(2) ☐ Qualification is required for doing business in other states.

(3) ☐ Regular reporting to governmental entities is required.

(4) ☐ Stock transfers are subject to securities law regulation.

(5) ☐ Strict qualification rules must be met on a continuing basis, which among other things limit the number and types of shareholders.

(6) ☐ The distribution of property by an S corporation to its shareholders is generally a taxable event for income tax purposes.

§ 4:2. CHECKLIST OF TAX COMPLIANCE ISSUES FOR SOLE PROPRIETOR[5]

FEDERAL TAX COMPLIANCE CHECKLIST

1. ☐ Obtain employer identification number by filing Internal Revenue Service Form SS-4.

2. ☐ File income tax returns and pay taxes.

   a. ☐ Pay quarterly estimates of tax on April 15, June 15, September 15, and January 15 with Form 1040ES if the tax liability for the year on income from self employment and other income not subject to withholding will exceed $500.

   b. ☐ File annual income tax returns for the prior year on Form 1040 by April 15, reporting income or loss from the sole proprietorship on Schedule C, and pay the tax due on the taxable income on the return.

   c. ☐ If a deduction is taken for a home office, attach Form 8829 to the Form 1040.

   d. ☐ Report income from the sole proprietorship as self-employment income on Form 1040, Schedule SE, and pay self-employment tax thereon.

3. ☐ File annual information returns.

   a. ☐ Information returns on Form 1099 must be sent to certain persons to whom $600 or more is paid in connection with the sole proprietor's business during a year. These forms must be sent to recipients by January 31 of the year following the year of payment.

   b. ☐ Copies of all Forms 1099 must be filed with the Internal Service along with a transmittal on Form 1096 by February 28.

4. ☐ File employment tax returns and pay taxes.

   a. ☐ Obtain from each employee a Form W-4 indicating the number of withholding allowances claimed.

   b. ☐ If any employee claims to be exempt from withholding, a new Form W-4 must be obtained by February 15 of each year.

   c. ☐ Withhold appropriate amounts for FICA tax, Medicare tax, and income tax withholding from each paycheck given to an employee.

   d. ☐ File 941 on a quarterly basis, on April 30, July 31, October 31, and January 31 and pay the employer's share of FICA and Medicare tax with those returns as well as remitting withholdings from employees' paychecks.

   e. ☐ If FICA tax, Medicare tax, and income tax withholdings will equal or exceed $1,000 for any quarter, taxes must be deposited on a monthly or more frequent basis along with Form 8109.

   f. ☐ Provide employees with a Form W-2, showing their compensation and withholdings for the prior year, by January 31 of each year.

g. ☐ File all forms W-2 with the Internal Revenue Service with form W-3 by February 28.

h. ☐ File Form 940 or Form 940-EZ by January 31 of each year and pay federal unemployment (FUTA) tax with that return.

§ 30:3. CHECKLIST FOR PURCHASING FRANCHISE AND REVIEWING FRANCHISE DOCUMENTS[6]

CHECKLIST FOR PURCHASING A FRANCHISE AND REVIEWING FRANCHISE DOCUMENTS

I. Preliminary Suggestions.

A. Involvement of Professional Assistance. Prospective franchise purchasers are typically inexperienced in business matters, emotionally driven, and locked into a particular offering. Many times they are resistant to obtaining the necessary professional assistance. There is no substitute for good legal advice or financial assistance. A franchise purchaser should employ competent legal counsel and a professional accountant.

B. Encourage "Comparison Shopping." It is common for a franchise purchaser to first involve an attorney after the client has selected a specific franchise opportunity. Despite this, it is always best to encourage the franchisee to look at the various franchise offerings in a given or related industry to determine the best price, market power, and other items which will make his or her business successful. There are a number of resources available for a client to search franchise offerings in a given industry.

II. Review of Disclosure Documents and Franchise Agreement.

A. Disclosure Documents. Disclosure documents are the crux of the franchise protection laws. Documents which disclose approximately 20 categories of information about the franchisor are required under the FTC Rule and most state laws. These are the ABCs of the opportunity. Nothing will provide the client with more information about the franchisor than the disclosures. Therefore, it is important to *insist* that the prospective franchisee thoroughly read all documents provided by the franchisor. Some of the important items that the franchise purchaser and the practitioner should study are:

1. Evaluate the stability of the franchisor.

2. How long has the business been in operation?

3. Is the business previously operated by the franchisor closely related to the type of franchise business now offered?

4. Determine the total investment including initial franchise fees, royalties, and advertising fees that will make up the capital investment.

5. Determine how much working capital the franchisee will need along with inventory costs and maintenance.

6. What requirements are imposed upon the franchisee in regard to training, monthly accounting, payment of royalties, contributions to advertising funds, operating in accordance with the franchisor's manual, business hours to be maintained, and any obligations to take on new products or services as dictated by the franchisor?

B. Franchisee Involvement in Investigation. There is a lot of "leg work" or "phone work" to be done when buying a franchise. The client should always be encouraged to do as much investigation as possible. Encouraging the franchise purchaser to obtain information on the general business background of the franchisor beyond what is offered in the disclosure documents is always recommended. In addition, the purchaser should contact every franchisee of the franchisor in person or by telephone to discuss information which the franchisor is unwilling or unable to provide. The information provided by the franchisor's existing franchisees is the most valuable information a purchaser can obtain. Because franchisees have been through the process that your client now is going through, they are generally willing to cooperate with a franchise purchaser. Also encourage your client to visit an existing franchise operation to study whether it will be successful and is the type of business the purchaser desires to operate. Some of the questions that a purchaser might ask existing franchisees include:

1. How long did it take them to break even?

2. How much money did they originally invest?

3. How much profit are they making based upon actual sales, etc.?

4. What ongoing assistance has the franchisor provided?

5. How is the quality of the services or products provided by the franchisor?

6. Has the franchisor conducted regular meetings with the franchisee and kept all promises in regard to continuing support?

7. Is the franchisee aware of any other franchisees who may not be satisfied or who have had problems with the franchisor?

8. What, if any, terms of the franchise agreement may be negotiable?

9. Does the franchisor appear to be concerned with the long-range development of the system?

C. Investigate the Franchisor through Governmental Sources. Because registration of a franchise offering is required in some states, a franchisee should check with the state administrator or attorney general to determine if the franchisor has complied with the state's laws and registered the offering as is required. Also, the franchise purchaser is well advised to inquire of the various states in which the franchisor operates to determine if any complaints have been filed with state administrators concerning the franchisor or the operation of its system.

D. Earnings Claims. Franchise purchasers should be very cautious of any statements made by a franchisor which focus upon the amount of profit or earnings a franchisee may earn. Often times, purchasers rely upon these statements when the franchisor intends only to provide an estimate or forecast of what it believed their franchise units should do. Earnings claims are carefully regulated by the FTC and various states but if earnings claims are made, franchise purchasers should insist upon substantiating documentation and data if the same is not supplied with the claim. Any substantiating data or information should be thoroughly reviewed by a professional accountant and counsel to determine if the information itself has any relationship to the type of unit or operation the franchise purchaser intends to operate. The best source for information concerning how well the franchise may do is from existing franchisees, however.

III. Franchise Agreement.

A. Negotiating with the Franchisor. The first thing to realize before a franchise purchaser begins his or her search for a franchise opportunity is that since the franchisor has prepared the disclosure documents and the franchise agreement, the purchaser is at a distinct disadvantage. The reason for this is that the franchisor and its legal advisors have prepared the contract. They have invested a great deal of time and money to structure the contract for their own protection. This is not to say that the contract is unfair, only that an imbalance usually exists. Although many franchisors adamantly refuse to negotiate the terms and conditions of their franchise offerings, a purchaser should not hesitate to negotiate items which are of importance to the franchise purchaser. The lack of maturity of the system, the lack of a presence of the system in the franchise purchaser's intended territory, and a number of other intangible factors may make the franchisor more flexible than the purchaser is initially led to believe. Franchise purchasers should attempt to negotiate each and every item which is of importance.

B. Choice of Law and Venue Selection. Because the franchise agreement is drafted by the franchisor and provided to the franchisee, it is customary for the franchisor to insist upon the application of its home state's law to the interpretation of the contract and, in some instances, to insist upon the litigation or arbitration of any disputes between the party to occur in the franchisor's home state. The franchisee should attempt to negotiate these clauses, but franchisors are normally adamant in maintaining this advantage. The franchise purchaser should take this into account at the outset and determine the cost and inconvenience of this disadvantage should a future dispute arise with its franchisor.

§ 30:5. FRANCHISE AGREEMENT[7]

FRANCHISE AGREEMENT

DATE: _____

PARTIES: [Name of Franchisor],

a[n] _____ [state of incorporation]

corporation (Franchisor)

Address:

[Franchisor's Address]

[Name of Franchisee] (Franchisee)

Address:

[Franchisee's Address]

RECITALS:

A. Franchisor is the owner of the name and trademark "_____®" and related logo types and is the owner of a system to offer franchise businesses to *[describe franchise business]*.

B. The Franchise program, includes but is not limited to: common use and promotion of the name _____®.

C. Franchisee warrants and represents that the Franchisee is familiar with Franchisor and its operation, has reviewed the Offering Circular provided by Franchisor, and has been provided with such other information concerning the operation of a franchise as Franchisee requested.

D. Franchisee warrants and represents that the Franchisee does not wish to obtain the franchise for speculative or investment purposes and has no present intention to sell or transfer or attempt to sell or transfer said franchise in whole or in part. Franchisee understands and acknowledges the importance of the high and uniform standards of quality, appearance, and service imposed by Franchisor in order to maintain the value of Franchisor's name and the necessity of operating the franchise in compliance with Franchisor's standards.

AGREEMENTS:
SECTION 1. FRANCHISE

1.1 *Grant of Franchise.* Franchisor hereby grants to Franchisee the exclusive right and license to operate a _____ business for a term of five years from the date of this Agreement in Franchisee's exclusive area and to use the Franchisor's method of advertising, trade name, logos, and the rights enumerated herein solely in a _____ business and in no other manner.

1.2 *Franchisee's Area.* Franchisee acknowledges that Franchisor's method is designed to operate on the basis that each Franchisee is assigned a specific exclusive geographical area in which each Franchisee must use its best efforts to develop and service in accordance with Franchisor's standards and specifications. Therefore, the license granted herein is specifically limited to the right to operate the _____ business within the Franchisee's Area, more fully set forth in Section 21.2 of this Agreement.

SECTION 2. INITIAL FRANCHISE FEE AND TERM

2.1 *Initial Franchise Fee.* The Franchisee shall pay to Franchisor an initial franchise fee, payable concurrently with the execution of this Agreement, of $_____, which fee is fully earned by Franchisor upon the signing of this Agreement and is nonrefundable.

2.2 *Term.* The term of this Agreement and the right to operate the franchise granted herein shall commence as of the date of acceptance, as indicated herein upon final execution hereof by Franchisor, and shall continue in effect for five years, unless a termination or breach shall occur as provided.

SECTION 3. OTHER FEES AND OTHER CONTINUING CHARGES

3.1 Royalty

3.1.1 *Monthly Royalty.* In addition to the initial franchise fee, Franchisee shall pay Franchisor a monthly royalty payment equal to five percent of monthly gross sales from Franchisee's business. Gross sales is defined in Section 3.1.2.

3.1.2 *Gross Sales.* For the purpose of this Agreement, gross sales shall mean all receipts, whether in cash or on credit: (i) from Franchisee's business; (ii) from all other activities of every type and description done by Franchisee or any person employed by Franchise, under the name _____ or in connection with any of its trademarks or service marks; and (iii) from any other related business operated by Franchisee or any person employed by Franchisee whether or not the name and marks of Franchisor are used.

3.1.3 *Payment.* The monthly royalty payments shall be due and payable without invoice or other notice from Franchisor on the 15th day of the month following the month for which payment is due, upon the form prescribed by Franchisor.

3.1.4 *Late Charge and Costs.* If royalty payments are not fully paid on or before the date when due, Franchisee agrees to pay Franchisor a later charge equal to two percent per month on all amounts due and unpaid. In addition,

Franchisee agrees to reimburse Franchisor for all costs of collection, including attorney's fees, of any amounts due under this Agreement.

3.2 *Advertising.* Franchisee shall pay Franchisor a monthly advertising fee equal to one percent of monthly gross sales (as defined in Section 3.1.2) from Franchisee's business. This amount shall be due and payable without invoice or other notice from Franchisor on the 15th day of the month following the month for which payment is due, upon the form prescribed by Franchisor. Payment shall be made separately from other payments to Franchisor and shall be paid to "Ad-Fund." Franchisor shall place all advertising fees received from Franchisees in a segregated advertising fund, the proceeds of which shall be expended solely upon advertising for Franchisees, subject to reasonable administrative fees and costs charged by Franchisor. The advertising fee and fund are more fully described in Section 7.3 of this Agreement.

SECTION 4. NATURE AND VALUE OF FRANCHISE NAME, TRADEMARKS, TRADE SECRETS, AND GOOD WILL

4.1 *Authorized Use.* The franchise granted hereby authorizes the Franchisee to use Franchisor's trademarks, know-how, and trade secrets in the operation of a business as set forth in this Agreement.

4.2 *No Transfer.* Nothing contained in this Agreement or done pursuant to this Agreement shall be deemed to give the Franchisee any right or interest in any of the trademarks, trade secrets, and know-how of Franchisor. Franchisee agrees further, having under this Agreement received secrets, know-how, experience, and assistance, now and hereafter provided by Franchisor, for the purpose of establishment and operation of a _____ business and having been granted participation in the commercial benefits of the good will provided by Franchisor, that Franchisee will not at any time divulge any secret or confidential information concerning the business of Franchisor and that upon termination or transfer of Franchisee's franchise, Franchisee will not at any time thereafter in any manner use, copy, or imitate any of the trademarks of Franchisor or trade upon Franchisor's good will. The Franchisee further agrees that in the event of a violation of any of Franchisee's obligations under this Section 4.2, Franchisor may immediately obtain an injunction from a court of competent jurisdiction without any requirement of bond, in addition to any other remedies.

4.3 *Benefit.* Any use of the Franchisor's trademarks by a Franchisee shall inure to the benefit of Franchisor.

4.4 *Limitations on Use.* The Franchisee agrees that the trademarks, secrets, and know-how of Franchisor may be used only for the purpose of operating a _____ business in the agreed territory and shall not be used by Franchisee for any purpose or in any manner not authorized by Franchisor and that, at all times during the entire term of this agreement, the Franchisee will diligently and loyally use the Franchisee's best efforts to promote such business and to enhance the good will of, and customer demand for, the franchise business.

4.5 *Name.* The trademarks, including without limitation, the mark _____® or any variation thereof, shall not be used as a part of the firm or corporate name of the Franchisee but shall be distinguished and set apart from the firm or corporate name of any Franchisee.

4.6 *Other Goods or Services.* In no way are any of Franchisor's trademarks or trade name to be used or misrepresented as names or marks for the sale of any goods or services not specified in this Agreement.

4.7 *State Registration.* Franchisee shall take steps to register, if not previously registered, the trademark of _____® with the state in which said Franchisee is located. Said registration shall be in the name of Franchisor and shall be at the Franchisee's expense. Franchisee shall notify Franchisor of the registration and shall provide all documentation of same to Franchisor.

4.8 *Infringement.* In the event of any infringement of, or challenge of the Franchisee's use of any name or mark, the Franchisee shall immediately notify Franchisor, and Franchisor will have sole discretion to take such action as it deems appropriate. While Franchisor is not required to defend the Franchisee against any infringement, unfair competition, or other claim respecting the Franchisee's use of any name or mark, Franchisor is obligated to indemnify the Franchisee against, and to reimburse the Franchisee for, all damages for which Franchisee is found liable in any proceeding arising out of the use of any name or mark and for all costs reasonably incurred by the Franchisee in the defense of any such claim, provided that the Franchisee has notified Franchisor of such claim as described above and provided Franchisee made an effort to register the trademark _____® as provided in Section 4.7. The Franchisee agrees not to contest, directly or indirectly, Franchisor's ownership, title, right, or interest in its names or marks, trade secrets, methods, procedures, and advertising techniques which are part of the franchise business or contest Franchisor's sole right to register, use, or license others to use such names and marks, trade secrets, methods, procedures, and techniques.

SECTION 5. RELATIONSHIP OF THE PARTIES

5.1 *Independent Contractor.* The nature of the relationship between Franchisee and Franchisor is and shall be an independent contractor and nothing herein contained shall be construed so as to create an agency relationship, a partnership, or joint venture between Franchisor and Franchisee. Neither Franchisor nor the Franchisee shall act as agent for the other and neither the Franchisee nor Franchisor shall guarantee the obligations of the other or in any way become obligated for the debts or expenses of the other unless agreed to in writing.

5.2 *Operation of Franchisee's Business.* Franchisor shall not regulate the hiring or firing of a Franchisee's employees. The conduct of the Franchisee's business and employees and the solicitation of customers by Franchisee and Franchisee's employees shall be determined in its own judgment and discretion, subject only to the Policy and Procedures Manual as it may be adopted or revised from time to time by Franchisor.

SECTION 6. OBLIGATIONS OF FRANCHISOR

Franchisor agrees, in consideration of Franchisee's promises contained in this Agreement, to assist Franchisee in providing the Franchisee with the following services:

6.1 *Training Program.* Franchisor will operate a one (1) week training program for the Franchisee at _____ or any other location that Franchisor may later choose. The training program will consist of Franchisor's operational procedures, marketing system, operation, basic bookkeeping, and accounting, and all aspects of general operations. No additional fee is charged for training. However, Franchisee shall be responsible for all travel, lodging, and sustenance expenses for Franchisee or any employee.

6.2 *Promotional or Merchandising Methods.* Franchisor may from time to time offer Franchisee suggested promotional or merchandising methods. Any such promotion or merchandising methods will be offered at the discretion of Franchisor according to the currently approved Policy and Procedures Manual of Franchisor.

6.3 *Consultation and Advice.* Franchisor shall provide ongoing consultation and advice to Franchisee.

6.4 *Continuing Assistance.* Franchisor may, in its discretion, provide continuing assistance to Franchisee in such areas set forth in the training program or which may arise from time to time. Franchisor may conduct quarterly sales and franchise consultation meetings at _____. (Attendance by Franchisee is voluntary.)

6.5 *Marketing.* Franchisor shall establish Franchisee's exclusive territory and shall assist Franchisee with the identification of and analysis of the initial targeted minimum households required to begin the operation of Franchisee's business. Franchisor shall also assist Franchisee with the purchase of the necessary mailing lists and other components necessary to the operation of the business.

6.6 *Initial Supplies.* Franchisor shall supply and provide Franchisee's initial supply of [describe goods provided]. After the initial supply, Franchisee shall pay the prices then in effect for said items to Franchisor. Franchisor will derive income from the sale of these items to Franchisee.

6.7 *Policy and Procedures Manual.* Franchisor shall develop and provide a Policy and Procedures Manual for the management and operation of Franchisee's business which may be updated from time to time.

6.8 *Advertising.* Franchisor may assist, but is not required to assist, Franchisee in obtaining national or regional advertising accounts and coordinate the placement of said advertisements among and between all Franchisees who desire to accept or secure said advertisers or advertisements in accordance with this Agreement.

SECTION 7. OBLIGATIONS OF THE FRANCHISEE

Franchisee agrees, in consideration of Franchisor's promises contained in this Agreement, as follows:

7.1 *Payments.* Franchisee shall pay promptly to Franchisor (or its designated suppliers) any fees due hereunder, as well as charges for any products or services furnished by Franchisor (or its designated suppliers) at Franchisee's request, including but not limited to (i) the initial franchise fee set forth in Section 2.1; (ii) the royalty payments as set forth in Section 3.1; (iii) the advertising fee as set forth in Section 3.2; and (iv) any other charges incurred under this Agreement by Franchisee.

7.2 *Reports.* Franchisee shall report to Franchisor by the 15th day of the following month, on forms required by Franchisor, the amount of monthly gross sales and royalty payments due for the previous month. In addition, Franchisee shall report to Franchisor, on forms prescribed by Franchisor, the general financial condition of Franchisee's business specifying expenses, costs, income, profit, and so forth on January 30th, April 30th, July 30th and October 30th of each year for the previous quarter of operation prior to each such date.

7.3 *Advertising Fund.* Franchisee shall contribute one percent of the monthly gross sales from the Franchisee's business to an advertising fund administered and maintained by Franchisor. The fund shall be maintained in a segregated bank account under Franchisors' control, designated as "Ad-Fund." None of the funds are refundable to Franchisee. Franchisor shall use the proceeds of the fund and any interest earned upon said proceeds solely and exclusively for advertising on behalf of Franchisees, subject to reasonable administrative fees and costs charged by Franchisor. Franchisee agrees and acknowledges that

Franchisor will administer the fund and the distribution of proceeds for advertising within its absolute discretion. Franchisor reserves the right to apply the proceeds of the fund in whatever manner it deems beneficial to all Franchisees, including an uneven distribution of the proceeds so as to accomplish different goals in different markets. Franchisee acknowledges and agrees that Franchisor may purchase advertising in combination with advertising for its company-owned retail stores (if any) and that any such costs for said advertising shall be allocated between Franchisor and the advertising fund on a per store basis for the relevant geographical area. Franchisee shall pay the one percent advertising contribution on the 15th day of the month following the month for which payment is due. Payment shall be due and payable without invoice or other notice from Franchisor and Franchisee is required to report gross sales and the advertising fee due upon the forms prescribed by Franchisor. Payment shall be made separately from other payments to Franchisor and shall be paid to "Ad-Fund."

7.4 *Harm to Business*. Franchisee shall not engage in any trade, practice, or other activity which is harmful to the good will or reflects unfavorably on the reputation of Franchisor or constitutes deceptive or unfair competition or is in violation of any applicable fair trade law.

7.5 *Policy and Procedures Manual*. Franchisee shall comply with the Franchisor's Policy and Procedures Manual (if adopted and as it may be revised from time to time) and with all rules and regulations for the good order, uniformity, or protection of the good will and reputation of Franchisor which may from time to time be declared in writing by Franchisor.

7.6 *Hold Harmless*. Franchisee agrees to hold harmless and protect Franchisor from and against any liability of any kind or nature resulting from the operation of the Franchisee's business. The Franchisee, prior to beginning the operation of Franchisee's business and thereafter, is required to maintain at Franchisee's expense, covering both the Franchisee and Franchisor as named insureds, in a form and with an insurer satisfactory to Franchisor, comprehensive general liability insurance with personal injury coverage of not less than one million dollars ($1,000,000) per occurrence and business interruption insurance in an amount of not less than $100,000 per occurrence. The insurance to be furnished by the Franchisee shall also include motor vehicle insurance with the following coverages and limits: bodily injury liability with limits of $100,000 for any one person and $300,000 for all persons as a result of any one occurrence, property damage liability with limits of $50,000 for any one occurrence, medical payments of $5,000 for each person and uninsured and underinsured coverage, and comprehensive coverage for the actual cash value of each vehicle and $100 deductible collision insurance. Franchisee is also required to maintain worker's compensation insurance, and Franchisor must be a named insured with Franchisee on each insurance policy except worker's compensation insurance. The cost of such insurance and the dates payments are due will vary from one insurer to another. The payments are made directly to the insurer and are ordinarily not refundable.

7.7 *Trademarks and Service Marks.* Franchisee agrees that from time to time Franchisor may reasonably adopt new or modified trademarks, service marks, or other marks, and Franchisee agrees at Franchisee's expense, to adopt, use, and display for the purposes of this Agreement any such changes as if they were a part of Franchisor's program at the time of the execution of this Agreement.

7.8 *Compliance with Law.* Franchisee shall comply with all federal, state, and local laws and regulations, and shall obtain, and all times maintain, any and all permits, certificates, or licenses necessary for the full and proper conduct of the business.

7.9 *Annual Audit.* Franchisee shall conduct an annual audit which, along with the Franchisee's company books, shall be submitted to Franchisor for review within 60 days after December 31 of each year. Said audit shall contain complete and accurate financial statements of Franchisee's business, including a statement of profit and loss and a balance sheet, all prepared in accordance with generally accepted accounting principles.

7.10 *Training Program*

7.10.1 *Franchisee.* Franchisee shall attend a one week training program at Franchisor's headquarters prior to the opening of the franchise.

7.10.2 *Others.* If the trained Franchisee leaves the franchise business, another person shall take Franchisor's training course so that at least one manager at the franchise business has had the training course. If such other person is required to take the training course, a fee of not more than $1,000 for each additional person taking the course shall be charged Franchisee. The additional training fee shall be due and payable by Franchisee prior to the training session.

7.11 *Manager*

7.11.1 *Supervision.* The franchise business must be at all times under the direct supervision of a Franchisee who has completed the training program.

7.11.2 *Identity.* Franchisor must be informed of the identity of any manager, whether the Franchisee is an individual, corporation, or partnership, who is at any time utilized or employed by Franchisee.

7.12 *Office Equipment.* Franchisee shall be required to install and maintain a separate telephone line (or lines), dedicated to the operation of the business, as well as an answering machine for times when the telephone is unable to be answered directly. Territories of 250,000 households or more are required to install and maintain a facsimile machine to communicate with Franchisor and lease or purchase a copy machine. Territories of less than 250,000 households must have access to both facsimile and copying services. All Franchisees shall be required to purchase or lease a portable VHS video playback/monitor and to own or lease a motor vehicle for the purpose of making sales calls, although a specific make or model is not required.

SECTION 8. TERM AND RENEWAL

8.1 *Term.* The term of the Franchise Agreement is five years from the date of execution of the Franchise Agreement. Additional licenses for territories will be governed by separate Franchise Agreements and with termination dates established therein.

8.2 *Commencement of Business.* Franchisee is required to commence business operations within one week of the conclusion of Franchisee's training program.

8.3 *Option to Renew.* Franchisee has an unlimited option to renew the franchise relationship for successive additional five year terms. The Franchisee must give Franchisor at least six months' notice of its intention to exercise its option to renew. Said renewal will be granted if all the conditions of Section 8.4 have been met.

8.4 *Conditions of Renewal.* The Franchisee will be allowed to renew Franchisee's franchise relationship with Franchisor provided that:

8.4.1 *No Breach or Default.* The Franchisee is not in breach of any of the terms or conditions of this Agreement and is not in default of any of the provisions of this Agreement requiring payments to be made to Franchisor (or its designated suppliers). Franchisee shall be current on all royalty payments, supply payments, commission payments, and any other fee or payment required hereunder;

8.4.2 *Renewal Franchise Agreement.* The Franchisee executes a Renewal Franchise Agreement and other legal instruments then customarily used by Franchisor even though the terms, including the amount of royalty fees and other charges, may be materially different from the agreements now in use. Failure or refusal to execute such instruments within 30 days after delivery to the Franchisee shall be deemed an election not to renew the franchise; and

8.4.3 *Renewal Fee.* The Franchisee pays the renewal fee, not to exceed $1,000.

8.5 *Required Notice.* If state or local law requires that Franchisor give notice to Franchisee of nonrenewal for noncompliance with this Agreement or the Policy and Procedures Manual prior to the expiration of the term, this Agreement shall remain in effect on a month-to-month basis until Franchisor has given Franchisee the notice required by law.

SECTION 9. TERMINATION

9.1 *Termination by Franchisee*

9.1.1 *Permitted Termination.* If the Franchisee is in compliance with the Franchise Agreement and Franchisor breaches the Agreement and fails to cure such breach within 45 days after written notice of such breach is delivered to Franchisor, the Franchisee may terminate the Franchise Agreement and the franchise, effective 10 days after delivery of written notice to Franchisor of such termination.

9.1.2 *Termination in Violation of Agreement.* A termination without complying with these requirements or for any reason other than breach of the Franchise Agreement and failure to cure by Franchisor shall be deemed a termination by the Franchisee not in accordance with the provisions of the Franchise Agreement.

9.2 *Termination by Franchisor.* Franchisor may terminate the Franchise Agreement and the franchise immediately and without other cause, effective 30 days after delivery of notice of termination to the Franchisee, if the Franchisee:

9.2.1 *Assignment for Benefit of Creditors.* Makes an assignment for the benefit of creditors or an admission of his inability to pay his obligations as they become due;

9.2.2 *Bankruptcy or Similar Proceeding.* Files a voluntary petition in bankruptcy or any pleading seeking any reorganization, arrangement, composition, adjustment, liquidation, dissolution, or similar relief under any law, or admitting or failing to contest the material allegations of any pleading filed against him, or is adjudicated as bankrupt or insolvent;

9.2.3 *Failure to Operate Business.* Fails to continuously and actively operate the business;

9.2.4 *Inaccurate Statements.* Submits two or more statements, one or more annual financial statements, sales or income tax returns, or supporting records to Franchisor that understate by two percent or more the royalties due or materially distorts any other material information;

9.2.5 *Breach of Payment or Reporting Obligations.* Consistently fails to submit when due periodic or annual financial statements or other information or fails to pay when due royalty fees or other fees;

9.2.6 *Health and Safety Problems.* Violates and fails to cure or consistently violates any health or safety law, ordinance, or regulation or operates the business in a manner that presents a health or safety hazard to its customers or the public;

9.2.7 *Unauthorized Assignment.* Makes an unauthorized assignment of the Franchise Agreement, the franchise, or ownership of the franchise;

9.2.8 *Failure to Comply with Agreement.* Repeatedly fails to comply with the Franchise Agreement, whether or not such failures are corrected, after notice thereof is delivered to the Franchise;

9.2.9 *Misrepresentations.* Has made any material misrepresentations or misstatements on Franchisee's application for the franchise or with respect to the ownership of the Franchisee;

9.2.10 *Criminal Misconduct.* Has engaged in criminal misconduct relevant to the reputation or operation of the business;

9.2.11 *Failure to Adhere to Agreement.* Fails to adhere to any material provision of the Franchise Agreement including, but not limited to, all payments Franchisee is required to pay to Franchisor as specified in Sections 3 and 7 of this Agreement, or any specification, standard, or operating procedure prescribed by Franchisor and does not correct such failure within fifteen (15) days after notice of same by Franchisor;

9.2.12 *Noncompliance with Law.* Fails to correct any noncompliance with any law or government regulation within five days of notice by the appropriate government agency or by Franchisor;

9.2.13 *Failure to Meet Minimum Standards.* In the event performance of Franchisee falls below the minimum operation standards set forth in this Agreement or in any Policy and Procedures Manual, Franchisee will be notified in writing setting forth such deficiency and, at the option of Franchisor, Franchisee may be placed on probation for a period of not less than 30 days and not more than 90 days. If such deficiency is not corrected within said probationary period, Franchisor may, at its option, terminate this Agreement.

9.3 *Termination by Franchisor and Franchisee.* This Agreement may be terminated by mutual written consent of the parties upon such terms and conditions as they may mutually agree.

9.4 *Posttermination Obligations of Franchisee.* On the termination or refusal to renew or extend the Franchise Agreement by Franchisor, the Franchisee shall cease to be an authorized Franchisee and shall:

9.4.1 *Payment of Fees and Charges.* Pay fees and charges due within seven days;

9.4.2 *Discontinue Use of Marks.* Immediately and permanently discontinue the use of all names and marks indicating or tending to indicate that the Franchisee is an authorized Franchisee. All signs, stationery, letterheads, forms, manuals, printed matter, and advertising containing Franchisor's marks shall promptly be surrendered to Franchisor. Franchisor shall pay Franchisee's costs for all such items surrendered;

9.4.3 *Cease Advertising.* Cease all advertising as an authorized Franchisee, including, but not limited to, the immediate removal of all signs from its premises;

9.4.4 *Return of Franchisor's Property.* Immediately return all Franchisor's Policy and Procedures Manuals, books, films, cassettes, forms, or brochures to Franchisor;

9.4.5 *Books and Records.* Maintain all books, records, and reports required by Franchisor for a period of not less than one year after termination;

9.4.6 *Permit Inspection.* Allow Franchisor to make final inspection of said books and records during normal business hours within a one-year period for the purpose of verifying that all fees or other expenses due Franchisor have been paid;

9.4.7 *Cease Representations Regarding Relationship.* Refrain from doing anything that would indicate that it is or ever was an authorized Franchisee;

9.4.8 *Covenant Not to Compete.* Abide by all provisions of the covenant not to compete under Section 18;

9.4.9 *Assignment of Property.* At the option of Franchisor assign the leased premises and telephone numbers of the franchise business to Franchisor or any party designated by it.

9.5 *Franchisee's Business Property.* Upon termination or refusal to renew or extend the Franchise Agreement by Franchisor or by the Franchisee, the

Franchisee retains (unless the leased premises are, upon Franchisor's option, assigned to Franchisor or a party designated by it) its business property, location, site, furnishings, inventory, etc. except that all indications of Franchisor's affiliation must be removed.

SECTION 10. DEATH OF FRANCHISEE

10.1 *Successor.* In the event of the death of the Franchisee (who owns or controls 50% or more of the franchise business) during the term of this Agreement, Franchisor agrees that such person as shall be determined by Franchisee's will, or, in the event of Franchisee's intestacy, under the law of succession in effect in the state in which the deceased Franchisee's property interest in the franchise is located, to be the successor to the interest in the deceased Franchisee's property interest in the franchise (hereinafter referred to as "Successor"), shall be granted a franchise for the balance of the term of this Agreement subject to the following:

10.1.1 *Application and Qualification.* Successor may apply to Franchisor for acceptance by Franchisor and, if determined to be qualified in accordance with then prevailing standards, and upon compliance with the conditions described in subparagraph (c) below, such Successor shall be granted the franchise for the balance of the term, for the previously agreed territory.

10.1.2 *Alternative for Qualification.* If Successor is not willing or able to qualify as a Franchisee, such Successor may apply to Franchisor for acceptance by Franchisor by designating an individual employed by such Successor to be qualified in accordance with the then prevailing standards, and upon compliance with the conditions described in Section 10.2 below, such Successor shall be granted the franchise for the balance of the term, for the previously agreed territory.

10.2 *Acceptance of Successor.* The acceptance of the Successor as a Franchisee is subject to the following conditions:

10.2.1 *Delinquent Obligations.* Payment of delinquent obligations of the deceased Franchisee or his or her estate, if any, pertaining to this Agreement;

10.2.2 *Assumption by Successor.* Written assumption by the Successor, in forms furnished or approved by Franchisor of the obligations of the Franchisee under this Agreement;

10.2.3 *Execution of Other Documents.* Execution by Successor of such other documents as may be reasonably required by Franchisor;

10.2.4 *Training Requirements.* Compliance with the training requirements for franchisees set forth in this Agreement, and the payment of a training fee of not more than $1,000 prior to the training session.

10.3 *Transfer to Others.* Any proposed transfer of this Franchise by the legal representative of the estate of the deceased Franchisee to a person other than a Successor who qualified as a Franchisee, in accordance with Sections 10.1 and 10.2, shall be subject to the provisions governing assignment as set forth elsewhere in this Agreement.

10.4 *Failure to Transfer.* If no Successor shall have qualified and no transfer of the franchise shall have otherwise been accomplished consistent with the foregoing provisions within six months from the date of death of the Franchisee, Franchisor shall have the right to terminate this Agreement but may exercise any option it possesses under this Agreement or under the terms of the Franchisee's lease in order to maintain the operation of the business as a company-owned operation.

10.5 *Court Order.* Franchisor shall have the right to require a certified copy of an order of the court having jurisdiction over the deceased Franchisee's estate in which the Successor shall be determined, and may rely on such certified copy for the purposes of this paragraph. If not furnished with such certified copy of a court order, or in the event of a legal contest, Franchisor may decline, without liability, to recognize the claim of a party to be Successor. Franchisor shall not be liable to any heir, next of kin, devisee, legatee, or legal representative of a deceased Franchisee by reason of acceptance of a surviving spouse or child of the deceased Franchisee as Successor, provided such acceptance is not contrary to the order of a court of competent jurisdiction served on Franchisor.

10.6 *Interim Operation.* During the interim period from the date of death of Franchisee until qualification of Successor, or until a transfer of the franchise shall have otherwise been accomplished consistent with this Section 10, the legal representative shall operate under this Franchise Agreement through an individual who has the requisite qualifications for interim management thereof, as determined by Franchisor, it being understood that should the legal representative have failed to designate an individual so qualifying within 90 days after the death of the Franchisee, Franchisor shall have the right to terminate this Agreement but may exercise any option it may possess under this Agreement or under the terms of the Franchisee's lease in order to maintain the operation of the business as a company-owned operation.

10.7 *State Law.* In the event any provisions of this Agreement pertaining to renewal, termination, or modification conflict with any controlling state law, such provision shall be subordinate to such state law, to the extent there is a conflict.

SECTION 11. ASSIGNMENT OF THE FRANCHISE

11.1 *Agreement Is Personal.* This Agreement is personal, being entered into in reliance upon and in consideration of the skill, qualifications, and representations of, and the trust and confidence reposed in, Franchisee and Franchisee's present partners or officers (if Franchisee is a partnership or corporation), who will actively and substantially participate in the operation of the franchise business.

11.2 *Limitations on Transfer.* Neither this Agreement, the franchise, nor any part of the ownership of the franchise (which shall mean and include voting stock, securities convertible thereto, proprietorship interest, and general partnership interest) may be voluntarily, directly, or indirectly assigned or otherwise transferred or encumbered by the Franchisee or its owners (including without limitation by will, declaration of or transfer in trust, or by the laws of intestate succession) except as provided herein without the prior written approval of Franchisor, and any such assignment, transfer, or encumbrance without such approval constitutes a breach of this Agreement. Franchisor will not, however, unreasonably withhold consent to an assignment if the conditions specified below are met:

11.2.1 *Satisfaction with Assignee.* Franchisor is satisfied with the character, business experience, and credit rating of the proposed assignee (and its partners, officers, and/or controlling stockholders);

11.2.2 *Payment of Debts.* Payment of all outstanding debts to Franchisor (or its designated suppliers) by the assigning Franchisee;

11.2.3 *Release.* A general release of claims by the franchise and Franchisee;

11.2.4 *Execution of Agreement.* Assignee's execution of the then current Franchise Agreement;

11.2.5 *Transfer Fee.* Payment by assignee of a $1,000 transfer fee;

11.2.6 *Training Program.* Attendance by the proposed assignee or a managing employee at the next available New Franchise Training Program at assignee's expense and the payment of a $1,000 training fee prior to the training session;

11.2.7 *Compliance with Law.* Completion of the steps necessary, if any, to comply with the Federal Trade Commission Rules and/or state laws regarding franchising.

11.3 *Incorporation of Franchisee's Business.* If the Franchisee is a sole proprietorship or partnership, and if the conditions of Sections 11.2.1–11.2.4 and 11.2.7 (except 11.2.5 and 11.2.6) are met, Franchisor will consent to the assignment without payment of a transfer fee of this Agreement to a corporation formed, owned, and controlled solely by the Franchisee to operate the franchise business, provided such assignment shall not relieve the original Franchisee of the obligations of this Agreement.

11.4 *Transfer of Interests in Franchisee's Business.*

11.4.1 *Corporation.* If the Franchisee is a corporation, any merger thereof, or sale or transfer of more than 49% of any one class of stock or any series (whether related or unrelated) or sales or transfers totalling in the aggregate 49% or more of any one class of stock in such corporate Franchisee, whether by operation of law or otherwise, shall be deemed an attempted assignment of this Agreement requiring the prior written consent of Franchisor.

11.4.2 *Partnership.* If the Franchisee is a partnership, the sale or transfer of any general partner's interest or the sale or series of sales or transfers of limited partnership interests totalling in such aggregate 49% of such interests (including transfers of shares in corporate partners) whether by operation of law or otherwise, shall be deemed an attempted assignment of this agreement and shall require the prior written consent of Franchisor.

11.4.3 *Aggregation of Transfers.* For the purpose of determining whether 49% or more of the interests of any class of shares or of general partnership interests have been transferred, all transfers (whether related or unrelated) shall be aggregated. Any proposed transfer involving less than 49% but more than 25% of the stock or general partnership interests of the Franchisee shall be reported by the Franchisee to Franchisor at lease 20 days in advance of any such transfer but shall not be subject to the approval of Franchisor.

11.5 *Assignment by Franchisor.* Franchisor reserves the right to assign the Franchise Agreement provided that such assignment shall not affect the rights and privileges of the Franchisee under the agreement.

11.6 *Right of First Refusal.* Franchisor has the right of first refusal on any proposed assignment by Franchisee. Franchisee shall serve upon Franchisor a written notice setting forth all of the terms and conditions of the proposed assignment, a suitable current financial statement regarding the proposed assignee, and all other information requested by Franchisor concerning the proposed assignee. Said notice shall provide Franchisor with sufficient time to enable Franchisor to comply with all disclosure requirements with respect to any intended assignee. Within 20 days after receipt of such notice (or if Franchisor requests additional information, within 15 days after receipt of such additional information), Franchisor may either consent or refuse to consent to the assignment or, at its option, accept the assignment to itself upon the same terms and conditions specified in said notice. Consent to an assignment upon the specified terms and conditions shall not be deemed to be a consent to an assignment upon any other terms or conditions, nor to any other person, nor to any other subsequent assignment.

SECTION 12. REMEDIES FOR BREACH, ATTORNEY FEES, AND FORCE MAJEURE

12.1 *Remedies.* Franchisee expressly consents and agrees that Franchisor may, in addition to any other available remedies, obtain an injunction without bond to terminate or prevent the continuation of any existing default or violation, and to prevent the occurrence of any threatened default or violation of this Agreement.

12.2 *Attorney's Fees.* If any legal action shall be instituted to interpret or enforce the terms and conditions of this Agreement, the prevailing party shall be entitled to recover its costs and reasonable attorney's fees.

12.3 *Force Majeure.* Neither Franchisor or Franchisee shall be liable to each other, or be deemed in breach or default of any obligation contained in this Agreement, for any delay or failure to perform for difficulties of performance occasioned by war, law, regulations or order of public authority, labor troubles, shortages of materials, acts of God, or other causes amounting to Force Majeure.

SECTION 13. MODIFICATIONS

13.1 *Terms and Conditions.* This Agreement contains all of the terms and conditions agreed upon by the parties hereto. No promises or representations have been made other than as herein set forth.

13.2 *Modifications.* Any modification or change in this Agreement must be in writing executed by Franchisee and an officer of Franchisor authorized by the Board of Directors of Franchisor. No field representative or any other employee of Franchisor has the right or authority to make oral or written modifications of this Agreement, and any such modifications shall not be binding upon either party hereto.

SECTION 14. WAIVER

No waiver of any breach of any condition, covenant, or agreement contained in this Agreement shall constitute a waiver of any subsequent breach of the same or any other condition, covenant, or agreement.

SECTION 15. MISCELLANEOUS

15.1 *Governing Law.* This Agreement shall be governed by the laws of the State of _____, and Franchisee expressly and freely agrees that should any legal action against Franchisor be necessary, all such action shall be taken exclusively in the State of _____. Franchisee hereby submits himself/herself/itself to the jurisdiction of the courts of _____ County, _____.

15.2 *Partial Invalidity.* In case any one or more of the provisions of this Agreement or any application thereof shall be invalid, illegal, or unenforceable in any respect, the validity, legality, and enforceability of the remaining provisions contained in this Agreement and any other application thereof shall not in any way be affected or impaired thereby.

15.3 *Headings.* Section and subsection headings are for reference purposes only and shall not in any way modify or limit the statements contained in any section or subsection.

15.4 *Number and Gender.* All words in this Agreement shall be deemed to include any number or gender as the context or sense of this Agreement requires. All references herein to Franchisee or Franchisor shall include the plural if there be more than one, and the masculine, feminine, or neuter as the case may be.

15.5 *Conflict with Manual.* In the event of any conflict between this Agreement and the Policy and Procedures Manual, this Agreement shall control.

SECTION 16. AUTHORITY AND ACCEPTANCE

16.1 *Warranty of Authority.* Each of the undersigned parties warrants that he/she/it has full authority to sign and execute this Agreement.

16.2 *Acceptance.* This Agreement shall become valid on the date it is accepted by Franchisor. Franchisor will notify Franchisee of such acceptance by sending Franchisee an executed copy of the Agreement. If this Agreement is not accepted by Franchisor within 60 days of receipt, then all monies paid hereunder shall be returned to the Franchisee and this Agreement shall be null and void, unless the parties agree in writing to a longer period.

SECTION 17. DISCLAIMER OF WARRANTIES AND ENTIRE AGREEMENT

17.1 *Representations.* Franchisee represents, warrants, and acknowledges that Franchisor, its officers, employees, and/or agents, have made no representations or warranties, expressed or implied, as to the profitability of a franchise business. Franchisee further acknowledges that Franchisee has conducted Franchisee's own independent investigation as to the desirability of entering into this transaction and that Franchisee has had full opportunity to seek independent legal counsel and financial advice with respect to entering into this Agreement. Franchisee specifically states that Franchisee has not relied upon oral or verbal representations of Franchisor, its officers, employees, and/or agents in deciding to purchase this franchise.

17.2 *Uniform Offering Circular.* FRANCHISEE ACKNOWLEDGES THAT HE/SHE/IT HAS RECEIVED, AT THE EARLIER OF THE FIRST PERSONAL MEETING WITH FRANCHISOR OR TEN (10) BUSINESS DAYS PRIOR TO THE EXECUTION BY FRANCHISEE OF THIS AGREEMENT OR PAYMENT OF ANY CONSIDERATION TO FRANCHISOR, A COPY OF THE CURRENT FRANCHISOR'S UNIFORM FRANCHISE OFFERING CIRCULAR FOR THE STATE IN WHICH FRANCHISEE'S AREA IS LOCATED.

17.3 *Understanding of Agreement.* FRANCHISEE STATES THAT HE/SHE/IT HAS RECEIVED, READ AND UNDERSTOOD THIS AGREEMENT, AND HAS BEEN ACCORDED AN AMPLE OPPORTUNITY AND A PERIOD OF NOT LESS THAN FIVE (5) BUSINESS DAYS AFTER RECEIPT OF A FINAL COPY OF THIS AGREEMENT TO CONSULT WITH ADVISORS OF HIS OR HER OWN CHOOSING CONCERNING THE POTENTIAL BENEFITS AND RISKS THAT MAY BE INVOLVED IN ENTERING INTO THIS AGREEMENT AND BECOMING A FRANCHISEE.

17.4 *Financial Statements.* FRANCHISEE HAS PROVIDED FRANCHISOR WITH ACCURATE FINANCIAL STATEMENTS, WHICH PRESENT A TRUE REPRESENTATION OF FRANCHISEE'S FINANCIAL CONDITION.

17.5 *Stock Certificate Legend.* Franchisee, if it is a corporation, acknowledges that no stock of the corporation may be transferred without Franchisor's prior approval in accordance with Section 11. Franchisee agrees to place the following legend on all certificates of stock in the corporation:

The transfer of this stock is subject to the terms and conditions of a Franchise Agreement with _____, a[n] _____ [state of incorporation] corporation, as Franchisor.

17.6 *Entire Agreement.* This Agreement represents and constitutes the entire agreement between the parties. All other representations or negotiations, past or present, verbal or written, are merged herein.

SECTION 18. AGREEMENT NOT TO COMPETE OR DISCLOSE

18.1 *Covenant Not to Compete.* As long as this Agreement shall be in effect, and for a period of two years thereafter, regardless of the cause of termination, the Franchisee shall not in any capacity, directly or indirectly, engage or be financially interested in or associated with any business similar or substantially similar to a _____ business within a 50 mile radius of the exclusive territory granted Franchisee, any exclusive territory granted to other Franchisees, or any company-owned location, or employ or seek to employ any person who at the time of his employment is employed, or at any time six months prior thereto has been employed, by any other franchise business or by Franchisor.

18.2 *Nondisclosure.* At no time, except in the normal course of the Franchisee's business hereunder, shall the Franchisee disclose to any person any information or knowledge concerning the methods of promotion, sale, or distribution used by Franchisor.

18.3 *Remedies.* In addition to any other remedies available, Franchisor shall be entitled to obtain an injunction without bond to terminate or prevent the continuation of any existing or continuing default or violation of Sections 18.1 or 18.2.

SECTION 19. NOTICES

19.1 *Form.* Any notices to be given hereunder shall be in writing, and may be delivered personally, or by certified or registered mail, with postage fully prepaid. Any notice delivered by mail in the manner herein specified shall be deemed delivered five days after mailing or, if earlier, on actual receipt.

19.2 *Addresses.* Any notices to be delivered to Franchisor shall be addressed to *[address]*. Any notice to Franchisee shall be delivered to the address set forth in the first paragraph of this Agreement.

19.3 *Change of Notice Address.* The address specified herein for service of notices may be changed at any time by the party making the change giving written notice to the other party.

SECTION 20. EXCLUSIVE PROPERTY

The form and content of this Agreement are the exclusive property of Franchisor and may not be reproduced in part or in whole by Franchisee.

SECTION 21. ADDITIONAL REPRESENTATIONS

21.1 *Franchisee's Representations and Warranties.* Franchisee makes the following additional warranties and representations:

21.1.1 *Form of Business Organization.* Franchisee is a _____ *[corporation, partnership, or sole proprietorship]*.

21.1.2 *Beneficial Ownership.* If Franchisee is a corporation or partnership, there is set forth below the name and address of each shareholder or partner in the franchise holding 10% or more interest in the corporation or partnership.

NAME ADDRESS NO. OF SHARES/PERCENTAGES

_____ _____ _____

_____ _____ _____

_____ _____ _____

21.2 *Protected Territory Description.* Franchisor agrees that no other franchise or company-owned operation will be sold or operated in the protected territory consisting of: (Map attached)

The Minimum Number of Initial Targeted Households for Franchisee's exclusive territory is:_____.

[Signature by Franchisee]

Accepted on this _____ day of _____, 20__.

FRANCHISOR

BY   :_____

TITLE :_____

§ 37:2. CHECKLIST FOR DETERMINING EMPLOYEE STATUS[8]

CHECKLIST FOR DETERMINING EMPLOYEE STATUS

1. *Instructions.* Is the individual providing services required to comply with instructions from the person for whom the services are performed about when, where, and how the individual is to perform his or her work?

    Yes_____ No_____

2. *Training.* Is the individual required to undergo training, including working with an experienced individual, attending meetings, or reading instructions or other materials provided by the person for whom the services are performed?

    Yes_____ No_____

3. *Integration.* Are the services of the individual critical to the continuation or success of the business of the person for whom the services are performed?

    Yes_____ No_____

4. *Services Rendered Personally.* Is the individual required to provide his or her services personally?

    Yes_____ No_____

5. *Hiring, Paying, and Supervising Assistants.* Are the assistants who work with the individual hired, paid, or supervised by the person for whom the services are performed?

   Yes_____ No_____

6. *Continuing Relationship.* Is the relationship between the individual and the person for whom the services are performed a continuing relationship, including a relationship where work is performed at frequently occurring but irregular intervals?

   Yes_____ No_____

7. *Hours of Work.* Does the person for whom the services are performed establish hours of work for the individual?

   Yes_____ No_____

8. *Full Time Required.* Is the individual required to devote substantially full time to the business of the person for whom the services are performed?

   Yes_____ No_____

9. *Work on Premises.* Are the services of the individual performed on the premises of the person for whom the services are performed?

   Yes_____ No_____

10. *Order of Work.* Must the individual perform his or her services in an order or sequence set by the person for whom the services are performed?

    Yes_____ No_____

11. *Reports.* Is the individual required to provide regular or written reports to the person for whom the services are performed?

    Yes_____ No_____

12. *Payment by Hour, Week, or Month.* Is the individual paid by the hour, week, or month, as opposed to being paid by the job or on commission?

    Yes_____ No_____

13. *Travel or Business Expenses.* Does the person for whom the services are performed pay or reimburse the individual's travel or business expenses?

    Yes_____ No_____

14. *Tools or Materials.* Does the person for whom the services are performed furnish the tools or materials used by the individual in the performance of his or her services?

    Yes_____ No_____

15. *Investment.* Has the individual not made any significant investment in facilities used by the individual in performing his or her services?

    Yes_____ No_____

16. *Lack of Economic Risk.* Is there no possibility that the individual will suffer a significant economic loss in connection with the performance of the services (other than the risk of nonpayment for his or services)?

    Yes_____ No_____

17. *Single Employer.* Does the individual not perform more than de minimis services for persons other than the person for whom the services are performed?

Yes_____ No_____

18. *Services Available to General Public.* Does the individual *not* make his or her services available to the general public on a regular and consistent basis and *not* advertise the availability of those services?

Yes_____ No_____

19. *Right of Discharge.* Does the person for whom the services are performed have the right to discharge the individual performing the services?

Yes_____ No_____

20. *Right of Termination.* Does the individual performing the services have the right to terminate his or her relationship with the person for whom the services are performed at any time without penalty?

Yes_____ No_____

§ 46:2. SALE OF BUSINESS—TAX ISSUES CHECKLIST[9]

SALE OF BUSINESS TAX ISSUES CHECKLIST

I. Tax Objectives of the Parties.

    A. Seller.

        1.   If there will be a gain on the sale, the seller will want to realize capital gain rather than ordinary income.

        2.   If there is a loss on the sale, the seller will want to realize an ordinary loss rather than a capital loss.

        3.   If the sale involves a business operated by a corporation, the seller will want to avoid double tax on corporate income or gains.

    B. Purchaser.

        1.   The purchaser will want to maximize immediate or early-year deductions arising out of the sale.

        2.   If the purchase involves a loss corporation, the purchaser will want to preserve the tax benefit of the loss.

II. Tax Issues Common to All Types of Sales.

    A. Installment Sales.

        1.   If the purchase price for a business is paid in installments, installment reporting must be used for federal income tax purposes unless an election is made not to use installment reporting.

        2.   Minimum amounts of interest must be charged in an installment sale in order to avoid application of the imputed interest rules.

3. In an asset sale by a corporation, the right to use installment reporting may be available to shareholders of the selling corporation but only if the corporation is liquidated promptly in accordance with a plan.

4. The sale of installment obligations as a part of a sale of assets will constitute a disposition by the seller, triggering recognition of the deferred gain.

B. Covenants Not to Compete.

1. Covenants not to compete entered into in connection with a sale of business are, under current law, amortizable over 15 years, regardless of their term. Accordingly, a covenant not to compete is treated as the same from the buyer's standpoint as goodwill or other intangibles.

2. The party bound by a covenant not to compete has ordinary income, and the income is recognized when received by a cash basis taxpayer.

a. The consideration for a covenant not to compete is not subject to employment tax or self-employment tax.

b. Consideration for a covenant not to compete is also not subject to double tax in the context of a sale of assets by a corporation.

3. Covenants must have economic substance.

4. Deduction of the consideration paid by the purchaser may be denied if the consideration for the covenant constitutes excess parachute payments within the meaning of IRC §280G.

C. Consulting Agreements.

1. The purchaser may deduct compensation paid under a consulting agreement when the compensation is paid or accrued. It must be for true consulting.

2. Consultant has ordinary income when he or she receives payments of compensation under a consulting agreement.

a. The compensation is subject to self-employment tax (and may be subject to employment tax if the consultant is not classified as an independent contractor for employment tax purposes).

b. The compensation paid under a consulting agreement is not subject to double tax in the context of a sale of assets by a corporation.

3. Care must be taken if the consultant is to be treated as an independent contractor for income tax purposes.

III. Asset Sales.

A. Seller.

1. The amount and nature of the seller's gain or loss on the sale will depend upon an allocation of the sales price to individual assets.

2. The seller will favor allocation of purchase price to assets that produce capital gain, such as goodwill, other intangible assets, and real property that has been depreciated on a straight line basis.

3. The seller will not favor allocation of purchase price to inventory and personal property subject to depreciation recapture since this will result in ordinary income to the seller.

4. If the seller is a corporation and the sale involves substantially all of the corporation's assets, prompt liquidation may be desirable to avoid personal holding company tax and accumulated earnings tax.

B. Purchaser.

1. The amount and nature of the purchaser's deductions with respect to acquired assets will depend upon an allocation of the sales price to individual assets.

2. The purchaser will favor allocation of purchase price to assets such as inventory and depreciable personal property which give the purchaser immediate deductions or limit the buyer's ordinary income.

3. The purchaser will not favor allocation of purchase price to assets with lengthy depreciation periods, such as real property, covenants not to compete and goodwill.

C. Sales Price Allocation.

1. The sales price allocation by both the seller and purchaser must be made in accordance with the residual method under IRC §1060.

2. It is advisable to set forth an agreed purchase price allocation in the sale agreement.

IV. Stock Sales.

A. Seller.

1. A sale of stock will ordinarily result in capital gain or loss to the seller.

2. The gain on a stock sale may be ordinary income to the seller if the corporation is a collapsible corporation.

3. If there is a loss on the sale, all or a portion of the loss may be an ordinary loss under IRC §1244.

B. Purchaser.

1. The purchaser acquires a basis in the stock purchased equal to the price paid.

2. The sale of stock has no effect on the corporation's existing tax attributes, and thus does not generate increased deductions, even if the purchase price of the stock reflects a value for the assets exceeding their adjusted basis in the hands of the corporation.

C. Loss Corporations.

1. The use of net operating loss and capital loss carryovers of the acquired corporation following a stock sale are limited.

2. The use of such losses may be denied completely under IRC §269 if the principal purpose of the acquisition is tax avoidance.

D. Election of Asset Sale Treatment.

1. If the purchaser in a stock sale is a corporation, the purchaser may elect to treat a stock acquisition as an asset acquisition.

2. The election permits the basis of the assets of the acquired corporation to be stepped-up to reflect the purchase price for the stock, thus permitting greater depreciation deductions.

E. S Corporations.

1. If stock of an S corporation is being sold, the sale may result in termination of the S corporation election if the purchasers are not qualified to be S corporation shareholders.

2. In a stock sale involving an S corporation, an election to close the books in order to allocate the income of the year of sale should be considered.

V. Bootstrap Sales.

A. Seller.

1. The seller will have capital gain or loss on a sale of the seller's stock to the corporation so long as the sale qualifies as a complete termination of the seller's interest in the corporation.

2. Dividend treatment may result if the transaction is secured with a stock pledge and the seller acquires the stock in foreclosure.

3. The sequence of the sale and redemption in a bootstrap sale are unimportant so long as they are part of an integrated transaction.

B. Purchaser.

1. The purchaser in a bootstrap sale obtains a basis in the stock purchased from the corporation equal to the purchase price paid.

2. No increase in basis results from the consideration paid by the corporation for the redemption of the seller's stock.

VI. Like-Kind Exchanges.

A. Although uncommon, like-kind exchanges of business assets are possible.

B. Such transactions involve the exchange of assets of one business for the assets of another.

VII. Tax-Free Reorganizations.

A. Seller and Purchaser.

1. If a business sale is structured as a tax-free reorganization, such as a merger, there may be no gain or loss recognized by the seller for tax purposes on the transaction.

2. The purchaser also generally recognizes no gain or loss in a tax-free reorganization.

B. Corporate Participants.

1. The tax attributes of the acquired corporation will carry over and become attributes of the acquiring corporation.

2. The use of net operating loss and capital loss carryovers of the acquired corporation are limited.

§ 44:2. CHECKLIST OUTLINING STEPS[10]

CORPORATE LIQUIDATION CHECKLIST

I. Corporate Authorization.

    A. Corporation Has Not Issued Stock or Commenced Business.

        1. If the corporation has not issued stock *and* has not commenced business, a voluntary dissolution may be authorized by a majority of the incorporators under the Model Business Corporation Act.

        2. If the corporation has not issued stock *or* has not commenced business, a voluntary dissolution may be authorized by a majority of the incorporators or by a majority of the members of the initial board of directors under the Revised Model Business Corporation Act.

    B. Corporation has issued stock or has commenced business.

        1. If the corporation has issued stock and has commenced business, the approval of the shareholders is required for voluntary dissolution of the corporation. Under the Model Business Corporation Act, shareholder approval is required if the corporation has either issued stock or commenced business.

        2. Shareholder approval is obtained as follows:

            a. The board of directors of the corporation adopts a plan of liquidation and refers the plan to the shareholders for action.

            b. A majority of shareholders, and a majority of the holders of each class of shares entitled to vote as a class, approve the plan of liquidation.

II. Filings and Notice.

    A. Filings.

        1. Under the Model Business Corporation Act, a notice of intent to dissolve is filed initially with the secretary of state of the corporation's state of incorporation. Articles of dissolution are filed after the completion of the winding up and liquidation of the corporation.

        2. The filing of a statement of intent to dissolve is not required under the Revised Model Business Corporation Act. Under the Revised Model Business Corporation Act, articles of dissolution are filed by the corporation with the secretary of state of its state of incorporation following shareholder approval and before the corporation's business is wound up and the corporation liquidated.

    B. Revocation.

        1. The dissolution may be revoked prior to the filing of articles of dissolution under the Model Business Corporation Act.

        2. Under the Revised Model Business Corporation Act, the dissolution may be revoked within 120 days after the filing of articles of dissolution.

C. Notice.

1. The corporation must give notice of the dissolution to holders of known claims against the corporation. The notice must provide for a procedure and deadline for filing claims against the corporation.

2. In order to notify holders of unknown claims, notice of the dissolution is published by the corporation in a newspaper. This notice must also provide for a procedure for filing claims against the corporation.

III. Winding Up and Liquidation.

A. Cessation of Business.

1. The operation of the business of the corporation must cease on or before the filing of a notice of intent to dissolve under the Model Business Corporation Act or the filing of articles of dissolution under the Revised Model Business Corporation Act.

2. The only continuing activity of the corporation should be that necessary to wind up its affairs and distribute its assets in liquidation.

B. Assemble Assets.

1. The corporation must assemble its assets and sell or otherwise dispose of those assets that will not be distributed to shareholders or to claimants.

2. Particular care should be given to identifying assets such as prepaid items and contingent claims that might otherwise be overlooked.

C. Satisfy Obligations and Liabilities.

1. The corporation must pay or provide for payment of all corporate obligations and liabilities and all claims against the corporation.

2. In the case of disputed or contingent claims, provision may be made for payment by depositing funds into an escrow or liquidating trust.

D. Distribution to Shareholders.

1. The assets of the corporation remaining after payment of or providing for claims should be distributed to the shareholders.

2. All known assets should be transferred with appropriate forms of transfer or conveyance, such as deeds, bills of sale, or assignments.

3. Unknown assets can be transferred to shareholders by an assignment specifically covering such assets.

4. A statement of the fair market value of all assets transferred should be provided by the corporation to each shareholder. This statement will be required for the shareholders' income tax returns.

E. Stock Certificates.

1. All stock certificates of the corporation should be collected and canceled.

2. Stock certificates should be collected from shareholders in exchange for the assets distributed to them.

F. Timing.

    1.   If installment obligations of the corporation will be distributed in the liquidation, the liquidation should be completed within 12 months following the adoption of the plan of liquidation to enable noncorporate shareholders to report gain attributable to the installment obligations on the installment basis.

    2.   In other cases, the liquidation should proceed as quickly as possible. A protracted liquidation may result in the corporation's being subjected to personal holding company or accumulated earnings taxes.

IV. Tax Filings.

  A. Corporation.

    1.   Form 966 must be filed by the corporation with the Internal Revenue Service within 30 days after adoption of the plan of complete liquidation.

    2.   Forms 1099-DIV must be issued to all shareholders who have received $600 or more in the liquidation by January 31 of the year following the liquidation, and copies of these forms must be filed with the Internal Revenue Service, accompanied by Form 1096.

    3.   The corporation's final income tax return must be filed by the 15th day of the third month following the close of its final tax year, which will generally be the date on which its assets are distributed to shareholders.

  B. Shareholders.

    1.   Shareholders must report any gain or loss on the liquidation on their income tax returns for the year in which the liquidation occurs. If the shareholders have a loss, it may qualify as an ordinary loss under IRC §1244.

    2.   Shareholders must file certain information regarding the liquidation with those returns if the corporation is not liquidated within one year after adoption of the plan of liquidation.

§ 47:2. ASSIGNMENT FOR BENEFIT OF CREDITORS[11]

ASSIGNMENT FOR BENEFIT OF CREDITORS

DATE: _____

PARTIES: [Name of Corporation],

a[n] _____ [state of incorporation]

corporation (Debtor)

[Name of Assignee] (Assignee)

RECITALS:

A. The Debtor has its principal place of business in the city of _____, county of _____, and is engaged in the business of _____.

B. The Debtor is unable to pay its debts in the usual course of business and desires to dispose of its property and assets for the benefit of all its creditors, in proportion to the amount of their respective claims.

AGREEMENTS:
SECTION 1. ASSIGNMENT

The Debtor hereby grants, conveys, transfers, assigns, and sets over unto Assignee all of the Debtor's property, real, personal and mixed, of every kind and nature, and wherever situated, being all of the property described in the inventory attached to this Assignment as Exhibit A, together with all other property of any kind or nature, owned by the Debtor not listed on Exhibit A.

SECTION 2. SALE OF PROPERTY AND PAYMENT OF CLAIMS

The Debtor hereby authorizes and directs Assignee to sell and convert into money all of the Debtor's property in accordance with law, and after paying the proper costs and expenses of carrying out this trust, together with all claims and demands preferred according to law, pay the balance of the proceeds of such sale to all of the Debtor's creditors in proportion to the amount of their respective claims as the same shall be approved and established, and in general, to do any act or acts necessary, proper and expedient to be done in the premises according to law.

[Signatures]

ENDNOTES

[1] Am. Jur. Contract Forms §68:295.

[2] Am. Jur. Contract Forms §68:334.

[3] Advising Small Businesses: Forms §48:2 (1993).

[4] Advising Small Businesses: Forms §2:2 (1993).

[5] Advising Small Businesses: Forms §4:2 (1993).

[6] Advising Small Businesses: Forms §30:3 (1993).

[7] Advising Small Businesses: Forms §30:5 (1993).

[8] Advising Small Businesses: Forms §37:2 (1993).

[9] Advising Small Businesses: Forms §46:2 (1993).

[10] Advising Small Businesses: Forms §44:2 (1993).

[11] Advising Small Businesses: Forms §47:2 (1993).

GLOSSARY

Acceptance   Agreeing to an offer and thus forming a contract.

Agent   A person authorized by another person to act for him or her; a person entrusted with another's business.

Artificial person   An entity or "thing," especially a corporation, that the law gives some of the legal rights and duties of a person.

Asynchronous communication   The transmission of information as it is completed, rather than when the party to whom it is addressed is ready to receive it. Example: E-mail.

Authority   Permission to act; power to act.

Beneficiary   Anyone who benefits from something or who is treated as the real owner of something for tax or other purposes.

Bilateral contract   A contract that offers a promise in exchange for another promise.

Breach   Failure, without legal excuse, to live up to a significant promise made in a contract.

Brick and mortar   A business or other entity that maintains a physical structure with buildings, parking lots, and on-site employees.

Capacity   A person's mental and physical ability to understand the consequences of entering into a legally binding agreement.

Clause   A statement or sentence that is part of a legal document such as a contract, a will or a legal pleading.

Clear and convincing evidence   Proof that a particular set of allegations is likely true; it is a higher level of proof than preponderance of the evidence.

Code   A collection of laws.

Coercion   Compulsion or force; making a person act against free will.

Collateral   Money or property put up to back a person's word when out a loan.

Common stock   Shares in a corporation that depend on their value on the value of the company.

Condition   A future uncertain event that creates or destroys rights and obligations.

Condition precedent   A condition, fact, or occurrence that must occur before a contractual obligation is triggered.

Condition subsequent   If a certain future event happens, a right or obligation ends.

Consent Voluntary and active agreement.

Consideration The basic reason for a contract; a person gives up something of value in exchange for receiving something of value through the contract.

Contract An agreement between legally competent parties who have expressed intent to enter into agreement with one another in a form recognized by law.

Contract of adhesion A contract in which all the bargaining power favor one side.

Corporation An organization that is formed under state corporate law exists, for legal purposes, as a separate being or an "artificial person." The stockholders have no liability for corporate debts beyond the value of their stock.

Counteroffer A rejection of an offer and a new offer made back.

Detriment The bargained for exchange in a contract, where the parties take on some responsibility that they are not legally obligated to undertake.

Discharge To discharge a contract is to end the obligation by agreement or by carrying it out.

Dividend A share of profits or property; usually a payment per share of the corporation's stock.

Draft A bill of exchange or any other negotiable instrument for the payment of money drawn by one person on another.

Duress Unlawful pressure on a person to do what he or she would not otherwise have done.

Equity The name for a system of courts that originated in England to take care of legal problems when the existing laws did not cover some situations in which a person's rights were violated by another person.

Estoppel When a person is barred by prior actions from claiming a right or a duty against another person who relied, in good faith, on those actions.

Exclusion Keeping (or leaving) someone out.

Fraud Any kind of trickery used to cheat another of money or property.

General partnership An unincorporated business organization co-owned by two or more persons.

Guardian A person who has the legal right and duty to take care of another person or that person's property because that other person cannot.

Holder in Due Course Rule Under this rule, when a person acquires the instrument in good faith, he or she takes title free and clear of any defects or outstanding claims on it.

Identity theft   The process of obtaining a person's credit card and other identifying information, such as birth date and Social Security Number, to create bogus accounts that are then used to purchase items or obtain loans.

Injunction   A judge's order to a person to do or to refrain from doing a particular thing.

Internet Service Provider (ISP)   A business that provides Internet access through dial-up modems.

Jurisdiction   The persons about whom, and the subject matters about which, a court has the right and power to make decisions that are legally binding.

Laches   The legal doctrine that a delay (in pursuing or enforcing a claim or right) can be so long that the person against whom you are proceeding is unfairly hurt or prejudiced by the delay itself.

Limited liability   A legal concept that, when used in the context of business, refers to the protection of an investor's personal assets. Potential loss is limited to the total amount invested in the venture, not the investor's total personal assets.

Limited liability company   A limited liability company is a cross between partnership and a corporation owned by members who may manage the company directly or delegate to officers or managers who are similar to a corporation's directors.

Limited partnership   A partnership formed by general partners (who run the business and have liability for all partnership debts) and limited partners (who partly or fully finance the business, take no part in running it, and have no liability for partnership debts beyond the money they put in or promise to put in).

Liquidated damages   A specific amount of money agreed to in a contract as compensation for a breach of that contract.

Mailbox Rule   A rule that holds that an acceptance is legally valid at the time that it is posted; this rule is subject to several exceptions.

Material fact   A basic reason for a contract, without which it would not have been entered into.

Meeting of the minds   The general agreement between parties to a contract as to material terms.

Memorandum of contract   A writing that proves the existence of a contract.

Minor   A person who is under the age of full legal rights and duties.

Mistake   An unintentional error or act.

Mitigation of damages   The principle that a person suing for damages must have taken reasonable steps to minimize the harm done, or the amount of money awarded will be lowered.

Mutual assent   A party's willingness to enter into a contractual obligation and an agreement as to the general terms in the contract.

Mutuality of obligation   Describes the principle that, for a binding contract to exist, each side must have some obligation or duty to perform under the contract.

Mutuality of remedy   Under equity law, a principle that requires that both parties have a similar recourse through the courts.

Negotiable instrument   An unconditional promise or order to pay a fixed amount of money, with or without interest.

Note A written promise to pay a debt.

Offer   Make a proposal; present for acceptance or rejection.

Offeree   The person to whom the offer is made.

Offeror   The person making the offer.

Option   A contract in which one person pays money for the right to buy something from, or sell something to, another person at a certain price and within a certain time period.

Parol Evidence Rule   The principle that the meaning of a written agreement, in which the parties have expressly stated that it is their complete and final agreement, cannot be contradicted or changed by using prior oral or written statements or agreements as evidence.

Partial performance   Carrying out some, but not all, of a contract, or doing something in reliance on another's promise.

Power of acceptance   The right conferred on a person who has received a valid offer.

Preferred stock   A class of stock that entitles the holder to a stated dividend that must be paid before any dividend payment is made to holders of common stock. Holders of preferred stock generally do not have any voting rights in the corporation.

Prenuptial/antenuptial agreement   A contract between persons about to marry. It usually concerns the way that property will be handled during the marriage, the way it will be divided in case of divorce, and the limits on spousal support obligations.

Preponderance of the evidence   The greater weight of evidence, not as to quantity but as to quality.

Quantum meruit   "As much as he deserved." An old form of pleading used in a lawsuit for compensation for work done.

Quantum valebant   "As much as they were worth." An old form of pleading used in a lawsuit for payment of goods sold and delivered.

Quid pro quo   (Latin) "Something for something."

Ratification   Confirmation and acceptance of a previous act done by you or by another person.

Reformation   A procedure in which a court will rewrite or correct a written agreement to conform with the original intent of the persons making the deal.

Replevin   A legal action to get back personal property wrongfully held by another person.

Rescission   The annulment of a contract.

Revoking an offer   When the person making the offer terminates it before it has been accepted.

Secured transaction   A secured transaction is a secured deal involving goods or fixtures that is governed by Article 9 of the Uniform Commercial Code.

Security   A share of stock, a bond, a note, or one of many different kinds of documents showing a share in a company or a debt owned by a company or a government.

Shareholder   A person who owns shares in a corporation.

Skimming   Obtaining a person's credit card information by running the card through a hand-held device that stores the card information in downloadable form.

Specific performance   Being required to do exactly what was agreed to.

Statute of Frauds   Any of various states' law, modeled after an old English law, that require many types of contracts to be signed and in writing to be enforceable in court.

Strict construction   Strict construction of a law means taking it literally or "what is says, it means," so that the law should be applied to the narrowest possible set of situations.

Synchronous communication   The transmission of information when the party to whom it is addressed is ready to receive it. Example: telephone conversation.

Terminating the offer   To end an offer before any legal action has been taken on it.

Undercapitalization   Lacking enough cash or short-term profit to stay in business.

Undue influence   Abusing or misusing a position of trust to overcome a person's will, usually to the benefit of the person exerting the improper control.

Unilateral contract   A contract in which one party makes a promise in exchange for an action by the other party.

Unlimited liability   A concept that places all of a person's personal assets within reach of a civil judgment.

Virus   A computer program designed to destroy computer data and disable computer systems.

Void   Without legal effect.

Voidable   Describes something that is in force but can be legally avoided.

Waiver   A voluntary and intentional abandonment or relinquishment of a known right, claim, or privilege.

INDEX